BOUNTIFUL
HARVEST

BOUNTIFUL HARVEST

ESSAYS IN HONOR OF
S. KENT BROWN

Edited by
Andrew C. Skinner, D. Morgan Davis, and Carl Griffin

NEAL A. MAXWELL INSTITUTE
FOR RELIGIOUS SCHOLARSHIP

BRIGHAM YOUNG UNIVERSITY
PROVO, UTAH

Cover design by Stephen Hales Creative, Inc.

Frontispiece by Mark A. Philbrick

Neal A. Maxwell Institute for Religious Scholarship
Brigham Young University
Provo, UT 84602
maxwellinstitute.byu.edu

Printed in the United States of America
10 9 8 7 6 5 4 3 2 1

Library of Congress Cataloging-in-Publication Data

Bountiful harvest : essays in honor of S. Kent Brown / edited by Andrew C. Skinner, D. Morgan Davis, and Carl Griffin.
    p. cm.
Includes bibliographical references and index.
ISBN 978-0-8425-2804-7 (alk. paper)
1. Theology. 2. Church of Jesus Christ of Latter-day Saints. I. Brown, S. Kent. II. Skinner, Andrew C., 1951- III. Davis, D. Morgan, 1968- IV. Griffin, Carl W.
 BX8637.B63 2011
 230'.93--dc23

2011032826

CONTENTS

INTRODUCTION

For more than four decades S. Kent Brown has been a welcome presence on the Provo, Utah, campus of Brigham Young University (BYU), first as a student for a brief period and then as a teacher. As a professor of ancient scripture and Near Eastern studies he has devoted his academic life to expanding the borders of our knowledge about the history and religions of the Fertile Crescent and helping others to understand that part of the world. It is no exaggeration to say that thousands of students have benefited from his knowledge, wisdom, and kindness. Professor Brown is truly a gentleman and a scholar, a shrinking set in the world of academe today. Many on the BYU campus have known him not only as a teacher, but also as a constant and steady mentor and friend. Several others beyond Provo and even the United States have been privileged to call him a colleague and comrade in the common cause of lifting and building the world through careful and articulate scholarship. Truly, his reach is international.

It came as no surprise, therefore, that several of us wanted to extend our appreciation to him for all he has done by presenting a collection of essays in his honor as he approaches his eighth decade. This volume constitutes that offering. All of the authors are scholars who have had an association with Kent through the years; some were themselves students mentored by him.

The breadth of Kent Brown's expertise is impressive, as the bibliography of his works attests. He is arguably a world expert on early Christian literature and history, especially Coptic Christianity. Yet, the majority of his writings and other creative works have been geared to helping members of his own confessional affiliation, The Church of Jesus Christ of Latter-day Saints, to understand their faith tradition. Thus, Kent is equally at home in the text of the Book of Mormon as he is in the world of the New Testament. Latter-day Saints can be grateful that someone with Kent's discerning eye, scholarly ability, tremendous set of linguistic and historical-critical skills, and his deep commitment to their faith has expended so much careful effort to elucidate the underpinnings of their brand of Christianity.

No less an able administrator than scholar, Kent Brown served well the university community where he made his academic home the last three and a half decades until his retirement in 2009. The leadership positions he has held include department chair of Ancient Scripture, director of BYU's Jerusalem Center for Near Eastern Studies, director of Ancient Studies, and director of the Laura F. Willes Center for Book of Mormon Studies in the Neal A. Maxwell Institute for Religious Scholarship at BYU. After his "official" retirement, he responded to the university's special request and returned to Jerusalem once again to serve as the Jerusalem Center's academic coordinator and associate director. Kent has always taken very seriously the ideal of a consecrated life—giving back to the university his time, talents, and resources without expectation of reward. All who know him regard Kent Brown as a consensus builder and leader by example.

For years Kent served as editor of the Maxwell Institute's *Journal of Book of Mormon Studies*. He has corresponded with a wide variety of authors and writers, mature scholars to beginning students, professionals to laypersons. They and the journal are better because of his editorial oversight.

Kent Brown was also among the first of his colleagues at the Maxwell Institute to appreciate the power of visual media to illuminate and instruct a new generation of learners raised in the digital world. He conceived, cowrote, and coproduced four documentary films, two of which have helped to change the way Latter-day Saints understand Book of Mormon geography in an ancient setting. For all of his work on the text and history of the Book of Mormon, he still regards it as one of the most fruitful arenas for the LDS scholar. The *Golden Road*, a documentary on the fabled incense trail that ran from southern Arabia to the Mediterranean, has been warmly received by those in modern Middle Eastern countries associated with the ancient trade route.

All of the foregoing helps to explain the eclectic contents of the present volume. Kent Brown has touched upon so many topics associated with the ancient Near East, and become a valued colleague of such a diverse group of scholars, that the essays in this volume are something of a capsulized summary of his career and interests. These essays, however, reflect only a small number of the scholars who have come within Kent's orbit of influence and have desired to honor him. Many more, while wanting to recognize his achievements, were prevented from submitting formal papers for a variety of understandable reasons. However, the spirit of their well-wishes also accompanies this volume, which we have entitled *Bountiful Harvest* to reflect both the richness of Kent's career and the abundance of our esteem for him.

We extend our deep appreciation to the dedicated production staff who have contributed so much labor and talent to this volume. Shirley S. Ricks (production editor) and Elin Roberts (office manager) have been indispensable fellow laborers throughout. Our thanks likewise to Alison V. P. Coutts (typesetting, indexing); Paula W. Hicken and Sandra A. Thorne (proofreading); Rebekah Atkin, Julie Davis, and Daniel B. McKinlay (source checking); and Stetson Robinson (indexing). These and other staff at the Maxwell Institute have all labored generously and cheerfully on this project, as an expression of collegial affection.

All of us extend to our friend, S. Kent Brown, heartfelt congratulations on a life well lived and a career well blessed, and hope for him continued happiness and success. Those of us who know Kent well also wish health and long life to the secret behind his accomplishments—his eternal companion Gayle. Together they epitomize the Lord's promise: "Give, and it shall be given unto you; good measure, pressed down, and shaken together, and running over, shall men give into your bosom. For with the same measure that ye mete withal it shall be measured to you again" (Luke 6:38).

Andrew C. Skinner
D. Morgan Davis
Carl Griffin
August 2011

CHAPTER 1

"FAITH ALONE" IN ROMANS 3:28 JST

Kevin L. Barney

Professor S. Kent Brown was one of my principal mentors when I was an undergraduate at BYU in the early 1980s. I took a number of classes from him and then worked as his teaching assistant for almost two years. Over the ensuing more than a quarter century I have followed his scholarship with great interest. His work is consistently crafted with care, reason, and thoughtful inquiry and is a worthy model for any young scholar to emulate. The most enjoyable academic experience of my life was the semester I studied Coptic with Professor Brown on a noncredit basis. The class met on Wednesday evenings in the Richards Building, and I would often bring my baby daughter, who would sleep in a corner as a small group of us sat around a desk plumbing the depths of this Christian-era form of the Egyptian language. It was not a language I needed for my particular course of study; for me the class required self-motivation and was an exercise in learning for its own sake, which I thoroughly enjoyed. It was my opinion then, and remains so today, that S. Kent Brown was and is among the very finest professors to ever set foot on the Provo campus, and I am pleased to add this small offering to the Festschrift in his honor.

The word *solifidianism*, sometimes spelled *solafidianism*, was a neologism coined in the early seventeenth century to refer to the doctrine or tenet of justification "by faith alone" (*sola fide*),[1] one of the "five solas"[2] or Latin slogans that emerged as a description of the basic theological insights of the Protestant Reformation.

For members of the Church of Jesus Christ of Latter-day Saints, *salvation* as a theological technical term may have different meanings, depending on whether we mean to emphasize that *from* which we are saved (death and hell) or that *to* which we are saved (heaven). In the former sense, Mormons are almost universalists, since as a result of the grace of Jesus Christ all will be resurrected and all but a very few will inherit a kingdom of glory in the eternities. For most Christians, being saved from death and hell and being saved to heaven are the same thing (since heaven is a single place and condition), but since Mormons accept a variegated heaven, the second sense of salvation for them differs from the first. In this second, more common sense, salvation usually refers in Mormon discourse to being exalted in the highest heaven, the celestial kingdom. In this sense, Mormon theology is clearly *synergistic* (from the Greek preposition *syn* "with" + the noun *erga* "works"), where deeds (such as salvific ordinances) work together with faith in Jesus Christ to effect salvation. In this, the Mormon conception of salvation is like that of Roman Catholics or the Orthodox traditions, which are also synergistic. In contrast, it is unlike that of most Protestants, who view the Mormon concept of salvation in the former sense as too broad and in the latter sense as too narrow. Mormon theology clearly rejects solifidianism, which has historically been a point of significant contention with Protestant critics of the Church of Jesus Christ.[3]

---

1. The first occurrence listed in the *Oxford English Dictionary* is from 1628: "To the conuiction of that lewd slander of solifidianisme," citing Bp. Hall, *Righteous Mammon*, 728. *The Compact Oxford English Dictionary*, 2nd ed. (Oxford: Clarendon, 1989), 1823.

2. The other four are *sola scriptura* ("by scripture alone"), *sola gratia* ("by grace alone"), *solus Christus* ("Christ alone") and *soli Deo gloria* ("glory to God alone").

3. For a brief overview, see Alma P. Burton, "Salvation," in *Encyclopedia of Mormonism*, 4:1256–57. For the classic expression of salvation in the former sense, see

With that background, let us turn our attention to the Joseph Smith Translation (JST) of Romans 3:28.[4] The table below gives first the King James Version (KJV) of Romans 3:27-31 (to provide a little context), then only those verses of the JST (as printed in the 1944 Inspired Version edition published by the then Reorganized Church of Jesus Christ of Latter Day Saints, now Community of Christ) that vary from the KJV (with the revisions marked), and finally the same passage in the New Revised Standard Version, the most recent scholarly translation in the KJV tradition:

Romans 3:27-31

KJV	JST	NRSV
27. Where is boasting then? It is excluded. By what law? of works? Nay: but by the law of faith.		Then what becomes of boasting? It is excluded. By what law? By that of works? No, but by the law of faith.
28. Therefore we conclude that a man is justified by faith without the deeds of the law.	Therefore we conclude that a man is justified by faith *alone* without the deeds of the law.	For we hold that a person is justified by faith apart from works prescribed by the law.
29. *Is he* the God of the Jews only? *is he* not also of the Gentiles? Yes, of the Gentiles also:		Or is God the God of Jews only? Is he not the God of Gentiles also? Yes, of Gentiles also,

---

LeGrand Richards, *A Marvelous Work and a Wonder* (Salt Lake City: Deseret Book, 1950), 262-81. For explicit rejections of solifidianism, see Daniel C. Peterson and Stephen D. Ricks, *Offenders for a Word: How Anti-Mormons Play Word Games to Attack Latter-day Saints* (Provo, UT: FARMS, 1998), 138-47, and Craig L. Blomberg and Stephen E. Robinson, *How Wide the Divide? A Mormon and an Evangelical in Conversation* (Downers Grove, IL: InterVarsity, 1997), 148-49. For a discussion of Mormon soteriology using the vocabulary of the philosophy of religion, see Blake T. Ostler, *Exploring Mormon Thought: Of God and Gods* (Salt Lake City: Kofford Books, 2008), 321-58.

4. This particular emendation was not included among the approximately six hundred selections from the JST incorporated in footnotes or the special appendix to the 1979 edition of the Bible published by the Church of Jesus Christ; therefore, many members of the church are unfamiliar with it.

30. Seeing *it* is one God, which shall justify the circumcision by faith, and uncircumcision through faith.	Seeing ~~it is one God,~~ ~~which shall~~ *that* ***God will***[a] justify the circumcision by faith, and uncircumcision through faith.	since God is one; and he will justify the circumcised on the ground of faith and the uncircumcised through that same faith.
31. Do we then make void the law through faith? God forbid: yea, we establish the law.		Do we then overthrow the law by this faith? By no means! On the contrary, we uphold the law.

a. This revision would appear to be a simplifying paraphrase meant to avoid the awkwardness of the KJV. Note how the NRSV greatly improves upon the strained KJV construction.

A few verses earlier the JST makes a change similar to that in verse 28: "***Therefore***[5] being justified ~~freely~~ *only* by his grace[6] through the redemption that is in Christ Jesus" (Romans 3:24 JST).

Below I give the Greek text of verse 28 together with my own translation:

logizometha gar dikaiousthai pistei anthrōpon chōris ergōn nomou	For we are of the opinion that a person is acquitted[b] by faith independently of deeds required by the Law [Torah].

b. In the sense of being pronounced righteous by God. I have used *acquitted* in order to avoid the theological baggage that comes with the more traditional *justified*.

The standard critical edition of the Greek New Testament[7] reports only three small textual variations in this verse. (1) The most significant of these is whether the conjunction near the beginning of the verse should be *gar* "for" or *oun* "therefore" (the evidence

---

5. This revision is reminiscent of the variant reading *oun* at the beginning of verse 28 as discussed below.

6. Replacing the adverb *only* for *freely* is suggestive of a *sola gratia* concept, or the first sense of *salvation* in Mormon theology.

7. *Novum Testamentum Graece*, 27th ed. (Stuttgart: Deutsche Bibelgesellschaft, 1993), 415.

favors the former).[8] (2) Some manuscripts spell *logizometha* as *logizōmetha* (with an *omega* in lieu of an *omicron*), thus putting that verb in the subjunctive mood, and (3) a few manuscripts in lieu of *pistei anthrōpon* ("a person by faith") have *anthrōpon dia pisteōs* ("a person through faith"). As one can see, there is no manuscript support for a Greek word corresponding to the English *alone* added by the JST. Had the word *alone* been specifically and literally in the Greek text, presumably we would find some sort of textual evidence for the presence of *monon* (the neuter of the adjective *monos* used as an adverb), as in James 2:24, *kai ouk ek pisteōs monon* "and not by faith viewed in isolation" [KJV "and not by faith only"].[9]

When evaluating a JST textual emendation such as this, we of course should not limit ourselves to considering only possible textual restorations. The revisions of the JST have great value apart from only that one possibility. The types of changes we find in the JST may include the following: (1) restorations of original text, (2) text paralleling nonoriginal ancient textual variants, (3) alternate translations without positing any change in underlying text, (4) historical corrections of incorrect text, (5) harmonizations of biblical

---

8. The manuscript attestation of *gar* is slightly superior to that for *oun*, and the context favors *gar*, for verse 28 gives a reason for the argument in verse 27, not a conclusion from it. "Since verse 28 opens a new lesson (for the third Saturday after Pentecost), the Greek lectionaries omit the conjunction altogether," as there is no need in that context to connect verse 28 with the preceding verse. Bruce M. Metzger, *A Textual Commentary on the Greek New Testament* (New York: United Bible Societies, 1975), 509.

9. Of course, a complete absence of any textual evidence whatsoever is not in and of itself necessarily dispositive, since the reading could have been lost prior to the copying of any extant manuscript. But given that the JST is not a pure textual restoration, we cannot simply assume that any particular textual revision in the JST represents text that was originally present. If one wishes to conjecturally suggest that a particular JST revision reflects original text in the absence of textual evidence, at the very least one should put forward a rationale for either early intentional or accidental omission by scribes. I see no obvious likelihood of an unintentional omission of *monon* in this passage had it been an original part of the text. Conceivably *monon* could have been intentionally deleted as a partial harmonization with James (where *faith* and *alone* are juxtaposed in a negative sense), but this would be a complete speculation. The more parsimonious explanation is that the presence of *alone* is to be accounted for at the translational rather than the textual level.

text with other biblical text or with revealed doctrine, and (6) midrashic commentary (much like the *targumim* and the genres of "rewritten Bible" and *pesharim* attested among the Dead Sea Scrolls).[10] Perhaps the best single explanation of this diversity in JST readings was offered long ago by Richard Lloyd Anderson:

> In no case did Joseph Smith work with any original language to reach these results. In fact, Greek variant readings simply do not exist for most changes made, whether here or elsewhere in the Inspired Version. Such evidence proves that Joseph Smith worked on the level of meaning and doctrinal harmonization, not narrow textual precision. This is the most dramatic example of the Prophet presenting historical material with long explanations that go far beyond any original writing. This suggests that the Prophet used his basic document—in this case the King James Version—as a point of departure instead of a translation guide. Thus his sweeping changes are only loosely tied to the written record that stimulated the new information. The result is content oriented. One may label this as "translation" only in the broadest sense, for his consistent amplifications imply that the Prophet felt that expansion of a document was the best way to get at meaning. If unconventional as history, the procedure may be a doctrinal gain if distinguished from normal translation

---

10. Kevin L. Barney, "Reflections on the Documentary Hypothesis," *Dialogue* 33/1 (2000): 76-77, and "Isaiah Interwoven," *FARMS Review* 15/1 (2003): 382. This is my adaptation of the seminal formulation in Robert J. Matthews, *"A Plainer Translation": Joseph Smith's Translation of the Bible: A History and Commentary* (Provo, UT: BYU Press, 1985), 253. Another characterization of the emendations is offered by Philip L. Barlow, *Mormons and the Bible: The Place of the Latter-day Saints in American Religion* (New York: Oxford University Press, 1991), 51-56, in which he divides the emendations into six categories: (1) long-revealed additions with little or no biblical parallel, (2) "common sense" changes, (3) interpretive additions, (4) harmonizations, (5) changes otherwise not easily classified, and (6) grammatical improvements, technical clarifications, and modernization of terms (by far the most common type of change).

procedure, for paraphrase and restatement are probably the best way to communicate without ambiguity. The result may be the paradox of having less literally the words of Bible personalities while possessing more clearly the meanings that their words sought to convey. Thus Joseph Smith's revisions can best be judged on a conceptual, but not a verbal level.[11]

So if the addition of *alone* does not reflect a textual restoration, how should we characterize it? Why did Joseph add that word to the text, and what nuance did he seek to convey by the emendation? The possible key to providing an answer to these questions is to be found in the German translation of the New Testament by Martin Luther (1483-1546) and his subsequent writings.

Luther began translating the New Testament into German in 1521 during the time he was sequestered at the Wartburg Castle; he published it in September 1522, six months after his return to Wittenberg. In 1534 he and six other collaborators would publish a complete German translation of the Bible, and he continued to refine the translation for the balance of his life. Other German translations of the Bible had previously appeared, but they were slavish renderings of the Latin Vulgate. Luther's fresh and literate translation of the New Testament was the first to actually render the Greek text into German; he used Erasmus's second edition of the Greek New Testament published in 1519 (which laid the foundation for what would eventually become known as the *Textus Receptus*).

In his initial 1522 publication, Luther rendered Romans 3:28 as follows: *So halten wyrs nu, das der mensch gerechtfertiget werde, on zu thun der werck des gesetzes, alleyn durch den glawben* ("Now we hold that Man is perfected/finished/justified, without doing the work of the law, *alone* [*alleyn*] through faith"). Luther's *Aus der Bibel*,

---

11. Richard Lloyd Anderson, "Joseph Smith's Insights into the Olivet Prophecy: Joseph Smith 1 and Matthew 24," in *Pearl of Great Price Symposium: A Centennial Presentation* (Provo, UT: Brigham Young University, 1976), 50.

published in 1546 just before his death, renders the verse as follows: *So halten wir es nu, Das der Mensch gerecht werde, on des Gesetzes werck, **alleine** durch den Glauben* ("Now we hold that Man becomes just without the work of the law, ***alone*** [*alleine*] through faith"). This rendering also uses the word *alone* (in this version spelled *alleine*).[12]

The first question raised by this similar use of the word *alone* is whether Joseph borrowed it from Luther (directly or indirectly) or whether Joseph's usage is independent of Luther's. A direct borrowing is quite unlikely, given that the source would have been written in German. We know that late in his life Joseph studied German with Alexander Neibaur and did some reading in Luther's translation (which he viewed quite favorably), as recounted in the Thomas Bullock report of the King Follett Discourse (7 April 1844): "I have been readg. the Germ: I find it to be the most correct that I have found & it corresponds the nearest to the revns. that I have given the last 16 yrs."[13] But Joseph's emendation was made on Folio 4 of New Testament Manuscript 2, which would have been dictated some time during the first six months or so of 1832 (from January/February 1832 to between 20 and 31 July 1832), which was long before Joseph had gained the capacity to read any German.[14]

---

12. *D. Martin Luthers Werke, Kritische Gesamtausgabe* (Weimar: Böhlaus, 1883-), *Die Deutsche Bibel*, 7:38–39 (these two editions are on facing pages, with 1522 on p. 38 and 1546 on p. 39) [the Weimar edition is referenced herein as *Werke*].

13. Andrew F. Ehat and Lyndon W. Cook, eds., *The Words of Joseph Smith: The Contemporary Accounts of the Nauvoo Discourses of the Prophet Joseph* (Provo, UT: BYU Religious Studies Center, 1980), 351.

14. See Scott H. Faulring, Kent P. Jackson, and Robert J. Matthews, eds., *Joseph Smith's New Translation of the Bible: Original Manuscripts* (Provo, UT: BYU Religious Studies Center, 2004), 69. Although Joseph occasionally made revisions to the manuscript during the remainder of his life, these were pinned to the original manuscript. Romans 3:28 was on the original manuscript and was not one of these pinned revisions. For the twenty-three pinned revisions, see p. 73. H. Michael Marquardt has suggested that Romans 7 may have been modified "during February or early March, 1832"; if so, that would be a *terminus ad quem* for establishing the date of Romans 3 JST. See Ronald V. Huggins, "Joseph Smith's 'Inspired Translation' of Romans 7," *Dialogue* 26/4 (1993): 163 n. 8.

Some sort of indirect borrowing is more likely, if difficult to establish. The parallel between the JST and Luther is even closer than would be suggested by the 1944 Inspired Version's "justified by faith alone," because the insertion point for the word *alone* in the Joseph Smith marked Bible suggests that he intended the revision to read rather "justified alone by faith," which is an exact English parallel to Luther's German.[15] The debate over Luther's translation was, however, mostly limited to Lutherans and Catholics—high church traditions to which Joseph had had little exposure by this time—and most of the debate had taken place long before in Latin and German. None of the sources I have checked that would have been most readily available to Joseph during this time period make any reference to this translation. So while it remains possible that Joseph got the idea to insert the word *alone* at this specific point in Romans 3:28 from some secondary English source that was available to him, as of yet such a source has not been identified and the revision appears to have been made independently.[16]

---

15. See Faulring, Jackson, and Matthews, *Original Manuscripts*, 482-83.

16. Huggins, "'Inspired Translation' of Romans 7," 159-82, suggests the following as the most likely possibilities for external works that may have had an influence on JST Romans, given their popularity, accessibility, and for some their grounding in the Methodist and Campbellite traditions: (1) Alexander Campbell, ed., *The Sacred Writings of the Apostles and Evangelists of Jesus Christ, Commonly Styled The New Testament. Translated from the Original Greek, by George Campbell, James MacKnight, and Philip Doddridge, Doctors of the Church of Scotland. With Prefaces to the Historical and Epistolary Books; and an Appendix, Containing Critical Notes and Various Translations of Difficult Passages* (Buffaloe, VA [now Bethany, WV]: Alexander Campbell, 1826); (2) Adam Clarke, *The New Testament of Our Lord and Saviour Jesus Christ. The text carefully printed from the most correct copies of the present Authorized Version. Including the marginal readings and parallel texts. With a Commentary and Critical Notes* (in six volumes of approximately 1,000 pages each) (New York: Emory and Waugh, 1831); (3) Matthew Henry, *A Commentary on the Holy Bible . . . with Practical Remarks and Observations*, 6 vols. (London: Ward, Lock, Boden, 1706); or (4) John Wesley, *Explanatory Notes upon the New Testament* (London: Thomas Cordeux, 1813). None of these sources mentions Luther's translation of Romans 3:28. Luther's version with *allein* is described in Charles Hodge, *Commentary on the Epistle to the Romans* (Philadelphia: Williams and Martien, 1864), 100, the first edition of which was published in Philadelphia in 1835, but that is three years after Joseph dictated Romans 3 JST in 1832. Moses Stuart, *A Commentary on the Epistle to the Romans, with a Translation and Various Excursus* (Andover: Flagg and Gould, 1832), 172,

Although we have no explanation from Joseph as to why he added the word *alone* to Romans 3:28, we do have a lengthy letter from Martin Luther himself largely devoted to his rationale for making the same change to the text: his *Sendbrief vom Dolmetschen*[17] ("An Open Letter on Translating"), which he sent on 12 September 1530 to his good friend Wenceslaus Link, who forwarded it three days later (with his own brief introduction) to be published by the Nürnberg printer Johan Petrius. (This letter is referenced herein as the *Open Letter*.) The *Open Letter* and subsequent reactions to it may offer us some insight into the reasons behind Joseph's emendation of this particular text.

In 1530, Charles V, Emperor of the Holy Roman Empire, called together the princes of his German territories in a Diet at Augsburg to seek unity among them in fending off the attacks of Turkish armies in eastern Austria. He called upon the Lutheran nobility to explain their religious convictions, with the hope that the controversy swirling around the challenge of the Reformation might be resolved. To that end, Philip Melanchthon, a close friend of Luther

reflects the following sentence: "Luther translates *pistei*, ALLEIN *durch den Glauben*, i.e. by faith *only*." This book is an unlikely source for Romans 3:28 JST, given that that verse was dictated early in the year and Stuart suggests a different word (*only*) and a different insertion point than that followed in the JST. Doubtless there were English sources prior to 1832 that mention Luther's insertion of *allein* in his translation, but generally these would have appeared in more technical literature (like Stuart and Hodge). I have not yet found one that would be obviously available to Joseph Smith at that time.

17. The most relevant extracts from this letter are set forth in appendix A. The German text given in the appendix derives from the Weimar edition (see *Werke* 30:627-46) with the original spelling restored as reprinted in the edition of Erwin Arndt, *Martin Luther. Sendbrief vom Dolmetschen und Summarien über die Psalmen und Ursachen des Dolmetschens. Mit einem Anhang ausgewählter Selbstzeugnisse und übersetzungsproben* (Halle/Saale: Max Niemeyer Verlag, 1968). The English translation used in this article is that of Michael D. Marlowe (June 2003) posted at http://www.bible-researcher.com/luther01.html (accessed 24 June 2010), which is a revision of both the translation done by Gary Mann for Project Wittenberg and the traditional English translation of Charles M. Jacobs, revised by E. Theodore Bachmann, "On Translating: An Open Letter," in *Luther's Works: Word and Sacrament*, ed. E. Theodore Bachmann (Philadelphia: Muhlenberg, 1960), 35:175-202.

and a professor of New Testament at Wittenberg University, was called upon to draft what would become known as the Augsburg Confession. Luther was residing at Coburg Castle (which he dubbed "the Wilderness"), where he remained from 23 April to 4 October 1530, yet four days' journey away from the Diet (as he remained under the ban of the Empire and was not welcome at the official meeting in Augsburg).

Anxious about the outcome of the Diet, Luther kept busy in the Wilderness. His principal activity during this time was to be translation. As he wrote Melanchthon on the day of his arrival, "Out of this Sinai we shall make a Zion and build three tabernacles: One to the Psalter, one to the Prophets, and one to Aesop."[18] He began by translating the Prophets, finishing Jeremiah, portions of Ezekiel, and the Minor Prophets while at the castle. Near the end of his stay, he chose to write the *Open Letter* largely to address criticism he had received for his translation of Romans 3:28. In form it is a response to an inquiry from a friend identified as "N.," although this may simply have been a literary invention.

The tone of the *Open Letter*, especially its beginning, is angry, sarcastic, and defensive. For instance, Luther repeatedly uses some form of the word *Esel* "donkey" as a pejorative for his religious opponents. There is, however, a certain historical context that helps to explain his pique. Duke George of Saxony had prohibited the circulation of Luther's translation in his territory and commissioned Jerome Emser (1478-1527) to prepare a new one. Rather than crafting a completely new translation, however, Emser merely adapted the Luther translation, providing a more traditional introduction and glosses for controversial passages (derived from the Vulgate and the late medieval German Bible). This was presented as a "correction" of Luther's errors, but Luther rightly saw it as plagiarism on a massive scale, and he was furious over it. In the *Open Letter* Luther

---

18. Margaret A. Currie, trans., *The Letters of Martin Luther* (London: Macmillan, 1908), 208.

refuses to call Emser by name, referring to him only obliquely as "that scribbler from Dresden." Luther gamely laughed at the irony of prohibiting his New Testament when it was published under his name, but making it required reading when it was published under the name of another.

Luther begins his response to criticisms of his translation by asserting that the papists cannot translate, as they do not know German well enough to do so. He did the best that he could, and no one is compelled to read it. Any other translator is free to try to do better. He observes that Jerome went through the same thing when he prepared the Vulgate. When you do something publicly, you open yourself to ample criticism. People are quick to criticize, even when they do not have the capacity to do better themselves. Luther then offers his first formal response to the question raised, as follows: "If your papist wishes to make a great fuss about the word *sola* (*alone*), say this to him: 'Dr. Martin Luther will have it so, and he says that a papist and donkey are the same thing.' *Sic volo, sic iubeo, sit pro ratione voluntas.*"[19] This of course was not a serious response, but simply his opening salvo for rhetorical effect.

For the benefit of the person to whom he sent the letter and their own people, however, he turned serious and offered essentially four reasons for his translation. First, he pointed out that his translation had been widely misunderstood as contemplating the Latin *sola*, an adjective modifying the noun *fide* "faith." In fact, however, his translation contemplated the Latin *solum* or *tantum*, and the word *allein* "alone" was an adverb modifying the verb. This is a subtle distinction, but one that his critics had failed to observe in their overly simplistic reading of his text.

---

19. Juvenal, *Saturae* 6.223: "I will it; I command it; my will is reason enough!" In its original context this was part of a diatribe against marriage and women; these are the words spoken by a woman who wants to have one of the slaves crucified for no good reason, against her husband's protests. Luther liked to use this quotation as a characterization of what he viewed as the capricious, unlimited power of the pope.

Second, Luther argued that the insertion of *alone* was necessary to reflect accurately Paul's meaning in a clear and vigorous German. This is a basic principle of translation, that sometimes one must depart from the literal meaning of words in order to clarify the intended sense in the new language. Luther explained that it was the nature of German that when speaking of two things, one of which is affirmed and the other denied, one uses the word *allein* "only" along with the word *nicht* "not" or *kein* "no." For example, "The farmer brings *allein* grain and *kein* money." To be sure, one could say "The farmer brings grain and *kein* money," but adding the word *allein* makes the force of *kein* clearer and more complete.

Third, Luther made an argument that the word *allein* is *theologically* necessary to show that works of any kind were completely excluded from justification. He tried to make it clear that works are important and he was not objecting to the moral law as such, but works played no role in justification, which in his view was only by faith. (This argument would of course be stoutly rejected by Luther's Catholic critics.)

Fourth and finally, Luther protests that he is not the only one or the first to juxtapose *alone* and *faith*. He asserted that Ambrose, Augustine, and many others had employed similar usage long before his translation of Romans 3:28. So Luther appealed to the precedent of the church fathers. (We shall examine this point further below.)

The *Open Letter* conveyed Luther's own defense of his translation, but it did not put a stop to the controversy, which continued to swirl for some time. A dissertation completed almost a century and a half later[20] summarized additional arguments favoring the Luther translation that had been brought forward by Luther apologists:

---

20. Johann Ludwig Schleenaker, "Disputatio Theologico-Apologetica pro genuina B. Lutheri versione: So halten wir es nun daß der Mensch gerecht werde ohne des Gesetzes Werck, allein durch den Glauben, Rom III, 28" (dissertation, University of Strassburg, 1660). My summary of these additional points in favor of the inclusion of *alone* in Romans 3:28 from the dissertation is based on James Morison, *A Critical Exposition of the Third Chapter of Paul's Epistle to the Romans* (London: Hamilton, Adams, 1866), 377–81.

1. The Vulgate frequently inserts the word *only* for emphasis, although there is no corresponding word in the original language. For example, consider 1 Samuel 10:19:

Hebrew	KJV	Vulgate	Douay-Rheims (English translation of the Vulgate)
we'attem hayyom me'astem 'eth- 'eloheykem 'asher- hu' moshiya' lakem mikal-ra'otheykem wetsarotheykem	And ye have this day rejected your God, who himself saved you out of all your adversities and your tribulations	*Vos autem hodie proiecistis Deum vestrum, qui* **solus** *salvavit vos de universis malis et tribulationibus vestris*	But you this day have rejected your God, who *only* hath saved you out of all your evils and your tribulations

2. In quoting Deuteronomy 6:13 in Matthew 4:10, the Savior used *only*, even though there was no corresponding word in the Hebrew:

Hebrew (Deuteronomy 6:13)	KJV (Deuteronomy 6:13)	Greek (Matthew 4:10)	KJV (Matthew 4:10)
'eth-YHWH 'eloheyka tiyra' we'otho tha'abod ubishmo tishshabe'a	Thou shalt fear the LORD thy God, and serve him, and shalt swear by his name	*kurion ton theon sou proskunēses, kai autō* **monō** *latreuseis*	Thou shalt worship the Lord thy God, and him *only* shalt thou serve

3. The Septuagint repeatedly introduces a word for *alone/only*, even though it is not present in the Hebrew. For example, consider Leviticus 11:36:

Hebrew	KJV	Septuagint (LXX)	Brenton's Translation of LXX
'ak ma'yan ubor miqwah-mayim yihyeh tahor wenoge'a benib- latham yitema'	Nevertheless, a fountain or pit, wherein there is plenty of water, shall be clean: but that which toucheth their carcase shall be unclean	**plēn** *pēgōn hudatōn kai lakkou kai sunagōgēs hudatos estai katharon ho de haptomenos tōn thnēsimaiōn autōn akathartos estai*	*Only* if the water be of fountains of water, or a pool, or confluence of water, it shall be clean; but he that touches their carcases shall be unclean

4. The Peshitta uses the same liberty in Romans 4:5.

5. Even Catholic translations after Luther, such as that of Johann Dietenberger (1534), had used this same liberty, as in Mark 13:32, where Dietenberger added *only*.

6. In the Nürnberg Bible of 1483 the corresponding passage in Galatians 2:16 is translated *"only through faith"* (**nur** *durch den Glauben*), and the same passage is translated in the Italian Roman Catholic version, published in Venice in 1546, *ma* **solo** *per la fide di Giesu Christo.*

7. Many of the church fathers were accustomed to use the expression *by faith only* when discussing justification. So were Ambrosiaster and others.

Note that the Luther apologists repeated and stressed the point Luther himself had made, that there was ample precedent among the church fathers for a similar usage juxtaposing in some fashion the words *alone* and *faith*. A serious examination of this claim was made by Robert Bellarmine (1542-1621), who was a Jesuit and a cardinal and who would eventually be canonized as a saint in 1930. Bellarmine wrote the massive *Disputationes de controversiis christianae fidei*, which were first published at Ingolstadt from 1581 to 1593. Bellarmine's erudite and learned *Disputationes* represented a major threat to the Reformation, so much so that several universities established professorial chairs for the specific purpose of responding to them. In his *De justificatione* 1.25, Bellarmine provides a specific catalog of *loci* among the church fathers where the words *alone* and *faith* had indeed been juxtaposed, showing that both Luther and his defenders were correct in their claim that such passages existed. But in each case he went on to demonstrate that the juxtaposition of those words did not necessarily have the solifidian force Luther ascribed to it. Catholics accepted those writings of the church fathers, but understood the "faith" in other senses than did Luther, such as the dogmatic faith of the Catholic Church—and all that that entailed—or what later theologians would call "living faith."

Largely as a result of Bellarmine's work, scholarly Catholic objections to Luther's translation of Romans 3:28 eventually dissipated. Catholic scholars did not really react to Luther's second defense (that *alone* was necessary for sense), and they certainly rejected his third defense grounded in theology. But the first defense (that Luther intended *alone* as an adverb and not as an adjective) helped. Ultimately it was the fourth defense (the precedent of the usage of the church fathers) that was decisive in largely mooting the debate about Luther's translation of Romans 3:28. (See further appendix B.) The situation was perhaps best captured by a statement attributed to Erasmus: *Vox* sola, *tot clamoribus lapidata hoc seculo in Luthero, reverenter in patribus auditur* ("The word *alone*, which has been received with such a shower of stones when uttered in our times by Luther, is yet reverently listened to when spoken by the Fathers").[21] In a recent review of the matter, the Catholic scholar Joseph Fitzmyer concluded on these grounds that the Luther translation was acceptable and was not "church-divisive."[22]

In summary, we began by positing that the addition of *alone* to Romans 3:28 JST most likely is to be accounted for not at the textual level of inquiry but at the translational level. We observed that Luther made the same insertion in his translation, but that the German *Luther Bibel* could not be the direct source for Joseph's revision. Although there might be an indirect, secondary English source that was available to Joseph in this instance, I have as yet been unable to locate such a source, and so Joseph's emendation appears to be independent of Luther's translation. Fortunately for

---

21. Fred Augustus Gottreu Tholuck, *Exposition of St. Paul's Epistle to the Romans: With Extracts from the Evangelical Works of the Fathers and Reformers* (Philadelphia: Sorin and Ball, 1844), 113, attributed this to Erasmus, *Ecclesiastes: sive de ratione concionandi* 1.3. Morison, *Critical Exposition*, 379, correctly observes that this citation (which is repeated by various authors in the literature) is mistaken, but wherever Tholuck got the statement it was an accurate assessment of the situation at that time.

22. Joseph A. Fitzmyer, *Romans: A New Translation with Introduction and Commentary* (New York: Doubleday, 1983), 362. See also Stanislas Lyonnet, *Études sur L'Épître aux Romains* (Rome: Pontifical Biblical Institute, 1989), 116–21.

us, Luther's translation was quite controversial, which resulted in scholarly literature examining it.

We described Luther's *Open Letter*, in which he defended his translation, as well as subsequent scholarship on the question. Joseph's theology was not solifidian, and so, much like Luther's Catholic opponents, he could not have been influenced by something like Luther's third, theologically based argument. Luther's fourth argument of patristic precedent, which is the one that finally carried the day with scholarly Catholics, is one that would have had no influence on the unschooled Joseph, who had no access to the writings of the church fathers and could not have read them in their Greek and Latin publications even if he had. But the Catholic acquiescence on this point teaches us that we too do not need to read the juxtaposition of *faith* and *alone* in Romans 3:28 JST in a solifidian sense, as Joseph certainly did not intend those words to be taken in such a way.[23] Luther's first argument, that he intended an adverb and not an adjective, is one that is matched by Joseph, as the insertion point in his marked Bible makes it clear that *alone* in Romans 3:28 JST was intended to be an adverb, not an adjective.

The major insight from the intellectual history regarding Luther's translation that we can apply to a better understanding of this JST revision is Luther's second defense, that the addition of *alone* was necessary for sense so as to represent Paul's meaning in clear and vigorous language. As we have seen, using *alone/only* in such a way is actually a translator's device attested elsewhere for providing a sense of emphasis in the target language of the translation. As well articulated by Morison, "The word does not modify in the least the doctrinal idea of the Apostle. It simply gives a little more edge or emphasis to it,—emphasis that was doubtless in

---

23. For instance, we could read *faith* here not merely as a passive belief, but in an active sense in which action is implied, perhaps better represented in English with something like *faithfulness*.

thorough accordance with the thought and feeling of the inspired writer."[24]

This JST revision certainly benefits from the Luther precedent, which helps to establish its *bona fides* as a (periphrastic) translation. Further, the literature concerning Luther's translation helps us to understand and appreciate how the word *alone* was meant to function in the JST. But in a way, the JST returns the favor. I get the impression that people tended not to take Luther's second defense very seriously, at least at first, because they assumed that his *real* reason for adding the word was his third defense grounded in his theological commitments. It seems to me that Romans 3:28 JST is about as strong a demonstration as any Luther apologist could hope for that Luther's second defense had genuine merit. This is because Joseph's theology was *not* solifidian, so he certainly was *not* attempting to press a solifidian agenda with that revision. This is made clear by numerous revisions in the JST New Testament, including Romans; one illustration from Romans 4:16 JST should suffice to establish this point:

> Therefore it is *ye are justified* of faith, that it might be by *and works, through* grace, to the end the promise might be sure to all the seed; not to that *them* only which is *who are* of the law, but to that *them* also which is *who are* of the faith of Abraham; who is the father of us all.

The JST revision of Romans 3:28 only works if it is understood as being made for sense, emphasis, and clarity. Luther was not translating for the elite, but rather he was attempting to make his language clear, as he writes in his *Open Letter*, "for the mother in the home, the children in the street, the common man in the marketplace." Joseph Smith was of humble origins and was just such a common man. And to his eye and ear, apparently quite independently of

---

24. Morison, *Critical Exposition*, 377–78.

Luther, the word *alone* was necessary in this verse for it to ring right in his native tongue (in Joseph's case, English).[25]

In conclusion, the effect of Joseph's insertion of *alone* in Romans 3:28 JST is, I believe, well captured by this text from a popular Bible commentary on that verse:

> There is no problem in adding the word "alone" to the word "faith"—a tradition that goes way back beyond Luther, at least to Aquinas—as long as we recognize what it means: not that a person is "converted" by faith alone without moral effort. . . , nor that God's grace is always prior to human response . . . but that the badge that enables all alike to stand on the same, flat ground at the foot of the cross, is faith.[26]

Kevin L. Barney is a partner in Kutak Rock LLP.

---

25. There are two other translations that also use *allein/alone* in Romans 3:28, in each case in parentheses: Otto Kuss, *Der Römerbrief* (Regensburg: Verlag Friedrich Pustet, 1963), 174, and Ernst Käsemann, *Commentary on Romans*, ed. and trans. Geoffrey W. Bromiley (Grand Rapids: Eerdmans, 1994), 101.

26. *The New Interpreter's Bible* (Nashville: Abingdon, 2002), 10:482.

Appendix A

Relevant Extracts from Luther's *Open Letter*

[Greeting]

Ich hab ewer schrifft empfangen mit den zwo Questen odder fragen / darin ihr meines berichts begert. Erstlich / Warümb ich zun Römern am dritten Capitel die wort S. Pauli / Arbitramur hominem iustificari ex fide absque operibus legis / *also verdeudscht habe. Wir halte / das der mensch gerecht werde on des gesetzs werck / allein durch den glauben Und zeigt darneben an / wie die Papisten sich über die massen unnütz machen / weil im Text Pauli nicht stehet das wort /* Sola (allein) *Und sey solcher zusatz von mir nicht zu leiden / inn Gottes worten etc.*

I received your letter with the two questions,[c] or inquiries, requesting my response. In the first place, you ask why in translating the words of Paul in the 3rd chapter of the Epistle to the Romans, *Arbitramur hominem iustificari ex fide absque operibus legis,*[d] I rendered them, "We hold that a man is justified without the works of the law, by faith alone," and you also tell me that the papists are causing a great fuss because Paul's text does not contain the word *sola* (*alone*), and that my addition to the words of God is not to be tolerated.

c. The second question was whether the departed saints intercede for us, which Luther addresses briefly at the end of the *Open Letter*, and which is beyond the scope of this essay.

d. A Latin rendering of Romans 3:28, which matches precisely neither the Vulgate, which reads *arbitramur enim iustificari hominem per fidem sine operibus legis*, nor Erasmus's Latin version, which reads *arbitramur igitur fide iustificari hominem absque operibus legis*. See Heinz Bluhm, *Luther Translator of Paul: Studies in Romans and Galatians* (New York: Lang, 1984), 106.

[Seven paragraphs, to the effect that Papists can't translate into German; he's not forcing anyone to read his translation; they can do their own; Jerome was criticized, too; the scribbler from Dresden and his prince; put his translation side by side against his and see for yourself how the scribbler plagiarized.]

Und das ich widder zur sachen kome / Wenn ewer Papist sich viel unnütze machen wil mit dem wort (Sola / Allein) *so sagt ihm flugs also / Doctor Martinus Luther wils also haben / und spricht / Papist und Esel sey ein ding /* Sic volo / sic iubeo / sit pro ratione voluntas. *Denn wir wöllen nicht der Papisten schuler noch iünger / sondern ihre meister und richter sein / Wöllen auch ein mal stoltzieren un pochen mit den Esels köpffen / Und wie Paulus widder seine tollen heiligen sich rhümet / so wil ich mich auch wider diese meine Esel rhümen / Sie sind Doctores? Ich auch. Sie sind gelert? Ich auch. Sie sind Prediger? Ich auch. Sie sind Theologi? Ich auch. Sie sind Disputatores? Ich auch. Sie sind Philosophi? Ich auch. Sie sind Dialectici? Ich auch. Sie sind Legenten? Ich auch. Sie schreiben bücher? Ich auch.*

But I will return to the subject at hand. If your papist wishes to make a great fuss about the word *sola* (*alone*), say this to him: "Dr. Martin Luther will have it so, and he says that a papist and a donkey are the same thing." *Sic volo, sic iubeo, sit pro ratione voluntas.* For we are not going to be students and disciples of the papists. Rather, we will become their teachers and judges. For once, we also are going to be proud and brag, with these blockheads; and just as Paul brags against his mad raving saints, I will brag against these donkeys of mine! Are they doctors? So am I. Are they scholars? So am I. Are they preachers? So am I. Are they theologians? So am I. Are they debaters? So am I. Are they philosophers? So am I. Are they logicians? So am I. Do they lecture? So do I. Do they write books? So do I.

[Two paragraphs, to the effect that he can translate, they cannot; let this be the answer to your first question.]

Euch aber und den unsern wil ich anzeigen / warümb ich das wort (Sola) hab wöllen brauchen / Wiewohl Roma. 3. nicht Sola / *sondern* solum *odder* tantum *von mir gebraucht ist / Also fein sehen die Esel meinen Text an. Aber doch hab ichs sonst anderswo /* sola fide *gebraucht / und wil auch beide* Solum *und* Sola *haben. Ich hab mich des gevlissen im dolmetschen / das ich rein und klar deudsch geben möchte.*

For you and our people, however, I shall show why I used the [German equivalent of the] word *sola*—even though in Romans 3 it was not [the equivalent of] *sola* I used but *solum* or *tantum*. That is how closely those donkeys have looked at my text! Nevertheless I have used *sola fides* elsewhere; I want to use both *solum* and *sola*. I have always tried to translate in a pure and clear German.

*Also habe ich hie Roma. 3. fast wol gewust / das im Lateinischen und Griechischen Text / das wort (*Solum*) nicht stehet / und hetten mich solchs die Papisten nicht dürffen leren. War ists / Diese vier buchstaben* Sola *stehen nicht drinnen / welche buchstaben die Eselsköpff ansehen / wie die kue ein new thor / Sehen aber nicht / das gleichwol die meinung des Texts inn sich hat / und wo mans wil klar und gewaltiglich verdeudschen / so gehöret es hinein / den ich habe Deudsch / nicht Lateinisch noch Griechisch reden wöllen / da ich deudsch zu reden im dolmetschen furgenomen hatte. Das ist aber die art unser Deudschen sprache / wen sich ein rede begibt / von zweien dingen*

I know very well that in Romans 3 the word *solum* is not in the Greek or Latin text—the papists did not have to teach me that. It is fact that the letters *s-o-l-a* are not there. And these blockheads stare at them like cows at a new gate, while at the same time they do not recognize that it conveys the sense of the text—if the translation is to be clear and vigorous [*klar und gewaltiglich*], it belongs there. I wanted to speak German, not Latin or Greek, since it was German I had set about to speak in the translation. But it is the nature of our language that in speaking about two things, one which is affirmed, the other denied, we use the

/ der man eins bekennet / und das ander verneinet / so braucht man des worts solum (allein) neben dem wort (nicht odder kein) Als wen man sagt / Der Bawr bringt allein korn und kein gelt / Item / ich hab warlich itzt nicht gelt / sondern allein korn / Ich hab allein gessen und noch nicht getruncken / Hastu allein geschrieben und nicht uberlesen? Und der gleichen unzeliche weise inn teglichem brauch.

word *allein* [only] along with the word *nicht* [not] or *kein* [no]. For example, we say "the farmer brings *allein* grain and *kein* money"; or "No, I really have *nicht* money, but *allein* grain"; I have *allein* eaten and *nicht* yet drunk"; "Did you write it *allein* and *nicht* read it over?" There are countless cases like this in daily usage.

Inn diesen reden allen / obs gleich die Lateinische oder Griechische sprache nicht thut / so thuts doch die Deudsche / und ist ihr art / das sie das wort (Allein) hinzu setzt / auff das / das wort (nicht odder kein) deste völliger und deutlicher sey / Den wiewol ich auch sage / Der Bawer bringt korn und kein gelt / So laut doch das wort (kein gelt) nicht so völlig und deutlich / als wenn ich sage / Der Bawer bringt allein korn und kein gelt / und hilfft hie das wort (Allein) dem wort (kein) so viel / das es eine völlige Deudsche klare rede wird / denn man mus nicht die buchstaben inn der Lateinischen sprachen fragen / wie man sol Deudsch reden / wie diese Esel thun / Sondern man mus die mutter ihm hause / die kinder

In all these phrases, this is a German usage, even though it is not the Latin or Greek usage. It is the nature of the German language to add *allein* in order that *nicht* or *kein* may be clearer and more complete. To be sure, I can also say, "The farmer brings grain and *kein* money," but the words "*kein* money" do not sound as full and clear as if I were to say, "the farmer brings *allein* grain and *kein* money." Here the word *allein* helps the word *kein* so much that it becomes a completely clear German expression. We do not have to ask the literal Latin how we are to speak German, as these donkeys do. Rather we must ask the mother in the home, the children on the street, the

auff der gassen / den gemeinen man auff dem marckt drümb fragen / und den selbigen auff das maul sehen / wie sie reden / und darnach dolmetschen / so verstehen sie es denn / und mercken / das man Deudsch mit ihn redet.

common man in the marketplace. We must be guided by their language, by the way they speak, and do our translating accordingly. Then they will understand it and recognize that we are speaking German to them.

[Eight paragraphs going over other examples, such as the abundance of the heart example; the loss of ointment example; the hail Mary example; it would take him a year to explain rationale behind all of his word choices; he had no ulterior motives; the sealed/signified example.]

Das sey vom dolmetschen und art der sprachen gesagt / Aber nu hab ich nicht allein der sprachen art vertrawet und gefolget / das ich zun Römer am dritten / Solum (allein) habe hinzu gesetzt / Sondern der Text und die meinung S. Pauli foddern und erzwingens mit gewalt / Denn er handelt ja daselbs das heubtstück Christlicherl lere / Nemlich / das wir durch den glauben an Christum / on alle werck des gesetzs gerecht werden / und schneidt alle werck so rein abe / das er auch spricht / des gesetzes (das doch Gottes gesetz und wort ist) werck nicht helffen zur gerechtigkeit / Und setzt zum Exempel Abraham / das der selbige sey so gar on werck gerecht worden / das auch das höhest werck / das dazumal new gepoten ward von Gott / fur

So much for translating and the nature of language. However, I was not depending upon or following the nature of the languages alone when I inserted the word *solum* in Romans 3. The text itself, and Saint Paul's meaning, urgently require and demand it. For in that passage he is dealing with the main point of Christian doctrine, namely, that we are justified by faith in Christ without any works of the Law. Paul excludes all works so completely as to say that the works of the Law, though it is God's law and word, do not aid us in justification. Using Abraham as an example, he argues that Abraham was so justified without works that even the highest work, which had been

und uber allen andern gesetzen und wercken / Nemlich / die beschneittung / ihm nicht geholffen habe zur gerechtigkeit/ Sondern sey on die beschneittung / und on alle werck gerecht worden / durch den glauben / wie er spricht / Cap. 4. Ist Abraham durch die werck gerecht worden / So mag er sich rhümen / Aber nicht fur Gott / Wo man aber alle werck so rein abschneit / da mus ja die meinung sein / das allein der glaube gerecht mache / Und wer deutlich und dürre von solchem abschneiten der werck reden wil / der mus sagen / Allein der glaube / und nicht die werck machen uns gerecht / das zwinget die sache selbs / neben der sprachen art.

commanded by God, over and above all others, namely circumcision, did not aid him in justification. Rather, Abraham was justified without circumcision and without any works, but by faith, as he says in chapter 4: "If Abraham were justified by works, he may boast, but not before God." So, when all works are so completely rejected—which must mean faith alone justifies—whoever would speak plainly and clearly about this rejection of works will have to say "Faith alone justifies and not works." The matter itself and the nature of language requires it.

[Three paragraphs, to the effect that people object that this suggests no need for good works; not just any works but works of the Law; why all this ranting and raving?]

Auch bin ichs nicht allein / noch der erste / der da sagt / Allein der glaube macht gerecht / Es hat fur mir Ambrosius / Augustinus / und viel andere gesagt / Und wer S. Paulum lesen und verstehen sol / der mus wol so sagen / und kan nicht anders / Seine wort sind zu starck / un leiden kein / ja gar kein werck / Ists kein werck / so mus der glaube alleine sein.

Furthermore, I am not the only one, nor the first, to say that faith alone makes one righteous. There was Ambrose, Augustine and many others who said it before me. And if a man is going to read and understand St. Paul, he will have to say the same thing, and he can say nothing else. Paul's words are too strong—they allow no

O, wie solt es so gar eine feine / besserliche / unergerliche lere sein / wenn die leute lernten / das sie nebe dem glauben / auch durch werck from möchten werden / das wer so viel gesagt / das nicht allein Christus tod unser sunde weg neme / sondern unser werck thete auch etwas dazu / Das hiesse Christus tod fein geehret / das unser werck ihm hülffen / und kündten das auch thun das er thut / auff das ihm gleich gut und starck weren / Es ist der Teuffel / der das blut Christi nicht kan ungeschendet lassen.

Weil nu die sache im grund selbs foddert / das man sage / Allein der glaub macht gerecht / Und unser deudschen sprachen art / die solchs auch lernt also aus zusprechen / Habe dazu der Heiligen Veter Exempel / und zwinget auch die fahr der leute / das sie nicht an den wercken hangen bleiben / den des glaubens feilen / und Christum verlieren / sonderlich zu dieser zeit / da sie so lang her der werck gewonet / un mit macht davon zu reissen sind. Sso ists nicht allein recht / sondern auch hoch von nöten / das man auffs aller deutlichst und völligst eraus sage / Allein der glaube on werck macht frum / Und rewet mich / das ich nicht

works, none at all! Now if it is not works, it must be faith alone. Oh what a fine, constructive and inoffensive teaching that would be, if men were taught that they can be saved by works as well as by faith. That would be like saying that it is not Christ's death alone that takes away our sin but that our works have something to do with it. Now that would be a fine way of honoring Christ's death, saying that it is helped by our works, and that whatever it does our works can also do—which amounts to saying that we are his equal in strength and goodness. This is the very devil's teaching, for he cannot stop abusing the blood of Christ.

Therefore the matter itself, at its very core, requires us to say: "Faith alone justifies." The nature of the German language also teaches us to say it that way. In addition, I have the precedent of the holy fathers. The dangers confronting the people also compel it, for they cannot continue to hang onto works and wander away from faith, losing Christ, especially at this time when they have been so accustomed

auch dazu gesetzt habe / alle und aller / also on alle werck aller gesetz das es vol und rund eraus gesprochen were / darümb sols inn meinem Newen Testament bleiben / und solten alle Papstesel toll und töricht werden / so sollen sie mirs nicht eraus bringen. Das sey itzt davon gnug / Weiter wil ich (so Gott gnade gibt) davon reden im büchlin / De iustificatione.

to works they have to be pulled away from them by force. It is for these reasons that it is not only right but also necessary to say it as plainly and forcefully as possible: "Faith alone saves without works!" I am only sorry I did not also add the words *alle* and *aller,* and say, "without *any* works of *any* laws." That would have stated it with the most perfect clarity. Therefore, it will remain in the New Testament, and though all the papal donkeys go stark raving mad they shall not take it away. Let this be enough for now. God willing, I shall have more to say about it in the treatise *On Justification.*[e]

e. Although there are some extant fragments of it in the form of notes and outlines, this tract was never completed.

[Eleven paragraphs addressing the second question, on whether the departed saints intercede for us.]

Appendix B
Juxtapositions of *Faith* and *Alone* in
Theological Traditions Predating Luther[27]

1. Origen, *Commentarius in Epistolam ad Romanos,* cap 3[f]

Et dixit (Apostolus) sufficere solius fidei justificationem ("And the apostle says that justification by faith alone is sufficient")

2. Hilary, *Commentarius in Matthaeum* 8:6[g]

et remissum ab eo quod lex laxare non poterat. Fides enim sola justificat. ("and this was forgiven by him [Christ], because the Law could not yield, for faith alone justifies.")

3. Basil, *Homilia de humilitate* 20.3[h]

Haec est perfecta, et integra gloriatio in Deo, quando neque ob justitiam suam quis se jactat: sed novit quidem se ipsum verae justitiae indignum, sola autem fide in Christum justificatum. ("In this is the perfect and complete boasting in God,

---

27. The first eight illustrations were listed and discussed by Robert Bellarmine (1542-1621), *Controversarium de justificatione* 1.25, in *Decimae quartae controversiae generalis de reparatione gratiae controversia secunda principales de justificatione impii et bonis operibus generatim quinque libris explicata* (Paris: Vives, 1870), 6:204-7. (Greek passages are given in Bellarmine's Latin translation.) Stanislas Lyonnet added item 9 in his *Quaestiones in epistolam ad Romanos,* prima series, 2nd ed. (Rome: Pontifical Biblical Institute, 1962), 114-18. Items 10 and 11 were suggested by Fitzmyer, *Romans,* 360-61. This list is meant to be illustrative, not exhaustive. In the notes to this appendix, the abbreviation PG stands for J. P. Migne, ed., *Patrilogiae Cursus Completus, Series Graeca,* published by Migne's own publishing house in Paris in 166 volumes from 1857 to 1866; PL stands for Migne, ed., *Patrilogiae Cursus Completus, Series Latina,* published in 217 volumes from 1844 to 1849; and CSEL stands for *Corpus Scriptorum Ecclesiasticorum Latinorum,* a series begun in 1864 with the goal of superseding PL, published by a committee of the Austrian Academy of Sciences.

that no one is extolled on account of his own righteousness, but we know that he, being destitute of real righteousness, is justified by faith only in Christ.")

4. Ambrosiaster, *In Epistolam ad Romanos* 3.24[i]

sola fide justificati sunt dono Dei ("through faith alone they have been justified by a gift from God")

5. John Chrysostom, *Homilia in Epistolam ad Titum* 3.3[j]

Si credis fidei, cur alia infers, quasi fides justificare non sufficiat sola? ("If you believe in faith, why do you add other things, as if faith alone were not sufficient to justify?")

6. Cyril of Alexandria, *In Ioannis Evangelium* 10.15.7[k]

Hominem per solam fidem inhaerere Christo. ("Man clings to Christ by faith alone.")

7. Bernard, *In Canticum sermones* 22.8[l]

solam justificatus per fidem ("is justified by faith alone")

8. Theophylact, *Expositio in Epistolam ad Galatas* 3.12-13[m]

Fides sola habet in se justicandi virtutem ("Faith alone has within itself the power of justifying")

9. Thomas Aquinas, *Expositio in Epistolam 1 ad Timotheum* cap. 1, lect. 3

Non est ergo in eis [moralibus et caeremonialibus legis] spes iustificationis, sed in sola fide, Rom. 3.28: "Arbitramur justificari hominem per fidem, sine operibus legis" ("Therefore the hope of justification is not found in them [the moral and ceremonial requirements of the law], but in faith alone, Rom. 3:28: "We consider a human being to be justified by faith, without the works of the law.")

10. Marius Victorinus, *In Epistolam Pauli ad Galatas*, ad 2:15-16

Ipsa enim fides sola iustificationem dat—et sanctificationem ("For faith itself alone gives justification and sanctification")

11. Augustine, *De fide et operibus* 22.40[n]

Licet recte dici pussit ad solam fidem pertinere dei mandata, si non mortua, sed viva illa intellegatur fides, quae per dilectionem operator ("Although it can be said that God's commandments pertain to faith alone, if it is not a dead [faith], but rather understood as that live faith, which works through love")

f. Cf. PG 14:952.
g. Cf. PL 9:961.
h. Cf. PG 31:529C.
i. Cf. CSEL 81.1.119, 130.
j. Cf. PG 62:679 (in Latin translation but not in Greek text).
k. Cf. PG 74:368.
l. Cf. PG 183:881.
m. Cf. PG 124:988.
n. Cf. CSEL 41.84-85.

CHAPTER 2

๖☛

"REST ASSURED, MARTIN HARRIS WILL BE HERE IN TIME"

Susan Easton Black and Larry C. Porter

I seek out my sheep, and will deliver them out of all places where they have been scattered in the cloudy and dark day. (Ezekiel 34:12)

The name of Martin Harris is well known to the worldwide membership of the Church of Jesus Christ of Latter-day Saints as one of the Three Witnesses of the Book of Mormon. What is not well known is that Martin Harris was the only one among the Three Witnesses or the Eight Witnesses of the Book of Mormon to journey to the Salt Lake Valley, though he was not willing to come until 1870, in the eighty-eighth year of his life.

"The Old Spirit of Mormonism Here"

Elder David B. Dille[1] of Ogden, Utah, was called on a mission to England at the April general conference of the Church of

---

1. David Buel Dille (5 April 1812–1 January 1887)—farmer, stonemason, wheelwright, assessor, politician—was born at Euclid, Cuyahoga County, Ohio, the son of David Dille and Mary Sailor. He married Harriet Lucretia Welch on 16 March 1837 in Euclid, Ohio. He was baptized by Elder Bushrod W. Wilson and gathered with the Saints at Nauvoo in 1842. He was endowed in the Nauvoo Temple on 1 January 1846. He traveled in the James Pace Wagon Company (David Bennett's Division) to Salt Lake City, arriving 15 September 1850. Dille located at Farr's Fort, Weber County, Utah. On

Jesus Christ of Latter-day Saints in 1852. He accepted the call but found it necessary to delay his departure until the spring of 1853 when he and two other elders literally "got up a team together" to cross the plains. Elder Willard G. McMullin furnished the carriage, Charles R. Dana provided one mule, while David B. Dille supplied another mule and all the harnesses. Elder Dille left the Rockies with just forty-five cents in his pocket.[2]

En route to the East, forty-one-year-old Dille visited his brothers and sisters in Euclid, Ohio, a Cuyahoga County township, about thirteen miles west of Kirtland. Knowing that Martin Harris lived nearby, and "having business" with him, Elder Dille went to Kirtland to see the seventy-year-old Book of Mormon witness. While yet a non-Mormon, Dille had worked on the Kirtland Temple with his brother Samuel Dille, both of whom had been hired by the Mormons as stonecutters. David and his wife, Harriet Lucretia Welch, were eventually converted to the Mormon faith by Elders Bushrod W. Wilson and Linsay A. Brady. Elder Wilson baptized the couple. Elder Dille affirmed, "My first gathering with the saints was at Nauvoo, Illinois in the summer of 1842."[3]

Now, as a Mormon elder from Utah, Dille waited upon Martin Harris at his residence two miles east of the village. Dille found Martin at home with his wife, Caroline, and their little daughter

---

26 January 1851, when Lorin Farr became the stake president of the Weber Stake of Zion, covering Weber County, Utah, he selected David B. Dille as his second counselor. Dille served a mission to Great Britain, 1853–57. He was buried in the Neeley Idaho Cemetery. See David B. Dille, "Reminiscences, 1886," MS 1107, Church History Library, The Church of Jesus Christ of Latter-day Saints, Salt Lake City, Utah (hereafter Church History Library); John Parley Clay and Martha Ann Clay, *The Life of David Buel Dille, 5 April 1812–1 January 1887* (Logan, UT: Clay's Printing, 2002), chaps. 2–3; Amy Oaks Long, David J. Farr, and Susan Easton Black, *Lorin Farr: Mormon Statesman* (Salt Lake City: Winslow Farr Sr. Family Organization, 2007), 60; Milton R. Hunter, *Beneath Ben Lomond's Peak: A History of Weber County 1824–1900* (Salt Lake City: Deseret News Press, 1945), 432.

2. Dille, "Reminiscences, 1886," 3; Clay and Clay, *Life of David Buel Dille*, 15.

3. Dille, "Reminiscences, 1886," 1, 3; Clay and Clay, *Life of David Buel Dille*, 12; Jay D. Andrews, *Early Descendants of David Dille, Sr.,* vol. 2 (Yorktown, VA: by the author, 1997), 34.

Sarah. Although Martin was in bed at the time and had resolved not to "admit anyone into his room for three days," he allowed his old acquaintance to enter. "His good wife introduced me to him, he received me very coldly but told me to take a seat," recalled Dille. "I obeyed." After a few moments, Martin inquired, "How are they getting along at Salt Lake?" Dille answered, "Fine, delightfull." Dille's response was not satisfactory to Martin. He came to the point: "How are they getting along with polygamy?" Dille said, "Them that was in it was very comfortable." Martin pressed him for a better answer: "How do you reconcile polygamy with the doctrine taught by one of the old prophets?" Dille replied, "Mr. Harris, if necessary take what you call polygamy to fulfill that prophecy. . . . There is more females born into the world than there is males and besides the many thousands of young men slain in battle, leaving the ladies without a mate." After reflecting upon his answer, Martin said, "It is so but I never thought of it in that light before." He then interrupted their conversation to ask Caroline to bring him breakfast before again turning to Elder Dille. "I have not eaten anything for three days but the old spirit of Mormonism has cured me," he claimed. Martin then entreated the missionary, "You must stay with me all day." Having made other plans, Dille told Martin that he would be visiting "Bro. Whiting that afternoon." And then Martin invited him to "stay till noon and we will get you a good dinner and I will go with you." Dille replied, "You can't go, you are sick."[4]

At this, Martin sprang out of bed and began to put on his clothes while saying, "sick, no, you have brought the old spirit of Mormonism here and it has cured me." After dinner, both men called upon Brother Whiting. It was in the Whiting home that Martin spoke at length of the coming forth of the Book of Mormon:

> Do I not know that the Book of Mormon is true? Did I not
> hear the voice of God out of heaven declaring that it was

---

4. Dille, "Reminiscences, 1886," 3-4.

truth and correctly translated? Yes[,] I did[,] and you know
I did for I see you have the spirit of it. . . .[5] I know that the
plates have been translated by the gift and power of God,
for his voice declared it unto us. . . . And as many of the
plates as Joseph Smith translated I handled with my hands,
plate after plate.[6]

Martin then estimated the dimensions of the plates: "I should think
they were so long [demonstrating with his hands], or about eight
inches, and about so thick, or about four inches; and each of the
plates was thicker than the thickest tin." Dille asked him if he "ever
lost 3,000 dollars by the publishing of the Book of Mormon." Martin replied, "I never lost one cent. Mr. Smith . . . paid me all that I
advanced, and more too."[7]

That evening Elder Dille preached in a house built by Hyrum
Smith in Kirtland. After listening to his address, Martin said, "Just
let me go with you to England, I see you can preach. You do the
preaching and I will bear testimony to the Book of Mormon and we
will convert all England." Elder Dille replied, "You can not go, you
are too crooked." Martin queried, "Will I ever be any straighter?"
Dille told him, "Go to Salt Lake and get straightened up and then
[you] could go." Convinced that a better life awaited him in the

---

5. Dille, "Reminiscences, 1886," 4.

6. Elder Dille gave this "Additional Testimony" of his conversation with Martin
Harris in a manuscript dated 15 September 1853, which was later found and published
in the *Millennial Star*; see "Testimonies of Oliver Cowdery and Martin Harris," *Millennial Star* 21 (20 August 1859): 545-46. The manuscript was apparently prepared not
long after his interview with Harris as he didn't leave the port at Philadelphia on the
steamboat *City of Glasgow* until 18 October 1853.

7. As if to suggest that Martin "received a portion of the profits accruing from the
sale of the book"—his response lacks sufficient detail to fully assess the exact status of
his return on the $3,000 advance "and more too." The complex nature of the distribu-
tion and sales of copies of the Book of Mormon, and the decided dearth of accurate
records make it very difficult to compute income ascribed to the respective parties
associated with the volumes. As reported, however, Martin sounded a positive note
of satisfaction with the end results. David B. Dille, "Additional Testimony of Martin
Harris (One of the Three Witnesses) to the Coming Forth of the Book of Mormon,"
Millennial Star 21 (20 August 1859): 545.

West, Martin said, "I have got a good farm, I will advertise it for sale immediately and when you get back you will find me there."[8] In spite of his promise, Martin remained in Kirtland.

The next missionaries to arrive in Kirtland were Elders Thomas Colburn and W. W. Rust. In October 1854 at a conference held in St. Louis, these elders were called to find the "lost sheep" in the northeastern states. In an attempt to fulfill that assignment, Colburn and Rust journeyed to Kirtland, where they "found a few that called themselves Saints, but very weak, many apostates," among whom was Martin Harris. Elder Colburn, like Elder Dille before him, had known Martin years before. Colburn had been baptized in 1833 and had marched with Martin in Zion's Camp in 1834. It seemed natural for him to search out an old friend. Colburn had a "lengthy interview" with Martin. He sent news of their discussion to Elder Erastus Snow, editor of the *St. Louis Luminary*. Excerpts of his interview were printed in the *Luminary*:

> At first [Martin Harris] was down on polygamy, but before we left he informed me that he never should say a word against it. He confessed that he had lost confidence in Joseph Smith, consequently, his mind became darkened, and he was left to himself; he tried the Shakers, but that would not do, then tried Gladden Bishop, but no satisfaction; [he] had concluded he would wait until the Saints returned to Jackson Co., and then he would repair there. He gave us a history of the coming forth of the Book of Mormon; his going to New York and presenting the characters to Professor Anthon, etc.; concluded before we left that "Brigham was Governor," and that the authorities were there, and that he should go there as soon as he could get away.[9]

8. Dille, "Reminiscences, 1886," 4; Dille observed that Martin was then on "a valuable farm of 90 acres." "Additional Testimony," 546.

9. Letter of Elder Thomas Colburn to Erastus Snow, 2 May 1855, *St. Louis Luminary* 1/24 (5 May 1855): 2. See "Francis Gladden Bishop," Leonard J. Arrington Papers,

Yet once again, Martin did not make good on his promise. He refused to leave his beloved Kirtland.

"An Official Divorce Decree Was Not Found"

His promise to migrate to the Salt Lake Valley and his failure to keep that promise not only frustrated visiting missionaries, it led to disappointment and irreconcilable marital strife. For years, his wife, Caroline, had urged him to take their family to the Rocky Mountains, and for just as many years Martin had refused her entreaties. But in 1854, he promised Caroline that he would make good on his promise and take the family to the Salt Lake Valley. Yet as time passed, Martin did not tell friends that he was moving west nor did he try to sell his house or farm holdings in Kirtland. Nothing in his actions suggested that his family would soon be settled in the Rockies. In fact, he spoke with those outside his family circle of becoming a self-appointed guide in the Kirtland Temple.

Frustrated and unable to see any solution to the growing schism between Martin and herself, Caroline determined to make plans of her own. She insisted that Martin take her and the children to Pottawattamie County, Iowa, where her sister Louisa Young Littlefield and her family lived. At some juncture in the time period Martin agreed to her plea. It may well be that Martin and Caroline's sale of some ninety acres of land in Kirtland Township Lot 45 to Isaac Moneysmith on 9 October 1855, and another one-half acre of ground in that same township to William W. Hadden and Nelson I. Hadden on 29 April 1856 are directly connected to expense monies for Caroline and the family's western journey and keep in 1856.[10] Martin obviously felt an obligation to shepherd his expectant wife

---

Mormon History Topics, box 84, fd. 24, Special Collections and Archives, Merrill-Cazier Library, Utah State University, Logan, Utah (hereafter USU Special Collections).

10. Deed Record Book M, Lake County Recorder's Office, pp. 481–82, 9 October 1855, Painesville, Ohio; Deed Record Book N, Lake County Recorder's Office, pp. 48–49, 29 April 1856, Painesville, Ohio.

and the children from Kirtland to Iowa where her family members could give her the necessary assistance.

At age seventy-three, Martin transported Caroline and the children to Crescent City, Rocky Ford (Rockford) Township, Pottawattamie County. There Martin is identified as head of the household by the 1856 Iowa State census taker.[11] For a brief period, he stayed in Crescent City with Caroline and their children, residing right next door to his sister-in-law and her husband, Lyman O. Littlefield, a printer who became publisher of the Crescent City *Oracle*. Interestingly, on the other side of Caroline's dwelling place lived Russell King Homer, longtime friend and the man to whom Martin had sent a copy of the Book of Mormon via a "stranger" when Homer lived in Pennsylvania. In that small Iowa community, Martin's last child, Ida May, was born on 27 May 1856. After these familial events, concern over land holdings, monies, and other obligations in Kirtland

---

11. See Iowa State Census, 1856, Iowa State Collection, 1836-1925, Rocky Ford (Rockford) Township, Pottawattamie County, Iowa State Archives, Des Moines, Iowa. This census for Rockford Township was concluded by 29 August 1856. It lists Martaine [Martin] Harris (73) as the head of the household, his wife Caroline Harris (40), and the children, Martan [Martin] Harris [Jr.] (18), J[ulia] L[acothia] Harris (13), J[ohn] W[heeler] Harris (10), S[olomon Wheeler] Harris (2), and J[I]. C[?] Harris (0) [meaning less than a year old]. This last child is actually the infant Ida May Harris, a female, born to Caroline and Martin in Iowa on 27 May 1856. Another daughter, Sarah Harris, born in 1849, and age 1 year in the 1850 Census of Kirtland, Ohio, had died sometime in childhood and is not listed in this 1856 census. The time and place of her death is unknown. Noel R. Barton, genealogical specialist, the Joseph Smith Papers Project, informed us that "ordinarily the fact that Martin is listed by the census taker in Rockford Township as the head of the household would indicate that he was physically present with the family in Iowa. Otherwise, Caroline would have been listed as the family head." Personal interview of author with Noel R. Barton, 18 February 2010, Family History Library, Salt Lake City, Utah. David H. Pratt, emeritus professor of history at BYU and also a genealogist, informed us that after examining the Iowa 1856 census listing with Martin designated as head of the household, and looking at the attendant circumstances, he is convinced that Martin was personally present for the enumeration. "Martin Harris was definitely in Iowa in 1856. He had sired his last child with Caroline [Ida May]. They had moved west to Iowa where Caroline had family and friends for her departure." Personal interview with David H. Pratt, 30 November 2010 and 3 December 2010. See also Rachel Maretta Homer Crockett, *Homer Family History* (Salt Lake City, UT: by the author, 1942), 15; *History of Pottawattamie County, Iowa* (Chicago: Baskin, Historical Publishers, 1883), 290-91.

caused Martin to leave Iowa and return home. He was again re-siding in Kirtland by 24 April 1857, as recorded in the *Painesville Telegraph* on 30 April: "Martin Harris, of the Latter Day Saints, on Friday last [the 24th], baptized a happy convert in the river, near the Geauga Mills."[12] Although his reasons for returning had much to do with temporal affairs, it led to a marital separation, the duration of which neither Martin nor Caroline had perhaps fully anticipated. After about twenty years of marriage, Martin Harris and Caroline Young ended their marriage vows by separation in 1856. Biographer William H. Homer Jr. claimed that differences between the mar-riage partners was the cause of their separation.[13] Martin pointed to Brigham Young and Mormonism as the cause. Whatever the reason or reasons, Caroline and her four children, ages approximately one to eighteen, chose to remain in Pottawattamie County while Mar-tin Harris returned to Kirtland, some eight hundred miles distant.

On 16 July 1857, A. Milton Musser, a returning missionary from England, informed William Appleby, assistant editor of the *Mor-mon* in New York City: "It may be pleasing for you to learn that the family of Martin Harris (one of the three witnesses to the Book of Mormon) is in Pottawattamie, and purpose migrating to Zion next spring."[14] Although his announcement was met with excitement by Appleby and others, it proved premature, for Caroline and her chil-dren had put down roots in Crescent City, a Mormon settlement. In the interim period to 1859, the family biographer of Martin Harris Jr., Naomi Harris Morris, explained: "Many times the mother and her son, Martin Jr., prevailed upon the father to join one of the

12. *Painesville Telegraph* 35 (30 April 1857): 3.

13. William H. Homer Jr., "'. . . Publish It upon the Mountains': The Story of Mar-tin Harris," *Improvement Era*, May 1955, 345-46.

14. Letter of Amos M. Musser to William I. Appleby, president of the Eastern States Mission and assistant editor of the *Mormon*, 16 July 1857, in "Correspondence of Elder A. M. Musser," *Mormon* [New York City], 15 August 1857, 3.

companies coming west. But their pleadings were to no avail; . . . he returned to the old home in Kirtland."[15]

It was not until the early summer of 1859, three years after arriving in Iowa, that Caroline and her family began the final leg of their journey to the Salt Lake Valley. She joined with her sister, Louisa Young Littlefield, and family for the trek out of Crescent City. This afforded her not only their society but the added security provided by the presence of Louisa's capable husband, Lyman O. Littlefield. They were attached to the ox team company of the Captain Horton D. Haight/Frederick Kesler freight train. The company broke camp at Florence, Nebraska, on 6 June 1859. On their journey westward, the company entry of 28 June 1859 notes, "Caroline Harris got very ill and was almost on the point of death in consequence of an unexpected haemorroage." On 30 June the company moved forward, leaving Caroline and her children in the care of the Littlefields. Caroline survived the hemorrhage ordeal and on 18 July, assisted by the Littlefields, caught up with the main body of the camp.[16] The Haight ox team company reached the Salt Lake Valley on 1 September 1859. President Brigham Young's history recorded, "About 5 P.M. the church train went into the President's yard." That evening, "Martin Harris Jur was introduced to G[eorge] A. S[mith] by Prest. Young, he is the oldest son of Martin Harris by his second wife, daughter of John Young." The Frederick Kesler freight train came into Salt Lake the following day, September 2.[17]

---

15. Norma H. Morris, "The Life of Martin Harris Jr., Son of Martin Harris, A Witness of the Book of Mormon," typescript, p. 1, BX 8670 .Ala no. 327, L. Tom Perry Special Collections, Harold B. Lee Library, Brigham Young University (hereafter Perry Collections).

16. Frederick Kesler Papers 1837-1899, MS 7651, microfilm reel 1, vol. 2, Church History Library; Letter of Frederick Kesler, Ft. Laramie, to Brigham Young, Salt Lake City, 22 July 1859, Brigham Young Office Files 1832-1878, CR 12341, Microfilm reel 37, box 27, fd. 2, Church History Library; Horace S. Eldredge, "Crossing the Plains Narrative," Horace S. Eldredge Journal, 1 June 1859-1 September 1859, Church History Library.

17. Historian's Office Journal, Thursday, 1 September 1859, Church History Library; Journal History of the Church, 1 September 1859, p. 1; Frederick Kesler Papers

In the valley, Caroline and her family were welcomed into the home of her father, John Young. Although Caroline had planned to stay with her father for some time, the attentions of forty-five-year-old widower John Catley Davis cut her stay short.[18] In 1854 Davis, a convert from Birmingham, England—accompanied by his wife, Phoebe Oxenbold Davis, and their seven children—immigrated to America. En route to the valley, Phoebe and two of the children, John Edward and Phoebe, died of cholera in July 1854 and were buried at St. Louis, Missouri. Another child, Frederick William, died of consumption in July 1858 as the family was making preparations to cross the plains. John and the remaining four children later continued their journey to the Salt Lake Valley from the Mormon outfitting post at Florence (Nebraska) with the Edward Stevenson Company, 26 June 1859. John arrived in Salt Lake City on 19 September 1859, three days behind the main company because their wagon had broken down. The family settled in the Salt Lake 17th Ward, where Davis worked as a lock- and gunsmith and was known as a man of good repute.[19]

Following a brief courtship, Caroline Young Harris and John Catley Davis were married at the home of the bride's parents, John and Theodocia Young, on 16 January 1860. Lyman O. Littlefield, Caroline's brother-in-law, performed the ceremony. John and Caroline received their endowments and two months later were sealed in celestial marriage by the bride's uncle, President Brigham Young, at the Salt Lake Endowment House on 1 March 1860.[20] Their right

---

1837-1899, MS 7651, microfilm reel 1, vol. 2, Diaries 1857-1899, 2 September 1859.

18. John Catley Davis (21 April 1814-18 February 1879) is a native of Handsworth, Staffordshire, England. He married Phoebe Oxenbold (Oxenbould) on 24 August 1840 in Handsworth. He died in Brigham City, Box Elder County, Utah, 18 February 1879, and was interred in the Brigham City Cemetery. See John Catley Davis Family Group Record, FamilySearch Ancestral File.

19. Susan Woodland Howard, "John Catley Davis and Phoebe Oxenbold Davis," http://penwood.famroots.org/john_and_phoebe_davis.htm, pp. 1-10; Frank Esshom, *Pioneers and Prominent Men of Utah* (Salt Lake City, UT: Utah Pioneers Book, 1913), 489, 839.

20. "Married," *Deseret News*, 1 February 1860, 384; Endowment House Marriage Record, 1 March 1860, Family History Library, Salt Lake City, Utah. John Catley Davis's

to marry has been questioned since an official divorce decree from Martin Harris has not been found.[21] Caroline's lengthy separation from Martin in both time and distance appeared very final—all marital ties had long been severed. For her it was improbable that she would ever see him again. With both Caroline and John in need of mutual support for their respective families, John's advances were welcome.[22] At the time of their marriage, no questions were asked concerning a writ of divorcement; such formalities were often overlooked in pioneer Utah. One child was born to their union—Joseph Harris Davis on 19 November 1860 in Payson, Utah. He lived only two days, dying on 21 November. After the death of their infant son, Caroline and John returned to Salt Lake City and once again resided in the Salt Lake 17th Ward.[23]

In 1867, after only seven years of marriage, Caroline and John Davis separated. Among the circumstances leading to their separation was a dispute involving Brigham Young. William H. Homer Jr. explains:

---

deceased wife, Phoebe Oxenbold, was sealed to her husband at the same time. On that same date, 1 March 1860, Elijah Walter Davis, the nineteen-year-old son of John Catley Davis, was sealed to Julia Harris, the eighteen-year-old daughter of Martin and Caroline Harris.

21. Family biographers suggest that "one could correctly assume that the laws of the frontier at this time gave Caroline proper license for her remarriage. According to recorded statements, when a three-year period of time had elapsed during which a woman had received no support from her husband, she was legally free to contract another marriage." See Madge Harris Tuckett and Belle Harris Wilson, *The Martin Harris Story: With Biographies of Emer Harris and Dennison Lott Harris* (Provo, UT: Vintage Books, 1983), 69.

22. Dennis A. Wright, "Caroline Young Harris: The Kirtland Wife of Martin Harris," in *Regional Studies in Latter-day Saint Church History: Ohio and Upper Canada*, ed. Guy L. Dorius, Craig K. Manscill, and Craig James Ostler (Provo, UT: BYU Religious Studies Center, 2006), 117; see chapter on William H. Homer Jr. in Wayne Cutler Gunnell, "Martin Harris—Witness and Benefactor to the Book of Mormon" (master's thesis, Brigham Young University, 1955), 125.

23. Nell Sumsion, "Notes on Genealogy of Martin Harris, One of the Witnesses of the Book of Mormon," Genealogical Society of Utah, 21 March 1933, in Gunnell, "Martin Harris—Witness," 122; 1860 US Federal Census, Payson, Utah, 25 August 1860; 1870 US Federal Census, 17th Ward Salt Lake City, Utah, 2 July 1870.

An altercation arose between Mr. Davis and Brigham Young regarding title to land. Caroline supported the views of Brigham Young. Mr. Davis became so enraged that he threatened to leave the Church. John Young, Caroline's father and Brigham's brother, intervened as mediator and the dispute was settled. Thus, seeds of dissention were early sown in the Davis household. Disagreements multiplied and finally resulted in the couple's separation.[24]

Instead of moving back in with her father, Caroline moved north to Smithfield, Cache County, to be near her eldest son, Martin Harris Jr.[25] In Smithfield, she was known as Caroline Harris, not Caroline Davis.[26]

"Wherever He Turned, Life Had Changed"

During these years of difficulty and disappointment that had beset Caroline in the West, Martin too experienced troubles of his own in Kirtland. Many things were in a state of flux, and conditions were constantly changing. The absence of his family was a hard and lonely test. His diminishing financial resources and limitations of advancing age all took their toll. He continued his association

---

24. Letter of William H. Homer Jr., Cody, Wyoming, to Preston Nibley, Salt Lake City, Utah, 31 December 1959, in "William H. Homer research papers, 1867–1965," MSS 825, box 1, fd. 2, p. 3, Perry Collections; John Davis moved to Pleasant Grove, where he lived with his daughter Elizabeth Davis Stewart. According to his granddaughter, a Mrs. Atwood, in February 1878 John left Pleasant Grove, hoping to visit his children in Idaho. When he reached Brigham City, Utah, he became very ill and died. His obituary notice appeared in the *Deseret News*: "Died: At Brigham City, February 16th, 1878, after a prolonged illness, John C. Davis. He joined the Church in Birmingham, England, at an early day, lived the life of a Latter-day Saint, was ordained a High Priest, and died firm in the faith of the gospel." *Deseret News*, 29 May 1878, 271.

25. Her sons John and Solomon Harris resided in the Snake River Valley in Idaho. See "The Forgotten Woman: Letter of Leander S. Harris [to Nell Sumsion]," 19 January 1952. Sumsion, in writing on behalf of the Genealogical Society of Utah, attached Leander Harris's letter to her "Notes on Genealogy of Martin Harris," cited in Gunnell, "Martin Harris—Witness," 126.

26. According to her granddaughter, Sariah Steel of Goshen, Utah, Caroline "was never known by the name of Davis, either in the family circle or among neighbors or friends." Tuckett and Wilson, *Martin Harris Story*, 71.

with the local congregation of the Church of Christ, which circle of friends gave him some conversation and also provided an outlet for preaching. But it was his testimony of the Book of Mormon that kept Martin from becoming a solitary recluse and drifting into comparative obscurity. His powerful testimony, born of his calling as one of the Three Witnesses, kept him in the forefront. As in times past, many came to Kirtland to measure his experience. Believers, the undecided, or skeptics came to laud, inquire, or deride his testimony of an angel, gold plates, and the coming forth of the Book of Mormon. Too, Martin had an insatiable desire to exhibit the Kirtland Temple, the House of the Lord, and the inspired message that it represented to the world. For this task he felt a personal proprietorship and dedicated himself to that work.

Kirtland continued to be a touchstone for individuals and organizations hoping to generate or regenerate their particular religious creed. In October of 1855 William Smith had come to Kirtland and joined with Martin Harris and others in an attempt to reconstitute a church based on the principles of the original organization founded by Joseph Smith. At that time they went to great lengths to itemize those principles. Martin was elected president of their conference, which was held in the Kirtland Temple. However, Stephen Post, secretary of the conference, stipulated that "it was not found expedient to organize" at that time. Instead, the founders resolved to convene "in general conference and Solemn Assembly at the House of the Lord in Kirtland Ohio on the 6th day of Apr. 1856. Then and there to set in order all things not in order in the Church of Jesus Christ."[27]

The anticipated 1856 conference failed to materialize. Stephen Post was there for the conference, but it didn't transpire according to the 1856 appointment. He returned to his home in Erie, Pennsylvania, with the dejected observation, "I find Kirtland apparently a

---

27. Stephen Post Papers 1835-1921, MS 1304, box 6, fd. 3, 3-8 October 1855, Church History Library.

land barren of faith as people without a shepherd."[28] However, William attempted to regenerate his plan once again in 1857. According to Post, "In Sept [1857] Wm Smith got up a revelation appointing me [Stephen Post] a printer to the church &c he is trying to organize as president in Kirtland Ohio."[29]

But it was apparently not until 1858 that a makeshift organization took place at Kirtland involving Martin Harris and William Smith. On 18 May 1858, Dr. Jeter Clinton, who was just returning from a mission in the east, reported to Pres. Brigham Young "that Martin Harris and Wm Smith were at Kirtland, [and] had organized a Church of their own."[30] Similarly, we learn from a 22 June 1858 journal entry of Wilford Woodruff that Enoch Beese and other missionaries coming from England to Utah took occasion to stop in Kirtland. Elder Beese reported to Pres. Young's office that "Martin Harris had reorganized the Church in this place with 6 members. Appointed Wm. Smith their Leader Prophet Seer & Revelator. In [a] few days Harris drove Wm. Smith out of the place & damned him to Hell."[31] William's aspirations for presidency were short-lived at the hands of a disgruntled Martin Harris.

Martin Harris was naturally the subject of numerous interviews locally during the succession of Kirtland years in the 1850s and 1860s. Some of these interviews were recorded and published, providing invaluable insights into the man and the period. In late January 1859, one of the more informative interviews was granted to Joel Tiffany (editor of *Tiffany's Monthly* published in New York City), who visited Martin in Kirtland. Mr. Tiffany affirmed, "The following narration we took down from the lips of Martin Harris, and read the same to him after it was written, that we might be

---

28. Stephen Post Papers 1835-1921, 5-11 April 1856.
29. Stephen Post Papers 1835-1921, 25 October 1857.
30. Brigham Young, "Historian's Office Journal," Tuesday, 18 May 1858, Church History Library.
31. Wilford Woodruff, *Wilford Woodruff's Journal*, ed. Scott G. Kenny (Midvale, UT: Signature Books, 1984), 5:198-99.

certain of giving his statement to the world." Tiffany listened as Martin spoke of Joseph Smith Jr., an angel, and gold plates, without offering his own personal commentary.[32]

Most interviews and verbal exchanges concerning the faith, however, were never printed. Nevertheless, so many opportunities to express his views were proffered him by 1860 that Martin felt very confident in posting his daily occupation as that of "Mormon Preacher."[33] A striking example of the profound effect Martin had on certain visitors to Kirtland when bearing testimony of the validity of the Book of Mormon is readily apparent in the experience of David H. Cannon in 1861. Elder Cannon, a returning missionary from the British Isles, called to see Martin at the home of his son George B. Harris, where Martin was then residing.[34] Harris took him to the temple where David affirmed:

> He testified to me in all solemnity . . . that the angel did appear with the plates from which the Book of Mormon was translated, and testified that they contained a history of the ancient inhabitants of this continent, and that they had been translated by the gift and power of God. There was a feeling [that] accompanied his testimony, when he bore it, that I have never experienced either before or since in any man that I ever heard bear testimony.[35]

As Martin Harris exercised his calling as a witness the Spirit attended him and gave confirmation to the hearer.

---

32. Report of Joel Tiffany's January 1859 interview with Martin Harris in "Mormonism—No. II," *Tiffany's Monthly* (New York) 5/4 (August 1859): 163-70. Tiffany had expressed his personal views of the nature of Mormonism in a previous issue of his magazine and also alluded to the fact that Martin had "conversed with us many times upon the subject." See "Mormonism," *Tiffany's Monthly* (New York) 5/1 (May 1859): 46-51.

33. U.S. Federal Census, Kirtland, Lake County, Ohio 1860.

34. U.S. Federal Census, Kirtland, Lake County, Ohio, 1860, lists Martin Harris, age 77, "Mormon Preacher," as a resident in the household of his son, George B. Harris.

35. Beatrice Cannon Evans and Janath Russell Cannon, *Cannon Family Historical Treasury* (Salt Lake City: George Cannon Family Association, 1967), 250.

Martin continued to deal in realty on a very limited scale as long as he was able. It is interesting that during this period he acquired two one-half acre lots immediately adjoining the Kirtland Temple to the west along Whitney Street (now Maple Street). Lot No. 3 was purchased from Martha Frost on 17 October 1857; Lot No. 2 was procured from Hiram and Electa Stratton, 20 October 1857.[36] Personal circumstances, however, soon necessitated their sale. Martin deeded Lot No. 2 to his son George B. Harris on 10 December 1859 for the consideration of $200.00, and Lot No. 3 to Hiram Dixon on 11 November 1863 for the consideration of $125.00.[37]

Martin had become an object of charity. His financial base was virtually gone by 1860. He lived in the home of his forty-seven-year-old son, George, and his wife, Mary Jane Thompson Harris. James McKnight, in a 27 February 1862 letter to the editor of the *Millennial Star*, reported, "Of [Martin's] property there is little or none left. He has now no home; his son, a worthless scapegrace, with whom he lived, being in prison, and the house deserted."[38] McKnight may not have been acquainted with all of the extenuating circumstances affecting his description. Just six days before his letter was written, 21 February 1862, George B. Harris and his wife were in a divorce hearing at Painesville. The court found George "guilty of Extreme Cruelty" and granted the petitioned-for divorce decree to Mary Jane. Whether or not there was any "prison" time associated with the "Extreme Cruelty" aspect of the divorce proceedings or a separate situation entirely, we are unaware.[39] Whatever the condi-

---

36. Martha Frost to Martin Harris, Lot 3, Deed Record Book S, p. 277, Lake County Recorder's Office, Painesville, Ohio; and Hiram and Electa Stratton, Lot 2, Deed Record Book N, pp. 589-90, Lake County Recorder's Office, Painesville, Ohio.

37. Martin Harris to George B. Harris, Lot No. 2, Deed Record Book T, pp. 524-25, Lake County Recorder's Office, Painesville, Ohio; Martin Harris to Hiram Dixon, Lot No. 3, Deed Record Book X, pp. 462-63.

38. James McKnight, letter to George Q. Cannon, 27 February 1862, published in "Correspondence: America," *Millennial Star* 24 (19 April 1862): 251.

39. Journal No. F, pp. 349-50, Lake County Clerk of Courts, West Annex, Painesville, Ohio.

tion, that same year George B. Harris enlisted at Painesville in the U.S. Army on 12 August 1862 as a private in Company I of the 52nd Regiment of Ohio Volunteer Infantry. At the time of his enlistment, George stood 5' 7", had a light complexion, brown eyes, and dark hair. His stated occupation was a "Seaman." George enrolled in the military to fight for the northern cause in the Civil War. However, bronchitis and general debility landed him in General Hospital for two months, and for a time at the Convalescent Barracks in Nashville, Tennessee. There George was released from active duty on 2 February 1863 with a "Certificate of Disability for Discharge" and returned to Kirtland. Although doctors had hoped for his complete recovery, George died at Kirtland in 1864.[40]

Martin had not been left entirely homeless through the process of the 1862 divorce between his son George and daughter-in-law Mary Jane. At the divorce proceedings Martin was identified in court as still having some ownership rights in the property that he had previously sold to his son. Relative to the disposition of property regarding Mary Jane Thompson Harris and Martin Harris, the Court "ordered and decreed" that:

> The said plaintiff [Mary Jane] have and enjoy with the right to sell and dispose of all the personal property now in her possession and that she have and enjoy as for alimony one undivided half of the premises described in said petition Consisting of the house and lot in Kirtland in Common with Martin Harris he having appeared and Consented thereto, during their joint lives and in the Case of the death of Either the survivor is to have and Enjoy said premises during his or her natural life and at death of the survivor

40. George B. Harris, "Army of the United States, Certificate of Disability for Discharge," National Archives, Record Group 15 (Department of Veterans Affairs), invalid pension, app # 29,712; *Official Roster of the Soldiers of the State of Ohio in the War of the Rebellion, 1861-1866*, vol. 4 (Akron, OH: Published by Authority of the General Assembly, 1887), 669. The grave site of George B. Harris is presently unknown.

the said House and lot to Rest in fee simple in said Alma
Harris the Child of said Mary J and George B. [consider-
ation was also given to "any other Child that may hereafter
be born as the issue of said marriage"].[41]

Mary Jane gave birth to a second child, Henry Harris, shortly thereafter. Thus for an extended period of time Martin was living in a
household consisting of his daughter-in-law Mary Jane Thompson
Harris and her two children, Alma M. Harris and Henry Harris.[42]

In an effort to support himself without undue assistance Martin leased ninety acres of farmland in Kirtland commencing in
1865.[43] Unfortunately he was too old and too tired to work the land
as he desired and his financial situation was such that it was difficult to hire a helping hand. Near the same time, Pomeroy Tucker,
a Palmyra, New York, journalist, wrote an 1867 exposé on Mormonism in which he painted Martin as he remembered him in the
early days of the Restoration, a "prosperous, independent farmer,
strictly upright in his business dealings, and, although evidencing
good qualifications in the affairs of his industrial calling, yet he was
the slave of the peculiar religious fanaticism controlling his mental
organization"—all in the past tense.[44] Tucker failed to write anything of Martin's present condition.

Christopher Crary, a Kirtland and township trustee during this
difficult time for Martin, describes just how desperate the situation
had become regarding his personal plight:

---

41. Journal No. F. pp. 349-50, Lake County Clerk of Courts Office, West Annex,
Painesville, Ohio.

42. William H. Homer Research Papers, MSS 825, box 1, fd. 1 and fd. 2, Perry Col-
lections. Interestingly, this source reveals that Alma M. Harris later went west to
Lewisville, Idaho, in 1885 and there married Ida May Harris, the daughter of Martin
Harris and Caroline Young Harris, in 1886.

43. Rhett Stephens James, "Martin Harris," in *Encyclopedia of Mormonism* (New
York: Macmillan, 1992), 4:576.

44. Pomeroy Tucker, *Origin, Rise, and Progress of Mormonism* (New York: Appleton,
1867), 50.

In 1867 or 1868, while acting as township trustee, complaint was made to me that Martin Harris was destitute of a home, poorly clothed, feeble, burdensome to friends, and that he ought to be taken to the poor-house. I went down to the flats to investigate, and found him at a house near the Temple, with a family lately moved in, strangers to me. He seemed to dread the poorhouse very much. The lady of the house said she would take care of him while their means lasted, and I was quite willing to postpone the unpleasant task of taking him to the poor-house. Everybody felt sympathy for him. He was willing to work and make himself useful as far as his age and debility would admit of.[45]

Adding to the everyday burdens created by having suffered for so long the afflictions of extreme poverty, which had affected him both body and soul, Martin was informed of the death of his brother Preserved Harris, who passed away in Mentor, Ohio, on 18 April 1867. In what would later prove to be another pivotal year, Martin was informed that his brother Emer had succumbed in Logan, Utah, on 28 November 1869. Time was exacting a significant toll on those who had been so close to him across the years.[46] His

45. Christopher G. Crary, *Pioneer and Personal Reminiscences* (Marshalltown, IA: Marshall Printing, 1893), 44–45. George Levi Booth of Mentor, Ohio, interview by M. Wilford Poulson, 20 August 1932. "Poulson, 'Question: Was Martin Harris ever a public charge in his old age here in Kirtland?' Booth, 'Answer: No. he was not. There were people who would not have allowed that to take place.'" See M. Wilford Poulson Collection, Poulson interview, MSS 823, 20 August 1932, box 9, fd. 32, Perry Collections.

46. Preserved died at his home in Mentor, Ohio. He was buried in the Mentor Municipal Cemetery. Emer died at the home of his son Alma Harris in Logan, Utah. He was buried in the Logan City Cemetery. The plaque on his monument reads: "Emer Harris, born at Cambridge, New York, May 29, 1781. A direct descendent of Thomas Harris who came to America with Roger Williams in 1631 for religious freedom. Through influence of his brother Martin, the witness to the Book of Mormon, Emer received [the] first bound copy. He was baptized into the Church in 1831 by Hyrum Smith, called on mission by revelation in 1832 (D.&C. sec. 75:32 [30]), worked on Nauvoo and Kirtland Temples, suffered persecution and mobbings in Missouri and Nauvoo, came to Utah in 1852. Pioneered Ogden, Provo and Southern Utah. Ordained

life, however, was about to be transformed yet again in a very unexpected fashion.

"A Poorly Clad, Emaciated Little Man"

In mid-December 1869 Elder William H. Homer,[47] a returning British missionary en route to his home and family in Utah, stopped in Kirtland overnight. He was accompanied as far as Kirtland by his cousin, James A. Crockett of Summit Township, Crawford County, Pennsylvania, not a member of the Church. The weary travelers asked "[their] landlord who was custodian of the Mormon Temple." Homer recalled that the landlord "informed us that Martin Harris was custodian, and pointed out to us where we would find the old gentleman." On 14 December 1869[48] the two visitors knocked on the door of the cottage where the witness resided and found the eighty-six-year-old Martin to be "a poorly clad, emaciated little man, on whom the winter of life was weighing heavily." Homer affirmed, "In his face might be read the story of his life. There were the marks of spiritual upliftment. There were the marks of keen dissappointment. There was the hunger strain for the peace, the contentment, the divine calm that it seemed could come no more into his life." To Homer, Martin was "a pathetic figure, and yet it was a figure of strength. For with it all there was something about the little man which revealed the fact that he

---

patriarch 1853. The father of 15 children. Died in Logan November 28, 1869 in his 89th year."

47. William Harrison Homer Sr. (13 July 1845–28 January 1934) was born near Quiver, Mason County, Illinois, son of Russell King Homer and Eliza Williamson. He married Susanna Rebecca Raymond on 8 February 1870 in Salt Lake City. William died in Orem, Utah, and is buried in the Salt Lake City Cemetery; see "William Harrison Homer," in Rachel Maretta Homer Crockett, *Homer Family History* (Salt Lake City, UT: by the author, 1942), 56–61; William Harrison Homer, Family Pedigree Chart, Family-Search Ancestral File.

48. The date that Homer and Crockett visited the Kirtland Temple with Martin Harris is verified as 14 December 1869. Both men took occasion to sign the Kirtland Temple Visitor's Register. Crockett signed first, and dated his signature: "December 14th 1869 J.A. Crockett of Summit [township] Crawford Co Pennsylvania." Homer's inscription reads "W. H. Homer Salt Lake City Utah, Territory." Ron Romig, ed., *Martin Harris's Kirtland* (Independence, MO: John Whitmer Books, 2007), 92.

had lived richly, that into his life had entered such noble experiences as come to the lives of but few."[49]

Elder Homer introduced himself to Martin "as a brother-in-law of Martin Harris, Jr.,—as he [Martin Jr.] had married my eldest sister—and as an Elder of the Church who was returning from a foreign mission."[50] Martin snapped, "One of those Brighamite 'Mormons,' are you?" He then "railed impatiently against Utah and the founder of the 'Mormon' commonwealth." To Homer, "Martin Harris seemed to be obsessed. He would not understand that there stood before him a man who knew his wife [Caroline] and children, who had followed the Church to Utah."[51] After a time, Martin asked, "You want to see the Temple, do you?" Elder Homer nodded. "I'll get the key," said Martin. According to Homer, Martin now "radiated with interest." He led Homer and his cousin into the Kirtland Temple and "through the rooms of the Temple and explained how they were used. He pointed out the place of the School of the Prophets. He showed us where the Temple curtain had at one time hung. He related thrilling experiences in connection with the history of the sacred building."[52] While speaking of the neglected state of the temple, Martin again railed "against the Utah 'Mormons'" and said that a "gross injustice had been done to him. He should have been chosen President of the Church."[53] It was then that Martin seemed "somewhat exhausted."[54]

---

49. William H. Homer [Sr.], "The Passing of Martin Harris," *Improvement Era*, March 1926, 468-69; William H. Homer, "The Last Testimony of Martin Harris," pp. 1-6, notarized typescript sworn by William H. Homer, 9 April 1827, MSS 236, Perry Collections. The story by Homer of visiting Martin Harris was largely reprinted by his son, William H. Homer Jr., in "'. . . Publish It upon the Mountains': The Story of Martin Harris," *Improvement Era*, July 1955, 505-6.

50. Homer, "Passing of Martin Harris," 469; Homer Jr., "'Publish It upon the Mountains,'" 505.

51. Homer, "Passing of Martin Harris," 469.

52. Homer, "Passing of Martin Harris," 469; Homer Jr., "'Publish It upon the Mountains,'" 505.

53. Homer, "Passing of Martin Harris," 469.

54. Homer, "Passing of Martin Harris," 469; Homer Jr., "'Publish It upon the Mountains,'" 505.

While they were resting, Homer asked, "Is it not true that you were once very prominent in the Church, that you gave liberally of your means, and that you were active in the performance of your duties?" Martin replied, "That is very true." He mused, "Things were alright then. I was honored while the people were here, but now that I am old and poor it is all different." Homer reported that when questioned about his belief in the Book of Mormon, "the shabby, emaciated little man before us was transformed as he stood with hand outstretched toward the sun of heaven."

> "Young man," answered Martin Harris with impressiveness, "Do I believe it! Do you see the sun shining! Just as surely as the sun is shining on us and gives us light, and the [moon] and stars give us light by night, just as surely as the breath of life sustains us, so surely do I know that Joseph Smith was a true prophet of God, chosen of God to open the last dispensation of the fulness of times; so surely do I know that the Book of Mormon was divinely translated. I saw the plates; I saw the Angel; I heard the voice of God. I know that the Book of Mormon is true and that Joseph Smith was a true prophet of God. I might as well doubt my own existence as to doubt the divine authenticity of the Book of Mormon or the divine calling of Joseph Smith."[55]

To Homer, "it was a sublime moment. It was a wonderful testimony." Indeed, "it was the real Martin Harris whose burning testimony no power on earth could quench." Homer claimed that hearing him testify was "the most thrilling moment" of his life.[56] It was then that Martin turned to Elder Homer and asked, "Who are you?" Homer explained for the second time his relationship. "So

---

55. Homer, "Passing of Martin Harris," 469-70; Homer Jr., "'Publish It upon the Mountains,'" 505.

56. Homer, "Passing of Martin Harris," 470.

my son Martin married your sister," repeated the old man, shaking his hand.

"You know my family then?" "Yes," he replied, "Wouldn't you like to see your family again?" Martin admitted that he would "like to see Caroline and the children" but lamented that his impoverished circumstances prevented such a visit. "That need not stand in the way," Homer said. "President Young would be only too glad to furnish means to convey you to Utah."[57] The mere mention of Brigham Young angered Martin. "Don't talk Brigham Young," he warned. Martin then declared, "He would not do anything that was right." Homer suggested that Martin "send him a message by me." Martin refused. Yet he did admit, "I should like to see my family."[58] Homer entreated him again to convey a message to President Young. Martin replied,

> You call on Brigham Young. Tell him about our visit. Tell him that Martin Harris is an old, old man, living on charity with his relatives. Tell him I should like to visit Utah, my family, my children—I would be glad to accept help from the Church, but I want no personal favors. Wait! Tell him that if he sends money, he must send enough for the round trip. I should not want to remain in Utah.[59]

When Elder Homer reached his home in Utah, he told his father, Russell King Homer, of his visit with Martin Harris. Enthused by the account, his father suggested that they set out together to tell President Young of the visit. Homer recalled, "The president received us very graciously [in his office]. He listened attentively to

---

57. Homer, "Passing of Martin Harris," 470; Homer Jr., "'Publish It upon the Mountains,'" 506.

58. Homer, "Passing of Martin Harris," 470.

59. Homer, "Passing of Martin Harris," 470; Homer Jr., "'Publish It upon the Mountains,'" 506. Homer concluded, "For 25 [32] years he had nursed the old grudge against the leaders of the Church, probably because nobody had had the patience with him that I had shown." Homer, "Passing of Martin Harris," 470-71; Homer Jr., "'Publish It upon the Mountains,'" 506.

my recital of my visit with Martin Harris." During the recitation, "President Young asked questions now and again, to make clear on certain points," before saying, "I want to say this: I was never more gratified over any message in my life. Send for him! Yes, even if it were to take the last dollar of my own. Martin Harris spent his time and money freely when one dollar was worth more than one thousand dollars are worth now. Send for him! Yes indeed I shall send! Rest assured, Martin Harris will be here in time."[60]

"A Great Desire to See Utah, and His Children"

In February 1870, fifty-year-old Elder Edward Stevenson,[61] returning from the east to Salt Lake City, journeyed to Kirtland in hopes of finding Martin Harris. Stevenson, like David Dille and Thomas Colburn before him, had earlier become acquainted with the Book of Mormon witness. "While I was living in Michigan, then a Territory, in 1833, near the town of Pontiac, Oakland Co.," Stevenson penned, "Martin Harris came there and in a meeting where I was present bore testimony of the appearance of an angel exhibiting the golden plates and commanding him to bear a testimony of these things to all people whenever opportunity was afforded him to do so."[62] Thirty-six years later, after fulfilling a mission to

---

60. Homer, "Passing of Martin Harris," 471; Homer Jr., "'Publish It upon the Mountains,'" 506. See Preston Nibley, *The Witnesses of the Book of Mormon* (Salt Lake City: Stevens and Wallis, 1946), 115-23.

61. Edward Stevenson (1 May 1820-27 January 1897) first heard the gospel preached by Elders Jared Carter and Joseph Wood. He was baptized on 20 December 1833 in Silver Lake, Michigan, by Japheth Fosdick. Stevenson endured the trials associated with the Mormon era in Missouri and Illinois. In 1847 he was a pioneer to the Salt Lake Valley. He was appointed an alternate member of the First Council of Seventy in June 1879, nine years after bringing Martin Harris to the Salt Lake Valley. He was called as one of the seven presidents of the Seventy on 7 October 1894. See Edward Stevenson Collection, MS 4806, Church History Library; and "Edward Stevenson," Leonard J. Arrington Papers, box 94, fd. 8, USU Special Collections.

62. Letter of Edward Stevenson to the editor of the *Deseret News*, 30 November 1881, in "One of the Three Witnesses," *Deseret News*, 28 December 1881, 762; A year later in October 1834, Edward Stevenson had the opportunity of meeting Joseph Smith, Hyrum Smith, Oliver Cowdery, and David Whitmer at Pontiac, Michigan, and hearing the testimony of those witnesses. See *History of the Church,* 2:168-69; Edward

the Eastern States, Stevenson met Martin once again on 11 February 1870. Stevenson saw Martin coming out of the Kirtland Temple and observed, "He took from under his arm a copy of the Book of Mormon, the first edition, I believe, and bore a faithful testimony." He heard Martin say "it was his duty to continue to lift up his voice as he had been commanded to do in defence of the Book that he held in his hand, and offered to prove from the Bible that just such a book was to come forth out of the ground." Martin confessed to Stevenson that "he was daily bearing testimony to many who visited the Temple."[63]

Although Stevenson recognized the power of Martin's testimony, the circumstances in Martin's life left Stevenson with a sense of pity for the once prosperous farmer. Edward bore witness to Martin of the truthfulness of the Latter-day work—a witness he had gained "through obedience to the Gospel."[64] Stevenson further stated, "I felt to admonish him to the renewal of his duties and more advanced privileges of gathering to Zion and receiving his endowments and blessings." Martin was impressed by the power that attended his testimony and boldly declared that "whatever befell him he knew that Joseph was a Prophet, for he had not only proved it from the Bible but that he had stood with him in the presence of an angel, and he also knew that the Twelve Apostles were chosen of God."[65] His last statement was not repetitive of his testimony of the coming forth of the Book of Mormon. It was an expressed conviction of the calling of the Twelve. This testimony spoke volumes to Stevenson. By implication, it meant that Martin knew the

Stevenson, *Reminiscences of Joseph, the Prophet, and the Coming Forth of the Book of Mormon* (Salt Lake City: by the author, 1893), 4–5; Bertha S. Stevenson, "The Third Witness," *Improvement Era*, August 1934, 458.

63. Stevenson, "One of the Three Witnesses," *Deseret News*, 28 December 1881, 762–63. On that day, 11 February, Elder Stevenson signed the Kirtland Temple Register, see M. Wilford Poulson Collection, MSS, box 5, fd. 4, Perry Collections.

64. Stevenson, "One of the Three Witnesses," *Deseret News*, 28 December 1881, 763.

65. Edward Stevenson, "The Three Witnesses to the Book of Mormon. No. II.," *Millennial Star* 48 (7 June 1886): 366.

keys for leading the Lord's kingdom in the latter days rested with the Twelve. It meant that Martin knew the truth of God lay in the Church of Jesus Christ of Latter-day Saints.

For Martin, exchanging testimonies with Stevenson may not have been noteworthy. It may have been like so many encounters before—forgotten. But this was not so for Elder Edward Stevenson. Long after he returned to Salt Lake City, thoughts of Martin Harris surfaced. Rather than ignore what he believed were impressions, he wrote a letter to Martin recalling their meeting in Kirtland. Martin responded with a letter of his own, stating: "When I read your letter I had a witness for the first time that I must gather with the Saints to Utah."[66] A series of letters passed between the two men. The thread that bound their correspondence was Martin's repeated desire to migrate west.[67] Stevenson shared one of Martin's letters with Brigham Young. After reading the letter, President Young, through his counselor George A. Smith, suggested that Stevenson set up a subscription fund to financially assist Martin Harris on his journey to the Salt Lake Valley. Stevenson liked the suggestion and went to work, soliciting the necessary funds. President Young was among the immediate contributors and gave twenty-five dollars. Others contributed more or less and soon a subscription of nearly two hundred dollars was raised.[68]

With funds in hand, on 19 July 1870 Stevenson boarded a railroad car in Salt Lake City bound for the east. He first elected to make a hurried trip through Ohio to western New York where he visited the Hill Cumorah at Manchester before calling "for [his] charge at Kirtland."[69] By 7 August, Stevenson reached the agrarian community and there found Martin "anxiously waiting" for him.[70]

66. Journal History of the Church, 27 May 1884, 7.

67. Andrew Jenson, "The Three Witnesses," *The Historical Record* (Salt Lake City: by the author, 1886-1890), 6:215.

68. Stevenson, "One of the Three Witnesses," *Deseret News*, 28 December 1881, 763.

69. Stevenson, "The Three Witnesses to the Book of Mormon. No. II.," 366.

70. Stevenson, "The Three Witnesses to the Book of Mormon. No. II.," 366. The day after his arrival, Stevenson learned that the Kirtland Temple was available for

Martin, age eighty-eight, having no real wealth to speak of, was then living on the goodwill and charity found in the household of Joseph C. Hollister, age eighty-four, and his wife, Electa Stratton Hollister, age sixty-six.[71]

Martin was "elated with his prospective journey" and expressed confidence that neither age nor health could deter its success. To prove the matter, he boasted of having recently worked "in the garden, and dug potatoes by the day for some of his neighbors."[72] He later confided to Edward Stevenson that in preparation for his forthcoming departure for the west he experienced a most taxing incident. In the process of going from house to house to bid longtime friends farewell, he became "bewildered, dizzy, faint and staggering through the blackberry vines that [were] so abundant in that vicinity, his clothes torn, bloody and faint, he lay down under a tree to die. After a time he revived, called on the Lord, and finally at twelve midnight, found his friend, and in his fearful condition was cared for and soon regained his strength." Martin believed that the incident was a "snare of the adversary to hinder him from going to Salt Lake City."[73]

---

religious meetings. He secured the temple and preached on that Sunday morn. At the conclusion of his sermon, those in attendance voted to return for a second meeting that afternoon. According to Stevenson, the second one was "well attended." See Homer Jr., "'Publish It upon the Mountains,'" 506, who says, "Both meetings were well attended." Stevenson signed the Kirtland Temple Register on 7 August 1870. M. Wilford Poulson Collection, MSS 823, box 9, fd. 32, Perry Collections.

71. See United States Federal Census, 1870, Kirtland Township, Lake County, Ohio.

72. Stevenson, "One of the Three Witnesses," *Deseret News*, 28 December 1881, 763.

73. Stevenson, "One of the Three Witnesses," *Deseret News*, 28 December 1881, 763. A slightly different account appears in Stevenson, "The Three Witnesses to the Book of Mormon. No. II.," 366. In the latter account, Martin Harris related that "he went to bid adieu to some old friends previous to his departure. His way led him through a woodland field, in which he lost his way. Wandering about, he became bewildered, and came in contact with briars and blackberry vines, his clothes were torn into tatters, and his skin lacerated and bleeding. He laid down under a tree in despair, with little hope of recovery. It was about midnight, when he was aroused, and called upon the Lord and received strength; and about one o'clock, a. m., he found his friends.

Martin recited another incident to Edward Stevenson. From the recorded description it is difficult to distinguish whether this event was in any way associated with his departure or if it happened "on one occasion." It may have been an earlier snare designed to entrap him. During their journey west he confided in Edward Stevenson that:

> On one occasion several of his old acquaintances made an effort to get him tipsy by treating him to some wine. When they thought he was in a good mood for talk, they put the question very carefully to him: "Well, now, Martin, we want you to be frank and candid with us in regard to this story of your seeing an angel and the golden plates of the Book of Mormon that are so much talked about. We have always taken you to be an honest, good farmer and neighbor of ours, but could not believe that you ever did see an angel. Now Martin, do you really believe that you did see an angel when you were awake?" No, said Martin, I do not believe it. The anticipation of the delighted crowd at this exclamation may be imagined. But soon a different feeling prevailed when Martin Harris, true to his trust, said, "Gentlemen, what I have said is true, from the fact that my belief is swallowed up in knowledge; for I want to say to you that as the Lord lives I do know that I stood with the Prophet Joseph Smith in the presence of the angel, and it was in the brightness of day."[74]

With that same determination, he claimed that nothing could prevent him from going west—neither bewilderment nor designing friends. No matter the difficulty, he would board a train bound for Zion in the Rockies. Believing his stubborn tenacity, Stevenson

---

When he related this circumstance he said the devil desired to prevent him from going to Zion."

74. Stevenson, "The Three Witnesses to the Book of Mormon. No. II.," 367. Martin then went on to explain that "although he drank wine with them as friends, he always believed in temperance and sobriety."

sent a letter to the *Deseret News* informing the editor of their travel plans:

> Martin Harris, who still lives here [Kirtland], is tolerably well, and has a great desire to see Utah, and his children that live there; and although the old gentleman is in the 88th year of his age, he still bears a faithful testimony to the authenticity of the Book of Mormon, being one of the three original witnesses. He says he saw the plates, handled them and saw the angel that visited Joseph Smith, more than 40 years ago. I have made arrangements to emigrate him to Utah, according to his desire, and will start in about two weeks.[75]

Miles of Railroad Track to Cross

Nine days after Elder Stevenson arrived in Kirtland and on the very day the *Deseret News* printed his letter, he and Martin Harris boarded a train bound for Chicago. With miles of railroad track to cross, there were many occasions for conversation. None was more significant to Stevenson than Martin's memories of Joseph Smith. He recalled that Martin said, "Joseph Smith, the Prophet, was very poor, and had to work by the day for his support, and he (Harris) often gave him work on his farm, and that they had hoed corn together many a day." Martin said that "[Joseph] was good to work and jovial and they often wrestled together in sport, but the Prophet was devoted and attentive to his prayers."[76]

When the train arrived at the Chicago Depot on 21 August 1870, the passengers bound for Salt Lake City disembarked to await a train heading west. Upon learning of a delay, Stevenson and Martin checked into the popular American Hotel in downtown Chicago. Before retiring for the evening, Martin was "delighted to find

---

75. Letter of Edward Stevenson, 10 August 1870; see "Kirtland, Ohio," *Deseret News*, 24 August 1870, 341.

76. Stevenson, "The Three Witnesses to the Book of Mormon. No. III.," *Millennial Star* 48 (21 June 1886): 389.

crowds that would listen to him. All seemed astonished to hear him relate the story of his part in the bringing forth of the Book of Mormon."[77] After being comfortably situated in their room, Stevenson wrote to Elder George A. Smith: "I am well, as also Martin Harris, who is with me, although he is now in the 88th year of his age and rather feeble. But he walks along remarkably well. . . . He stands his journey, thus far, quite well, and feels filled with new life at the idea of going to the valleys of Utah, to see his children and friends." Stevenson confided, "[Martin] is coming to the conclusion, after trying everything else—although he has always borne a faithful testimony to the truth of the Book of Mormon—that the work of the Lord is progressing in the tops of the mountains and that the people are gathering in fulfilment of prophecy."[78]

The next day, the two men boarded a westbound train. One of the principal train stops on their route was Des Moines, Iowa. When Martin and Stevenson disembarked at the train depot, instead of seeking lodging as before, Stevenson escorted Martin to the *Daily Iowa State Register* office. There an editor of the *Register* listened and then questioned Martin about his testimony of the coming forth of the Book of Mormon. The editor was so intrigued by his words that on 26 August 1870, he printed in the *Register*, "Martin Harris, one of the *three witnesses* of the Mormon Bible, called at our sanctum yesterday. Mr. Harris is now in his 88th year, hale and hearty, with many interesting things to relate in reference to the finding of the tablets of the testament. We shall have occasion to mention some of these in another issue."[79] As promised, in the Sunday morning edition, 28 August 1870, an extensive account of his conversation with Martin was printed. It included, "The old gentleman evidently loves to relate the incidents with which he was personally connected and he does it with wonderful enthusiasm." Martin spoke of the Book

---

77. Homer Jr., "'Publish It upon the Mountains,'" 506-7.

78. Edward Stevenson, letter to George A. Smith, 21 August 1870, *Deseret Evening News*, 27 August 1870, p. 3.

79. *Daily Iowa State Register* (Des Moines), 26 August 1870, 4.

of Mormon and gave a valuable observation concerning the record itself. As reported, "Mr. Harris describes the plates as being of thin leaves of gold, measuring seven by eight inches and weighing altogether, from forty to sixty pounds."[80]

With more than a day remaining in Des Moines, Martin took advantage of other opportunities to bear his testimony. James M. Ballinger, president of the Des Moines Iowa Branch, invited him to speak to his congregation. He responded by bearing "testimony as to viewing the plates, the angel's visit, and visiting professor Anthony [Anthon]." His brief mention of Professor Charles Anthon captured the fancy of branch members, especially his recounting of "a certificate, etc., as to the correctness of the characters, [Anthon] asked him to fetch the plates for him to see. Martin said that they were sealed, and that an angel had forbidden them to be exhibited. Mr. Anthony [Anthon] then called for the certificate, tore it up and consigned it to the waste basket, saying, angels did not visit in our days, etc."[81]

The next day Stevenson baptized Sally Ann Ballinger Fifield, the forty-nine-year-old sister of President Ballinger, in the Des Moines River. Seeing an opportunity for discussing the doctrine of baptism, Stevenson tried to teach Martin of "the necessity of being rebaptized." Troubled by the inference, Martin said that "he had not been cut off from the Church"; therefore, there was no need of being rebaptized.[82] Stevenson begged to differ. Martin replied that "if it was right, the Lord would manifest it to him by His spirit."[83] Since a manifestation did not occur, he refused to enter baptismal

---

80. *Daily Iowa State Register* (Des Moines), 28 August 1870, 4.

81. Stevenson, "One of the Three Witnesses," *Deseret News*, 28 December 1881, 763.

82. Stevenson, "One of the Three Witnesses—Incidents in the Life of Martin Harris," *Millennial Star* 44 (6 February 1882): 87. Martin's statement that he "had not been cut off from the Church" was true in the sense that he had not been excommunicated since his rebaptism in Kirtland in 1842. See Thomas G. Truitt, "Was Martin Harris Ever Excommunicated from the Church?," *Ensign*, June 1979, 34-35.

83. Stevenson, "The Three Witnesses to the Book of Mormon. No. II.," 367; cf. Stevenson, "One of the Three Witnesses," 87.

waters that day.[84] Members of the Des Moines branch contributed "a new suit of clothes" to him. Of their generosity, Stevenson penned, "[This] very much helped the feelings and appearance of the old gentleman."[85] To Martin, this was more than a singular gift. He was overcome by their generosity and "felt to bless them" before departing with Stevenson and two members of the Des Moines branch for the depot.[86]

At the depot, they boarded their Pullman passenger car bound for Utah. There were other stops along the way and more people to meet, but it was not until 29 August, when the train stopped at Ogden, Weber County, that another reporter took interest in Martin, and wrote a note, albeit brief. The *Ogden Junction* reported, "Martin Harris arrived, (with Elder Edward Stevenson) whose name is known almost throughout the world as one of the witnesses of the Book of Mormon. They left Kirtland on the 19th of August."[87] On 30 August the *Deseret Evening News* printed: "By a telegram, per Deseret Telegraph Line, received at half-past three o'clock this afternoon, we learn that Martin Harris, accompanied by Elder E. Stevenson, of this city, arrived at Ogden, by the 3 o'clock train, he comes to this city to-morrow morning."[88]

"Arrival in This City, of Martin Harris, One of the Three Witnesses"

The train actually pulled into the Salt Lake Depot at 7:30 p.m. that same evening, Wednesday, 30 August 1870. The Stevenson and Harris party had not delayed their coming until the following day but had continued through to Salt Lake from Ogden. Newspaper

---

84. Stevenson, "One of the Three Witnesses," 87. See Stevenson, "The Three Witnesses to the Book of Mormon. No. II.," 367.

85. Stevenson, "The Three Witnesses to the Book of Mormon. No. II.," 366; Stevenson, "One of the Three Witnesses," 86.

86. Stevenson, "One of the Three Witnesses," 86.

87. *Ogden Junction*, 29 August 1870, as quoted in Stevenson, "One of the Three Witnesses," 86.

88. *Deseret Evening News*, 30 August 1870, 3. This announced delay in the time of their arrival in Salt Lake proved to be incorrect.

reporters were understandably anxious to announce the arrival of the only witness of the Book of Mormon to enter the Salt Lake Valley. The *Salt Lake Herald* responded the morning of the 31st: "Martin Harris, one of the three witnesses of the book of Mormon, arrived in Salt Lake City last night, accompanied by Elder Edward Stevenson."[89] George Q. Cannon, editor of the *Deseret Evening News,* devoted a lengthy column of newsprint to his arrival. He related, "Considerable interest has been felt by our people in the arrival in this city, of Martin Harris, one of the three witnesses of the Book of Mormon. He arrived here at 7,30, p. m. yesterday, in the company of Elder Edward Stevenson." Over the process of time "he has never failed to bear testimony to the divine authenticity of the Book of Mormon. He says it is not a matter of belief on his part, but of knowledge."[90] Whether reading the telegrapher's message or the newsprint of the day, residents in the Salt Lake area were abuzz with news of Martin's arrival. But to assure that his arrival was officially reported, Stevenson led him to the Church Historian's office where an authoritative record was made.[91]

Edward Stevenson and Martin Harris were invited to address the congregation gathered in the Salt Lake Tabernacle on Sunday morning, 4 September 1870. Stevenson spoke first, followed by Martin Harris, and Pres. George A. Smith concluded the meeting.[92] Martin's remarks and personal testimony were carefully recorded

---

89. From an interview that took place at the *Salt Lake Daily Herald* office on 2 September 1870. An article highlighting the interview appeared the following day and also included, "Mr. Harris is now 88 years of age, and is remarkably lively and energetic for his years. He holds firmly to the testimony he has borne for over forty years, that an angel appeared before him and the other witnesses, and showed them the plates upon which the characters of the Book of Mormon were inscribed. After being many years separated from the body of the Church, he has come to spend the evening of life among the believers in that Book to which he is so prominent a witness." *Salt Lake Daily Herald,* 3 September 1870, 3.

90. See *Deseret Evening News,* 31 August 1870, 2; cf. *Salt Lake Daily Herald,* 3 September 1870, 3.

91. Journal History of the Church, 31 August 1870, 1.

92. "Sabbath Meetings," *Deseret Evening News,* 5 September 1870, 2.

by Edward Stevenson as he wrote, "Salt Lake City Sept 4, [1870] Sunday morning Testimony of Martin Harris Written By my hand from the Mouth of Martin Harris." Martin declared:

> In the year 1818=52 years ago I was Inspired of the Lord & Taught of the Spirit that I Should not Join any Church although I was anxiousley Sought for By many of the Sectarians I Was Taught I could not Walk together unless agreed What can you not be agreed in[?] in the Trinity because I can not find it in any Bible find it for me & I am ready to Receive it 3 persons in one god—one personage I can not concede to for this is Anti christ for Where is the Father & Son I have more Proof to Prove 9 Persons in the Trinity than you have 3 How Do you Do so[?]—John Tells us of the 7 Spirits sent into all the World—if you have A Right to make A Personage of one Spirit I have of the 7—& the father and Son are 2 more Making 9—other Sects the Episcopalians also tried me they say 3 Persons in one god Without Body Parts or Passions I Told them Such A god I Would not be afraid of I could not Please or offend him [I] would not be afraid to fight A Duel with sutch A god—the Methodists teach two [illegible word] them exceed form one I told them to [retract] it or I Would sue them for Riley their Minister made them give it up to me saying god would hold me accountable for the use I made of it—all of the sects caled me "Bro" [Brother] because the Lord had enlightened me the Spirit told me to Join None of the Churches for none had Authority from the Lord for there Will not be A True Church on the Earth until the Words of Isaiah shall be fulfilled=When Interrogated & I told them if any church [be] the Church of Christ the Christians then claime me But join and lectuien [?] as much as any other The time has not come for you to take that name. at Antioch they were called Christians in Derision—No thanks for your name—So remained for there was No authority for the Spirit

told me that I might just as well Plunge myself into the Water as to have any one of the sects Baptise me So I Remained until the Church Was organized By Joseph Smith the Prophet Then I was baptised by the Hands of Oliver Cowdery By Joseph Smith's command Being the first after Joseph & Oliver Cowdery & then the Spirit Bore Testimony that this was all right & I Rejoiced in the Established Church Previous to my being Baptised I became A Witness of the Plates of the Book of mormon in 1829 in March the People Rose up & united against the Work gathering testimony against the Plates & Said they had testimony enough & if I did not Put Joseph in Jail & his father For Deception, they Would me So I went from Waterloo 25 miles South East of Palmyra to Rogerses Suscotua [Seneca?] Co. N. Y. & to Harmony, Pensylvania 125 miles & found Joseph[.][93] Rogers unknown to me had agreed to give my Wife 100 Dollars if it was not A Deception & had Whet his Nife [knife] to eat the [illegible word] of the Plates as the Lord had forbid Joseph exhibiting them openly.

Martin's Wife had hefted them & felt them [the gold plates] under cover as had Martin & [this disconnected sentence on the fifth page abruptly ends his transcript of Martin's words and any remaining pages of text are missing].[94]

Conclusion

Following his tabernacle address, there were many opportunities for Martin to speak—types of opportunities that were never enjoyed by other witnesses of the Book of Mormon. Martin was

93. We believe that Martin is essentially saying that he went 25 miles from Palmyra southeast to Waterloo, Seneca County, which is the correct distance and direction, and then from Waterloo to Harmony, Pennsylvania, which is close to 100 miles more or a total of 125 miles traveled overall.

94. Edward Stevenson Papers Collection, MS 4806, reel 9, box 9, fd. 7, 5pp, Church History Library. Martin was again in the Salt Lake Tabernacle on Sunday, 9 October 1870, bearing testimony of the "divine authenticity" of the Book of Mormon following the remarks of Elder John Taylor. *Deseret News*, 12 October 1870, 419.

beset with numerous invitations to express his experiences from the earliest days of the Restoration. He accepted quite a number, but certainly not all since the long journey from Ohio and the fanfare surrounding his arrival had begun to take a heavy toll on his health. Stevenson perhaps said it best: "Considering his great age, much charity was necessary to be exercised in his behalf."[95] It was his grandniece, Irinda Crandall McEwan,[96] who offered to help until his family from Smithfield came to take him to their home. She and her husband of three years, Joseph T. McEwan, a pressman for the *Salt Lake Herald*, had moved to Salt Lake City in 1870. The McEwans provided shelter, food, and kindness to Martin.

"While he was there, hundreds of people came to see him, including President Brigham Young, to talk over with him the details regarding his contact with the Book of Mormon story and of the appearance of the Angel to him." Irinda McEwan recalled, "Anyone who heard Martin Harris describe the scenes and bear his testimony to the truthfulness of the Book of Mormon could not help but be deeply impressed with his sincerity and his absolute conviction of the truth of what he was saying."[97]

Of those who called at the McEwan home, none was of greater significance to Martin than his estranged wife, Caroline, who

95. Stevenson, "The Three Witnesses to the Book of Mormon. No. III.," 390.

96. Irinda Naomi McEwan (18 August 1851-12 January 1935), daughter of Spicer Wells Crandall and Sophia Kellogg. Her grandmother, Naomi Harris, was the sister of Martin Harris. See Theria McEwan Selman, "History of Irinda McEwan, 1928," in authors' possession.

97. Franklin S. Harris, "Minutes of Harris Family Reunion," 3 August 1928, Geneva Resort, Utah County, Utah, USU Special Collections. Franklin S. Harris, president of Brigham Young University, records her words in his summary of a speech by Irinda McEwan at a Harris family reunion. See Selman, "History of Irinda McEwan." On that same occasion, Mrs. Sariah Steele of Goshen, Utah, told of her experiences with her grandfather Martin "whom she knew when she was a little girl. She had sat on his lap many times and heard him bear fervent testimony to the truthfulness of the Book of Mormon record and of the part he played in connection with the testimony of the three witnesses. She said that anyone who had ever come in contact with him and had heard him bear his testimony was thoroughly impressed with his sincerity and with the truthfulness of the story which he told." See also Franklin S. Harris Papers, MSS 340, box 2, fd. 4, Perry Collections.

came to see him.[98] It had been over eleven years since she had seen the father of her children. There was much to share and forgive. Unfortunately, a record of their conversation was not preserved. The same is true of other conversations that took place in the McEwan home.

We are grateful for the careful record of Martin's days in Salt Lake City as found in the writings of Edward Stevenson. Stevenson often visited Martin in the McEwan home and frequently brought him to his own residence. There, much like on their journey to Salt Lake City, the two men spoke of the gospel. In one conversation, Martin said that "the Spirit of the Lord had made it manifest to him, not only for himself personally, but also that he should be baptized for his dead, for he had seen his father [Nathan Harris] seeking his aid. He saw his father at the foot of a ladder, striving to get up to him, and he went down to him taking him by the hand and helped him up."[99] He reminded Stevenson of having been taught "a principle that was new to him—baptism for the dead, as taught and practiced by the ancient Saints, and especially taught by Paul the Apostle in the 15th chapter of 1st Corinthians: 'Else what shall they do which are baptized for the dead, if the dead rise not at all? why are they then baptized for the dead?'"[100] He then expressed a desire to be baptized for the remission of sins and baptized by proxy for his father.

A joyous Stevenson hurried to inform Latter-day Saint leaders of Martin's intention. Each responded with enthusiasm. On the day of his baptism, Saturday, 17 September 1870, Elders George A. Smith (president of the quorum), John Taylor, Wilford Woodruff, Orson Pratt, and Joseph F. Smith of the Quorum of the Twelve Apostles and also John T. D. McAllister gathered near the baptismal font at the Endowment House to witness the event. Naomi Harris Bent, a sister of Martin, was also in attendance. Edward Stevenson

---

98. See Sumsion, "Notes of the Genealogy of Martin Harris," as cited in Gunnell, "Martin Harris—Witness," 122.

99. Stevenson, "The Three Witnesses to the Book of Mormon. No. II.," 367.

100. Stevenson, "One of the Three Witnesses," 87.

baptized Martin Harris. John Taylor, Wilford Woodruff, Joseph F. Smith, and Orson Pratt confirmed him a member of the Church of Jesus Christ of Latter-day Saints, Orson Pratt being voice.[101] Edward Stevenson later observed, "The occasion was one which interested all present, and reminded us of Christ's parable of the lost sheep."[102] Martin then entered the font and was baptized for his deceased father, Nathan Harris, and his uncle, Solomon Harris.[103] His sister, Naomi Harris Duel Kellogg Bent,[104] was baptized by proxy for two of her own sisters, Sophia and Lydia Harris, and also for Harriet Fox Kellogg, who was the first wife of Naomi's deceased husband Ezekiel Kellogg.[105] She and Martin were then confirmed by the same brethren, with Joseph F. Smith being voice.[106] Martin was again in the Endowment House on 21 October 1870 for the purpose of obtaining his own endowment.[107]

---

101. Journal History of the Church, 17 September 1870, 1.

102. Stevenson, "The Three Witnesses to the Book of Mormon. No. II.," 368.

103. Salt Lake Temple and Endowment Records, Baptisms, Records for the Dead, 12 September 1870, p. 184, microfilm #1149519, Special Collections, Family History Library, Salt Lake City; Stevenson, "The Three Witnesses to the Book of Mormon. No. II.," 368.

104. *Pioneer Women of Faith and Fortitude* (Salt Lake City, UT: International Society Daughters of Utah Pioneers, 1998), 1:237.

105. Salt Lake Temple and Endowment House Records, Baptisms, Records of the Dead, 12 September 1870, p. 184; Journal History of the Church, 17 September 1870, microfilm #1149519, Special Collections, Family History Library, Salt Lake City; Elder Stevenson wrote of Martin's initial failure to understand the doctrine of vicarious work for the dead: "I wish to add that Brother Harris having been away from the Church so many years did not understand more than the first principles taught in the infantile days of the Church, which accounts for his not being posted in the doctrine of the Gospel being preached to the spirits who are departed, which was afterwards taught by Joseph Smith the Prophet." Stevenson, "The Three Witnesses to the Book of Mormon. No. II.," 367.

106. Members of the Harris family were imbued with a desire to see to the ordinance work for their kindred dead. On 12 October 1870, Martin Harris Jr., son of Martin Sr. and Caroline, was baptized for his half-brother George B. Harris, the son of Martin Sr. and Lucy Harris, and also his great-grandfather Samuel Kimball (1757-1780), grandfather of his mother Caroline; see Salt Lake Temple and Endowment House Records, Baptisms, Records for the Dead, 12 October 1870, p. 234, microfilm #1149519.

107. Salt Lake Temple and Endowment House Record, Endowment Records Living, 31 October 1868-11 November 1872, Book G, 21 October 1870, p. 208.

This was a time of rejoicing for many to see a witness of the Book of Mormon participate in sacred covenants. Martin's response to such proceedings was, "Just see how the Book of Mormon is spreading."[108] A few days later, he made a similar statement in the company of Edward Stevenson, George A. Smith, and John Henry Smith on the way to the warm springs just north of Salt Lake City. As the carriage in which they were riding reached a summit, curtains were raised so that the passengers could have a panoramic view of the city below. To Martin, who could see the Tabernacle and the Salt Lake Temple under construction, as well as the expansive city, the scene was "wonderful." He exclaimed, "Who would have thought that the Book of Mormon would have done all this?"[109] Martin was now back. Brigham Young's prophecy, "Rest assured, he will be here in time,"[110] had been fulfilled. Martin had become the only one of the Three Witnesses to personally observe the growth of the Church in the West. For him, this was a day of great rejoicing.

After spending over a month and a half in Salt Lake City, Martin accepted the invitation of his son Martin Jr. to live with him in Smithfield, Cache County. From 1870 to 1874 Martin lived with his son's family in Smithfield. In October 1874 Martin moved with them to Clarkston, Cache County. Just ten months after moving to Clarkston, in early July 1875, Martin was stricken with paralysis.[111] William Harrison Homer Sr. and William's mother, Eliza Williamson Homer, were the only persons present with Martin at the moment of his passing. Martin Jr. and wife Nancy had gone to milk the cows and do the evening chores. William affirmed:

---

108. It is not certain whether this statement was made by Martin at his own baptism or at another baptismal service. Stevenson, "The Three Witnesses to the Book of Mormon. No. III.," 390.

109. Stevenson, "The Three Witnesses to the Book of Mormon. No. III.," 390; see Journal History of the Church, 1 June 1877, 1-2.

110. W. H. Homer, "Passing of Martin Harris," 471.

111. See Homer Jr., "'Publish It upon the Mountains,'" 525; for details of his paralysis and final illness, see Letter of Martin Harris Jr. to George A. Smith, 10 July 1875, Clarkston, Utah, George A. Smith Papers, MS 1322, Church History Library.

I stood by the bedside holding the patient's right hand and my mother at the foot of the bed. Martin Harris had been unconscious for a number of days. When we first entered the room the old gentleman appeared to be sleeping. He soon woke up and asked for a drink of water. I put my arm under the old gentleman, raised him, and my mother held the glass to his lips. He drank freely, then he looked up at me and recognized me. He had been unconscious several days. He said, "I know you. You are my friend." He said, "Yes, I did see the plates on which the Book of Mormon was written; I did see the angel; I did hear the voice of God; and I do know that Joseph Smith is a Prophet of God, holding the keys of the Holy Priesthood." This was the end. Martin Harris, divinely-chosen witness of the work of God, relaxed, gave up my hand. He lay back on his pillow and just as the sun went down behind the Clarkston mountains, the soul of Martin Harris passed on.[112]

At about a quarter to eight in the evening of 10 July 1875, Martin died in his ninety-third year.[113]

His funeral was held on 12 July 1875 at the Clarkston meeting-house. "We had a good attendance and a large turn out for a small town like Clarkston," wrote Martin Jr. "Every respect that could be paid to him was manifested by the people."[114] There was only one problem—"they were going to put a Book of Mormon in [Martin's] hand, and they forgot the book." While the mourners waited, Martin Jr. went to fetch the book. Upon returning, he placed the Book of Mormon in Martin's right hand and a copy of the Doctrine and Covenants in his left. Martin was buried in the Clarkston Cemetery

---

112. William Harrison Homer [Sr.], "The Passing of Martin Harris," *Improvement Era*, May 1926, 472. Compare also William Harrison Homer Sr., "The Last Testimony of Martin Harris," a notarized statement of this account (with slight variations), signed by William Harrison Homer Sr., 9 April 1927, MSS 236, p. 5, Perry Collections.

113. Letter of Martin Harris Jr. to George A. Smith, 10 July 1875.

114. Martin Harris Jr., "Funeral," *Deseret Evening News*, 17 July 1875, p. 3, col. 4.

north of town. A simple wooden marker inscribed with the words "One of the Three Witnesses of the book of Mormon" was placed above his grave.[115]

Susan Easton Black is professor of church history and doctrine at Brigham Young University.

Larry C. Porter is professor emeritus of church history and doctrine at Brigham Young University.

---

115. "Presiding Bishopric," Clarkston Cemetery Project File, 1940-1950, CR 4117; Letter of Martin Harris Jr. to George A. Smith, 13 July 1875, Clarkston, Utah, George A. Smith Papers, MS 1322, Church History Library.

CHAPTER 3

ॐ

SEEING THE HAND OF GOD IN ALL THINGS: A DIFFERENT APPROACH TO EVIL AND SUFFERING

M. Gerald Bradford

The Lord gave, and the Lord hath taken away; blessed be the name of the Lord. (Job 1:21)

One way or another, all of us face the challenge of coming to terms with the reality of evil and suffering. Those of us who believe in God confront the added burden of accounting for our belief in light of it. For centuries, the established way of doing this, especially for those theologically or philosophically inclined, has been to try to justify the ways of God or "to explain God's goodness and power and reconcile these with the evident evil in the created world."[1] Some are convinced this is a dead end. They choose to deal with evil and suffering differently. I have come to identify with

---

I have known Kent Brown for more than thirty years. We first met at Brigham Young University in the early 1970s, shortly after he joined the faculty. Over the years I kept track of him mainly through his writings, particularly on the Book of Mormon. Finally, in the mid-1990s, I had the good fortune of linking up with him when we both worked on the *Journal of Book of Mormon Studies* and later when he became associated with BYU's Neal A. Maxwell Institute for Religious Scholarship. Kent is a friend and colleague and has been a genuine mentor to me. I am pleased to submit a paper to this collection in his honor. It is adapted from a chapter in a book I am writing entitled *The Hope That Is in Me: Thoughts on Being a Latter-day Saint in the Twenty-first Century*.

1. John Cobb Jr. and Truman G. Madsen, "Theodicy," in *Encyclopedia of Mormonism*, ed. Daniel H. Ludlow (New York: Macmillan, 1992), 4:1473.

a version of this alternative approach, thanks, in part, to insights from two philosophers: James E. Faulconer and D. Z. Phillips.[2]

In this paper I reconstruct Faulconer's and Phillips's criticisms of the traditional approach to the problem of evil. I then summarize how they confront the challenge in different ways (by rethinking what it means to do theology in one case and by putting forward an alternative view of religious beliefs in the other). Faulconer questions the entire intellectual approach to the issue (what he calls the "problem of theodicy"). He argues that the best way to deal with evil and suffering is by practical, concrete means. Phillips argues that those who use their religious beliefs as a means of trying to explain how things are, fare poorly when it comes to confronting evil and suffering compared to those who understand such beliefs as a distinctive form of response to a world in which such negative

---

2. It is heartening to discover how others—fellow Latter-day Saints and those of other faiths—in the course of thinking through matters of interest to them, can be of genuine help in coming to see things one prizes in a new light. James E. Faulconer addresses the problem of evil in his article, "Rethinking Theology: The Shadow of the Apocalypse," in *Faith, Philosophy, Scripture* (Provo, UT: Neal A. Maxwell Institute, 2010), 109-36. Faulconer is a longtime friend and colleague. He is professor of philosophy at Brigham Young University and is writing some important things dealing with two broad topics: modernity (and its next-of-kin postmodernity) and theology. D. Z. Phillips's insights on the problem of evil are spelled out in the context of his thoughts about religious beliefs. See his chapter, "Believing in God," in *Introducing Philosophy: The Challenge of Scepticism* (Oxford: Blackwell, 1997), 143-65. Phillips, the well-known Welsh philosopher of religion, died in 2006. He wrote over twenty books, most of them on the philosophy of religion and ethics. Raimond Gaita, in an obituary that appeared in the *Guardian*, 21 August 2006, points out that because Phillips resisted so relentlessly the desire that philosophy should underwrite theories of religious belief, or even the beliefs themselves, he was often accused of irrationalism or what others came to refer to as "Wittgensteinian fideism." According to Gaita, Phillips "never denied that sincerely religious people believe in the reality of their God," but he "did deny that philosophers understand clearly enough what it means to believe such things." I think Gaita gets Phillips right on this score. As we shall see, Phillips is a critic of conventional accounts of what it means to believe in God and urges his fellow philosophers and the rest of us to think about the subject differently. I have been reading Phillips for a long while now. The way he deals with this issue is one of the things that drew me to him in the first place, that and the fact that I had an opportunity, years ago, to take a seminar from him when he was a visiting professor at the University of California, Santa Barbara. I find in him something rare—a rigorous philosopher who tries hard to understand what it means for others to adhere to religious beliefs.

things happen. Finally, with their help, I describe how I approach evil and suffering. By emphasizing the things I choose to do in living my life in covenant with God (more so than my beliefs about him and a host of other subjects)—that is, by appreciating what it means to be solely dependent upon him, by worshipping him with full intent, by striving day in and day out to relate with him and others in a manner that I hope is acceptable, and then by responding to the world from this vantage point—I find I am able to see his hand in all things and thus can better grapple with the negative aspects of life.

The Traditional Approach to Evil and Suffering

There are all kinds of obstacles to belief in God. For many, the most pronounced is the reality of evil and suffering in the world. Some who once believed have lost their faith as a result of encountering it. Others see the massive death and destruction caused by natural disasters and the mayhem and devastation resulting from the actions of individuals or groups directed toward others and cannot find it within them to believe.

For a long while now, theologians and philosophers have wrestled with what has come to be called the problem of evil. It can be stated quite simply. Believers are said to adhere to four propositions: God is all-loving, he is all-powerful, he is all-knowing, and evil exists. The problem is, as Faulconer points out, if God is all of these things, then the existence of evil is inexplicable since "God *could* create a world without evil—he has the power and the knowledge to do so—and he *would* create it, for his love would require that he do so. . . . Therefore, the existence of God is incompatible with the existence of evil. For many, the suppressed conclusion is that it is irrational to believe in God if one recognizes the existence of evil, as most people do."[3]

---

3. Faulconer, "Rethinking Theology," 125.

The way out of this intellectual dilemma, for many, is to employ a class of arguments—known as "theodicies"—meant to explain or justify God in the face of evil either by qualifying the various divine attributes or by interpreting evil and suffering in alternative ways.[4] According to Faulconer, theologians and philosophers use such arguments to achieve various ends. Some, for instance, deny the reality of evil. Others note that the problem itself is flawed since it requires that God do what is logically contradictory. Some question the quantity of suffering in the world and conclude that, despite appearances to the contrary, this is the "best of all possible worlds" (which merely denies evil by other means). Still others search for a solution by qualifying, in one way or another, God's power or goodness.

For Faulconer, the problem is not with these arguments per se. Rather, it is with the whole enterprise of approaching God and evil in this fashion, what he calls the "problem of theodicy."[5] What we need to do, he argues, is not turn our back on the problem but to see it in a new light—as one "that makes things more difficult."[6] If we see the problem of theodicy as "a philosophical goad, a spur, an itch that will not go away,"[7] we will discover a number of things:

---

4. Some Latter-day Saint thinkers rely on theodicies. Truman G. Madsen's well-written essay "Evil and Suffering," in his book *Eternal Man* (Salt Lake City: Deseret Book, 1966), 53–61, is a good example. Madsen dismisses many prevailing views of evil, puts forth his own definition of it, and argues that a correct understanding of God, of our own eternal nature, and of decisions we made in our premortal life, coupled with an acknowledgment of the ultimate sacrifice that the Savior has made in our behalf, can resolve the matter. I am certain his argument carries weight, especially among fellow Latter-day Saints for whom religious beliefs function as hypotheses and who thus rely on explanations such as this. There was a time when I tried to come to terms with negative things this way, in particular, by relying on Madsen's article. But no more. I understand such things differently now and approach God differently.

5. Faulconer, "Rethinking Theology," 124. That is, he approaches the issue in a fundamentally different way than, say, the authors of the article cited in note 1 above. Cobb and Madsen identify a handful of these arguments, briefly describe them, and say how Latter-day thinking on related matters alters or strengthens them. But they never call into question this particular approach to evil and suffering.

6. Faulconer, "Rethinking Theology," 129.

7. Faulconer, "Rethinking Theology," 132.

For one, that dealing with God and evil is not, as Faulconer puts it, purely a theoretical problem.

> In the end, it *is* a problem for action, and philosophical speculation has little place among the actions required when we respond concretely to suffering and evil. At the second coming not only will every knee bow and every tongue confess, but also the lame and the halt will be cured. Confession and cure show themselves in the type and shadow of our concrete responses to suffering rather than in rational speculation. They show themselves in the confession we make and the succor we offer in a world remade by our encounter with God.[8]

Furthermore, we will realize that the problem challenges our faith, even as it points out the need for it. Every call, Faulconer maintains, invites a response on our part, and, in so doing, disturbs our status quo. In this sense, the problem calls us, challenges our faith, and invites us to respond. It invites us to live in the world and to see it differently—as a world that is "awaiting the second coming" even if it has been "figured by the presence of Christ."[9] Faulconer acknowledges (as does Phillips) that some lose their faith in the face of evil and suffering (Phillips calls these "limiting cases"). But most of us, Faulconer observes, continue to believe even as we struggle intellectually with such things. We struggle *because* we believe, *because* we have faith. And, importantly, we find the need to confront evil to be a real one, rather than merely an intellectual one, and this further evidences that we have faith. Thus,

> by continuing to be a problem—by the fact that we seem unable to find any solution to the problem of theodicy that does not merely shift it some place else where it reappears in

---

8. Faulconer, "Rethinking Theology," 131, last emphasis added.
9. Faulconer, "Rethinking Theology," 133.

a new and slightly different guise—the problem of theodicy shows us the necessity of trust as well as the limits of reason. *The problem of evil and suffering is intractable to our powers of reason. As believers we find ourselves foolish before it. Ultimately the only thing to which it is tractable is moral and faithful response: action.*[10]

Also, according to Faulconer, if we deal with the problem as merely a theological or philosophical one (what earlier he referred to as a theoretical problem), rather than a religious one (that is, as a practical problem), we will find that we are attempting to rationally represent God in such a way that he allows the evil we encounter to continue. We create a god in our own image, an idol, and then, on the basis of this, try to solve the problem. That is, we try to make it go away. We pretend that the enemy of God is either unreal or not really an enemy.[11] We try, Faulconer says, "to integrate evil into our understanding, to make sense of it and make it part of the wholeness of our existence. It is evil to do so precisely because evil *cannot* be made sense of, cannot be justified. *It is evil to explain evil, to tame it, no longer to be horrified by it. If evil ceases to be horrible, but instead makes sense, then we cease to struggle with it.*"[12]

For Faulconer, once we come to live in the world differently and thus come to see it differently (what he means by living within the "shadow of the apocalypse," the subtitle of his article), we come to understand that this demands of us a practical, concrete struggle with evil, not just abstract thought about it (which may be relevant but is never enough).

Our horror in response to transcendent evil is one with our eschatological hope for the good of the kingdom that is to come, and that hope makes no sense apart from the fight

---

10. Faulconer, "Rethinking Theology," 133, emphasis added.
11. See Faulconer, "Rethinking Theology," 129.
12. Faulconer, "Rethinking Theology," 134, last emphasis added.

against evil. Only if the problem of theodicy is genuinely a problem—only if all solutions ultimately fail in this world without the Apocalypse, the Revelation of Jesus Christ—can we continue to know that evil is genuinely evil.[13]

Faulconer makes the following observation about the problem of theodicy (one that echoes one of Phillips's key insights, as we shall see):

Sometimes we treat scripture and revelation as if they were simplified scientific explanations of things, or poetic philosophizing, but I think that is a mistake, and sometimes a serious one. For it assumes that the rationality characteristic of science is the measure of all discourse. *Though religious discourse may offer us explanations, its purpose is not explanatory, but soteriological: It is concerned, not with telling us how the world and the things in the world are (at least not in the way that science and philosophy do), but with telling us about God's power to save and how we can be saved.* . . . Given its purposes, revelation ignores the problem of theodicy—which, since theodicy is a philosophical/theological problem rather than a religious one, is not the same as ignoring the problem we face in reconciling the evil we encounter with our faith in God.

That religion ignores the problem is deeply suggestive. Of course revelation is not blind to suffering. Christian revelation often reminds us that we must be deeply concerned with suffering, especially with the suffering of others and with our own spiritual suffering. God wills neither, and he offers answers to both. *But Christian concern is with the proper, Christ-like response to that suffering, not with explaining its logical compatibility with God's existence.* One can even imagine a Christian arguing that, as a speculative

13. Faulconer, "Rethinking Theology," 134.

rather than a practical problem, the problem of theodicy distracts us from the existential problem.[14]

Like Faulconer, Phillips thinks the trouble lies with the problem itself. But unlike Faulconer, he thinks it ought to be rejected out of hand since it leaves the believer adhering to a senseless position. As he puts it, "If we reflect on the reality of evil, we shall come to see that belief in God [viewed from this traditional perspective] is empty."[15]

According to Phillips, the obstacle facing those who deal with the problem of evil in the usual manner is that the arguments relied on are problematic and invariably fail since, one way or another, they either falsify the reality of evil, wrongly attempt to justify it, demean the suffering of others, or a combination of all three.[16] What is more, this line of reasoning amounts to claiming that, judged by normal standards of human decency, God is found wanting.[17]

But the real culprit in all of this, for Phillips, is a particular understanding of religious beliefs and the fact that it contributes to the presumption that we can somehow explain the ways of God.

---

14. Faulconer, "Rethinking Theology," 129–30, emphasis added.

15. Phillips, *Introducing Philosophy*, 152.

16. On pp. 152–56 in his book *Introducing Philosophy*, Phillips faults a number of these arguments, ranging from those that claim that evil and suffering are somehow instrumental toward achieving a higher good, to those that contend that evil and suffering are needed so that we can develop as free individuals, or that the amount of suffering in the world may only be a matter of our viewing it from our finite, limited perspective, or that without the suffering of others, there would be no opportunity for us to develop our own moral responsibility, or, finally, that the greater good that will come from the evil and suffering in the world will only be achieved in heaven.

17. Phillips warns against pushing the analogy between God and man too far. "If we judge God by the standards of moral decency, God must stand condemned. God does not intervene in circumstances in which any half-decent human being would, and uses human beings as means to a further end in ways which are clearly immoral. On the other hand, if we say that it is a mistake to judge God by human standards, that God is somehow beyond the reach of moral criticism then, again, the consequences for religion are dire. There is a place beyond morality, beyond the ordinary language of decency and indecency, where God might be located, but it is the place reserved for the monstrous and the horrific. So the choice [following this traditional line of reasoning] is either to find God guilty by our moral standards, or to find him too monstrous to be worthy of ordinary condemnation" (Phillips, *Introducing Philosophy*, 155–56).

He arrives at his conclusion this way: Before pointing out flaws in a number of theodicies, he looks at traditional arguments used to prove the existence of God, borrowing a page from most standard textbooks in the philosophy of religion, ones that convey a sense of how moderns tend to think and talk about God. He notes that those who put forth such arguments are, in effect, testing hypotheses.[18] But the trouble is, there seems to be no way of checking such claims and if this is the case,

> what sense does it make to speak of hypotheses at all in this connection? The position is not that we must remain agnostic about any hypothesis proposed. The point is that since *anything* can be proposed, the whole enterprise is shown to be a senseless aping of those contexts in which hypotheses are properly advanced and in which there are resources for their proper consideration.[19]

Then he offers this important observation,

> From the suggestion that to believe in God is to advance a hypothesis about the existence of something, to the efforts to express this hypothesis in the argument from design and the cosmological argument, and finally to the efforts to confront the problem of evil, by advancing hypotheses which would justify the presence of evil, one common assumption runs through all the arguments—that religion offers us an *explanation* of human life.[20]

---

18. I suspect that most Christians (including most fellow Latter-day Saints) may think of religious beliefs this way. This may account, in part, for why most think of being religious as adhering to a set of beliefs, more so than paying attention to what they are required to do. On this view, being religious is primarily a cognitive activity, a matter of the mind, more so than a practical concern, a matter of the heart. In other words, religion, for many, is on a par with science. For a long while this was how I viewed such beliefs, how they functioned in my life, and thus how I tried to come to terms with negative things.

19. Phillips, *Introducing Philosophy*, 150.

20. Phillips, *Introducing Philosophy*, 156.

For Phillips, the question is, why do those who think this way also think that trying to explain something will always make things better? According to our authority, the greatest divide in the philosophy of religion, one not always recognized, "is not between those who give religious explanations and those who give secular explanations of the contingencies of human life. *The divide is between those who think it makes sense to look for explanations in these contexts, and those who do not.*"[21]

Phillips sees the issue this way:

> Faced by the vicissitudes of life, the blind forces of nature, unpredictable visitations of disease and death, the fickleness of human beings and the interventions of bad luck, people have asked, "Why is this happening to us?" It is important to note that this question is asked *after* what we normally call explanations have been answered.[22]

In other words, those who ask such questions, under such circumstances, are not asking for further explanations. Rather, their doing so is a plea on their part to make sense of things in a different way. Some never find such a way. But others of us do. The same vicissitudes of life, the same limitations of time and space, the same encounters with the forces of nature, the same confrontations with the horrendous acts of others that cause some to despair of ever finding any meaning in such things are experienced by others of us as full of meaning. How is this possible? Phillips's answer (coupled with Faulconer's insistence that there is an important distinction between dealing with God and evil theoretically or intellectually and dealing with them in terms of how one comes to live one's life in covenant with God) amounts to a distinctively different approach to evil and suffering.[23] It is the one that I follow. In the balance of

---

21. Phillips, *Introducing Philosophy*, 156.
22. Phillips, *Introducing Philosophy*, 157.
23. It rests, in large part, on an alternative, less common view of religious beliefs that he puts forward, one that sees such beliefs not as a means of explaining how

this paper I will spell out what I mean by this, first by agreeing with Faulconer's contention that our concrete responses to evil and suffering, rather than our rational speculations about it, are what is required of us and then by saying how, in following Phillips's lead, I have come to realize that believing in God in the face of evil and suffering makes sense—provided I respond to or view the world in a particular way.

A Different Approach to Evil and Suffering

In the course of arguing that the only kind of theology worthy of our consideration is one that reveals God, one that enables us to hear his call and respond properly by living in the world differently (what he calls "apocalyptic theology"),[24] Faulconer deals with some issues in a manner that has contributed to my particular approach to evil and suffering.[25] For instance, he notes that those who think

---

things are but as *forms of response* or *modes of acceptance* of a world in which evil and suffering happen and are only too real. Like I said, I have come to identify with something like this view of religious beliefs. For me, such beliefs are better understood as part of, or better still, as a consequence of the way I strive to live my life in covenant with God. Living my life this way, rather than trying to reconcile my beliefs about God and evil, is what enables me to deal with the challenge of evil and suffering.

24. Faulconer, "Rethinking Theology," 117.

25. According to Faulconer, any theology worthy of the name, must be a type, a figure, or a shadow of the apocalypse. If, in the last analysis, it remains merely a matter of learning—of acquiring this, that, or another fact—then it is really more about us than God. As he puts it, If the Good News and God's kingdom are invisible in a theology, then it cannot really be talk about God. "What we say may concern itself with his effects in this world or with our ideas and understanding of him. It may be about our doctrines, our understanding of his revelation. . . . [It] *may be about many things, but it is not about him if it does not reveal him, and it does not reveal him if it does not announce the nearness of his kingdom*" (Faulconer, "Rethinking Theology," 113, emphasis added). What is more, we need to appreciate that such an announcement comes to us as a call. If we hear it and if we respond properly, we experience, here and now, the kingdom of God. "Thus, the revelation of the reign of God is not only something far away in time, something to be awaited, but something here and now" (Faulconer, "Rethinking Theology," 110). When we become part of the kingdom of God his rule over us begins. Such an experience, importantly, *"does not so much refer to the end of the world, though it also refers to that, as it refers to the moment when the nearness of the kingdom of God is revealed to the believer and the believer's life is oriented by that kingdom rather than by the world. . . . If we see the world through religious eyes, we see the imprint of God's work in everything"* (Faulconer, "Rethinking Theology," 110, emphasis added).

about theology along traditional lines—as that which organizes and examines a set of beliefs—may not fully grasp his notion of theology since they see only one basic kind, the kind that defines religion as adhering to a belief or set of beliefs. Of course, as he points out, religion entails beliefs, but it cannot be reduced to them. And in a religious tradition like our own where priesthood is essential and ordinances are required, beliefs are not sufficient to define religion. In an important sense they may not even come first.[26]

Also, Faulconer observes that scriptures teach that

> The Lord commands ancient Israel, "Ye shall be holy ["set apart," "consecrated"]: for I the Lord your God am holy" (Leviticus 19:2). Similarly, during his ministry in Israel, he commands, "Be ye therefore perfect [or "whole"], even as your Father which is in heaven is perfect" (Matthew 5:48), and he repeats that command when he comes to the Nephites (3 Nephi 12:48).[27]

This means, according to our guide, that "to be in Israel, ancient or modern, is not only to hold a set of beliefs, but to make and keep covenants with God. It is to enter into a formal relation with him in which we imitate him." For Latter-day Saints at least, *"covenant rather than belief is the heart of religion. It is probably true that no covenants fail to entail beliefs, but the important point is that religious beliefs do not matter if they are not intimately bound up with covenants."*[28]

What is more, Faulconer insists that any theology, worthy of the name,

> must go beyond learning to the gospel, to the *revelation* of Christ. It must be not only about beliefs; it must also be testimony. *For Latter-day Saints, apocalyptic theology must go beyond learning and even testimony to being part of covenant*

---

26. See Faulconer, "Rethinking Theology," 122.
27. Faulconer, "Rethinking Theology," 123, brackets in original.
28. Faulconer, "Rethinking Theology," 123.

life, for we cannot reveal God by re-presenting him in an idol of
some sort, but he reveals himself in our covenant life.[29]

His observation that "we cannot reveal God by re-presenting
him in an idol of some sort, but he reveals himself in our covenant
life" is crucial, for me at least, because it is true. In striving to do all
that is required of me to live my life in covenant with God, that is,
in living my life differently and thus responding to or viewing the
world differently, I have discovered that it is by this means (not by
dwelling on my beliefs about him or by trying to reconcile them
in various ways) that he makes himself known to me. It is by this
means that I am able to see his hand in all things. It is by this means
that I struggle to come to terms with the negative things in life in
ways that are both meaningful and lasting.

To give a full account of what is entailed in my doing this would
be involved, owing to a number of factors and influences; it would
also go beyond the scope of this paper. Suffice it to say, it begins
with my living a covenantal life with God, and it ends, importantly,
with my being convinced that my religious beliefs do not function
for me as hypotheses. That is, I have quit asking for explanations
when faced with all manner of things that happen to me and to
others. Instead, I have learned, in Phillips's words, to respond to
or accept this fallen world as one in which such negative things are
inevitable.

Like virtually everyone else, I experience the world, most of
the time, as admittedly peaceful and beautiful, even majestic. But,
on occasion, as we all know, it can be a frightening and dreadful
place, where the forces of nature combine in a flurry of violence
and destruction, disease and death. Likewise, I find myself, most of
the time, surrounded by evidence of human goodness—everything
from ongoing efforts to improve all aspects of the human condition, to seemingly endless acts of kindness and charity shown to

---

29. Faulconer, "Rethinking Theology," 123, most emphasis added.

me and my loved ones. Yet, as we are reminded all too often, the world can also be a place where humans are capable of treating others in the worst possible ways by committing unspeakable acts of horror, cruelty, and mayhem.

But there is more to it than this. In experiencing the world this way I am keenly aware that there is something deeper (as Phillips puts it) in my encounter with it, both in the sense that I try to respond to it as a whole, as it were, and in such a way as to evidence a form of patience on my part, and also in the sense that I experience something more (what Faulconer calls "the nearness of the kingdom of God").[30] Living my life in covenant with God (with all that this implies) means that I struggle to respond to or view the world from this perspective, *not the other way around.* Consequently, I not only experience a mixed world but also a new one that is coming into being and thus can see "the imprint of God's work in everything"[31]—his hand, if you will, in what is both beautiful and ugly in nature as well as kind and cruel in the actions of others. Others view the world the same way. Some have a gifted way of expressing it. David B. Hart, an Eastern Orthodox theologian, puts it this way:

> The Christian vision of the world, however, is not some rational deduction from empirical experience, but is a moral and spiritual aptitude—or, rather, a moral and spiritual labor [that is, a conviction on the part of the individual that living his life in terms of God and the things of God is what he ought to do]. The Christian eye sees (or should see) a deeper truth in the world than mere "nature," and it is a truth that gives rise not to optimism but to joy.[32]

---

30. See note 25 above; Faulconer, "Rethinking Theology," 109.

31. Faulconer, "Rethinking Theology," 110.

32. David B. Hart, *Doors of the Sea: Where Was God in the Tsunami?* (Grand Rapids: Eerdmans, 2005), 58.

He quotes religious authorities in his own tradition to further illustrate this point and then, in his own eloquent way, makes this observation,

> To see the world as it should be seen, and so to see the true glory of God reflected in it, requires the cultivation of charity, of an eye rendered limpid by love. . . . But what the Christian should see, then, is not simply one reality: neither the elaborate, benign, elegantly calibrated machine of the deists, smoothly and efficiently accomplishing whatever goods a beneficent God and the intractable potentialities of finitude can produce between them; nor a sacred or divine commerce between life and death; nor certainly "nature" in the modern, mechanistic acceptance of that word. Rather, the Christian should see two realities at once, one world (as it were) within another: one the world as we all know it, in all its beauty and terror, grandeur and dreariness, delight and anguish; and the other the world in its first and ultimate truth, not simply "nature" but "creation," an endless sea of glory, radiant with the beauty of God in every part, innocent of all violence. To see in this way is to rejoice and mourn at once, to regard the world as a mirror of infinite beauty, but as glimpsed through the veil of death; it is to see creation in chains, but beautiful as in the beginning of days.[33]

The everyday world that I encounter is indeed one "in all its beauty and terror, grandeur and dreariness, delight and anguish," but, more importantly, it also reveals a new world that is being born, one that is "radiant with the beauty of God in every part."

In talking this way about the world, in saying things like, "I see the hand of God in all things"—that is, in describing my particular approach to evil and suffering—I do not want to be misunderstood.

33. Hart, *Doors of the Sea*, 60–61.

When I say that I can see God even in the sometimes violent and destructive acts of nature, I mean that such occurrences dramatically manifest the power and force of creation itself and, hence, reveal something of the Creator. When I come across accounts of individuals committing dreadful and inexcusable acts against others and I speak of seeing God in such things, I do not mean to suggest that he is behind such outbursts of evil or the accompanying suffering that results. On the contrary. For me, all such negative things can and ought to be traced back to their ultimate source, the evil one.[34] When I say that I see God in such things, I am trying to convey the idea that in living my life the way I do, I view the whole world as symbolically ordered for me by God and the things of God, with all that this entails.[35]

In ordering my life this way I do not take a quietistic or indifferent approach to instances of evil and suffering. Just the opposite. When faced with natural calamities, I join with others in doing what I can to help those caught up in such disasters. When confronted with instances of human evil, I thwart them as best I can (ever mindful that whatever I do rarely seems to be enough). In this vale of tears, no matter what we do to fight against it or try to lessen

34. To the extent I am able to come to terms with the massive amount of evil and suffering in this world, especially that inflicted by humans on other innocent humans, it is only by tracking such things back to God's enemy. At the same time, for me at least, all that is good and true and beautiful comes ultimately from God. I am aware of the range of concerns that some have when these cardinal qualities are raised. Is something good, true, or beautiful because it comes from God or is it such in and of itself and therefore God endorses it? Dealing with such issues is interesting, even challenging, but for me, at the end of the day, beside the point. What God has come to mean to me is not so much the result of such theological reasoning as it is a consequence of my trying to live my life in terms of him and things associated with him and my trying to grasp the portrait of him that is revealed in the scriptures and in the teachings of latter-day prophets. For me, God is the source of everything good, true, and beautiful. In other words, I agree with the teachings of Mormon, as recorded by his son (see Moroni 7:12–19).

35. Again, I do not want to be misunderstood. When I talk this way, I do not have in mind some kind of woolly, pantheistic notion of God. Rather, God, for me at least, really is distinct from his creation and yet is visible within it. This is the way the scriptures speak of God and the world, and I try to do the same.

its effect, there will always be more evil (and what, more times than not, seems like needless suffering) to contend with. Nevertheless, my course is clear. I must always do whatever I can to minimize and lessen such terrible things in my life and in the lives of those I come in contact with, in most instances by joining with others in this common cause, often by using various means provided by the Church of Jesus Christ of Latter-day Saints.

What is more, I take the approach I do to evil and suffering, in large part, precisely because the message of the Good News is true. That is, Heavenly Father, nearly two thousand years ago, acting through the Savior, began to do what he always promised he would do: deal with the sins of the world and restore justice and order to all of creation by beginning the process of bringing about a new earth and new heavens. As a result, the victory over evil, suffering, and death has been won. At that time, he set in place the means by which all those who respond to his call can be brought into a new and ever-lasting covenantal relationship with him and the Savior—something he has again restored to the earth in our day. The Spirit's influence in the hearts of those of us who hear and respond to God's call is such that we declare the Savior to be Lord over all, we accept him and this glorious message of redemption, we join the community of his covenant people, and we live this new way of life our entire lives in the hope of what is coming and because this is what is required of us. Despite the fact that all of us, like those who came before us and will follow after us, must endure the persistence of sin and evil, suffering and death in this life, some of us are better able to do this than others precisely because of the assurance we have of what has already been accomplished on our behalf by the Father and the Son. Furthermore, we are confident of what they will yet accomplish when the Savior is sent again to vanquish all this for good, subject all things unto him-self, and make "all things new."

At the same time, I acknowledge that what the scriptures and the latter-day prophets say about our dealings with certain kinds of suffering, certain kinds of evil, even death itself, is true: if properly discerned, understood, and approached, even these things can be turned to our good. Such is the grandeur of the plan of the Father we are in the midst of experiencing. In any event, I try never to minimize the reality or starkness of such evils or the grief and suffering they cause others and myself as a result. Indeed, I like to think it is precisely because of the way I try to relate properly with God and others and thus how I have come to view the world, that I take the position I do on the need to come to terms with these negative realities—in this particular way.[36]

For me at least, the difference between someone like myself and others (those who fail to find any meaning in their encounters with such negative things or those who do but only by using their religious beliefs as hypotheses, as a means of trying to explain them) lies in how I experience and interpret my dependence on God, how I have come to trust in him.[37]

---

36. As with virtually everyone else (but, unfortunately, not all), life is precious to me. I cling to it with all of my might and do all I can (relying on prayer and priesthood blessings, as well as medical science) to aid others and myself whenever it is threatened. At the same time, were I to find myself in a life-or-death situation my trust in God is such that if he spares my life then (in the words of William Clayton's hymn) "All is well. All is well." I will continue on my journey toward him. But if not, "Happy day! All is well." I will continue on my journey, but on the other side. One of the more provocative observations in what was rather (in my opinion) a disappointing four-hour documentary entitled "The Mormons" (aired on PBS, 30 April and 1 May 2007) was made by the literary critic Harold Bloom (who speaks with some authority, having written a book on the tradition, *The American Religion* [New York: Simon and Schuster, 1992]). Bloom asks, "What is the essence of religion?" And then he answers his own question: "Sigmund Freud said it was the longing for the father. Others have called it the desire for the mother or for transcendence. I fear deeply that all these are idealizations, and I offer the rather melancholy suggestion that they would all vanish from us if we did not know that we must die. Religion rises inevitably from our apprehension of our own death. To give meaning to meaninglessness is the endless quest of all religion. When death becomes the center of our consciousness then religion authentically begins. Of all religions that I know, the one that most vehemently and persuasively defies and denies the reality of death is the original Mormonism of the prophet, seer and revelator, Joseph Smith."

37. My dependence on God is not an obstacle to my sense of self or to my moral agency, as commonly argued. On the contrary. I interpret key scriptures as teaching that in the premortal realm one of our first inklings of identity was our rather

Phillips is helpful in thinking through what is required of me in responding to instances of natural evil. He asks us to contemplate a believer who finds himself caught in a small boat at sea in a storm. When this poor fellow says things like, "my life is in the hands of God," Phillips urges us to take him to mean that in the midst of all that he faces, the believer is not only struck by his dependence on God, but also by a sense of the majesty of God. This is part of what he means when he says that some believers respond to the world in a deeper way. For Phillips,

> The believer is the creature in the hands of the Creator; his life, whether he is going to live or die, is in God's hands. Not that externally related to this storm is a God who decides to send it *in order* to test the believer's faith, or *in order* to give the believer a sense of the majesty of God. . . . No, the majesty of God is revealed *in* the storm and the reaction to it. God's will is in the life or death of the person caught in the storm, in the same sense as it is in the storm itself.[38]

Our guide also reminds us that the scriptures, especially narratives such as the book of Job, teach us to deal with evil and suffering this way as well. Job came to see the wonder of it all in the face of all that he suffered. He eventually gave up on his friends (those he called "forgers of lies" and "physicians of no value," Job 13:4) and their seemingly endless, fruitless attempts at explaining

---

inchoate sense of self that emerged as a result of relationships we found ourselves in when Heavenly Father created us as his spirit children—ones primarily with him, but also with his Firstborn Son and with our other spiritual siblings. Now, as a fully embodied being, my very sense of who I am is grounded in such relationships—something that becomes more apparent the more I strive to live a covenantal life. My dependence solely on Heavenly Father and on the Savior is how I can be independent of other ideas, movements, or individuals who would have me reliant on them. It is what assures that I am free in the fullest sense of the term. Because of it, I define myself as a child of God, as a member of my own family, and as a member of the restored kingdom of God on earth. Because of it, I experience this life, despite everything else, as full of hope and meaning, purpose and joy.

38. Phillips, *Introducing Philosophy*, 160–61.

what was happening to him. He eventually (and this is key) stopped placing himself in the center of things and stopped asking, "Why is this happening to me?" Instead, he came to acknowledge his dependence on God. He came to see the world and all of its contingencies as gifts from God. He patiently admitted that God is at the center of all things. God makes the rain to fall on the just and the unjust. Job eventually confessed that everything that comes to him comes as a gift, as a form of grace, as an expression of God's love for him—the good things and the bad. Things that come as trials, things he did not want or like, are gifts, nonetheless. Job's wonder at the whole of creation, his newfound dependence on God who is at the center of all things, and his acceptance of what comes to him, good or bad, as gifts from God, is what he meant to express in his famous claim, "'The Lord gave, the Lord hath taken away; blessed be the name of the Lord.'"[39]

There are those, Phillips observes, who are fatalistic, who contend that whatever happens, happens and insist that those of us who talk about God in such situations change nothing. He rejects this view and so do I.[40] My birth and my death happen but what I make of them, how I respond to them, indeed, what I make of my life as a whole, makes all the difference. Job initially cursed the day he was born, and then he came to see his dependence on God and the wonder of it all. *Coming to God made this difference for him; it changed the meaning of things for him. Coming to so live in this world that, like Job, I can see the hand of the Lord in all things, makes all the difference for me as well.*

When encountering instances of human evil, Phillips likewise contends that it is the believer's dependence on God, his experience of the love and grace of God in his life, that distinguishes him from the conventional moral person. The latter fights against evil and strives mightily for the good but always acknowledges that he does

39. Phillips, *Introducing Philosophy*, 162; see 161-62.
40. See Phillips, *Introducing Philosophy*, 161-62.

such things on his own. Those of us who depend on God do these things as well. The difference is we confess that all that we do and whatever we achieve in this regard is because of him. This further evidences, according to Phillips, a deeper response to the world on our part, one that, among other things, reflects our strengths as well as our weaknesses as human beings.[41]

I like the way Phillips illustrates his point about our dependency on God. He notes that Peter promised he would never deny the Savior, and yet he did. The question is, when did he do this? "The popular answer is," Phillips says, "when he broke his promise. The deeper answer is: when he made it."[42] Peter's act of self-sufficiency, his putting himself at the center of things, as Job did initially, was his undoing. He ought always to have relied on God and trusted in him. Such dependence, such acknowledgment of God's grace and love in our lives, is what should inform all of our endeavors as followers of him. It is what steels us for our inevitable encounters with the evil one, particularly in the form of all manner of depraved human actions, and it is what enables us to do the right thing morally in our dealings with others, including being quick to forgive others while always seeking forgiveness from others and from God, as the Savior teaches us.[43]

As I noted above, Phillips cautions those of us who try to respond to the world in this way that every now and then some of us will face what he calls "limiting cases"—profound challenges to our faith, most often, it seems, in the form of situations in which the innocent are made to undergo untold suffering at the hands of

---

41. See Phillips, *Introducing Philosophy*, 162-63. Faulconer makes a similar distinction; see his article "The Concept of Apostasy in the New Testament," in *Early Christians in Disarray: Contemporary LDS Perspectives on the Christian Apostasy*, ed. Noel B. Reynolds (Provo, UT: BYU Press and FARMS, 2005), 133-63, especially 155-56.

42. Phillips, *Introducing Philosophy*, 163.

43. One of the most memorable talks on this great principle was given by President James E. Faust in the April 2007 general conference, not too long before his passing; it is a fitting tribute to this good man. See "The Healing Power of Forgiveness," *Ensign*, May 2007, 67-69.

others. Some who contemplate the magnitude and weight of such evil in the world, especially that which is visited upon innocent children, discover that it has crushed their faith.[44] For those of us fortunate enough to persist in our trust in God (it is a gift, after all), who continue to struggle to so live that we can see his hand even in the midst of such horrible things, the book of Job is again help-ful in suggesting at least part of what may be involved in our being able to do this. While Job was confronting all that had happened to him, his friends joined him and, at least initially (thank heaven) did what true friends do—they came "to mourn with him and to com-fort him. . . . [They] wept; and they rent every one his mantle, and sprinkled dust upon their heads toward heaven. So they sat down with him upon the ground seven days and seven nights, and none spake a word unto him: for they saw that his grief was very great" (Job 2:11-13).

When I encounter things that challenge my faith, that threaten to cause me to doubt God, I find solace in my experiences of him as one who does for me what Job's friends did for him—he abides with me when I need him, he suffers and weeps with me in my time of grief, and he says nothing when silence is what is called for.

For me at least, to see the hand of God in situations like these is to be at peace with the fact that my experiences with the divine do not explain such things as the wrongful suffering of innocent children (or anyone else) nor do they justify them in any way.[45] It

---

44. The twentieth century experienced two world wars and such atrocities as the Holocaust that emerged out of Nazi horrors in Europe during the second one and the ethnic and class genocide that took place during the same time but continued long afterward, resulting in the killing of tens of millions who lived under Communist domination in a swath stretching from the Gulag labor camps in the old Soviet Union, through China, and onto the killing fields of Cambodia. It may turn out to be the worst century in human history in this regard.

45. There is suffering and there is suffering. All of us experience it; it is part of the very point and purpose of life in this mortal realm. For most of us, the suffering we encounter and need to find the courage to endure, if properly approached and under-stood (that is, within our ongoing trust and dependence on God), can be ennobling, refining, even sanctifying. The Savior taught this. But other kinds of unspeakable

is to acknowledge that in these and other similar situations in life it is folly on my part to try to explain the ways of God. Rather, my course is to depend on him and wait patiently on him, in silence and in hope.⁴⁶

It seems clear that the Prophet Joseph Smith understood this. Writing from Liberty Jail in the winter of 1838-39, Joseph told how the Lord assured him that all the suffering and anguish he and the other members of the church were being forced to undergo at the time, at the hands of others, would "give [them] experience and be for [their] good" *if* they would "stand still" with the "utmost assurance" in God (D&C 122:7; 123:17). One of the many things he must have learned at that time about life in this lone and dreary world is the age-old truth we all need to learn, that we must "cheerfully do all things that lie in our power" and then wait on the Lord and trust in him (D&C 123:17).

---

suffering, imposed upon the innocent, are needless, pointless, and evil. I find that one of the many things the Holy Spirit does for me, if I am living the life I know I should, is help me recognize instances of the former and give me the needed strength to withstand them. He will also aid me in discerning instances of the latter and embolden me to fight against them with all of my might.

46. Phillips ends his chapter on this same note. Following up on what he said earlier about evil inflicted on innocent children, he observes that "to witness absolute evil, as we do in this persecution of children, is to feel at the same time that an absolute good is being outraged. An absolute good does not triumph when violated by absolute wrong: it suffers. It can offer no explanation, no end to which the evil is the means. On such matters, it is dumb. In the religious responses that we have been discussing, God and absolute good are one. If absolute good can suffer, so can God. The presence of the divine does not explain away the suffering or justify it in any way. The divine suffers. It was said by Jesus that to do this to children was to do it to him. The suffering of innocent children is the suffering of God at the same time. In Isaiah we read the following words: 'He was oppressed and he was afflicted, yet he opened not his mouth: he is brought as a lamb to the slaughter, and as a sheep before her shearers is dumb, so he opened not his mouth.' But confronted by the silence of God, we have seen many philosophers of religion react by saying: 'Well, if he did not open his mouth we will, and give you here, as elsewhere, the justification for this evil.' One way of understanding the arguments of this chapter is to wish that those philosophers had not spoken" (Phillips, *Introducing Philosophy*, 165).

Several years ago, Phillips gave a lecture, and part of it found its way onto the Internet.[47] In a simple yet dramatic fashion, he contrasts the two very different approaches to God, and hence, the two ways of viewing the world that I have sketched out in this paper. He began by noting that if one believes in God, he will, no doubt, be asked to give reasons for his belief. This is not unusual, Phillips says, since we think it reasonable to be asked to give reasons for our beliefs. This is something we take for granted.

Then he read an eloquent passage from one of the psalms:

> Whither shall I go from thy spirit? or whither shall I flee from thy presence?
>
> If I ascend up into heaven, thou art there: if I make my bed in hell, behold, thou art there.
>
> If I take the wings of the morning, and dwell in the uttermost parts of the sea;
>
> Even there shall thy hand lead me, and thy right hand shall hold me.
>
> If I say, Surely the darkness shall cover me; even the night shall be light about me.
>
> Yea, the darkness hideth not from thee; but the night shineth as the day: the darkness and the light are both alike to thee.
>
> For thou hast possessed my reins: thou hast covered me in my mother's womb.
>
> I will praise thee; for I am fearfully and wonderfully made: marvelous are thy works; and that my soul knoweth right well. (Psalm 139:7-14)

Here, Phillips notes, the psalmist speaks of the "inescapable reality of God." "Inescapable?" Phillips asks. "But what about the evidence?

---

47. "D. Z. Phillips and What It Means to Believe in God"; an audio recording of the lecture and a transcript are available at http://www.contra-mundum.com/?p=894 (accessed 10 June 2010). This Web page is the source for the following ideas and quotations from Phillips.

What about the reasons?" According to our guide, it would never occur to any prophet or writer in scripture

> to seek evidence for this existence of God, let alone to prove it. For them this would be quite pointless, even senseless. *The movement of thought in the Old Testament is not from the world to God, but from God to the world.* The whole world declared God's presence. Not because it gave excellent evidence for God's existence, but because the world was seen from the start as God's world.[48]

Phillips observes, in a nostalgic tone, how far away that view seems to most of us today. "That world is not our world. It hasn't been our world for quite some time. Ever since the Renaissance and through the Enlightenment, the view of the world as God's world has been under attack."

At this point, he notes that for us today it is natural to view religious beliefs as conjectures or hypotheses and to look for evidence to justify them. He points out how philosophers who write about such matters weigh the probabilities for and against God but never seem to agree. And then asks, "Is that our problem? A difficulty in weighing probabilities?" and answers his own query, "Surely not." Rather,

> Our difficulty is that the majority of us no longer naturally see the world as God's world. It's all too easy to escape from God's presence. If we ascend into the heavens, well even Bishops tell us He's not there. If we descend into the depths, again psychoanalysts tell us He's not there either. Our problem, it seems, is not how to escape from God but how to find him. We all too easily rise in the morning and lie down in darkness without him. The heavens no longer declare his glory for us, and the hills no longer sing for joy.[49]

---

48. "Phillips and What It Means to Believe in God," emphasis added.

49. "Phillips and What It Means to Believe in God"; Phillips earlier recited the following verses from the Psalms: "The little hills rejoice on every side. The pastures are

I think Phillips correctly portrays the modern perspective on the world. What he and Faulconer say about many if not most of us who are religious today is true. It used to be true of me. But not anymore. I have heard God's call, and my making every effort to live in covenant with him has made all of the difference: I think about him differently and, in turn, respond to or view the world differently. I agree with the psalmist. From the heights to the depths, God is there—"and that my soul knoweth right well" (Psalm 139:14).

M. Gerald Bradford is executive director of the Neal A. Maxwell Institute for Religious Scholarship at Brigham Young University.

---

clothed with flocks; the valleys also are covered over with corn; they shout for joy, they also sing. . . . Let the floods clap their hands: let the hills be joyful together. . . . O Lord, how manifold are thy works! in wisdom hast thou made them all: the earth is full of thy riches" (Psalms 65:12–13; 98:8; 104:24).

CHAPTER 4

ॐ

"Living in Negligent Ease": Evidence for al-Ghazālī's Crisis of Conscience in His *Iqtiṣād fī al-Iʿtiqād*

D. Morgan Davis

I wish to express my regard for S. Kent Brown, whose example of faith, scholarship, and goodwill have inspired and blessed me in myriad ways.

Abū Hamīd Muḥammad al-Ghazālī is by all accounts a pivotal figure in the history of Islamic thought. Born in 1058 and educated in northern Persia, he proved to be a precocious student. Eventually he was attracted to Baghdad, capital of the ʿAbbasid empire and the intellectual center of gravity of his time. There, in 1091, he was appointed by the Caliph's minister, Niẓām al-Mulk, to head the foremost legal school in the realm. But al-Ghazālī was more than a brilliant legal mind. He mastered a number of intellectual disciplines, making his mark on all of them through the numerous treatises he generated over a lifetime.[1] These cover a broad range of subjects—including

---

I would like to thank an anonymous reviewer for comments that helped me to clarify a number of points in this essay.

1. For a succinct catalogue of al-Ghazālī's works, see George F. Hourani, "A Revised Chronology of Ghazali's Writings," *Journal of the American Oriental Society* 104 (1984): 289-302. For a more recent and very thorough treatment of al-Ghazālī's oeuvre and his significance to Islamic intellectual history, see Frank Griffell, *al-Ghazālī's Philosphical Theology* (Oxford: Oxford University Press, 2009).

philosophy, theology, and mysticism, in addition to law—and his autobiography is one of the most intimate and compelling portraits of an intellectual's search for truth and authentic faith to be found anywhere in world literature. From our vantage today, al-Ghazālī's most lasting and therefore significant contributions were not his legal teachings but those that pointed out the fallacies of thinkers who, according to al-Ghazālī, had gone too far in accommodating pure Islamic ideals and Qurʾanic teachings to the philosophies of the Greeks. His later writings that argued for the union of mind, heart, and body in matters of faith—the Islamic concept of *niyya*, or right intention—challenged and deepened understandings of what it meant to live their faith. His writings in this vein still carry much weight, I believe, because al-Ghazālī famously lived what he taught. Forsaking the worldly fame and prosperity that he had achieved, hc departed Baghdad in order to pursue an intensely personal and spiritual path. The focus of this essay is to point out how one of al-Ghazālī's lesser-known works, *al-Iqtiṣād fī al-iʿtiqād* (Moderation in Belief),[2] connects to his momentous decision to renounce his post at the law school in Baghdad and how it yields tantalizing clues about his state of mind as he contemplated a radical change of life. In order to appreciate this connection, however, it will be useful first to briefly summarize a few key points of his biography and situate the writing of *al-Iqtiṣād* within that history.

Epistemological Crisis

In his autobiography, *al-Munquidh mīn al-dalāl* (Deliverance from Error),[3] al-Ghazālī writes about an important formative experience—an epistemological crisis—that took place while he was still a student. He tells of an early, God-given "thirst for grasping the real meaning of things," so that when he was "still quite

---

2. Al-Ghazālī, *al-Iqtiṣād fī al-itiqād*, ed. A. Çubukçü and H. Atay (Ankara, 1962).
3. The English translation of *al-Munquidh* cited in this essay is Richard J. McCarthy, ed. and trans., *al-Ghazali: Deliverance from Error* (Louisville, KY: Fons Vitae, 1998). All quotations from the *Iqtiṣād* in this essay are my translation from the Arabic.

young" he became unwilling to blindly accept inherited beliefs simply on the basis of authority. "For," he says, "I saw that the children of Christians always grew up embracing Christianity, and the children of Jews always grew up adhering to Judaism, and the children of Muslims always grew up following the religion of Islam."[4] It became al-Ghazālī's goal to critically separate out the true from the false or dubious of the received beliefs that people held from their parents or religious leaders. To do this, he determined that he would not accept any belief on the basis of authority or surmise but would rather rely only upon "sense-data and the self-evident truths." But then he began to question whether even these seemingly certain sources of knowledge were as unassailable as they at first appeared. "With great earnestness," he writes, "I began to reflect on my sense-data to see if I could make myself doubt them."[5]

By noticing such phenomena as the sundial's shadow that appears to stand still and yet over time proves to be in constant motion, or a star that appears tiny yet can be proven geometrically to be very distant and great in size, al-Ghazālī came to the point where he admitted:

> My reliance on sense-data has also become untenable. Perhaps, therefore, I can rely only on those rational data which belong to the category of primary truths, such as our asserting that "Ten is more than three," and "One and the same thing cannot be simultaneously affirmed and denied," and "One and the same thing cannot be incipient and eternal, existent and nonexistent, necessary and impossible."[6]

Al-Ghazālī's epistemological doubts reached a crisis when he came to question whether even this last pillar of knowledge—self-evident truths—could survive the thought experiment that pitted one's

4. McCarthy, *Deliverance from Error*, 54–55.
5. McCarthy, *Deliverance from Error*, 56.
6. McCarthy, *Deliverance from Error*, 56.

confidence in the "reality" of dreams against that of one's waking hours:

> Don't you see that when you are asleep you believe certain things and imagine certain circumstances and believe they are fixed and lasting and entertain no doubts about that being their status? Then you wake up and know that all your imaginings and beliefs were groundless and unsubstantial. So while everything you believe through sensation or intellection in your waking state may be true in relation to that state, what assurance have you that you may not suddenly experience a state which would have the same relation to your waking state as the latter has to your dreaming, and your waking state would be dreaming in relation to that new and further state? If you found yourself in such a state, you would be sure that all your rational beliefs were unsubstantial fancies.[7]

At this point, al-Ghazālī says he lost confidence even in logic and the power of the so-called self-evident truths to impart knowledge that was secure against all doubt. He tried, he says, to construct a proof for the efficacy of a priori truths in the waking state, but he had to admit that "the only way to put together a proof was to combine primary cognitions. So if, as in my case, these were inadmissible, it was impossible to construct the proof." He seemed stuck, and for nearly two months he continued to write and speak as though he were as certain as he had always been of his beliefs, but inwardly, he writes, "I was a skeptic."[8] His faith in his ability to know *anything* with certainty had been shaken.

According to al-Ghazālī, the resolution to this crisis of faith came—and could only have come—through divine intervention. Al-Ghazālī reports that, in the end, no proof or other argument

---

7. McCarthy, *Deliverance from Error*, 57.
8. McCarthy, *Deliverance from Error*, 57.

resolved the issue, but "a light which God Most High cast into [his] breast."[9] This was not a rational resolution to his crisis, but a spiritual one. Al-Ghazālī affirms that the return of his confidence in the relevance of sense-data and of logical reasoning to the quest for knowledge came because of a divine assurance that they were valid—a divine assurance which he then took to constitute an additional source of certain knowledge. Some truths were available through sense perception, others through logical reasoning, and others through spiritual means—the revelations of God to prophets and divine light cast into the hearts of sincere seekers of truth generally. This addition by al-Ghazālī of revelation/inspiration to sense perception and intellectual reason as a valid epistemic mode was a serious matter for him. He did not see it as merely auxiliary to other forms of gaining knowledge, but as affording access to a certain domain of truth that reason and sense perception by themselves simply could not reach. Unaided, reason and sense perception could not reliably intuit metaphysical truths in the first place. The most that could be expected of them was that they might confirm and flesh out the logical ramifications of certain metaphysical truths *after* these were made known by revelation/inspiration. This position set the stage for al-Ghazālī's famous attack on the thinking of the Muslim philosophers—the *falāsifah*—who subscribed to many Aristotelian doctrines about God and his relationship to the world that, in al-Ghazālī's view, patently contradicted the plain teaching of the revelations of Muḥammad.

Early in his career at Baghdad, al-Ghazālī set about familiarizing himself with the teachings and methods of the philosophers. He wrote a book, *Maqāṣid al-falāsifah* (The Aims of the Philosophers), summarizing their teachings in order to be sure he understood their positions and arguments in their strongest forms. Having laid this groundwork, he then set out to show where the philosophers' inordinate admiration for Greek thought had led them to privilege

---

9. McCarthy, *Deliverance from Error*, 57.

reason over revelation and had blinded them to the logical problems inherent in some of their conclusions. Al-Ghazālī's *Tahāfut al-falāsifah* (Incoherence of the Philosophers)[10] was a devastating critique of Hellenistic-style philosophizing within Islam. It was also a warning to others about the dangers of following reason and sense perception—which were invaluable in their proper place—into the metaphysical realm, to which those tools simply did not have adequate access. Using their own methods against them, al-Ghazālī showed where the *falāsifah* had arrived at positions that were logically problematic and blatantly at odds with the prophetic teachings of the Qur'ān. The *falāsifah* followed Aristotle in his doctrine of an uncreated, eternal world; of a Creator so wholly other than his creation that he could have no direct awareness or knowledge of any particular aspect of it; and of the fundamental baseness of the body that dissolves at death, not to be resurrected, freeing the mind at last to contemplate pure being. The Qur'ān, on the other hand, affirmed a God who created the heavens and the earth, who knew his creatures and their doings, and who would judge them in the day of bodily resurrection.

The *Tahāfut* was a game-changing attack on the philosophers that could not be ignored by any who would come after, but al-Ghazālī seems to have recognized that it also was in danger of creating the impression that he was out to discredit the use of sense-data and logic altogether, which was not his intent. These did have their place, and so, in the *Tahāfut* he stated that his intention was next to write a constructive work of theology—one that would demonstrate the proper use of reason in tandem with revelation to flesh out a true understanding of God and the world. That work, as it turns out, would be *al-Iqtiṣād fī al-i'tiqād*.[11]

---

10. Michael E. Marmura, ed. and trans., *Al-Ghazālī: The Incoherence of the Philosophers*, 2nd ed. (Provo, UT: Brigham Young University Press, 2000).

11. This point is not entirely uncontroversial, since *al-Iqtiṣād fī al-i'tiqād* is not the title that al-Ghazālī originally said in the *Tahāfut* he would write, though he did eventually write a treatise by that title—*Qawā'id al-'aqā'id* (Principles of Belief).

The *Iqtiṣād* has been called al-Ghazālī's "chief work of dogmatics,"[12] but in addition to the chronological placement of the *Iqtiṣād* soon after the *Tahāfut* and its probable role in al-Ghazālī's program of scholarly writing, personal events in the life of al-Ghazālī also form a very important background to the *Iqtiṣād*.

Crisis of Conscience

In July 1095, at the height of his academic prestige as the head lecturer in legal theory at the Niẓāmiyya school of jurisprudence in Baghdad, al-Ghazālī apparently had some kind of breakdown, which led him to conclude that he must leave his post. By his own account this was precipitated by convictions within his own heart that he was living a lie—that while outwardly he seemed to be the model of Muslim piety, in moments of pure honesty with himself he knew that much of what he did and had achieved was merely for the sake of public adulation and personal renown.

> I attentively considered my circumstances, and I saw that I was immersed in attachments, which had encompassed me from all sides. I also considered my activities—the best of them being public and private instruction—and saw that in them I was applying myself to sciences unimportant and useless in the pilgrimage to the hereafter. Then I reflected on my intention in my public teaching, and I saw that it was

Nevertheless, Michael E. Marmura has convincingly argued, on the basis of George F. Hourani's revised chronology of al-Ghazālī's works, that the *Iqtiṣād*, rather than the *Qawāʿid*, is really the work that best fulfills al-Gazālī's commitment to write a work of theology. This is so, Marmura argues, because it follows closely after the *Tahāfut* chronologically and because al-Ghazālī actually states in his preface to the *Iqtiṣād fī al-iʿtiqād* that he is writing it to establish "principles of belief"—that is, "*qawāʿid al-ʿaqāʾid*." As T. Gianotti has nicely put it, by using this phrase in opening his *Iqtiṣād fī al-iʿtiqād*, al-Ghazālī fulfills "the spirit of the promise" he made in the *Tahāfut*, if not "the letter." See Michael E. Marmura, "Ghazali's *al-Iqtiṣād fī al-iʿtiqād*: Its Relation to *Tahāfut al-Falasifa* and to *Qawāʿid al-aqāʾid*," *Aligarh Journal of Islamic Philosophy* 10 (2004): 1–12; Timothy J. Gianotti, *Al-Ghazālī's Unspeakable Doctrine of the Soul: Unveiling the Esoteric Psychology and Eschatology of the Iḥyāʾ* (Leiden: Brill, 2002), 68 n. 2.

12. W. Montgomery Watt, "al-Ghazālī," in *Encyclopaedia of Islam*, new ed., 1040.

not directed purely to God, but rather was instigated and motivated by the quest for fame and widespread prestige. So I became certain that I was on the brink of a crumbling bank and already on the verge of falling into the Fire unless I set about mending my ways.[13]

It is clear from al-Ghazālī's concern with worldly "attachments" in this and other statements, that he had already begun to be versed in the discipline of Sufism, or Islamic mysticism, while he was teaching in Baghdad. It seems that he found this path appealing though challenging, for he clearly found himself at odds with it in his professional lifestyle. In order to "mend his ways," al-Ghazālī became convinced that he would have to free himself of selfish attachments by actually renouncing them, including his academic position. For some time, however, he could not bring himself to do so. He vacillated between the allure of his prestigious seat and the pull of his conscience until, apparently, the conflict within him grew so intense that he became physically incapacitated, unable to speak, let alone to teach. As a result of this breakdown, he says, he finally made arrangements to leave. Under the guise of going on the hajj, he embarked on a spiritual quest that led him first to Damascus, where he studied under a Sufi master; then to Jerusalem, where he meditated in the cave under the Dome of the Rock; and eventually on to Mecca (twice) before returning to his home, now an adept of Sufi thought and practice. He would go on to write a number of mystical works as well as the *Iḥyaʾ ulūm al-dīn* (Revival of the Religious Sciences), a multivolume masterpiece that remains to this day one of the most influential treatises on Sufism and its proper place within the faith and practice of Muslims.

The Evidence from *al-Iqtiṣād*

But let us return to the moment of al-Ghazālī's crisis of conscience and the information that might be gleaned from the *Iqtiṣād*

---

13. McCarthy, *Deliverance from Error*, 78-79.

about his state of mind at that time. Montgomery Watt, following Maurice Bouges, indicates that the *Iqtiṣād* was "probably composed shortly before or shortly after [al-Ghazālī's] departure from Baghdad [c. 1095]."[14] George Hourani has argued that, along with one other work, the *Mīzān al-ʿamal*, the *Iqtiṣād* must have been completed before or during al-Ghazālī's famous crisis.[15] Hourani plausibly reasons that it was unlikely al-Ghazālī composed the *Iqtiṣād* after he began his journey, "for it is hard to believe that this prosaic piece of *kalām* [dogmatic Islamic theology] was one of the first products of his new life as a Ṣūfī."[16] In fact, he argues, the likelihood was that *Mīzān* was composed even after *Iqtiṣād* and still in the final year before al-Ghazālī left Baghdad. The seeming lack of coherence in *Mīzān* might even be an indication of al-Ghazālī's troubled state of mind at that time.[17] In any event, Hourani argues,

> Now that both *Iqtiṣād* and *Mīzān* have been placed with some confidence in the period when Ghazālī was approaching or actually immersed in the intense spiritual crisis of his life, the importance of these two works for understanding the evolution of his thought will readily be understood. Both of them therefore deserve more serious studies than they have hitherto received, and they should be read in the context of the author's revealing account of his state of mind at the time, narrated in *Munqidh [mīn al-ḍalāl]*, 122–30.[18]

---

14. Watt, "al-Ghazālī," 1040.

15. Some scholars have sought to suggest that there were other motives for al-Ghazālī's sudden departure. These are evaluated in Frank Griffel's recent and important monograph on al-Ghazālī. He concludes: "There is no testimony for al-Ghazālī's motivations other than the words we quoted from [his autobiography], and further conjecture disconnects itself from textual evidence. In the end, the reasons for al-Ghazālī's 'crisis' in Baghad are less interesting than the results." See Griffel, *al-Ghazālī's Philosophical Theology*, 43.

16. Hourani, "Revised Chronology," 294.

17. Hourani, "Revised Chronology," 295.

18. Hourani, "Revised Chronology," 294.

Though a full treatment of what the *Iqtiṣād* reveals about its author's state of mind at the time he wrote it must be deferred to later studies, two observations beyond those offered by previous scholars can be offered here.

First, the *Iqtiṣād* is written with students in mind. Its organization and tone reflect both a pedagogical and a polemical concern. It is composed as a primer on how to conduct a debate with one's ideological rivals. It is intended not so much for the actual convincing of real opponents but for study by the qualified believer who will one day, ostensibly, present similar arguments in actual debates or contests of ideology. For an audience, al-Ghazālī presumably had in mind his students at the Niẓāmiyya. In the course of his exposition, al-Ghazālī takes positions on a number of basic theological issues, dialectically presenting and then answering challenges to each of his claims—challenges such as had been or might have been raised by an incredulous "opponent." In most cases, al-Ghazālī is specifically envisioning an opponent either from among the extreme literalists (whom he identifies with the Hashwiyya and their reputation for anthropomorphism), the *falāsifah* (whom we have already mentioned), or the Muʿtazilites (an early school of rationalist theologians with doctrines to which al-Ghazālī's own school, the Ashʾarites, strongly objected). He offers his arguments and rebuttals, taking care to show at key moments that the soundness and superiority of his positions derive from striking a successful balance between reason and revelation. This is the "moderation in belief" for which the *Iqtiṣād* as a whole is named.

Second, early in the *Iqtiṣād*, al-Ghazālī spends a chapter arguing for the importance of the volume he is writing—that the study of God and his relation to his creation is deserving of serious attention, and that to waste time on pointless or frivolous topics while salvation hangs in the balance would be a grave error. It is here that al-Ghazālī makes what is perhaps the most direct allusion to his own state of mind as he composes the *Iqtiṣād*. He says that reports of prophets coming with signs and wonders, showing evidence that there might indeed be a God who rewards and punishes people with heaven or hell, have the power

> to tear peaceful security from the heart and to fill it with fear and trembling and to move it to study and pondering. [They can] snatch [the heart] from peace and stillness, and frighten it with the danger to which one is exposed while living in negligent ease.[19]

This passage bears a strong resonance with the personal account al-Ghazālī gives in the *Munqidh* of his six-month struggle to commit himself fully to the Sufi path of knowledge, a struggle that was underway, as best we can ascertain, when he wrote the passage just cited. Of this time, he writes in the *Munqidh*:

> One day I would firmly resolve to leave Baghdad and disengage myself from those circumstances, and another day I would revoke my resolution. . . . Mundane desires began tugging me with their chains to remain as I was, while the herald of faith was crying out: "Away! Up and away! Only a little is left of your life, and a long journey lies before you! All the theory and practice in which you are engrossed is eye-service and fakery! *If you do not prepare now for the afterlife, when will you do so? And if you do not sever these attachments now, then when will you sever them?*
>
> At such thoughts the call would reassert itself and I would make an irrevocable decision to run off and escape. Then Satan would return to the attack and say: "This is a passing state: beware, then, of yielding to it! For it will quickly vanish. Once you have given in to it and given up your present renown and splendid position free from vexation and renounced your secure situation untroubled by the contention

---

19. Al-Ghazālī, *Iqtiṣād*, 6-7.

of your adversaries, your soul might again look longingly at all that—but it would not be easy to return to it!"[20]

In both passages, vexation of spirit while one's standing before God remains in doubt is the theme. If read in this context, the passage from the *Iqtiṣād* may be seen as evidence of al-Ghazālī's sense of spiritual malaise in connection with his growing Sufi convictions—that to *know about* the existence of God and of the punishment or reward of the afterlife was not enough; he was responsible to *do* something about this knowledge by renouncing the world, seeking purity, and obtaining a more direct knowledge of God. "Once all of this has become clear for us," he continues, as though writing the *Iqtiṣād* to himself, "we would then undoubtedly be obliged—if we were prudent—to take our precautions and look to our souls and to despise this transitory world in comparison with that other, everlasting realm. Thus, the reasonable man sees to his destiny and is not deceived by his own works."[21] Surely al-Ghazālī saw himself as this reasonable man. His concern was that he lacked the will to overcome the deception of his own works—his position at the top of the Niẓāmiyya law school. But given the strength of his convictions, he must either do so or collapse in a state of cognitive paralysis. As he states in the *Iqtiṣād*, "There is no other course, once the impulse to find out [about these things] has occurred, than to instigate a quest for salvation."[22] According to our best estimates, less than a year after writing those words, al-Ghazālī did as he said he must. He quit his academic position, made arrangements for the care of his family, disappeared from the life of renown he had known since he was young, and embarked upon the Sufi path.

---

20. McCarthy, *Deliverance from Error*, 79, emphasis added.
21. Al-Ghazālī, *Iqtiṣād*, 8.
22. Al-Ghazālī, *Iqtiṣād*, 8.

Conclusion

Al-Ghazālī is a complex and problematicial figure. There is still considerable debate about a number of his positions with respect to the value of Greek-inherited ideas, formal dogmatic theology, theodicy, physical theory, and more. But these academic issues seem prosaic when compared to the compelling and very personal story of al-Ghazālī's own quest for truth and salvation. Written at the very meridian of his spiritual life, certain sections of the *Iqtiṣād fī al-iʿtiqād* appear to contain hints of what he was thinking as he neared that moment of crisis. They may be read as poignant meditations upon his own soul's predicament and as prologue to the life-changing decision that he ultimately made to renounce his worldly attainments and to devote himself to God.

D. Morgan Davis is an assistant research fellow at the Neal A. Maxwell Institute for Religious Scholarship.

CHAPTER 5

ᴈ☙

Usage of the Title *Elohim* in the Hebrew Bible and Early Latter-day Saint Literature

Ryan Conrad Davis and Paul Y. Hoskisson

Since the word *elohim* never occurs in any of our English Latter-day Saint scriptures[1] (though it appears more than twenty-six hundred times in the Hebrew text), it may seem unusual that Latter-day Saints use the term *elohim* at all. Yet use it we do.

For nearly one hundred years now, Latter-day Saints have understood, and more or less used, *elohim* as "the name-title of God the Eternal Father."[2] Yet historically they have not always used the term in this strict sense. In the nineteenth century, LDS literature employed *elohim* in a wider range of meanings than today, some of which might seem foreign to contemporary ears. Even more remarkable is that early LDS usage of the term mirrors in many respects its usage in the Hebrew Bible. In this essay in honor of S. Kent Brown, a friend and mentor, we explore how *elohim* is used in the Hebrew Bible and sample how early Latter-day Saints used the term.

---

1. Some search programs will turn up Mark 15:34 if *elohim* is typed in as the search word, but the word used in Mark, *eloi*, is hardly *elohim*. Mark 15:34 is a quotation from Psalm 22:1, where the word in Hebrew is *eli*, "my God." Additionally, the quotation in Mark is in Aramaic, not Hebrew.

2. James E. Talmage, *Jesus the Christ*, 2nd ed. (Salt Lake City: Deseret News, 1915), 38.

In 1916 the First Presidency, in an essay entitled "The Father and the Son: A Doctrinal Exposition by the First Presidency and the Twelve," issued a statement concerning the nature of the Godhead. The statement, published in the *Improvement Era*, set forth the official position of the church on the Father and the Son. "God the Eternal Father, whom we designate by the exalted name-title 'Elohim,' is the literal Parent of our Lord and Savior Jesus Christ, and of the spirits of the human race."[3] The statement also made it clear that "Christ in His preexistent, antemortal, or unembodied state . . . was known as Jehovah."[4] This is how Latter-day Saints use these terms in the church today.

With this statement, a clear distinction was made between the titles *elohim* and Jehovah as they apply to members of the Godhead. Today *elohim* and Jehovah are often used to differentiate for the listener or reader whether the reference is to the Father or to the Son. This unique separation of terms (which also separates the Latter-day Saints from all other groups who accept the Bible as scripture) does not find its roots in the Hebrew Bible or its English translations because the biblical evidence is at best ambiguous and at worst non-existent. After all, Latter-day Saint usage of these and other theological terms stems from the words of latter-day prophets, not the Bible. Therefore, we now turn to a brief summary of what can be determined about how the term *elohim* is used in the Hebrew Bible.

Hebrew Bible Usage of *elohim*

Because English translations of the Old Testament are of little use,[5] clarity about the biblical use of the term *elohim* can be found only in the Hebrew Bible. Like most languages, Hebrew has several

---

3. Dated 30 June 1916 and published as "The Father and the Son: A Doctrinal Exposition by the First Presidency and the Twelve," *Improvement Era*, August 1916, 934.

4. "The Father and the Son," 939–40.

5. The only help that the KJV translators offered is tangential. When they thought that any Hebrew term for deity referred to the God of Israel, they opted to capitalize the word, e.g., *God*, but they lowercased it whenever they thought the term in question referred to a non-Israelite deity.

words that can be translated as "god" or "gods." For instance, in addition to *elohim*, Hebrew uses various words, all of which can be and are translated as "God," "god," or "gods," such as *el*, a singular, and its plural form *elim*, and *eloah*, usually taken as the singular of *elohim*.[6] Even the Hebrew Tetragrammaton, usually translated as "LORD," but in four verses as "Jehovah" (Exodus 6:3; Psalm 83:18; Isaiah 12:2; 26:4), can be rendered as "GOD" (see, for example, Exodus 23:17). Of the more than 3,300 occurrences of *god* or *gods* in the English text of the King James Version of the Old Testament (hereafter KJV), it is impossible to know without checking the Hebrew text which instances represent the approximately 2,600 occurrences of *elohim*.

A close look at how *elohim* is used in Hebrew will help to make clear its range of meanings. In form, *elohim* looks like a Hebrew plural and can be translated as a plural. For example, Joshua 24:15 reads, "And if it seem evil unto you to serve the LORD (*yhwh* = Jehovah), choose you this day whom ye will serve; whether the gods (*elohim*) which your fathers served that were on the other side of the flood, or the gods (*elohim*) of the Amorites, in whose land ye dwell: but as for me and my house, we will serve the LORD (*yhwh*)."[7]

When the plural form is intended, which usually happens when *elohim* is used for a non-Israelite deity, it can be coupled with plural forms. For instance, in 2 Chronicles 25:15 not only is a plural verb used with *elohim* but also a plural pronoun: "Wherefore the anger of the LORD was kindled against Amaziah, and he sent unto him a

---

6. In addition to these four etymologically related words for deity, there are numerous other titles and epithets for the God of Israel, including "the most High" (*el elion*), "Lord," "Jehovah," and "Lord of Hosts." There are even instances where the term *elim* is not translated as "god(s)" but as some other term. See Psalm 29:1, where the Hebrew "sons of *elim*" is translated as "ye mighty." See also Psalm 89:6, where the Hebrew "sons of the *elim*" is translated as "sons of the mighty"; and Isaiah 57:5, where the Hebrew *elim* is translated as "idols."

7. These passages also illustrate the aforementioned King James convention of capitalizing *God* if thought to refer to Israel's deity but lowercasing it in reference to a non-Israelite deity.

prophet, which said unto him, Why hast thou sought after the gods (*elohim*) of the people, which could not deliver [plural] their [plural] own people out of thine hand?"

Though plural in form, *elohim* can take a singular verb and other singular attributives. Note this usage in Genesis 28:4, where *elohim* refers to the "God" of Abraham: "thou mayest inherit the land wherein thou art a stranger, which God (*elohim*) gave [singular] unto Abraham."[8] Other passages also use the singular, especially in reference to the God of Israel. Throughout Genesis 1, whenever *elohim* governs a verb, the verb is invariably a third person singular form. Furthermore, Exodus 6:2 states, "And God (*elohim*) spake [singular] unto Moses, and said unto him, I *am* the LORD (*yhwh*)." In this verse, *elohim*, besides taking a singular verb in Hebrew, *spake*, also takes the singular pronoun *I*. Thus in the Hebrew Bible, when *elohim* was thought to refer to the God of Israel the verb or attributives are usually singular, and when *elohim* seems to refer to a non-Israelite deity the verb or attributives are usually plural.

But there are enough exceptions to the usual Hebrew practice that no hard-and-fast rule can be formulated regarding singular/plural and Israelite/non-Israelite usage. Occasionally, when *elohim* refers to the God of Israel, plural attributives and verbs can be used. These instances are most often explained as being conditioned by their international context.[9] For example, when the Philistines hear that Israel is coming to battle against them, they exclaim, "Woe unto us! who shall deliver us out of the hand of these [plural] mighty [plural] Gods (*elohim*)? these *are* the Gods (*elohim*) that smote [plural] the Egyptians with all the plagues in the wilderness" (1 Samuel 4:8). Here the Philistines, who are likely polytheistic, impose perhaps their own views of deity upon Israelite deity.

---

8. Note though that *God* in the preceding verse is the translation of *el*, a singular form.

9. *Gesenius' Hebrew Grammar*, ed. E. Kautzsch, trans. A. E. Cowley (Oxford: Clarendon, 1970), §124, g (hereafter cited as GKC), §145, i.

Another example comes from Genesis 20:13. In speaking with Abimelech, Abraham uses the term *elohim*, but with a plural verb. This is usually translated as "God caused me to wander from my father's house." However, in the Hebrew it literally says that "Gods (*elohim*) caused [plural] me to wander from my father's house." Again, this plural usage can be explained by an international polytheistic setting in which *elohim* may have had a different meaning for Abimelech than it did for Abraham.

Because the general rule about the usage of the singular when referring to Israelite *elohim* and plural when referring to non-Israelite *elohim* is not consistent, and because *elohim* can be used for both Israelite and non-Israelite deities, the conclusion can be drawn that *elohim* is a generic term for any deity, whether Israelite or not, whether singular or plural. Recently Joel S. Burnett has convincingly shown that there are direct analogs to the generic use in Hebrew of *elohim*, both as an abstract term and as a singular and a plural noun. His evidence comes from Semitic languages closely related to Hebrew— namely, in the Late Bronze Age Babylonian dialect of the El Amarna tablets, in Iron Age Phoenician, and first-millennium Akkadian.[10] In his view, the Hebrew Iron Age usage of *elohim* as a singular and as a plural was simply a continuation of a Late Bronze Age Northwest Semitic grammatical convention or practice. Thus, whether the writers of the Hebrew Bible used *elohim* as a generic term for the God of Israel or for a non-Israelite deity, they were simply following the contemporary Semitic literary conventions of their day.[11]

Since *elohim* is a generic term for any deity, it should not be surprising that on occasion, contrary to the general rule, non-Israelite *elohim* can take singular verbs and attributives. The Hebrew Bible has the Philistines using the term to refer to Dagon, the main god they worshipped. The Philistines' leaders came together to offer "a great sacrifice unto Dagon their god (*elohim*), and to rejoice: for they

---

10. Joel S. Burnett, *A Reassessment of Biblical Elohim* (Atlanta, GA: SBL, 2001), 1–53.
11. Burnett, *Biblical Elohim*, 79–119.

said, Our god (*elohim*) hath delivered [singular] Samson our enemy into our hand" (Judges 16:23).

Conversely, if *elohim* is a generic term for any deity, it might be expected that when *elohim* refers to the God of Israel, it might on occasion govern plural forms. This seems to be the case in Exodus 32:4–5. When Aaron had produced the golden calf, the people exclaimed, "These [plural] be thy gods (*elohim*), O Israel, which brought [plural] thee up out of the land of Egypt." But lest anyone think the calf was anything other than a symbol of the God of Israel, the writers of the Hebrew Bible make it clear through Aaron's words that the calf symbolized none other than Jehovah, "And when Aaron saw [the calf], he built an altar before it; and Aaron made proclamation, and said, To morrow is a feast to the LORD (*yhwh*)."[12] Similar wording can be found in 1 Kings 12:28, where the first king of the northern kingdom, Jeroboam, erected golden calves for Israelite worship.[13]

According to Burnett, because *elohim* was used as a title for Jehovah in the northern kingdom, the northern prophets were concerned that Israel understand that their *elohim*, their deity, was Jehovah.[14] For example, in the days of Elijah some people in the northern kingdom were beginning to assume that Baal was the *elohim* of Israel. This can be seen in Elijah's imperative "How long halt ye between two opinions? if the LORD (*yhwh*) be God (*elohim*), follow him: but if Baal, then follow him" (1 Kings 18:21). Translated another way, "How long are you going to have two views? If Jehovah is *elohim*, follow him: but if Baal [is *elohim*], follow him." Elijah then devised a contest to determine the identity of the real *elohim* of Israel. He challenged the people, "Call ye on the name of your gods (*elohim*), and I will call on the name of Jehovah: and the God (*elohim*) that answereth [singular] by fire, let him be God (*elohim*).

---

12. See Paul Y. Hoskisson, "Aaron's Golden Calf," *FARMS Review* 18/1 (2006): 375–87.

13. It is irrelevant which passage is dependent on the other, 1 Kings 12:28 or Exodus 32:4–5. The point is that *elohim* governing the plural forms could be used for Israelite deity.

14. Burnett, *Biblical Elohim*, 107–19.

And all the people answered and said, It is well spoken" (1 Kings 18:24, our translation). When the story finishes with Elijah calling down fire from heaven, the people exclaim, "Jehovah, he is the God (the *elohim*); Jehovah, he is the God (the *elohim*)" (1 Kings 18:39, our translation).

Besides governing both singular and plural forms, *elohim* has another usage in the Hebrew Bible which is also analogous to general ancient Semitic usage. It has long been suggested that *elohim* is used as an abstract noun for the divine.[15] In other words, *elohim* may be translated as "godhead," "godhood" or "divinity." This usage falls under a well-defined category of Hebrew words that, when placed in a plural form, can have an abstract meaning.[16] For example, in Hebrew the plural of "young man" or "young woman" can mean "youth," the plural of "old man" can mean "old age," and the plural of "virgin" can mean "virginity."[17] The abstract meaning for *elohim* is found multiple times in the book of Exodus, and elsewhere, in reference to Jehovah. For example, Exodus 3:18 reads, "ye shall say unto him, The LORD (*yhwh*) God (*elohim*) of the Hebrews hath met with us." Here, the Hebrew word *elohim* is used as a modifier for Jehovah, and the phrase could be translated, among other possibilities, as "Jehovah, the God (the *elohim*) of the Hebrews," or as "the deity Jehovah of the Hebrews."

Moreover, because *elohim* can function as an abstract noun in Hebrew, it has a wider range of meanings than the other Hebrew terms for deity.[18] This is why *elohim* is sometimes used as we would use an adjective in English to indicate that the noun it modifies has divine qualities.[19] For example, the phrase "the angel of God" in Judges

---

15. GKC §124, g.

16. GKC §124, d.

17. בחור *young man* > בחורים and בחורות *youth*; זקן *old one* > זקנים *old age*; בתולה *virgin* > בתולים *virginity*; see GKC §124, d.

18. Burnett, *Biblical Elohim*, 57–60.

19. Sometimes nouns used as genitives take on adjectival qualities. GKC §128, p–u, examples include "man of words" = "eloquent man," "man of wrath" = "wrathful man," "possession of eternity" = "everlasting possession."

6:20 reads literally from the Hebrew, "the angel of the *elohim.*" The translation "divine messenger" would be equally as acceptable as the King James "angel of God." Genesis 32:1-2 reads literally in Hebrew, "And Jacob went on his way, and the angels of God (= messengers of *elohim,* or "divine messengers") met him. And when Jacob saw them, he said, This is God's host (literally, "the camp of *elohim*" = the divine host): and he called the name of that place Mahanaim."[20] Also, in Genesis 1:2 the Hebrew reads, "and the spirit/wind of *elohim* brooded [feminine singular, with reference to spirit/wind] upon the waters." The Septuagint translators understood this meaning of *elohim* in this verse to be the attributive use of the genitive and omitted the definite article before *theos,* prompting the translation "a divine wind was being carried along over the water."[21]

Additionally, though masculine plural in form, *elohim* can refer to either male or female deities in the singular. First Kings 11:33 reads, "Because that they have forsaken me, and have worshipped Ashtoreth the goddess (*elohim*) of the Zidonians, Chemosh the god (*elohim*) of the Moabites, and Milcom the god (*elohim*) of the children of Ammon, and have not walked in my ways, to do that which is right in mine eyes, and to keep my statutes and my judgments, as did David his father." In each instance the Hebrew word for "god" and "goddess" in this verse is *elohim.* Because Ashtoreth is singular (as are the other non-Israelite gods mentioned) and female, this verse demonstrates that *elohim* can be used for non-Israelite gods of either gender.

As the above discussion has shown, the uses and functions of the word *elohim* are manifold in the Hebrew Bible. The word can be translated as "god," "gods," "God," "divinity," "divine," "godhood,"

---

20. The words in the King James translation, *host* and *mahanaim,* are the same word in Hebrew, the former in the singular and the latter in the dual, מחנה, מחנים. It is possible that the dual is used because God's camp is one and Jacob's camp is another. Later Jacob splits his camp into two parts, mirroring the dual in this verse.

21. Albert Pietersma and Benjamin G. Wright, eds., *A New English Translation of the Septuagint* (New York: Oxford University Press, 2007), 6.

and "godhead." It can govern both plural and singular verbs and attributives, as well as being a singular abstract noun that takes a singular verb. It can denote both masculine and feminine gods. The Hebrew Bible also does not distinguish in person or being between this *elohim* and Jehovah, and therefore, *elohim* was used as the name/title that was given to Jehovah, the *elohim* of Israel.

With this broad range of usage of *elohim* in the Hebrew Bible in mind, we can now turn to beginnings of the usage of *elohim* in Latter-day Saint literature and to examples of the range of its usage among early Latter-day Saints.

Nineteenth-Century LDS Usage

Because early Latter-day Saints did not suddenly become *tabulae rasae* when they joined the church, they brought with them vocabulary and traditions that were familiar to them from their previous religious training. Indicative of general American usage, Noah Webster's 1828 edition of *An American Dictionary of the English Language* gives insight into the vernacular of the early nineteenth century American religious discourse. The entry for "Jehovah" reads, "The Scripture name of the Supreme Being"[22]—that is, Jehovah is the scriptural name for God. The entry under "God" explains, "The Supreme Being; Jehovah; the eternal and infinite spirit, the creator, and the sovereign of the universe."[23] This definition fits squarely within the Trinitarian views of God held by most Christians in early America. It seems likely that this early American usage influenced early LDS usage of divine names. Indeed, American usage may explain Erastus Snow and Benjamin Winchester's 1841 statement in the *Times and Seasons*: "We believe in God the Father, who is the great Jehovah and head of all things, and that Christ is the Son of God."[24]

---

22. Noah Webster, *An American Dictionary of the English Language* (New York: Converse, 1828), s.v. "Jehovah."

23. Webster, *American Dictionary*, s.v. "God."

24. Erastus Snow and Benjamin Winchester, "An Address to the Citizens of Salem (Mass.) and Vicinity," *Times and Seasons* 3/1 (November 1841): 578.

Webster's 1828 dictionary lacks an entry for *elohim*, suggesting that *elohim* was not at all in common usage in America. The paucity of entrees for *elohim* in the *Oxford English Dictionary* would also suggest that *elohim* was not a regular part of British religious discourse either. It would seem then that any use of *elohim* in American English might be conditioned by its meaning and usage in the Hebrew Bible, rather than by any longstanding English tradition. In other words, Jehovah and *God* were the common names in America for deity, and *elohim* was relatively unknown. It would not be surprising then if whatever usage was made of *elohim*, it would have been synonymous with the general American usage of Jehovah and *God*. Therefore, even though the topic of this paper is *elohim*, we will necessarily point out that *elohim* and Jehovah are often interchangeable in early LDS usage, in direct analogy to their use in the Hebrew Bible.

The range of early LDS usage of *elohim* showed remarkable variety. There is no better place to begin a selective citation of these usages than with the Prophet Joseph Smith, who appears to have been the first to introduce the term to the church. On 20 November 1835, he received from Oliver Cowdery "a Hebrew bible, lexicon & grammar" in anticipation of the formal Hebrew instruction he would eventually receive under Joshua Seixas.[25] Joseph devoted much time to studying Hebrew even before Seixas arrived. He often recorded in his journal that he had "spent the day in reading Hebrew."[26] Along with other church members, he received about two months of formal instruction under Professor Seixas.[27] It seems likely that in Seixas's

25. *The Personal Writings of Joseph Smith*, ed. Dean C. Jessee (Salt Lake City: Deseret Book, 1984), 91.

26. Smith, *Personal Writings*, 93, 98, 104, 120.

27. Included among this group were Brigham Young and Heber C. Kimball. The duration of the course was 26 January–29 March 1836. D. Kelly Ogden, "The Kirtland Hebrew School (1835-36)," in *Regional Studies in Latter-day Saint Church History, Ohio*, ed. Milton V. Backman Jr. (Provo, UT: Dept. of Church History and Doctrine, Brigham Young University, 1990), 63-87.

class Joseph first encountered the Hebrew word *elohim*.[28] Yet it was not until a few years later that he began using the word in his writings and sermons. Latter-day Saints who are familiar with contemporary LDS usage may find his use of the term somewhat surprising.

The Prophet, after the manner of the Hebrew Bible, employed on occasion the terms *elohim* and Jehovah interchangeably for the God of Israel. For example, in a letter to Major General Law dated 14 August 1842, in keeping with common American usage, he used the title Jehovah for God the Father, but also equated Jehovah with *elohim*: "Let us plead the justice of our cause; trusting in the arm of Jehovah, the Eloheim, who sits enthroned in the heavens."[29] Here we have usage exactly analogous to the Hebrew Bible: "Jehovah, the *elohim* of the Hebrews." Just over a week later, Joseph, in supplicating God in prayer, equated Jehovah and *elohim* again: "O, thou who seeeth and knoweth the hearts of all men; thou eternal, omnipotent, omnicient, and omnipresent Jehovah, God; thou Eloheem, that sitteth, as saith the psalmist; enthroned in heaven; look down upon thy servant Joseph, at this time; and let faith on the name of thy Son Jesus Christ, to a greater degree than thy servant ever yet has enjoyed, be conferred upon him."[30] It is clear that the Prophet, by equating *elohim* and Jehovah, used the terms differently than Latter-day Saints do today.

Joseph's first semipublic use of *elohim* suggests, but does not force, the conclusion that he knew of its plural sense. On 4 May 1842, in a meeting with several of the brethren, he set forth the order pertaining to "all those plans and principles by which any one is enabled to secure the fullness of those blessings which have been prepared for the Church of the First Born, and come up and abide

---

28. In the grammar written by Joshua Seixas and probably used by Joseph Smith, this entry occurs as a definition for *elohim*: "God; a sing. noun with a *plur. form*." Joshua Seixas, *A Manual Hebrew Grammar for the Use of Beginners* (Andover, MA: Gould and Newman, 1834), 85.

29. *History of the Church*, 5:94.

30. Smith, *Personal Writings*, 536. The prayer was written on 23 August 1842.

in the presence of the Eloheim in the eternal worlds."[31] The use of the definite article *the* might suggest that the Prophet intended a plural meaning for *elohim*, in which case the Prophet was probably referring to the Gods of eternity. If he had meant the singular exclusively, the definite article would not have been necessary.

In subsequent discourses Joseph Smith explicitly drew attention to the plural meaning of *elohim*. In April of that same year, the Prophet gave his famous King Follett discourse. Though he does not mention *elohim*, in speaking of the creation process he drew on the term's plural sense to explain Genesis 1:1, "The head one of the Gods brought forth the Gods. . . . Thus the head God brought forth the Gods in the grand council."[32] Two months later, on 16 June 1844, Joseph again translated this verse: "In the beginning the head of the Gods brought forth the Gods. . . . In the beginning the heads of the Gods organized the heavens and the earth."[33] The word that is translated as "Gods" corresponds with *elohim* in the Hebrew Bible. In the same speech the Prophet continued by calling attention to the plural meaning of *elohim* to establish the doctrine of a plurality of Gods, declaring, "In the very beginning the Bible shows there is a plurality of Gods beyond the power of refutation. . . . The word Eloheim ought to be in the plural all the way through—Gods,"[34] meaning that *elohim* ought to be rendered as plural at least in the creation account, if not also in other biblical passages.

Even though he referred to Jehovah as *elohim* and used Jehovah as a term for God the Father in many instances, at some point

---

31. *History of the Church*, 5:2. The transcription of Willard Richards's diary that he kept for Joseph Smith, from which this account is taken, reads, "all those plans & principles by which any one is enabled to secure the fullness of those blessings which has been prepared for the church of the first born, and come up ~~into~~ and abide in the presence of ~~God~~ the Eloheim in the eternal worlds." See Andrew F. Ehat, "'Who Shall Ascend into the Hill of the Lord?' Sesquicentennial Reflections of a Sacred Day: 4 May 1842," in *Temples of the Ancient World: Ritual and Symbolism*, ed. Donald W. Parry (Salt Lake City: Deseret Book and FARMS, 1994), 51.

32. *History of the Church*, 6:307.

33. *History of the Church*, 6:475.

34. *History of the Church*, 6:476.

Joseph Smith made a clear distinction between *elohim* and Jehovah. For purposes unrelated to Hebrew Bible usage, Joseph Smith must have thought it important to distinguish between God the Father and Jesus Christ the Son. In a late reminiscence, Edward Stevenson remarked in his journal that "Joseph Smith was the first, whome I ever herd proclaim a plurality of Gods, he said that there was Elohiem God, and Jehovah God, and Michial God."[35] He also remembered that "Joseph the Seer, said, in the grand Council of Heaven, The Great Eelohéåm, directed Jehovah and Michaiel[?], for the Gods Counciled in the beginning of the Creation of This Earth."[36] A remark by Brigham Young in 1852 would seem to corroborate Edward Stevenson's later recollection: "It is true that the earth was organized by three distinct characters, namely, Eloheim, Yahovah, and Michael."[37] Here the delineation is clearly set forth in terminology that is similar to the usage that prevails in the church today.

Nevertheless, despite the clear separation that the Prophet and Brigham Young made between *elohim* and Jehovah on occasion, the two terms continued to be used inconsistently. For example, Joseph Smith used a variety of names to refer to God the Father. In the dedicatory prayer of the Kirtland Temple, for example, he seems to have addressed God the Father as "God of Israel" (D&C 109:1), "Holy Father" (vv. 4, 10, 14, 22, 24, 29, and 47), and "Jehovah" (v. 34).[38] Yet only a week later Joseph stated that he heard "the voice of Jehovah," that is Christ, speak to him when he appeared to him and Oliver in the Kirtland Temple (D&C 110:3). Thus in the first instance, Doctrine and Covenants 109, Jehovah was used as it commonly was in

---

35. *Autobiography of Edward Stevenson, 1820–1870*, ed. Joseph G. Stevenson (Provo, UT: Stevenson's Genealogical Center, 1986), 64, original spelling and conventions retained.

36. *Autobiography of Edward Stevenson*, 64.

37. Brigham Young, in *Journal of Discourses*, 1:51.

38. This is of course based on the assumption that the deity addressed is God the Father. At this early stage of LDS vocabulary usage, the Lord, through the Prophet, may have used these terms the way Americans in general used them, according to "the manner of their language, that they might come to understanding" (D&C 1:24).

America at that time, namely, as a name for the God of Israel. However, in the second instance, Doctrine and Covenants 110, Joseph seems to have departed from contemporary usage by identifying Christ as Jehovah.

Other church leaders also used *elohim* and Jehovah in a variety of ways. John Taylor in 1845 mirrored the language of Joseph in an editorial in the *Times and Seasons*. In translating Genesis 1:1, he stated, in language that would appear to be dependent on Joseph Smith's King Follett discourse: "In simple English, the Head brought forth the Gods, with the heavens and with the earth. The 'Head' must have meant the 'living God,' or Head God: Christ is our head."[39] In this interpretation John Taylor seems to equate Christ with the "Head God" who brought forth the other "Gods" (*elohim*). Normally, Latter-day Saints would equate the "Head God" with *elohim*—that is, God the Father, not with Jehovah/Christ.

Brigham Young on occasion associated *elohim* with God the Father. For example, he stated, "I want to tell you, each and every one of you, that you are well acquainted with God our heavenly Father, or the great Eloheim."[40] As explained above, Brigham's clear application of this term to God the Father seems to be the exception rather than the rule in the early days of the church. Often it was still used as a generic term for deity without any specific designation. For example, Brigham Young himself ten years later in 1867 used Jehovah and *elohim* synonymously when he said, "To secure His blessings the Lord requires the strict obedience of His people. This is our duty. We obey the Lord, Him who is called Jehovah, the Great I AM, I am a man of war, Eloheim, etc. We are under many obligations to obey Him."[41]

Heber C. Kimball in 1863 distinguished between Jehovah and *elohim* when he said, "We have been taught that our Father and God,

---

39. John Taylor, "The Living God," *Times and Seasons* 73 (February 1845): 809.
40. Brigham Young, in *Journal of Discourses*, 4:216.
41. Brigham Young, in *Journal of Discourses*, 12:99.

from whom we sprang, called and appointed his servants to go and organize an earth, and, among the rest, he said to Adam, 'You go along also and help all you can; you are going to inhabit it when it is organized, therefore go and assist in the good work.' It reads in the Scriptures that the Lord did it, but the true rendering is, that the Almighty sent Jehovah and Michael to do the work."[42] This clear differentiation between God the Father and Jehovah goes along with President Young's statement that "Elohim, Yahovah, and Michael" were the three distinct beings who organized the earth.

In all the examples we have provided so far, the distinction between *elohim* = God the Father and Jehovah = God the Son occurs in the context of the creation, which is the context in which Joseph first emphasized the plurality of Gods. John Taylor, however, seems to have used these terms without worrying about specific attribution. In 1872 he stated, "Who has controlled and managed the affairs of the world from its creation until the present time? The Great I am [a title of Jehovah], the Great Eloheim, the Great God who is our Father. We bow before him. Is it a hardship to reverence the Lord our God?"[43] Here he equates *elohim* with "the Great I am," an epithet that refers to Jehovah and comes out of Exodus 3:14. He also used the phrase "the Lord our God," which is usually the translation of the Hebrew "Jehovah our *elohim*." However, in 1882 in *The Mediation and Atonement*, John Taylor clearly identified Christ as Jehovah when he wrote, "He is not only called the Son of God, the First Begotten of the Father, the Well Beloved, the Head, and Ruler, and Dictator of all things, Jehovah, the I Am, the Alpha and Omega, but He is also called the Very Eternal Father."[44]

---

42. Heber C. Kimball, in *Journal of Discourses*, 10:235.

43. John Taylor, in *Journal of Discourses*, 15:217.

44. John Taylor, *An Examination into and an Elucidation of the Great Principle of the Mediation and Atonement of Our Lord and Savior Jesus Christ* (Salt Lake City: Deseret News, 1882), 138. This is also made clear about the same time in Franklin D. Richards and James A. Little, eds., *A Compendium of the Doctrines of the Gospel*, 2nd ed. (Salt Lake City: Deseret News, 1886), 12, and in James A. Little, "Jesus Christ—His Character and Attributes," *Juvenile Instructor* 16 (15 October 1881): 237.

John Taylor apparently did not always confine himself to a single narrow definition of Jehovah. In the words to a song first published in 1840 in Manchester, England, which was later ascribed to John Taylor,[45] the author had penned the following:

> As in the heavens they all agree,
> The record's given there by three . . .
> Jehovah, God the Father's one;
> Another, God's Eternal Son;
> The Spirit does with them agree,—
> The witnesses in heaven are three.[46]

Here Jehovah is used to refer to God the Father, according to the general American vernacular of the day. After going through numerous editions, this hymnal was replaced with the 1927 *Latter-day Saint Hymns*. No doubt because the 1916 First Presidency statement had changed LDS theological discourse, the words to this hymn were also changed. The line that read, "Jehovah, God the Father's one," was changed to read, "Our God, the Father, is the One."[47]

If John Taylor did write the words to the 1840 hymn that confused God the Father and Jehovah, then by at least 1884 he allowed a distinction between Jehovah and *elohim*. He spoke of how the Saints needed the support of "the Great Jehovah" and "were dependent upon Him." He then went on to say that the "work in which [the Saints] are engaged is one that has been introduced by

---

45. The Liverpool, England, 20th edition of 1890, ascribes the hymn to J. Taylor; see p. 435.

46. *A Collection of Sacred Hymns for the Church of Jesus Christ of Latter-day Saints, in Europe* (Manchester: Thomas, 1840), no. 254, pp. 295-96. By the time of the 13th edition of the hymnal in 1869 the wording was changed from "God's Eternal Son" to "His Eternal Son." This altered wording was retained at least as late as the 20th edition in 1890.

47. The 1890 20th edition of this LDS hymnal, still published in England, contains the same unaltered text as the 1840: "Jehovah, God the Father's one."

the Great Eloheim."[48] Though President Taylor does not explicitly distinguish between *elohim* as God the Father and Jehovah as God the Son, the context allows the reader to make the distinction.

Also in that same year, 1884, John Taylor remarked, "I have heard [Joseph] quote from the Hebrew Bible in support of a plurality of Gods, showing that the suffix 'mem' in the word Eloheim or God, ought to be rendered in the plural. . . . If, as stated, Jesus was with the Father in the beginning, there certainly was more than one God—God the Father, and God the Son."[49] President Taylor's point seems to be that the plurality of Gods demonstrated by the Hebrew word *elohim* comprises both the Father and the Son, which would be a usage similar to the Hebrew abstract meaning.

A few years after the turn of the century, Orson F. Whitney published a collection of poems, *Elias: An Epic of the Ages*. In the revised and annotated edition published in 1914, a footnote was added to explain *elohim*. The note reads: "The Hebrew plural for God. To the modern Jew it means the plural of majesty, not of number; but to the Latter-day Saint it signifies both. As here used it stands for 'The Council of the Gods.'"[50] The last part of the footnote may be an example of the Hebrew abstract meaning of *elohim*.

On the other hand, Franklin D. Richards clearly set forth that Jehovah is Christ. In 1885 he told the Saints that Jesus Christ's "name when He was a spiritual being, during the first half of the existence of the earth, before He was made flesh and blood, was Jehovah."[51] Despite this fact, just four months earlier, using the vernacular of the day, he seems to have associated Jehovah with God the Father when he said, "The Savior said He could call to His help more than twelve legions of angels; more than the Roman hosts; but He knowing the great purposes of Jehovah could go like a lamb

---

48. John Taylor, in *Journal of Discourses*, 25:305.

49. John Taylor, in *Journal of Discourses*, 25:213-14 (29 June 1884).

50. Orson F. Whitney, *Elias: An Epic of the Ages* (Salt Lake City: Whitney, 1914), 118. The original edition was published by Knickerbocker Press in New York, 1904.

51. Franklin D. Richards, in *Journal of Discourses*, 26:300.

to the slaughter."[52] Here we see the name Jehovah being coupled with established American patterns. Both the adjective *great* and the phrase *purposes of* are coupled with Jehovah and may represent a more generic usage of the term than we would use today.

Elohim was consistently used by President Wilford Woodruff in dedicatory prayers of the St. George and Salt Lake Temples in 1877 and 1893 respectively. Both of these prayers, like many dedicatory prayers today, were addressed to "Our Father in Heaven." The Salt Lake Temple dedicatory prayer continues, "We thank thee, O thou Great Elohim," clearly a reference to God the Father. At one point the Father is addressed as "O thou God of our fathers, Abraham, Isaac, and Jacob," a title that some would reserve for Jehovah. But Jehovah-Messiah-Christ-Son is never addressed or appealed to in the prayer, though the Son is mentioned several times. Throughout the prayer, it is the Father who is addressed.[53]

Earlier, in 1881, Elder Wilford Woodruff had published *Leaves from My Journal*, wherein he explained that "the Father and Son were revealed unto [Joseph], and the voice of the great Eloheim unto him was: 'This is my beloved Son, hear ye Him,'" with an obvious reference to the Father as *elohim*.[54]

The above quotations are not meant to suggest that nineteenth-century LDS usage of *elohim* and Jehovah was clearly defined. In

---

52. Franklin D. Richards, in *Journal of Discourses*, 26:172. This and the preceding passage were pointed out by Barry Bickmore in his essay "Of Simplicity, Oversimplification, and Monotheism," a review of *Monotheism, Mormonism, and the New Testament Witness*, by Paul Owen, *FARMS Review* 15/1 (2003): 215-58.

53. The dedicatory prayer offered on 1 January 1877 to dedicate portions of the St. George Temple is found in Matthias F. Cowley, ed., *Wilford Woodruff: History of His Life and Labors as Recorded in His Daily Journals* (Salt Lake City: Deseret News, 1909), 161-71. The dedicatory prayer for the Salt Lake Temple, offered on 6 April 1893, is found in James E. Talmage, *The House of the Lord: A Study of Holy Sanctuaries, Ancient and Modern* (Salt Lake City: Deseret News, 1912), 134. See also the reprint, James E. Talmage, *The House of the Lord: A Study of Holy Sanctuaries, Ancient and Modern* (Salt Lake City: Signature Books, 1998), 94-102. The quotations above are from the reprint, pages 94b, 95a and 97a respectively.

54. Wilford Woodruff, *Leaves from My Journal*, 2nd ed. (Salt Lake City: Juvenile Instructor Office, 1882), 86.

fact, most usages of these terms are ambiguous, denoting simply "God." Because they are often used in similar phrases and usually appear in contexts that often do not specify identity, it seems likely they were often used as generic names for deity without consistent specificity. This may explain why different denotations for Jehovah were used simultaneously and why both the plural and singular meanings of *elohim* were used.

Such interchangeability of terms no doubt led to questions among church members. In the April 1895 General Conference, President Woodruff counseled the elders of the church, "Cease troubling yourselves about who God is; who Adam is, who Christ is, who Jehovah is. For heaven's sake, let these things alone. Why trouble yourselves about these things? . . . God is God. Christ is Christ. The Holy Ghost is the Holy Ghost. That should be enough for you and me to know. . . . I say this because we are troubled every little while with inquiries from Elders anxious to know who God is, who Christ is, and who Adam is."[55]

The matter began to be laid to rest in the early 1900s when the meanings of the terms *elohim* and Jehovah as they are known within the church today were clearly set forth. Charles W. Penrose was adamant that church members understand and use these terms differentially. In September 1902, two years before his ordination to the apostleship, he published an *Improvement Era* article entitled "Our Father Adam." In it he explained that "Elohim, Jehovah and Michael were associated in that mighty work. When God spake 'in the beginning,' he gave direction to other divine persons and said, 'Let US do thus and so,' and they obeyed him and acted in harmony with Him. The Eternal Elohim directed both Michael and Jehovah, and the heavenly hosts obeyed them. When Adam was formed 'out of the dust of the earth,' he worshiped the great Elohim, the Eternal

---

55. Although the address was given on 7 April 1895, this portion was recorded in "Discourse by President Wilford Woodruff," *Millennial Star* 57 (6 June 1895): 355-56.

Father of us all."[56] The statement by the future apostle made it clear that *elohim* was a name or title for God the Father, separate and distinct from Jehovah, and he made the point in the context of the creation.

Only two months later in the November issue of the *Improvement Era*, W. H. Chamberlin, a teacher at Brigham Young College in Logan, Utah, wrote an article entitled "Use of the Word Elohim" in which he clearly stated that "Jehovah was a personal name applied to the Being who guided Israel, and afterwards lived on the earth as Jesus Christ."[57]

Several years later, Charles W. Penrose, this time as an apostle and member of the First Presidency, spoke in the October 1914 General Conference of "the great Elohim, the God of gods, the Father of our spirits, the Mighty and Eternal One to whom today we address our praises and our prayers."[58] Clearly, Elder Penrose wanted to emphasize for the Saints that *elohim* should be applied to God the Father.

To the growing amount of church material clarifying the matter was added *Jesus the Christ*, by James E. Talmage. This work, commissioned by the First Presidency and published in 1915, was foundational in establishing practice. In it Elder Talmage explained, "*Elohim*, as understood and used in the restored Church of Jesus Christ, is the name-title of God the Eternal Father, whose firstborn Son in the spirit is *Jehovah*—the Only Begotten in the flesh, Jesus Christ."[59] The clarity and precision articulated so well here by Elder Talmage, and which helped set the course for our contemporary usage, must have been refreshing to many church members.

---

56. Charles W. Penrose, "Our Father Adam," *Improvement Era*, September 1902, 876–77.

57. W. H. Chamberlin, "Use of the Word Elohim," *Improvement Era*, November 1902, 26.

58. Charles W. Penrose, in Conference Report, October 1914, 38.

59. Talmage, *Jesus the Christ*, 38.

These statements continued to build when President Penrose again clearly separated the terms *elohim* and Jehovah for members of the church. In the April 1916 General Conference, he declared:

> Now, who is this person, this Jesus Christ? Is He Adam or a son of Adam? Not at all. . . . Well, was Jesus Jehovah? Yes. . . . We are told by revelation that in the creation of the earth there were three individuals, personally engaged. This is more particularly for the Temple of God, but sufficient of it has been published over and over again to permit me to refer to it. Elohim,—not Eloheim, as we spell it sometimes— that is a plural word meaning the gods, but it is attached to the individual who is the Father of all, the person whom we look to as the great Eternal Father. Elohim, Jehovah and Michael, were engaged in the construction of this globe. Jehovah, commanded by Elohim, went down to where there was space.[60]

President Penrose in this rare instance referred to the temple for the source of the definition that we today take for granted. He then identified very clearly the three persons as God, Jesus Christ, and Adam. This distinction in terms seems to have most often been associated with the creation of the earth, and it seems that was in this isolated instance where these names were separated.

An additional authoritative statement appears to have been necessary. It came in the form, mentioned above, of an official statement of the First Presidency and Quorum of the Twelve dated 30 June 1916: "God the Eternal Father, whom we designate by the exalted name-title 'Elohim,' is the literal Parent of our Lord and Savior Jesus Christ, and of the spirits of the human race. . . . Christ in His preexistent, antemortal, or unembodied state . . . was known as

---

60. Charles W. Penrose, in Conference Report, April 1916, 18.

Jehovah."[61] This was a clear and official delineation of terms for the benefit of the church members.

In 1924 Elder Talmage made additions to his book *The Articles of Faith* in order to reflect this distinction. At the end of chapter 2, he added, "Note that distinction is not always indicated here [in this book] between the Eternal Father or Elohim and the Son who is Jehovah or Jesus Christ."[62] Further, where Genesis 11:5 is quoted, a parenthetical insertion next to "Lord" states, "i.e., Jehovah, the Son."[63] Elder Talmage also included the First Presidency statement in an appendix with a preface stating, "That Jesus Christ or Jehovah is designated in certain scriptures as the Father in no wise justifies an assumption of identity between Him and His Father, Elohim. This matter has been explained by the presiding authorities of the Church in a special publication."[64] Thus even after 1916 a conscious effort was made to emphasize the clarity that the First Presidency had brought to the definitions.

Summary and Conclusion

As detailed above, church members prior to the authoritative clarifications of the early twentieth century often used *elohim* and Jehovah interchangeably and inconsistently, much the same way they are used in the Hebrew Bible. Like much of the Christian world of the nineteenth century, Latter-day Saints did not always distinguish between Jehovah, God the Father, the God of Israel, *elohim* or simply God. However, the flexibility of use and at times the ambiguous phrasing of the nineteenth century that reflected general American usage and served the general Christian world well, fell short of the precision that the restoration of the gospel brought to LDS understanding of the Godhead.

---

61. "The Father and the Son," 934, 939–40: see notes 3–4 above.

62. James E. Talmage, *A Study of the Articles of Faith, Being a Consideration of the Principal Doctrines of The Church of Jesus Christ of Latter-Day Saints*, 12th ed. (Salt Lake City: The Church of Jesus Christ of Latter-day Saints, 1924), 49.

63. Talmage, *Articles of Faith*, 43.

64. Talmage, *Articles of Faith*, 465.

It is remarkable that early Latter-day Saints used the name Jehovah in reference to both God the Father and to his Son. Equally interesting is that *elohim* seems to have been used by Latter-day Saints for both God and gods, exactly as it is used in the Hebrew Bible—that is, as both a singular and a plural noun, a proper name and a common noun. Officially, this practice ended in 1916.

And finally, a word of caution here is appropriate. Since the modern Latter-day Saint usage of Jehovah and Elohim was not taken from the Hebrew Bible, it can create misunderstandings if imposed upon the Hebrew scriptural account. Thus if we try to exclusively assign actions to different members of the Godhead based on which divine name is used in the Hebrew Bible, the result, in many instances, will be chaos. Additionally, Doctrine and Covenants 20:28 states that "Father, Son, and Holy Ghost are one God."[65] In this same vein, Elder Bruce R. McConkie once said that "most scriptures that speak of God or of the Lord do not even bother to distinguish the Father from the Son, simply because it doesn't make any difference which God is involved. They are one. The words or deeds of either of them would be the same words and deeds of the other in the same circumstance."[66] Therefore, the issue of which name or title is assigned to which member of the Godhead is not one that Latter-day Saints should be overly concerned with. But it is helpful to know that the meaning of a word such as *elohim* is not always the same in all times and in all places.

Ryan Conrad Davis is a graduate student in ancient Near Eastern studies at the University of Texas at Austin. Paul Y. Hoskisson is professor of ancient scripture and director of the Laura F. Willes Center for Book of Mormon Studies at Brigham Young University.

---

65. See also 2 Nephi 31:21; Alma 11:44; 3 Nephi 11:27, 36; Mormon 7:7.

66. Bruce R. McConkie, "Our Relationship with the Lord," in *BYU 1981–82 Fireside and Devotional Speeches* (Provo, UT: University Publications, 1982), 101b.

CHAPTER 6

AN EGYPTIAN VIEW OF ABRAHAM

John Gee

My association with Kent Brown has been longer than either of us would wish to admit. Under his tutelage, I had my first classes in Coptic and early Christian history. Since joining the faculty at Brigham Young University, I have benefited from being a colleague, from serving on committees together, and most recently, from his being my department head. It is a pleasure to present this as a tribute to him, both because of my personal association and interests and because it gives me the chance to combine Coptic with Kent's Latter-day Saint interests.

For the second half of the twentieth century, Coptic studies have been dominated by interest in the Nag Hammadi Library, a collection of manuscripts in Lycopolitan and Sahidic dialects, whose contents can be characterized either as at least heretical or even bizarre. Their very strangeness draws interest. Before that time, the interest in Coptic literature focused on Coptic orthodoxy, whose texts at least make some modicum of sense. Unfortunately, orthodox Coptic literature has fallen on some hard times. The manuscripts are dispersed, largely unpublished, or published in some obscure place.

Extracanonical traditions about Abraham circulated in the ancient world from at least the third century BC on, and a number of these have been gathered in a volume.[1] The volume, however, does not contain any Coptic material because it had not yet been located. One missed account comes from a Coptic encomium that is found in three manuscripts; notice of one was published with a brief Latin summary first by Georgio Zoega in 1810,[2] another was published by W. E. Crum.[3] E. O. Winstedt published a composite text of the two manuscripts along with an English translation in 1908.[4] Winstedt made certain assumptions in the presentation of his text that can at least be questioned. Given the wider range of extracanonical traditions about Abraham, this text can be more securely placed within those traditions than it could when Winstedt published it. It deserves to be known to a wider audience.

Text

The text is fragmentary, but the story told about Abraham seems to be complete. I have kept Winstedt's punctuation but have omitted his superlinear marks as it is not clear to me that he has interpreted them correctly. Coptic manuscripts tend not to have spacing between words, and different editors have different preferences; I have used mine rather than Winstedt's. The text follows:

[...] ⲤⲰⲞⲨⲠ ⲘⲚ ⲠⲚⲞⲨⲦⲈ ⲚⲀⲂⲢⲀⲠⲀⲘ :— ⲀⲠⲢⲀϤ ϬⲈ ⲀⲂⲢⲀⲠⲀⲘ ⲈⲔⲬⲰ

ⲘⲘⲞⲤ ⲈⲢⲞϤ ϪⲈ ⲀⲨⲤⲰⲞⲨⲠ ⲘⲚ ⲠⲚⲞⲨⲦⲈ ⲚⲀⲂⲢⲀⲠⲀⲘ :— ⲞⲨⲔⲞⲨⲚ

ϬⲈ ⲈⲒⲈ ⲘⲚ ⲀⲀⲨ ⲚⲢⲰⲘⲈ ⲠⲒϪⲘ ⲠⲔⲀⲠ ⲘⲠⲈⲨⲞⲈⲒⲰ ⲈⲦⲘⲘⲀⲨ · ⲚⲤⲀ

ⲀⲂⲢⲀⲠⲀⲘ ⲘⲀⲨⲀⲀϤ · ⲈⲔⲦⲀⲒⲞ ⲘⲘⲞϤ ⲚⲦⲈⲒⲠⲈ ⲦⲎⲢⲤ :—

ⲤⲈ ⲠⲈϪⲀϤ ⲚϬⲒ ⲠⲈⲠⲢⲞⲫⲎⲦⲎⲤ ⲀⲀⲨⲈⲒⲀ · ⲞⲨⲚ ⲠⲀⲠ ⲚⲢⲰⲘⲈ ⲠⲒϪⲘ

ⲠⲔⲀⲠ ⲘⲠⲈⲞⲨⲞⲈⲒⲰ ⲚⲀⲂⲢⲀⲠⲀⲘ ∴ ⲀⲀⲀ ⲘⲠⲈⲀⲀⲨ ⲘⲘⲀⲨ ⲤⲞⲨⲈⲚ

_____

1. John A. Tvedtnes, Brian M. Hauglid, and John Gee, *Traditions about the Early Life of Abraham* (Provo, UT: FARMS, 2001).

2. Georgio Zoega, *Catalogus Codicum Copticorum Manuscriptorum qui in Museo Borgiano velitris adservantur* (Rome: Typis Sacrae Congregationis de Propaganda Fide, 1810), 548.

3. Walter E. Crum, *Catalogue of the Coptic Manuscripts in the British Museum* (London: British Museum, 1905), 141, no. 318.

4. E. O. Winstedt, "Coptic Saints and Sinners," *Proceedings of the Society of Biblical Archaeology* 30 (1908): 231-37, 276-83.

ⲚⲚⲞⲨⲦⲈ ⲚⲐⲈ | ⲚⲀⲂⲢⲀⲌⲀⲘ · ⲈⲂⲞⲖ ⲬⲈ ⲚⲈⲀⲂⲢⲀⲌⲀⲘ ⲬⲠⲒⲞ ⲘⲘⲞⲞⲨ ·
ⲘⲚ ⲚⲈⲨⲈⲒⲆⲰⲖⲞⲚ · ⲬⲈ ⲚⲌⲚⲚⲞⲨⲦⲈ ⲀⲚ ⲚⲈ · ⲀⲨⲰ ⲘⲠⲈⲨⲖⲞ
ⲈⲨⲬⲠⲒⲞ ⲘⲘⲞⲞⲨ · ⲰⲀⲚⲦⲞⲨϬⲰⲚⲦ ⲈⲢⲞⲨ ⲚⲤⲈ⳨ ⲔⲰⲌⲦ ⲈⲢⲞⲨ
⳨ ⲚⲦⲈⲢⲞⲨⲚⲞⲨⲬⲈ ⲆⲈ ⲚⲀⲂⲢⲀⲌⲀⲘ ⲈⲌⲞⲨⲚ ⲈⲠⲔⲰⲌⲦ · ⳨ ⲀⲨⲰ
ⲀⲠⲀⲄⲄⲈⲖⲞⲤ ⲘⲠⲬⲞⲈⲒⲤ ⲈⲒ ⲰⲀⲢⲞⲨ ⲚⲦⲈⲨⲚⲞⲨ · ⲀⲨⲰ ⲀⲨⲦⲞⲨⲬⲞⲨ
ⲌⲚⲠⲔⲰⲌⲦ · ⲘⲠⲈⲨⲬⲰⲌ ⲈⲢⲞⲨ ⲈⲠⲦⲎⲢⲨ : ⳨ ⲀⲨⲰ ⲀⲠⲈⲨⲤⲞⲈⲒⲦ
ⲈⲒ ⲈⲂⲞⲖ ⲌⲘⲠⲔⲀⲌ ⲦⲎⲢⲨ ⲚⲦⲘⲈⲤⲞⲠⲞⲦⲀⲘⲒⲀ · | ⲬⲈ ⲀⲠⲈⲨⲚⲞⲨⲦⲈ
ⲦⲞⲨⲬⲞⲨ ⲈⲠⲔⲰⲌⲦ ⲚⲤⲀⲂⲰⲢ ⲠⲢⲢⲞ · ⳨ ⲚⲦⲈⲢⲈⲠⲢⲢⲞ ⲆⲈ ⲤⲰⲦⲘ
ⲈⲠⲤⲞⲈⲒⲦ ⲚⲀⲂⲢⲀⲌⲀⲘ ⲬⲈ ⲀⲨⲞⲨⲬⲀⲒ ⲈⲠⲔⲰⲌⲦ · ⲀⲨⲰ ⲀⲨⲰⲒⲠⲈ
ⲚⲬⲞⲞⲨ ⲚⲤⲰⲨ · ⲬⲈ ⲚⲦⲞⲨ ⲠⲈⲚⲦⲀⲨⲦⲢⲈⲨ⳨ · ⲠⲔⲰⲌⲦ ⲈⲢⲞⲨ : ⳨

ⲚⲦⲈⲨⲚⲞⲨ ⲆⲈ ⲀⲠⲢⲢⲞ ⲤⲰⲞⲨⲌ ⲘⲘⲚⲦⲤⲚⲞⲞⲨⲤ ⲚⲀⲢⲬⲰⲚ ⲚⲦⲈ
ⲠⲖⲀⲞⲤ ⲠⲈⲬⲀⲨ ⲚⲀⲨ ⲬⲈ ⲂⲰⲔ ⲰⲀ ⲠⲈⲒⲢⲰⲘⲈ ⲬⲈ ⲀⲂⲢⲀⲌⲀⲘ
ⲚⲦⲈⲦⲚⲈⲒⲘⲈ ⲈⲦⲘⲈ ⲌⲚ ⲌⲰⲂ ⲚⲒⲘ · ⲬⲈ ⲚⲦⲀⲨⲞⲨⲬⲀⲒ ⲈⲠⲔⲰⲌⲦ
ⲚⲀⲰ ⲚⲌⲈ · ⲀⲨⲰ ⲞⲚ ⲬⲒ ⲚⲘⲘⲎⲦⲚ ⲚⲌⲚⲔⲈⲢⲰⲘⲈ ⲚⲬⲰⲰⲢⲈ ⲌⲒ
ⲦⲈⲌⲒⲎ · ⲘⲘⲞⲚ · ⲀⲒⲤⲰⲦⲘ ⲬⲈ ⲀⲚⲌⲈⲐⲚⲞⲤ ⲔⲰⲦⲈ ⲈⲢⲞⲨ · ⲘⲎⲠⲞⲦⲈ
ⲚⲤⲈⲦⲞⲢⲠⲨ ⲚⲦⲞⲞⲦⲦⲎⲨⲦⲚ · ⲰⲀⲚⲦⲈⲦⲚⲈⲒⲘⲈ ⲈⲦⲘⲈ ⲚⲚⲈⲒⲰⲀⲬⲈ
ⲦⲎⲢⲞⲨ.

ⲀⲨⲰ ⲚⲦⲈⲨⲚⲞⲨ ⲀⲠⲘⲚⲦⲤⲚⲞⲞⲨⲤ ⲚⲀⲢⲬⲰⲚ · ⲌⲰⲚ ⲈⲌⲞⲨⲚ
ⲈⲢⲞⲨ · ⲀⲚⲈⲬⲰⲰⲢⲈ ϬⲰⲰⲦ ⲈⲢⲞⲞⲨ — ⲀⲨⲰ ⲀⲨⲚⲀⲨ ⲈⲚⲈⲖⲖⲞⲤ
ⲈⲨⲤⲞⲞⲨⲌ ⲈⲌⲞⲨⲚ ⲈⲠⲈⲚⲈⲒⲰⲦ ⲀⲂⲢⲀⲌⲀⲘ · ⲠⲈⲬⲈ ⲚⲀⲢⲬⲰⲚ ⲚⲀⲨ ⲬⲈ
ⲠⲈⲚⲈⲒⲰⲦ ⲀⲂⲢⲀⲌⲀⲘ · ⲈⲨⲦⲰⲚ ⲠⲈⲔⲚⲞⲨⲦⲈ · ⲠⲀⲒ ⲚⲦⲀⲨⲦⲞⲨⲬⲞⲔ
ⲌⲘ ⲠⲔⲰⲌⲦ ⲦⲚⲚⲀⲨ ⲈⲢⲞⲨ | ⲌⲰⲰⲚ · ⲦⲚⲞⲨⲰⲰⲦ ⲚⲀⲨ :— ⲀⲨⲰ
ⲚⲄⲦⲀⲘⲒⲞ ⲚⲀⲚ ⲌⲰⲰⲚ ⲚⲞⲨⲚⲞⲨⲦⲈ ⲈⲨϬⲘϬⲞⲘ ⲚⲐⲈ ⲘⲠⲈⲔⲚⲞⲨⲦⲈ
· ⲚⲨⲦⲞⲨⲬⲞⲚ ⲈⲠⲔⲰⲌⲦ · ⲚⲐⲈ ⲚⲦⲀⲨⲦⲞⲨⲬⲞⲔ ⳨ ⲀⲨⲰ ⲚⲦⲈⲨⲚⲞⲨ
ⲀⲀⲂⲢⲀⲌⲀⲘ ⲚⲈⲦⲂ ⲢⲰⲨ ⲚⲤⲰⲨⲈ ⳨ ⲠⲈⲬⲀⲨ ⲚⲀⲨ ⲬⲈ Ⲱ ⲚⲈⲢⲰⲘⲈ
ⲚⲦⲘⲈⲤⲞⲠⲞⲦⲀⲘⲒⲀ · ⲘⲎ ⲦⲀⲤⲨⲚⲎⲐⲒⲀ ⲠⲈ ⲦⲀⲘⲒⲞ ⲚⲞⲨⲦⲈ · ⲚⲐⲈ
ⲚⲚⲈⲦⲚⲚⲞⲨⲦⲈ · ⲈⲒⲈ ⲚⲦⲀⲰⲘⲰⲰ ⲚⲀⲨ ⲌⲞⲖⲰⲤ ⳨ ⲠⲚⲞⲨⲦⲈ ⲠⲀⲒ
ⲚⲦⲀⲨⲦⲞⲨⲬⲞⲒ ⲈⲠⲔⲰⲌⲦ · ⲘⲠⲈⲠⲀⲈⲒⲰⲦ ⲚⲀⲨ ⲈⲢⲞⲨ ⲈⲚⲈⲌ · ⲞⲨⲆⲈ
ⲞⲚ ⲘⲚⲈⲨⲰⲘⲰⲈ ⲚⲀⲨ ⳨—

ⲠⲈⲬⲈ ⲚⲀⲢⲬⲰⲚ ⲚⲀⲨ ⲬⲈ ⲠⲈⲚⲬⲞⲈⲒⲤ ⲀⲂⲢⲀⲌⲀⲘ · ⲚⲦⲀⲚⲬⲞⲞⲤ
ⲈⲢⲞⲔ ⲬⲈ ⲈⲢⲈ ⲠⲈⲔⲚⲞⲨⲦⲈ ⲦⲀⲈⲒⲎⲨ ⲚⲌⲞⲨⲞ ⲈⲠⲰⲚ · ⲈⲦⲂⲈ ⲬⲈ
ⲀⲨⲦⲞⲨⲬⲞⲔ ⲈⲠⲔⲰⲌⲦ :—

ΠΕϪΕ ΑΒΡΑϨΑΜ ΝΑΥ ϪΕ ΠΑΝΟΥΤΕ ΑΝΟΚ ΤΑϬΙΗΥ ΠΑΡΑ ΠΝΟΥΒ

· ΜΝ ΠШΝΕ ΜΜΕ · ΜΝ ΝΚΑ ΝΙΜ ΝΤΕ ΠΕΙΚΟϹΜΟϹ ΑΛΛΑ ΕШϪΕ

ΤΕΤΝΟΥШШ ΕΝΑΥ ΕΠΑΝΟΥΤΕ · ΑΥШ ΝΤΕΤΝΕΙΜΕ ϪΕ ϤΤΑϬΙΗΥ

ΠΑΡΑ ΝΚΑ ΝΙΜ ΕΤϨΙϪΜ ΠΚΑϨ ⁙ ϬШШΤ ΝΗΤΝ ΕΝΕΙ ϨШΟΝ

ΝΤΑΠΑΝΟΥΤΕ ΤΑΜΙΟΟΥ ϨΝ ΤΠΕ · ΠΡΗ ΜΝ ΠΟΟϨ · ΜΝ ΝΕϹΙΟΥ

· ΜΝ ΝΕΚΛΟΟΛΕ ΝΑΗΡ ⁙ ΤΑΡΕΤΕΤΝΕΙΜΕ ϪΕ ΟΥΝ ϬΟΜ ΜΜΟϤ

ΕΤΟΥϪΟΙ ΕΠΚШϨΤ ⁙ ΝΤΕΥΝΟΥ ΑΥΟΥШШΤ ΝΑϤ ΝϬΙ ΜΜΗΗШΕ

ΕΥϪШ ΜΜΟϹ ⁙ ϪΕ ΠΕΝΕΙШΤ ΑΒΡΑϨΑΜ ΜΠΑΤΕΚΡ ϨΜΕ ΝΡΟΜΠΕ

ϨΟΛШϹ ΝΙΜ ⁵ΠΕΝΤΑϤΤΑΜΟΚ ΕΠΕΙ ШΑϪΕ ΠΑΙ ΑΚϪΟΟϤ ΕΡΟΝ

⁙ ΕШϪΕ ΠΕΚΝΟΥΤΕ ΑϤΤΑΜΟΚ ⁶ ΕΠΕΙ ΜΥϹΤΗΡΙΟΝ ΠΑΙ ·

ΤΝΟΥШШ ⁷ ϨШШΝ ΕΝΑΥ ΕΥΜΥϹΤΗΡΙΟΝ ΝΤΑϤΤΑΡΕΝΠΙϹΤΕΥΕ

ΕΡΟϤ ϨШШΝ · ΑΥШ ΝΤΕΥΝΟΥ ΑΑΒΡΑϨΑΜ ϹΑΚϤ ⁸ ΝϹΑ ΟΥϹΑ

ϨΜ ΠΟΥΕ ΑϤΠШΡШ ΝΝΕϤϬΙϪ ΕΒΟΛ ΑϤШΛΗΛ ΕϨΡΑΙ ΕΠΝΟΥΤΕ

⁙ ΑΥШ ΑϨΝΕΒΡΗϬΕ · ΜΝ ϨΝϨΡΟΥΒΑΙ ШΑ ϨΝ ΤΠΕ ⁹ ⁙ ΑΥШ

ΝΤΕΥΝΟΥ ΑΠΝΟΥΤΕ ШΑϪΕ ΜΝ ¹⁰ ΑΒΡΑϨΑΜ ΕϤϪШ ΜΜΟϹ ⁙

ϪΕ ΑΝΟΚ ΠΕ ΠΝΟΥΤΕ ΝΝΚΑ ¹¹ ΝΙΜ ⁙ ΑΥШ ΝΤΕΥΝΟΥ ΑΠϨΟ ¹²

ΝΑΒΡΑϨΑΜ ΕΡΟΥΟΕΙΝ ΝΘΕ ΜΠϨΟ ΝΟΥΑΓΓΕΛΟϹ ΝΤΕ ΠΝΟΥΤΕ ¹³ ·

ΕΤΒΕ ΠΕΟΟΥ ΜΠΝΟΥΤΕ ΝΤΑϤШΑϪΕ ΝΜΜΑϤ · ΑΥШ ΝΤΕΥΝΟΥ

ΑΜΜΗΗШΕ ϨΕ ΕϨΡΑΙ ΕϪΜ ΠΚΑϨ · ΜΠΟΥШϬΜϬΟΜ ¹⁴ ΕϬШШΤ ·

ΕϨΟΥΝ ϨΜ ΠϨΟ ¹⁵ ΝΑΒΡΑϨΑΜ · ΕΤΒΕ ΠΕΟΟΥ ΜΠΝΟΥΤΕ ΝΤΑϤШΑ ¹⁶

ΕϨΡΑΙ ΕϪШϤ ⁙ ΑΥШ ΝΤΕΥΝΟΥ ΑΥШШ ΕΒΟΛ ΕΥϪШ ΜΜΟϹ

ϨΝ ¹⁷ ΟΥϨΡΟΟΥ ΝΟΥШΤ · ϪΕ ΑΒΡΑϨΑΜ ΠΕШΒΗΡ ΜΠΝΟΥΤΕ

---

5. The British Museum fragment begins here with [ΠΕΝΤΑϤΤΑ]ΜΟΚ.
6. BM: ΑϤΤΑΜΑ[Μ]ΜΟΚ.
7. BM: ΤΕΝΟΥ [ΑΝΟΥШ]Ϣ.
8. BM: [ϹΟ]ΚϤ.
9. BM: ΑΥШ [Ν]ΤΕΥΝΟΥ [ΑϨΕΝ]ΕϤΡΗϬΕ [ΜΕΝ] ϨΝϨΡΟΥΒΑΙ ΜΕΝ ϨΕΝ[ϨΟΥ]ΜΠΕ ШΑ ϨΕΝ ΤΠΕ.
10. BM: ΜΕΝ.
11. BM: ΝΕΝΚΑ.
12. BM: ϨΑ.
13. BM: omits ΝΤΕ ΠΝΟΥΤΕ.
14. BM: ΜΠΟΥΕШϬΕΜϬΟΜ.
15. BM: ΕΠϨΟ.
16. BM: ΝΤΑ[Ϥ...].
17. BM: ϨΕΝ.

ⲥⲟⲡⲥ ⲙⲡⲉⲕⲛⲟⲩⲧⲉ ⲉⲧⲃⲏⲏⲧⲛ[18] ⲧⲉⲡⲉⲓϣⲧⲟⲣⲧⲣ ⲗⲟ[19] ⲙⲙϥⲩ

ϩⲓϫⲱⲛ · ⲧⲁⲣⲉⲛϣϭⲙϭⲟⲙ[20] ⲉϣⲁϫⲉ ⲛⲙⲙⲁⲕ :— ⲁⲩⲱ ⲛⲧⲟⲩⲛⲟⲩ

ⲁⲡⲛⲟⲩⲧⲉ ⲥⲙⲟⲩ ⲉⲡⲉⲛⲉⲓⲱⲧ ⲁⲃⲣⲁϩⲁⲙ ⲁϥ† ⲥⲁ ϩⲓ ⲭⲁⲣⲓⲥ ⲛⲁϥ

ⲙⲡⲙⲧⲟ ⲉⲃⲟⲗ ⲛⲟⲩⲟⲛ ⲛⲓⲙ ⸭ ⲁⲩⲱ ⲁⲡⲛⲟⲩⲧⲉ ⲟⲩⲱⲛϩ ⲉⲣⲟϥ[21]

ⲛϩⲛⲕⲉⲙⲩⲥⲧⲏⲣⲓⲟⲛ[22] ⲉⲛⲁϣⲱⲟⲩ ⲛⲁⲓ[23] ⲉⲩⲛⲁϣⲱⲡⲉ[24] ⲙⲙⲟϥ ⲛⲥⲁ

ⲑⲏ · ⲁⲩⲱ ⲛⲧⲉⲩⲛⲟⲩ ⲁϥϩⲟⲡϥ ⲉⲣⲟϥ ⸭⸭

ⲛⲧⲉⲩⲛⲟⲩ ⲇⲉ ⲁⲁⲃⲣⲁϩⲁⲙ ϣ ⲉⲃⲟⲗ ⲉϥϫⲱ ⲙⲙⲟⲥ ⲛⲟⲩⲟⲛ[25]

ⲛⲓⲙ · ϫⲉ ⲡⲣⲣⲟ ⲛⲛⲉϫⲱⲣⲉ ⲧⲏⲣⲟⲩ ⲙⲡⲕⲁϩ ⲛⲧⲉⲡⲉⲛⲛⲟⲩⲧⲉ

· ϫⲓⲥⲉ ⲙⲙⲟϥ :— ⲁⲩⲱ ⲁⲡⲉⲓ ϣⲁϫⲉ ⲡⲁⲓ ϣⲱⲡⲉ ⲉϥ†·[26] ⲥⲟⲉⲓⲧ

ⲉⲧⲃⲉ ⲁⲃⲣⲁϩⲁⲙ ϫⲉ ⲁⲛⲁⲣⲭⲱⲛ ⲙⲛ[27] ⲛⲗⲁⲟⲥ ⲥⲱⲟⲩϩ ⲙⲛ

ⲡⲛⲟⲩⲧⲉ[28] ⲛⲁⲃⲣⲁϩⲁⲙ · ϫⲉ ⲡⲣⲣⲟ ⲛⲛⲉϫⲱⲣⲉ ⲧⲏⲣⲟⲩ ⲙⲡⲕⲁϩ

ⲛⲧⲉⲡⲉⲛⲛⲟⲩⲧⲉ ϫⲓⲥⲉ ⲙⲙⲟϥ ⸭⸭

ⲁⲗⲏⲑⲱⲥ ⲅⲁⲣ ⲱ ⲡⲉⲡⲣⲟⲫⲏⲧⲏⲥ ⲉⲧⲟⲩⲁⲁⲃ ⲡⲉⲛⲉⲓⲱⲧ[29] ⲇⲁⲩⲉⲓⲇ

· ⲡⲕⲁⲗⲱⲥ ⲅⲁⲣ ⲧⲟⲟⲙⲉ ⲉⲣⲟⲕ ⲛⲛⲁⲩ ⲛⲓⲙ · ⲓⲛⲛϫⲧⲉⲕⲙⲛⲧϣⲱⲥ

ⲙⲙⲁⲛⲉⲥⲟⲟⲩ · ϣⲁⲧⲉⲕⲙⲛⲧⲡⲣⲟⲫⲏⲧⲏⲥ ⸭ ⲉⲃⲟⲗ ϫⲉ ⲟⲩⲁϩⲟ

ⲛⲱⲛϩ · ⲡⲉ ⲡⲉⲕⲁϩⲟ ⲱ ⲡⲣⲣⲟ ⲛⲇⲓⲕⲁⲓⲟⲥ ⲡⲉⲛⲉⲓⲱⲧ ⲉⲧⲟⲩⲁⲁⲃ

ⲇⲁⲩⲉⲓⲇ ⸭⸭

ⲁⲗⲏⲑⲱⲥ ⲱ ⲛⲉⲛⲉⲓⲟⲧⲉ ⲉⲧⲟⲩⲁⲁⲃ ⲛⲁⲡⲟⲥⲧⲟⲗⲟⲥ · ⲡⲉⲧϣϣⲉ ⲡⲉ

ⲛⲧⲉ ⲗⲁⲥ ⲛⲓⲙ · ϩⲓ ⲥⲡⲟⲧⲟⲩ ⲛⲓⲙ ϫⲱ ⲙⲡⲉⲧⲛⲧⲁⲉⲓⲟ ⸭ ⲉⲃⲟⲗ ϫⲉ

ⲁⲡⲉⲭⲥ ⲡⲉⲛⲱⲛϩ ⲧⲏⲣⲉⲛ ⲙⲟⲩⲧⲉ ⲉⲣⲱⲧⲛ ⲛϫⲓⲛⲉⲧⲉⲧⲛϣⲟⲟⲡ

ϩⲓϫⲙ ⲡⲕⲁϩ · ϫⲉ ⲛⲁⲥⲛⲏⲩ · ⲁⲩⲱ ⲛⲁϣⲃⲏⲣ ⸭ ⲭⲱⲣⲓⲥ ⲡⲛⲟϭ

ⲛⲉⲟⲟⲩ ⲛⲧⲁϥⲭⲁⲣⲓⲍⲉ ⲙⲙⲟϥ ⲛⲏⲧⲛ ⲙⲡⲙⲧⲟ ⲉⲃⲟⲗ ⲙⲡⲉϥⲉⲓⲱⲧ

· ⲙⲛⲛⲉϥⲁⲅⲅⲉⲗⲟⲥ ⲉⲧⲟⲩⲁⲁⲃ · ⲉϥϫⲱ ⲙⲙⲟⲥ · ϫⲉ ⲡⲁⲉⲓⲱⲧ

---

18. BM: ⲉⲧⲃⲏⲏⲧⲉⲛ.
19. BM: ⲗⲁ.
20. BM: ⲧⲁⲣⲉⲛϣϭⲉⲙϭⲟⲙ.
21. BM: ⲟⲩⲱⲛⲁϩ ⲉⲃⲟⲗ.
22. BM: ⲛϩⲉⲛⲕⲉⲙⲩⲥⲧⲏⲣⲓⲟⲛ.
23. Word omitted in BM.
24. BM: ⲉⲛⲁ[...]ⲉ.
25. BM: ⲉⲟⲩⲟⲛ.
26. BM: ⲁⲩⲱ ⲁⲡⲉ[ⲙ]ⲡⲁⲓϣ†.
27. BM: ⲙⲉⲛ.
28. BM: ⲙⲡⲛⲟⲩⲧⲉ.
29. The British Museum fragment ends with ⲡⲉⲛⲉⲓⲱ[ⲧ].

ϯΟΥⲰϢ · ϪⲈⲕⲀⲤ ⲠⲘⲀ ⲀⲚⲞⲕ Ⲉϯ ⲘⲘⲞϤ ⲘⲀⲢⲈ ⲚⲈⲦⲚⲞΥⲒ
ⲚⲈ ϢⲰⲠⲈ ⲚϨⲎⲦϤ · ϪⲈⲕⲀⲤ ⲈΥⲈⲚⲀΥ ⲈⲠⲈⲞⲞΥ ⲚⲦⲀⲕⲬⲀⲢⲒⲌⲈ
ⲘⲘⲞϤ ⲚⲀⲒ ⲈⲂⲞⲖ ϪⲈ ⲀΥϨⲀⲢⲈϨ ⲈⲠⲀϢⲀϪⲈ · ⲚⲐⲈ ϨⲰ ⲚⲦⲀⲒϨⲀⲢⲈϨ
ⲈⲠⲈⲕϢⲀϪⲈ ⁚— ⲠⲀⲈⲒⲰⲦ ⲈⲦⲞΥⲀⲀⲂ · ⲠⲞΥⲚⲞϤ ⲘⲠⲈⲕϢⲀϪⲈ ⲠⲈⲦ
ⲘⲈ · ⲀΥⲰ ⲀⲚⲞⲕ ⲘⲚ ⲚⲀⲠⲞⲤⲦⲞⲖⲞⲤ · ⲀⲚϨⲀⲢⲈϨ ⲈⲢⲞϤ ⁘ ϯⲦⲂⲂⲞ
ⲘⲘⲞⲒ ϨⲀⲢⲞⲞΥ ⲠⲀⲈⲒⲰⲦ · ϪⲈ ⲀΥϢⲰⲠⲈ ⲈΥⲦⲂⲂⲎΥ ϨⲚ ⲦⲘⲈ ⁘—
ⲠⲀⲈⲒⲰⲦ ⲚⲈⲚⲦⲀⲕⲦⲀϨⲘⲞΥ ⲦⲎⲢⲞΥ · ⲀⲒⲤⲀⲕⲞΥ ϢⲀⲢⲞⲒ ϨⲘ ⲠϢⲀϪⲈ
ⲚⲦⲀⲦⲀⲠⲢⲞ ⁘ ⲘⲠⲞΥϢⲒⲚⲈ ⲚⲤⲀ ⲖⲀⲀΥ ⲚⲦⲞⲞⲦ · ⲈⲒⲘⲎⲦⲒ ⲠⲈⲕⲢⲀⲚ
ⲘⲘⲀⲦⲈ · ⲈⲦⲢⲈⲕϨⲀⲢⲈϨ ⲈⲢⲞⲞΥ ϪⲈ ⲚⲚⲈⲖⲀⲀΥ ⲦⲀⲕⲞ ⲈⲂⲞⲖ ⲚϨⲎⲦⲞΥ
· ⲈⲒⲘⲎⲦⲒ ⲠϢⲎⲢⲈ ⲘⲠⲦⲀⲕⲞ · ⲈϢϪⲈ Ⲱ ⲚⲈⲚⲈⲒⲞⲦⲈ ⲈⲦⲞΥⲀⲀⲂ
ⲚⲀⲠⲞⲤⲦⲞⲖⲞⲤ · ⲀⲠϢⲎⲢⲈ ⲘⲠⲚⲞΥⲦⲈ ⲤΥⲚϨⲒⲤⲦⲀ ⲘⲘⲰⲦⲚ ⲘⲠⲘⲦⲞ
ⲈⲂⲞⲖ ⲘⲠⲈϤⲈⲒⲰⲦ ϪⲈ ⲀΥⲘⲈⲢⲒⲦ · ⲠⲈⲦϢϢⲈ ⲈⲢⲞⲚ ϨⲰⲰⲚ ⲠⲈ
· ⲈⲦⲢⲈⲚⲘⲈⲢⲈ ⲦⲎΥⲦⲚ ⲈⲠⲈϨⲞΥⲞ ⁘ ϨⲞⲦⲀⲚ ⲆⲈ ⲈⲕϢⲀⲚⲘⲈⲢⲈ
ⲞΥⲘⲀⲢⲦΥⲢⲞⲤ · ⲈⲒⲈ ⲞΥⲆⲒⲕⲀⲒⲞⲤ · ⲠⲰϤ ⲠⲈⲤⲞⲠⲤ ϨⲒϪⲰⲔ · ⲈⲂⲞⲖ
ϪⲈ ⲠⲈΥⲤⲞⲠⲤ ϬⲘϬⲞⲘ ⲘⲘⲀⲦⲈ ⲘⲠⲘⲦⲞ ⲈⲂⲞⲖ ⲚⲞΥⲞⲚ ⲚⲒⲘ ⁚—

ⲈⲕϢⲀⲚⲢ ⲞΥⲘⲚⲦⲚⲀ ϨⲘ ⲠⲢⲀⲚ · ⲚⲚⲈⲒ ⲀⲠⲞⲤⲦⲞⲖⲞⲤ ⲈⲦⲞΥⲀⲀⲂ ·
ⲔⲀⲚ ϨⲚ ⲞΥⲐΥⲤⲒⲀ ⲈⲔⲚⲀⲦⲀⲀⲤ ϨⲘⲠⲈΥⲢⲀⲚ · ⲔⲀⲚ ϨⲚ ⲞΥϪⲰⲰⲘⲈ
ⲈⲔⲚⲀⲦⲀⲀϤ ϨⲘ ⲠⲈΥⲢⲀⲚ · ⲚⲄⲦⲀⲀϤ ⲈϨⲞΥⲚ ⲈⲦⲈⲔⲔⲖⲎⲤⲒⲀ ·
ⲈⲦⲢⲈΥϢⲰ ⲚϨⲎⲦϤ · ⲔⲀⲚ ⲞΥⲖⲀⲀΥ ϨⲰⲖⲞⲤ · ⲈⲔⲚⲀⲦⲀⲀϤ ϨⲘ
ⲠⲈΥⲢⲀⲚ ⲔⲀⲦⲀ ⲤⲘⲞⲦ ⲚⲒⲘ ⁘ ⲔⲀⲚ ϨⲚ ⲞΥϢⲞⲠⲤ ⲈΥⲚⲀⲀⲀⲤ ϨⲘ
ⲠⲈΥⲢⲀⲚ ⲈⲚⲈϨⲎⲔⲈ · ⲘⲚ ⲚⲈϢⲘⲘⲞ · ⲘⲚ ⲚⲈⲦϢⲀⲀⲦ · ⲢⲀϢⲈ
ⲚⲀⲔ ϨⲰⲰⲔ Ⲱ ⲠⲀⲘⲈⲢⲒⲦ · ϪⲈ ⲀΥⲞΥⲰ ⲈΥⲤϨⲀⲒ ⲘⲠⲈⲕⲢⲀⲚ
ⲈⲠⲈΥϪⲰⲰⲘⲈ · ⲈⲂⲞⲖ ϪⲈ ϨⲚ ⲢⲈϤⲤⲞⲠⲤ ⲚⲈ ⲈΥϪⲎⲔ ⲈⲂⲞⲖ
⁚⁝ ⲚⲈⲆⲒⲔⲀⲒⲞⲤ ⲆⲈ ⲘⲚ ⲚⲈⲘⲀⲢⲦΥⲢⲞⲤ · ϨⲚ ⲢⲈϤⲤⲞⲠⲤ ϨⲰⲞΥ
ⲚⲈ ⁚⁝ ⲚⲈⲒⲀⲠⲞⲤⲦⲞⲖⲞⲤ ⲆⲈ ⲚⲦⲞⲞΥ ϨⲚ ⲢⲈϤϯ ϨⲀⲠ ⲚⲈ · ϨⲘ
ⲠⲈⲒⲀ ⲚⲒⲰⲤⲀⲪⲀⲦ ⁚⁝ ⲒⲰϨⲀⲚⲚⲎⲤ ⲠⲈΥⲀⲄⲄⲈⲖⲒⲤⲦⲎⲤ ⲈⲢⲘⲚⲦⲢⲈ
· ⲈϤϪⲰ ⲘⲘⲞⲤ · ϪⲈ ⲈⲢϢⲀⲚ ⲠϢⲎⲢⲈ ⲈⲢ ⲦⲎΥⲦⲚ ⲚⲢⲘϨⲈ ·
ⲞⲚⲦⲰⲤ ⲦⲈⲦⲚⲚⲀϢⲰⲠⲈ ⲚⲢⲘϨⲈ ⁚⁝ ⲦⲈⲒⲈⲚⲦⲞⲖⲎ ⲚⲦⲀⲠⲈⲒⲰⲦ
ⲦⲀⲀⲤ ⲘⲠⲈϤⲘⲈⲢⲒⲦ ⲚϢⲎⲢⲈ ⲀⲠϢⲎⲢⲈ ϨⲰⲰϤ ⲬⲀⲢⲒⲌⲈ ⲘⲘⲞⲤ
ⲚⲚⲈϤⲀⲠⲞⲤⲦⲞⲖⲞⲤ ⲈⲦⲞΥⲀⲀⲂ ⁚⁝ ⲈⲦⲂⲈ ⲠⲀⲒ ⲠⲈⲦⲈⲢⲈⲚⲀⲠⲞⲤⲦⲞⲖⲞⲤ
ⲚⲀⲀⲀϤ ⲚⲢⲘϨⲈ · ⲠϢⲎⲢⲈ ⲘⲠⲚⲞΥⲦⲈ ⲚⲀⲀⲀϤ ⲚⲢⲘϨⲈ ·
ⲠⲈⲦⲈⲢⲈⲚⲀⲠⲞⲤⲦⲞⲖⲞⲤ ⲚⲀⲔⲰ ⲚⲀϤ ⲈⲂⲞⲖ · ⲠⲈⲬⲤ ⲚⲀⲔⲰ ⲚⲀϤ
ⲈⲂⲞⲖ ϨⲰⲰϤ ⁚⁝ ⲀΥⲰ ⲠⲈⲦⲈⲢⲈⲚⲀⲠⲞⲤⲦⲞⲖⲞⲤ ⲚⲀϯ ⲔⲖⲎⲢⲞⲚⲞⲘⲒⲀ

ΝΑϤ · ΑΠϢΗΡΕ ΜΠΝΟΥΤΕ ✝ ΚΛΗΡΟΝΟΜΙΑ ΝΑϤ ⋮ ΑΛΛΑ
ΤΕΤΝCΟΟΥΝ Ϣ ΠΛΑΟC ΜΜΑΙ ΠΕΧC ΕΠΕΙ ϢΑΧΕ Ε✝ΝΑΧΟΟϤ
· ΧΕ ΝΝΕΤΝ CΑϢΤ · ΟΥΔΕ ΝΝΕΤΝΒΑΒϢϢΤ · ΑΛΛΑ ΝΘΕ
ΝΟΥΑΓΓΕΛΟC ΝΤΕΠΝΟΥΤΕ · ϢΕΠ ΠΑϢΑΧΕ ΕΡϢΤΝ · ΕΥΝΟΒΡΕ
ΝΝΕΤΝ✝ΥΧΗ · ΕΡϢΑΝ ΟΥCΟΝ · Η ΟΥCϢΝΕ Ν2ΗΤΤΗΥΤΝ
ΤΕ2Μ ΟΥΑ 2Μ ΠΡΑΝ ΝΝΕΙ ΑΠΟCΤΟΛΟC ΕΤΟΥΑΑΒ ⋮ ΕϤϢΠΕ
ΠΕΤΡΟC ΠΕ ΜΠΡΠΟΡΧϤ ΕΑΝΔΡΕΑC ΠΕϤCΟΝ ⋮ ΕΚϢΑΝ✝
ΝΟΥΑΓΠΗ 2Μ ΠΡΑΝ ΝΙϢ2ΑΝΝΗC · Μ[Π]ΕΚΠΟΡΧϤ ΕΙΑΚϢΒΟC
ΠΕϤCΟΝ ⋮ ΕΚϢΑΝΤΑΑC 2Μ ΠΡΑΝ ΜΦΙΛΙΠΠΟC · ΜΠΕΚΠΟΡΧϤ
ΕΒΟΛ ΕΒΑΡΘΟΛΟΜΑΙΟC · ΕΒΟΛ ΧΕ ΟΥΤϢ2Μ ΝΟΥϢΤ ΠΕ
⋮— ΕΚϢΑΝΤΑΑC 2Μ ΠΡΑΝ ΝΘϢΜΑC · ΜΠΕΚΠΟΡΧϤ ΕΒΟΛ
ΕΜΑΘΑΙΟC · ΕΒΟΛ ΧΕ ΟΥΚΟΙΝϢΝΙΑ ΝΟΥϢΤ ΤΕΤ2Ν ΤΕΥΜΗΤΕ
21 ΟΥCΟΠ ⋮— ΕΚϢΑΝΤΑΑC 2Μ ΠΡΑΝ ΝCΙΜϢΝ · ΜΠΕΚΠΟΡΧϤ
ΕΒΟΛ ΕΙΑΚϢΒΟC ΠϢΗΡΕ ΝΑΛΦΑΙΟC ⋮— ΜΠΕΚΝΑΥ ΕΠΕΤΡΟC ΧΕ
ΠΝΟϬ ΠΕ 2Ν ΝΑΠΟCΤΟΛΟC · ΑΥϢ ΧΕ ΑΡΕ ΝΕϤϢΟϢΤ ΝΝΜΠΗΥΕ
ΝΤΟΟΤϤ · ΝΤΕΤΝΘΕϢΡΕΙ ΝΙϢ2ΑΝΝΗC · ΧΕ ΕϤ2Ν ΤΜΝΤΑΤΜΟΥ
· ΝΤΕΤΝΚΑ ΠΚΕCΕΕΠΕ ΝΝΕΙ ΑΠΟCΤΟΛΟC ΝCϢΤΝ · ΜΜΟΝ
ΟΥΜΕ ΝΟΥϢΤ ΠΕΤΕΡΕ ΠΕΥΧΟΕΙC ΜΕ ΜΜΟΟΥ Ν2ΗΤϤ ⋮— ΑΥϢ
ΠΕΙ2ΜΟΤ ΝΟΥϢΤ ΠΕ ΝΤΑΠΧΟΕΙC ΧΑΡΙΖΕ ΜΜΟϤ ΝΑΥ ΤΗΡΟΥ
ΕϤΧϢ ΜΜΟC ΝΑΥ · ΧΕ ΤΕΤΝΝΑΟΥϢΜ ΝΤΕΤΝCϢ ΝΜΜΑΙ 2ΙΧΝ
ΤΕΤΡΑΠΕΖΑ ΝΤΑΜΝΤΕΡΟ ⋮—

Translation

My translation of the text follows:[30]

[. . .] "gathered with the God of Abraham" [Psalm 47:9].
And what is Abraham that you say of him that they gathered with the God of Abraham? And were there not any

---

30. I have settled on a compromise on the second-person singular pronouns which
are translated as thou, thee, thy, and thine when referring to deity. While my personal
preference would be to keep the distinction between singular and plural in the second
person, these days preserving the distinction is considered unacceptable. However,
the use of the plural English pronoun when addressing deity is too jarring to my sense
of English—hence the compromise.

men on the earth at that time save Abraham alone since you praise him to all this extent?

Yea, said the prophet David, there were many men on the earth at the time of Abraham, but none of them knew God like Abraham because Abraham mocked them and their idols: They are not Gods, and he did not cease mocking them, until they became angry with him so that they might set fire to him. But when Abraham was thrown into the fire, the angel of the Lord came to him in that moment and saved him from the fire. It did not touch him at all. And his fame came forth in all the land of Mesopotamia because his God saved him from the fire of Sabor the Pharaoh. When Pharaoh heard the fame of Abraham that he was safe from the fire and[31] he was ashamed to speak with him because he was the one who had caused them to set fire to him.

Then Pharaoh collected twelve rulers of the people. He said to them: Go to this man Abraham to learn the truth of everything. How was he saved from the fire? And also take with you other strong men on the way (indeed, I have heard that the people surround him) lest they seize him from you, until you learn the truth of all these things.

And then the twelve rulers approached him; the strong men saw him, and they saw the people gathered to our father Abraham. The rulers said to him: Our father Abraham, where is your God, that one who saved you in the fire, so that we may see him ourselves, and may worship him, and you may teach us of a god who is powerful like your God, so that he may save us from the fire like you were saved. And then Abraham smiled. He said to them: O men of Mesopotamia, is it my custom to fashion gods like your

---

31. Although the English here is awkward, the Coptic clearly has the unusual (for English) *and*.

gods? Then surely I would serve them completely. God is this one who saved me from the fire. My father never saw him; neither did he ever worship him.

The rulers said to him: Our lord, Abraham, didn't we tell you that your God is more honored than ours because he saved you from the fire?

Abraham said to them: But my God is more worthy of honor than gold and precious stones and anything of this world. But if you wish to see my God and to know that he is more worthy of honor than anything which is on the earth, look at the constellations that God created in the heaven; the sun and the moon and the stars and the clouds of the atmosphere let you know that he has power to save me from the fire. Immediately the crowds worshipped him, saying, Our father Abraham, you are not yet even forty years old. Who taught you this saying, this one you told us? If your God taught you this mystery, we ourselves wish to see a mystery so that he can make us believe him ourselves. And then Abraham withdrew himself to one side of the way and spread out his hands and prayed to God. And lightnings and thunders appeared in heaven and then God spoke with Abraham, saying, I am the God of everything. And then the face of Abraham shone like the face of an angel of God because of the glory of God who spoke with him. And immediately the crowd fell to the earth. They could not look in the face of Abraham because of the glory of God that appeared on him. And then they cried out, saying with one voice: Abraham, friend of God, entreat your god on our behalf so that this trouble over us might stop, that we might be allowed to speak with you. And immediately God blessed our father Abraham. He gave him beauty and grace in everyone's presence. And God revealed to him many other mysteries, those which shall happen to him afterwards, and then he hid himself from him.

Then Abraham cried out, saying to everyone: O Pharaoh of all the strong men of the earth of our God, exalt him! And saying this was what became famous about Abraham, that "the rulers of the people met with the God of Abraham" [Psalm 47:9] so that the Pharaoh of all the strong men of the earth of God exalted him.

For truly, O holy prophet, our father David, the good is appropriate for you at all times, from your shepherding of sheep to your prophecy because your treasury was a treasury of life, O righteous king, our holy father, David.

Truly, O our holy fathers, the apostles, what is proper is that which every tongue and every lip say for your glory because the Christ, the life of all of us, calls you "my brethren and my friends" since you were on earth, without the great glory which he granted to you in the presence of his father and his holy angels, saying: "My father, I desire that the place where I am, that these which are mine might be so that they may see the glory that thou hast granted me because they have kept my word as I myself have kept thy word. O my holy father, the joy of thy word is that which is true and I and my apostles have kept it. I purify myself for their sake, my father, because they have become pure in the truth. O my father, all those whom thou hast called, I have drawn to me by the word of my mouth. They have not sought anything really from me save thy name so that thou mayest keep them so that none of them perish[32] save the son of destruction."

---

32. For an examination of this term in earlier phases of Egyptian, see John Gee, "Trial Marriage in Ancient Egypt? P. Louvre E. 7846 Reconsidered," in *Res Severa Verum Gaudium: Festschrift für Karl-Theodor Zauzich*, ed. Friedhelm Hoffmann and Heinz-Josef Thissen (Leuven: Peeters, 2004), 224-30.

O our holy fathers, the apostles, if the Son of God commended you in the presence of his father because "they loved me," it is appropriate for us to love you more. When you love a martyr or a just man, his is the prayer on you because their prayer has great effect in the presence of everyone.

If you do mercy in the name of these holy apostles, even if in an offering which you give in their name, even in a book which you give in their name, and you put it in the church, so that they can read in it, even anything of any sort at all which you give in their name, even in a banquet which will be made in their name for the hungry and the stranger and the needy, then rejoice for yourself, O my beloved, because they have already written your name in their book because they are those who pray perfectly. And the righteous and the martyrs are those who pray. But these apostles, they are judges in the valley of Jehoshaphat. John the Evangelist testifies, saying: If the son made you free, you will actually become free. This commandment which the father gave to his beloved son, the son, himself, granted to his holy apostles. Therefore, him whom the apostles will make free, the Son of God himself will make free. Him whom the apostles will forgive, Christ himself will forgive. And to him to whom the apostles shall give an inheritance, the son will also give an inheritance. But you recognize, O Christ-loving people, this saying which I will say: Do not obstruct me, neither despise me, but like an angel of God receive my saying for the good of your souls. If a brother or sister among you call one in the name of these holy apostles, if it is Peter, do not separate him from Andrew, his brother. If you give alms in the name of John, do not separate him from James, his brother. If you give it in the name of Philip, do not separate him from Bartholomew because it is only one convocation.

> If you give it in the name of Thomas, do not separate it from Matthew because it is only one community and one occasion in their midst. If you give it in the name of Simon, do not separate him from James, the son of Alphaeus. You did not see Peter because he is the greatest among the apostles and because the keys of heaven are in his hands; nor did you look to John because he is among the immortal and leave out the rest of these apostles. No. It was only one love that their Lord loved them with, and this grace only is that which the Lord granted to all of them, telling them: You shall eat and drink with me at the table in my kingdom.

As is clear from the text, this story about Abraham is found inside a larger homily.

Philological Notes

One of the first concerns we have is knowing whether the story about Abraham is originally in Coptic or Greek or in some other language.

A number of features of the story in the text are striking. There is a limited amount of Greek vocabulary in the story itself; only seventeen words are of Greek origin (ⲀⲄⲄⲈⲖⲞⲤ, ⲀⲎⲢ, ⲀⲖⲖⲀ, ⲀⲢⲬⲰⲚ, ⲆⲈ, ⲈⲓⲆⲰⲖⲞⲚ, ⲌⲰⲰⲚ, ⲔⲞⲤⲘⲞⲤ, ⲖⲀⲞⲤ, ⲘⲈⲤⲞⲠⲞⲦⲀⲘⲒⲀ, ⲘⲨⲤⲦⲎⲢⲒⲞⲚ, ⲠⲒⲤⲦⲈⲨⲈ, ⲠⲀⲢⲀ, ⲤⲨⲚⲎⲐⲒⲀ, ⲬⲀⲢⲒⲤ, ⲈⲐⲚⲞⲤ, ⲞⲖⲰⲤ). The text even uses the native word for king, Ⲣ̄ⲢⲞ, which comes from *pr-ꜥꜣ*, Pharaoh,[33] even though it is not clear that the Pharaoh in the text was king over Egypt. He has normally been equated with one of many Persian kings named Shapur.[34] If this is the case, the name has passed through Greek and not directly through Syriac as an intermediary, and the lack of Greek loan words is all the stranger. The other possibility for the name is as a corrupt version of the Fourteenth

---

33. Jaroslav Černý, *Coptic Etymological Dictionary* (Cambridge: Cambridge University Press, 1976), 138–39.

34. Winstedt, "Coptic Saints and Sinners," 233.

Dynasty ruler *Sh̠3b-rꜥ,* about whom nothing is known other than his name.[35]

The story also contains only two sentences that use constructions with ⲛ̄ϭⲓ. The term ⲛ̄ϭⲓ derives from a native Egyptian term,[36] but it is used primarily for indicating the subject of a sentence, which is a nonnative use for this expression. It appears frequently in translation texts to preserve the syntax of the original Greek. Because of its use in translation texts, especially biblical texts, it passes into the Coptic language but is not used as frequently in native texts.

The vocabulary and syntax are signs that the story is not a translation but a retelling by native speakers that seems to come from an earlier period of Coptic.

Homilies

The story about Abraham is part of a larger homily.

The text begins on its third page with a fragmentary quotation of Coptic Psalm 46:9 (Hebrew 47:10; KJV 47:9): ⲛⲁⲣⲭⲱⲛ ⲛⲛⲁⲁⲟⲥ ⲁⲩⲥⲱⲟⲩ2 ⲉ2ⲟⲩⲛ ⲙⲛ ⲡⲛⲟⲩⲧⲉ ⲛⲁⲃⲣⲁⲁⲙ. "The rulers of the people gathered with the God of Abraham."[37] The story about Abraham is used to explain the wording in this particular Psalm. After the story about Abraham the homily shifts to extolling Jesus's apostles and urges treating them as a group. After that, the homily, at least as we have it, ends.

The end of the preserved text, however, does not seem to be the end of the homily. Coptic homilies customarily end with an exhortation and benediction on the hearers, and a doxology, for example:

---

35. For the name, see Jürgen von Beckerath, *Handbuch der ägyptischen Königsnamen,* 2nd ed. (Mainz: von Zabern, 1999), 108-9; for what is known about this ruler, see Kim S. B. Ryholt, *The Political Situation in Egypt during the Second Intermediate Period* (Copenhagen: The Carsten Niebuhr Institute of Near Eastern Studies, 1997), 379.

36. Černý, *Coptic Etymological Dictionary,* 119.

37. E. A. Wallis Budge, *The Earliest Known Coptic Psalter* (London: Kegan Paul, Trench, Trübner, 1898), 51; William H. Worrell, *The Coptic Psalter in the Freer Collection* (New York: Macmillan, 1916), 99.

> And we must produce fruit, and labour in the remem-
> brance of His commandments; and we must make ourselves
> ready for His glorious rest, and then nothing whatsoever
> shall give us offence; through Jesus Christ, our Lord, to
> Whom be the glory, and with Him the Father, and the Holy
> Spirit, for all ages of ages. Amen.[38]

This example shows that the customary ending for a homily is absent in the text, and thus the end of the text is not the end of the original homily. So this homily is missing both its beginning and end.

Traditions about Abraham

The text can also be seen in the light of other traditions about the biblical patriarch Abraham.

One of the more interesting features of the text is its mention that an angel saved Abraham from the fire. This is one of the unique and interesting features of the story, and it is missing from Zoega's notice. Zoega's entire notice reads as follows: "NUM. CCX-XII.* Folium unum lacerum, paginae г̄, л̄, characteres classis VI. De Abrahamo, ⲡⲉⲛⲉⲓⲱⲧ ⲁⲃⲣⲁⲍⲁⲙ, qui a Sapore rege Mesopotamiae in rogum conjectus salvus evasit, quo facto rex ad eum misit duodecim principes populi ut interrogarent, quis esset Deus ejus qui eum servaverat."[39] "Number 222*. One torn folio, pages г̄ [3], л̄ [4], in class VI characters. About Abraham, ⲡⲉⲛⲉⲓⲱⲧ ⲁⲃⲣⲁⲍⲁⲙ, who escaped

---

38. Athanasius, *On Mercy and Judgment*, fol. 86a-b, in E. A. Wallis Budge, *Coptic Homilies in the Dialect of Upper Eypgt* (New York: AMS 1977), 211. Cf. Athanasius, *Concerning the Soul and the Body*, fol. 162a, in Budge, *Coptic Homilies*, 274; Athanasius, *On the Labourers in the Vineyard*, fol. 115b-116a, in Budge, *Coptic Homilies*, 234; Theophilus, *On Repentance and Continence*, fol. 104b, in Budge, *Coptic Homilies*, 225; Proclus, *Installation Sermon*, fol. 122a-b, in Budge, *Coptic Homilies*, 240; Basil, *On the End of the World*, fol. 141b-142a, in Budge, *Coptic Homilies*, 257; Eusebius, *Concerning the Canaanitish Woman*, fol. 175a, in Budge, *Coptic Homilies*, 285; Flavianus, *Encomium on Demetrius*, fol. 45b, in E. A. Wallis Budge, *Coptic Martyrdoms* (London: British Museum, 1914), 408; Proclus, *Against the Dogma of Nestorius*, fol. 130a-b, in Budge, *Coptic Homilies*, 247; Timothy, *Discourse on the Abbaton*, fol. 32a-b, in Budge, *Coptic Martyrdoms*, 496; Apa John, *On Repentance and Continence*, fol. 60a-b, in Budge, *Coptic Homilies*, 191; Apa John, *Concerning Susanna*, fol. 76a-b, in Budge, *Coptic Homilies*, 203.

39. Zoega, *Catalogus Codicum Copticorum Manuscriptorum*, 548.

alive after being thrown into a funeral pyre by Sapore, the king of Mesopotamia, because of which, the king sent twelve princes of the people to him to inquire who is that God who saved him." The account's description of Abraham being saved by an angel contrasts with the other noncanonical accounts of the involvement of the angels in the attempted sacrifice of Abraham, which are related.

The story of Abraham being delivered from the fire in Chaldea is known in Christian sources both in the East and in the West. In the West, it was preserved by Jerome and a few French clergy. In the East, it had a history of more vigorous retelling. But none of the Christian traditions outside this Coptic text preserve any account of the involvement of angels.

A version of the Abraham story attributed to Eliezer ben Jacob held that the angel Michael descended to rescue Abraham from the fiery furnace, but this is a minority version to the rabbis' version that God himself rescued him.[40] Two rabbis named Eliezer ben Jacob are known. One is supposed to date from the first century and the other, a disciple of Akiba, from the second century. The recorded account dates somewhere between the fifth and tenth centuries.

The *Midrash Rabbah* Exodus claims that the angels Michael and Gabriel asked to save Abraham when he was cast into the furnace but that God himself decided to save him.[41] The recorded account may date as late as the twelfth century.

In the Babylonian Talmud, which dates between the fifth and eighth centuries, Gabriel alone asks God to save Abraham, but God himself intervenes.[42]

---

40. *Midrash Rabbah*, Genesis 44:13, in Tvedtnes et al., *Traditions about the Early Life of Abraham*, 99; *Midrash Rabbah*, Song of Songs 1:12.1, in Tvedtnes et al., *Traditions about the Early Life of Abraham*, 116; *Midrash Rabbah*, Song of Songs 3:11.1, in Tvedtnes et al., *Traditions about the Early Life of Abraham*, 117.

41. *Midrash Rabbah*, Exodus 18:5, in Tvedtnes et al., *Traditions about the Early Life of Abraham*, 103.

42. Babylonian Talmud, *Pesahim* 118a, in Tvedtnes et al., *Traditions about the Early Life of Abraham*, 120.

The medieval Jewish *Chronicles of Jerahmeel,* attributed to the twelfth-century Jerahmeel ben Solomon, tells the version of the story from *Midrash Rabbah* Exodus, elaborating the angels' involvement by having the angels (in the plural) quarrel and naming Michael and Gabriel specifically,[43] but also adds the version from the Babylonian Talmud.[44]

Ka'b al-Aḥbār, a seventh-century Yemenite Jew who converted to Islam, brought the Jewish accounts of the attempted sacrifice of Abraham into Islam. In Ka'b al-Aḥbār's account, Gabriel asks Abraham while he is flying through the air after having been launched from a catapult if he needs anything. Abraham denies it saying that he will give his request to God alone. God then heard and saved him.[45] Ka'b al-Aḥbār brings into Islam the tradition cited in the Babylonian Talmud that the angel Gabriel is involved and then God saved Abraham himself. This version of the story adds the picturesque element of the fire being so hot that Abraham must be delivered into the flames by a catapult.

The eighth-century Arabic author, Ibn Isḥāq, whose grandfather had been a Jewish slave from Babylon who converted to Islam, compiled a tremendous number of Islamic traditions. He had hung around the *warraqs,* who sold Jewish and Christian scriptures, commentaries, and apocryphal works, as well as copies of the Qur'an. In his version, it is not the angels who ask to be able to save Abraham but "heaven and earth and all the creatures in it except men and Jinn" who do so. But God himself steps in to save him and then sends the Angel of Shade to amuse Abraham in the fire.[46]

---

43. *Chronicles of Jerahmeel* 34:13, in Tvedtnes et al., *Traditions about the Early Life of Abraham,* 133.

44. *Chronicles of Jerahmeel* 35:3, in Tvedtnes et al., *Traditions about the Early Life of Abraham,* 134.

45. Ka'b al-Aḥbār 13–14, in Tvednes, et al., *Traditions about the Early Life of Abraham,* 301.

46. Extracts from Ibn Isḥāq, *Kitab al-mubtada',* 13–14, in Tvedtnes et al., *Traditions about the Early Life of Abraham,* 307–8.

The eighth-century historian Isḥāq ibn Bishr adds to the account of Kaʿb al-Aḥbār the detail that the angel Isrāfīl cooled the way before Abraham, and Gabriel and Isrāfīl brought Abraham clothing from paradise and kept him company the three days that he was in the fire.[47]

The tenth-century historian al-Ṭabarī repeats Ibn Isḥāq's story, ascribing it to him.[48] He says that the angel Gabriel quenched the fire by saying: "O fire! be coolness and peace for Abraham," and also includes some other comments by Ibn ʿAbbās about how the cold that God commanded to quench the fire would have killed Abraham had it not been followed by peace.[49]

Other Arabic authors repeat the story in al-Ṭabarī with variations. The eleventh-century theologian al-Thaʿlabī repeats al-Ṭabarī's story, which he ascribes to Ibn Isḥāq. The comments of Ibn ʿAbbās, he notes, are echoed in ʿAlī ibn Abī Ṭālib.[50] The eleventh-century chronographer al-Ṭarafī reports the story as taken from al-Ṭabarī.[51] The eleventh-century theologian al-Zamakhsharī repeats a shortened version of al-Ṭabarī's story.[52] The twelfth-century Imami scholar Rāwandī repeats the story from al-Ṭabarī but claims to have it from a very different chain of authority.[53] Other Arabic versions of the story occur later, but they need not concern us here.

An undated Hebrew text first published in the eighteenth century in Constantinople called *The Story of Abraham Our Father from*

---

47. Isḥāq ibn Bishr, *Mubtadaʾ al-dunyā wa-qiṣaṣ al-anbiyāʾ*, folio 168B, in Tvedtnes et al., *Traditions about the Early Life of Abraham*, 323.

48. Al-Ṭabarī, *Tārīkh al-rusūl wa-al-mulūk*, 252-70 (30), in Tvedtnes et al., *Traditions about the Early Life of Abraham*, 340-41.

49. Al-Ṭabarī, *Tārīkh al-rusūl wa-al-mulūk*, 252-70 (30-34), in Tvedtnes et al., *Traditions about the Early Life of Abraham*, 341-42.

50. Al-Thaʿlabī, *Kitāb ʿarāʾis al-majālis fī qiṣaṣ al-anbiyāʾ*, 2:10, in Tvedtnes et al., *Traditions about the Early Life of Abraham*, 364-65.

51. Al-Ṭarafī, *Qiṣaṣ al-anbiyāʾ*, 93-96, in Tvedtnes et al., *Traditions about the Early Life of Abraham*, 378.

52. Al-Zamakhsharī, *Al-Kashshāf ḥaqāʾiq al-tanzīl*, 2:578, in Tvedtnes et al., *Traditions about the Early Life of Abraham*, 412-13.

53. Rāwandī, *Qiṣaṣ al-anbiyāʾ*, 4, 6, in Tvedtnes et al., *Traditions about the Early Life of Abraham*, 415-16.

What Happened to Him with Nimrod preserves Kaʿb al-Aḥbār's account of the angel Gabriel conversing with Abraham as he is lying on the catapult.[54] This shows interaction from Muslim sources and a willingness to borrow back details from them.

The undated Hebrew text *Midrash of Abraham Our Father* takes the Babylonian Talmud's account and changes the angel from Gabriel to Michael, a slight return to the *Midrash Rabbah* versions attributed to Eliezar.[55]

Placing the Coptic account of the angel delivering Abraham from the fire into the other accounts of the angel's involvement with the deliverance of Abraham shows a stark contrast with most Jewish and Muslim versions of the story. The Coptic version somehow preserves a detail otherwise only preserved by Eliezar ben Jacob and rejected by the majority of the rabbis.

Martyrdoms

In our focus on this as an Abraham story, we should not forget that this story has some affinities with the rich tradition of Coptic martyrdoms. Coptic martyrdoms, as such accounts are called, take an almost sadistic pleasure in describing gruesome tortures inflicted on the martyrs. Burning the martyr is one of these tropes.

In the second martyrdom of Apa Victor, Victor is thrown into the furnace that heats the baths, and then "Michael the holy archangel came down from heaven and went into the furnace of the bath and spread under Apa Victor his holy cloak and caused the flame of the fire to become like the wind of the first hour. (ⲁϥⲃⲱⲕ ⲉ̅ϩⲟⲩⲛ ⲉⲡⲙ̅ⲧ̅ⲱⲕ ⲛⲧⲥⲓⲟⲟⲩⲛ. ⲁϥⲡⲱⲣϣ̅ ϩⲁⲣⲟϥ ⲛⲁⲡⲁ ⲃⲓⲕⲧⲱⲣ ⲛⲧⲉϥⲥⲧⲟⲗⲏ ⲉⲧⲟⲩⲁⲁⲃ. ⲁⲩⲱ ⲁϥⲧⲣⲉⲡϣⲁϩ ⲙ̅ⲡⲕⲱϩⲧ̅ ϣⲱⲡⲉ ⲛⲑⲉ ⲛⲟⲩⲧⲏⲩ ⲙ̅ⲡⲛⲁⲩ ⲛϣⲱⲣⲡ̅.)"[56] Again in the fourth martyrdom of Apa Victor, Victor

54. *The Story of Abraham Our Father from What Happened to Him with Nimrod* 32, in Tvedtnes et al., *Traditions about the Early Life of Abraham*, 174.

55. *Midrash of Abraham Our Father* 4, in Tvedtnes et al., *Traditions about the Early Life of Abraham*, 179.

56. Second Martyrdom of Apa Victor, fol. 13b–14a, in Budge, *Coptic Martyrdoms*, 24–25, 276–77.

is thrown into a furnace that has been heated for four days, but he is not harmed.[57] He is finally beheaded. The manuscript for Apa Victor dates to AD 951. The detail about Michael coming down and making the fire like the morning breeze is shared with the Islamic accounts about the sacrifice of Abraham.

An exceptional example is the martyrdom of Eustathius. This martyrdom is exceptional in many ways. First, it takes place during the reigns of Trajan and Hadrian rather than of Diocletian, when most Coptic martyrdoms are set. Second, it is modeled on the recognitions genre. Third, there are no protracted tortures; the family is put to death inside a burning bull.[58] The miracle, like that of Njál and his wife in *Brennu-Njals Saga,* is that the bodies are preserved.[59]

The treatment of human sacrifice by burning in the Abraham homily differs from those in the martyrdoms because Abraham is not repeatedly tortured and then put to death. He is saved by an angel and that is the end of the attempts on his life. More verbiage is spent on the aftereffects of the attempted burning than describing the act itself, which seems to be of excessive interest in Coptic martyrdoms.

Conclusion

The Coptic homily on Abraham interacts with various genres and types of stories available in Coptic and in the wider ancient world. Like most Egyptian stories about Abraham, it does not fit into the standard mold that we have come to expect from other Jewish, Christian, and Muslim accounts of Abraham's attempted sacrifice.

I am certain that Kent can think of other Egyptian accounts in which a king attempts to put Abraham to death only to have him

---

57. Fourth Martyrdom of Apa Victor, fol. 21b-22a, in Budge, *Coptic Martyrdoms,* 37-38, 290.

58. The Life of Saints Eustathius and Theopiste, fol. 20b-22a, in Budge, *Coptic Martyrdoms,* 125-27, 378-79.

59. *Brennu-Njals Saga* 128, 131. Interestingly, Njál and Bergthora and their grandson Thord are covered with an ox hide.

delivered by an angel and also have Abraham afterwards attempting to teach the king and his court about the true God through the use of astronomy.

John Gee is a senior research fellow and William (Bill) Gay Professor of Egyptology at the Neal A. Maxwell Institute for Religious Scholarship at Brigham Young University.

CHAPTER 7

ℨ☛

SOUTH ARABIAN POTTERY IN KHOR MUGHSAYL, OMAN: AN EARLY SETTLEMENT CONNECTION

William D. Glanzman

I have had the pleasure of knowing Professor Kent Brown personally since 2001, when we met and discussed various issues about the archaeology of South Arabia in the context of the annual meeting of the Seminar for Arabian Studies in Edinburgh. Subsequently, in 2005, I was asked by Kent to assist him in acquiring a permit to begin archaeological fieldwork in the Dhofar region of Oman, which was originally planned as a very brief and targeted expedition that followed up from Brigham Young University's earlier reconnaissance of the region from the perspectives of geology and botany. In 2006 we went to Oman for a series of meetings with H.E. Abdel Aziz Mohammed al-Rawas and Dr. Said Nasser Alsalmi in the Office of the Advisor to H.M. the Sultan for Cultural Affairs in Muscat, and with Mr. Hassan Abdullah Aljabri, Director of Land of Frankincense Sites, and Mr. Ghanim Said Ashanfari, the Site Supervisor in Salalah. Afterwards, our efforts were kindly rewarded, and the first field season of BYU's Dhofar project was launched in the summer of 2007, under Kent's coordination and codirectorship with Professor David J. Johnson from the Department of Anthropology at BYU, and myself representing Mount Royal's Department of Sociology and Anthropology. One of the interests of the project

that Kent relayed to me was whether or not there is evidence of occupation in the region dating to the sixth century BC.[1]

Khor Mughsayl and Its Exploration

The Mughsayl region of the Rakhyut drainage system is situated
approximately 40 km southwest of Salalah, which was known as
al-Balid in the earlier Islamic sources.[2] The Mughsayl region is defined by the Wadi Ashawq which trends east-west and runs roughly
parallel to the Dhofar coastline, where it turns southward toward
the coast.[3] Just as it turns, it has a confluence with one minor *wādī*
system and its tributaries emanating from the coastal mountains to
the north.[4]

The region was first explored archaeologically by Frank P. Albright in 1952-53, following the legendary, hasty escape from Marib
of the team led by Wendell Phillips.[5] Albright published in 1982 a

---

1. At present, we have undertaken three field seasons of the BYU Dhofar project. Team members in 2007 included: Professor S. Kent Brown as project coordina-
tor; retired geologist Professor William Revell Phillips; Professor David J. Johnson as
codirector and archaeologist; and Mr. Sidney Rempel, a PhD student at Arizona State
University, as archaeologist and surveyor. Team members in 2008 and 2009 included:
Professor Brown as coordinator; Professor Johnson as codirector and archaeologist;
Dr. W. D. Glanzman from Mount Royal as codirector, archaeologist, and ceramicist;
Ms. Gabrièle Gudrian from the University of Münster as registrar; and Mr. Sidney
Rempel as archaeologist and surveyor. During both 2008 and 2009 Mr. James Gee as-
sisted as a volunteer. In 2009 we also had Professor John Robertson of Mount Royal
assisted by his wife Evelyn Robertson as physical anthropologists and archaeologists.
In each field season our representative was Mr. Mohammed Aljahfli.

2. Frank P. Albright, *The American Archaeological Expedition in Dhofar, Oman, 1952-
1953* (Washington, DC: The American Foundation for the Study of Man, 1982), 51-69;
Juris Zarins, *The Land of Incense: Archaeological Work in the Governate of Dhofar, Sultanate
of Oman 1990-1995* ([Muscat]: Sultanate of Oman, 2001), 126.

3. Wm. Revell Phillips, "Mughsayl: Another Candidate for Land Bountiful," *Journal of Book of Mormon Studies* 16/2 (2007): 50.

4. Phillips, "Mughsayl," 50; David J. Johnson and W. D. Glanzman, *Excavations
and Survey around Khor Mughsayl; Brigham Young University 28 June-25 July 2008*. Report
submitted in 2008 to the Office of the Advisor to H.M. the Sultan for Cultural Affairs,
and to Mr. Hassan Abdullah Aljaberi, Director of Land of Frankincense Sites, and to
Dr. Said Nasser Alsalmi, Coordinator of Archaeological Work.

5. Albright, *American Archaeological Expedition*, 1; Wendell Phillips, *Unknown Oman*
(London: Longmans, 1966), 191; Zarins, *Land of Incense*, 96.

brief report on the materials from those explorations in Dhofar, a few of which have been reexamined by Paul Yule.[6] Prior to the arrival of the BYU expedition, the Mughsayl region was also cursorily reexamined by a survey team led by Juris Zarins in 1992–93 and again in 1995,[7] yet most of his survey collection remains unpublished.[8]

In the 2007 field season six major sites were located in a brief reconnaissance survey. During the past two field seasons we have expanded our efforts to include more geological reconnaissance, and we conducted trench excavations at several locations within Mughsayl.[9] During the 2007 field season, Brown, Johnson, and

---

6. Paul Yule and Monique Kervran, "More Than Samad in Oman: Iron Age Pottery from Suhār and Khor Rorī," *Arabian Archaeology and Epigraphy* 4 (1993): 79-83, figs. 3, 4; see Zarins, *Land of Incense*, 97. The publication of the Oman expedition of Wendell Phillips (see Phillips, *Unknown Oman*, 191) has not progressed for several reasons, one of which is the absence of Albright's and Cleveland's site notebooks, numerous artifacts, and many of their photographs from the official archives of the American Expedition for the Study of Man. In the early 1990s the author discussed by phone with Frank Albright the whereabouts of those records, but he was unable to recall. Later phone discussions with Ray Cleveland revealed that some of the documents and artifacts may have perished while under study in Palestine during the Israeli invasion of Jerusalem. Most of the material excavated from Khor Rori, however, seems to have survived. Prior to those discussions, the late Father Albert Jamme discussed the devastation caused by the fire in his office at the Catholic University of Washington, DC, during which some of the records may also have been lost.

7. Zarins, *Land of Incense*, 126, 128.

8. See Zarins, *Land of Incense*, fig. 33d, under "Mughsayl (49)," where at least 12 of the illustrated potsherds bear the site's prefix. Only seven artifacts were described in Albright's publication, *American Archaeological Expedition*, 113, catalog numbers 298-304.

9. Brown, Johnson, and I have focused excavations on three major sites: Site 2B, Site 2C, Site 3, and Sites 5E and 5W (see fig. 1). Site 2B is located on top of the tourist attraction known as al-Qaf (the "cave") at the al-Marneef promontory; this archaeological site is Zarins's "promontory fort" designated as "TA 93:50." (Zarins, *Land of Incense*, 128; see Phillips, "Mughsayl," 57, figs. 17 and 18.) Here, Johnson and Rempel uncovered very promising architectural remains that were barely exposed at the surface, suggesting the presence of something more than a watchtower. Site 2C is in the saddle below Site 2B and was briefly investigated in 2008. Sites 5E and 5W became a focus in 2008; we returned in 2009 to Site 5E, an ancient cemetery complex. (David Johnson, *Archaeological Preliminary Report, Excavations and Site Survey*, 2. Report submitted in 2007 to the Office of the Advisor to H.M. the Sultan for Cultural Affairs, and to Mr. Hassan Abdullah Aljaberi, Director of Land of Frankincense Sites, and to

Rempel excavated three trenches in the eastern part of Site 3, where they found substantial architectural remains largely covered up by deposition over the centuries.[10] In 2008 I continued excavation here with Trench 3D.[11] We have also examined a substantial cemetery complex (Site 5E) as well as structures and sedimentation (Site 5W) at the head of the modern nature preserve; other sites have also been explored by reconnaissance survey (namely, Sites 1, 4, and 6).[12]

Location and Exploration of Site 3

Site 3 (fig. 1) is easily found today atop a limestone outcrop that seems to be the eroded remnant of an uplifted ancient beach, about 500 m from the modern shoreline.[13] It is only about 100 m west of the modern nature preserve known as Khor Mughsayl.[14] The perennial flow of the Wadi Ashawq today is facilitated by modern water pumps. Around the base of the plateau on which Site 3 was built

Dr. Said Nasser Alsalmi, Coordinator of Archaeological Work; Johnson and Glanzman, *Excavations and Survey*.) On an elevated terrace about 8 m above sea level west of the "blowhole" at the base of al-Marneef, below Sites 2B and 2C, Zarins encountered leached lithic materials; no site designation is provided. Sites TA 95:233 and TA 95:238, which he encountered in 1995, are seemingly extraction sites for raw lithic materials just north of the *khōr* itself in a now dry extension of it. (Zarins, *Land of Incense*, 72.) These must be very close to our Sites 5E and 5W.

10. Johnson, *Archaeological Preliminary Report*, 2.

11. Johnson and Glanzman, *Excavations and Survey*, 9-14.

12. See Johnson, *Archaeological Preliminary Report*, 1.

13. Phillips describes the outcrop as a "plateau" ("Mughsayl," fig. 17); it seems to be an uplifted and eroded set of fossilized beach sediments (see fig. 1). See Zarins, *Land of Incense*, 26-31, 50, fig. 20, for a discussion of site location in relation to the geomorphology of the southern coast of Arabia, in particular the Salalah plain, during the remote prehistoric and Neolithic periods, and Zarins, *Land of Incense*, 67, 72, and figs. 25-28, for the relationship of Bronze Age site location to the geomorphological conditions of the Salalah plain, as well as mention of sites located on a terrace and in the dry lower reaches of Mughsayl. See also the discussion of Mauro Cremaschi and Alessandro Perego, "Patterns of Land Use and Settlement in the Surroundings of Sumhuram. An Intensive Geo-archaeological Survey at Khor Rori: Report of Field Season February 2006," in *A Port in Arabia between Rome and the Indian Ocean (3rd c. BC-5th c. AD)*. Khor Rori Report 2, ed. Alessandra Avanzini (Rome: L'Erma di Bretschneider, 2008), for Khor Rori, especially the similarity with the sites with respect to the development of the lagoon and its sandbar.

14. Phillips, "Mughsayl," fig. 21.

Figure 1. Photograph of Site 3 (center ground) from atop an undesignated site; view to SW. The promontory of al-Marneef is in the background, on top of which is Site 2B; Site 2C is in the saddle to its right. All photographs by the author unless otherwise noted.

are eroded caves, still unexplored archaeologically, that have been partially filled up with collapse debris and deposition; some have the remains of fish skeletons and wooden objects within them. To its north, between the outcrop and the low saddle, are the remains of field systems.[15] To the northwest are a series of structures that probably relate to the modern farmstead, and to the west beyond several Islamic and some scattered, possible pre-Islamic burials is a small *wādī* with a modern gas station on its west bank.[16]

Our Site 3 was partially excavated and documented by Albright in 1952, and he provided the designation "habitation" for the site, which he placed as ca. 500 m west of "Hôr Muġsayl" and ca. 400 m from the coastline.[17] Today the local inhabitants identify the nature preserve as Khor Mughsayl, while the modern community to the

15. Phillips, "Mughsayl," figs. 10, 20.
16. Phillips, "Mughsayl," fig. 17.
17. Albright, *American Archaeological Expedition*, 77. Albright erroneously refers to the site as located "southeast" of modern Salalah (ibid., 77). It is southwest of Salalah.

northeast along the coast is identified as al-Mughsayl.[18] In Arabic the basic meaning of *khōr* is "lagoon" or "estuary," a place where plant life is relatively abundant, which would include a place where a perennial freshwater source such as a river (Arabic *nahr*) flows into the sea,[19] as at Khor Rori. This term seems to have been pronounced as "*kho*" by non-Arabic-speaking indigenous inhabitants as recorded by the Bents in the 1890s;[20] we assume they refer here to the Jibbali, who are Mahra speakers.[21] Those meanings best fit the condition of the modern nature preserve and its immediately surrounding landscape, regardless of the flow of water down Wadi Ashawq.

Farmers with camel herds today are present in the Wadi Ashawq and the surrounding region. Given its position and relative ease of access into the Yemen, this *wādī* likely was one of the conduits for ancient camel caravans.[22] Virtually every day we saw herds of camels coming into the *khōr* to graze and access fresh water from the bed of the *wādī* (fig. 2). While the role of the camel herd seems to have changed along with implementing more modern means of wrangling, camels are still used to transport the harvest of frankincense from the trees in the hills above the coast. There are literally millions of frankincense trees growing in this region of Dhofar. In antiquity it was the point of origin for much of the famous trade in aromatics; its remnants are found in the frankincense *sūq* in Salalah. Many of the traditions of the indigenous people of Dhofar are still present today, and caravans traversed the region as recently as the journey of the Bents.

---

18. The meaning of the site's name, if Arabic (as opposed to a place name given by the local Jibbali population), may have something to do with a place of cleansing (personal communications with Gudrian, Johnson, and Ruth Altheim-Stiehl).

19. C. E. Bosworth and J. Burton-Page, "Nahr," in *Encyclopaedia of Islam*, 2nd ed., ed. P. Bearman et al. (Louvain: Brill, 1993), 7:909b.

20. For example, Theodore Bent and Mrs. Bent, *Southern Arabia* (London: Smith, Elder, 1900), 275.

21. Zarins, *Land of Incense*, 131–32.

22. Phillips, "Mughsayl," figs. 10, 11, and 20.

Figure 2. Camels and modern camel wranglers S of Site 3 are in the background; view to SSE. The expedition's white rental vehicle is parked beyond the collapse of Albright's Room L (Albright, *American Archaeological Expedition,* pl. 26, fig. 42).

Site 3 is only one of several archaeological sites near the mouth of the *khōr* of Wadi Ashawq. Informal surveys of the lower reaches of the Wadi Ashawq—part of the Rakhyut drainage system—by the BYU expeditions have revealed many other sites and surface remains, spanning remote prehistory through to the Islamic period.[23] Sites 5E and 5W, as well as a number of unexplored structures, are located adjacent to the head of the *khōr* proper. As yet, no geomorphological study has been conducted to determine the approximate location of the coastline in antiquity or of Site 3 in relation to it. It seems likely that the *khōr* silted up in recent time in a manner similar to that of Khor Rori some 80 km to the northeast, as both have a sandbar blocking the freshwater flow from the *khōr* into the sea.[24]

---

23. For example, a major occupational site with probable burial structures is located in a saddle on the lower shelf of the extension of the mountains that separates Wadi Ashawq from the coast. A cursory surface survey of this site revealed it has only pre-Islamic artifacts along with numerous sea shells strewn about its surface, except where a modern access road has cut into its northern and eastern portions. In 2008 and 2009 Rempel discovered lithics attributable to the Palaeolithic, Neolithic, and Chalcolithic periods along the banks and on a beach exposure of the tributary flowing south into the *khōr.*

24. Phillips, "Mughsayl," figs. 5, 17, and 21.

Albright's excavation of the habitation site, which he suggested may have been a fishing village, focused upon the extant western-most architectural complex atop the eroded outcrop. Here he discovered a series of rooms with mostly Islamic occupation, yet he speculated the presence of pre-Islamic occupation based on masonry characteristics.[25] Zarins surveyed this site and the adjacent areas during 1992, 1993, and 1995. Although he does not specifically locate or directly state which site is identified by his survey designation as the "Khor Mughsayl complex (TA 92:49),"[26] his citation to Albright's report makes that association clear. Hereafter, we shall refer to Albright's "habitation" and Zarins's "TA 92:49" as Site 3 of the BYU Dhofar project.

Stratified Sequence from Site 3

Site 3 was selected to excavate in part because Albright had excavated the first trenches at the site in 1952-53, and in part because it is such an easily encountered site near the *khōr* proper and close to the coastline. The BYU team excavated a series of three trenches in 2007 (Trenches 3A, 3B, and 3C), and in the 2008 field season we excavated a larger additional trench (Trench 3D; fig. 3). During the excavations

Figure 3. Kent Brown setting up for photographs of Trench 3D on Site 3; view to S, toward coast of Indian Ocean. Note the masonry debris of Albright's Rooms L on left and K on right (see Albright, *American Archaeological Expedition*, pl. 26, fig.42).

25. Albright, *American Archaeological Expedition*, 77-79.
26. Zarins, *Land of Incense*, 72, 128.

a relatively small quantity of potsherds was recovered from several deposits, some of which can be dated stylistically (see table 1). While absolute dates might be obtainable from ^{14}C analysis of some organic remains recovered in 2007, the analysis has yet to be undertaken; no coins or inscriptions have been found, and no glass or other datable artifact categories have been uncovered. For now, we must rely solely upon relative dating for the site's chronology, specifically upon stylistically datable pottery from stratified contexts.

Table 1. Comparative stratigraphy and chronology between trenches in Site 3 (2007-2008 field seasons), in reverse stratigraphic order (top to bottom) by locus.

Trench 3A	Trench 3B	Trench 3C	Trench 3D
000 (surface)	000 (surface)	000 (surface)	000 (surface)
---	---	---	A
001 (topsoil)	001 (topsoil)	001 (topsoil)	001 (topsoil)
L	A, I, IRPW, L, LH	I, IRPW, L	D, IRPW, L
007	003	003	003
D, I, L	IRPW, L	A, D, I, IRPW, L, LH, SCB	IRPW, L
009	004 / BR	005 / BR	002
D, IRPW, L	L	I, IRPW, L, LH	A, D, I, IRPW, L
010 / BR	---	---	005
IRPW, L			D, I, IRPW, L, LH
---	---	---	006
			I, L
---	---	---	009
			D, I, IRPW, L, LH
---	---	---	008
			D, IRPW, L
---	---	---	010 / BR
			L
---	---	---	011 / BR
			L

A	Imported East and South Asian glazed wares
D	"Local" fabric wares with "dot-in-circle" decoration
I	Imported Islamic glazed wares
IRPW	"Indian Red Polished Ware"
L	"Local" fabric wares (with shell and/or limestone inclusions)
LH	Decorated Lug Handle in "local" fabric
SCB	Pre-Islamic South Arabian Shallow Carinate Bowl
/ BR	Deposit rests on Bedrock
---	No deposits, or recovered potsherds

As table 1 reveals, we have Islamic-period glazed ware imports in all of the deposits of Trench 3C, and all of the deposits except the bottommost two in Trenches 3A, 3B, and 3D. The rows of this table do not reflect anything more than the sequence of deposits; due to intervening walls, no secure stratigraphic correlations can be drawn between the four trenches apart from topsoil and bedrock. In the stratified sequences, only those bottommost deposits lacking Islamic glazed wares may be candidates for a pre-Islamic establishment and use of the eastern portion of the settlement; all of the others represent a mixture, deriving from later occupation and use of the site. The datable imports so far suggest an Islamic period occupation between the tenth and thirteenth or fourteenth centuries AD, with a possible extension as late as the sixteenth century AD.[27]

So far, for parallels to probable pre-Islamic pottery we must rely almost exclusively upon Zarins's published survey and excavations. The comment by Zarins that his survey collection has definite parallels to his Iron Age B of Dhofar[28] can be accepted, however only with caution. The admixture of Islamic period imports in most of the excavated deposits makes it clear that one of two scenarios can be invoked to account for this site condition. On the one hand, the easternmost part of the site, at least, may have been heavily disturbed sometime after its initial occupation and use; that disturbance would have occurred during the Islamic period, yet our data cannot specify when. It is likely to have coincided with the major Islamic use of the westernmost part of the site, including the erection and use of a mosque, as well as an Islamic burial ground just outside and to the west of the mosque. On the other hand, it might also be the case that the wares Zarins cites continued in use into the early phases of the

---

27. William D. Glanzman, *Second Initial Report on the Excavated Pottery from Khor Mughsayl, Sultanate of Oman: BYU Project 2007 (Trenches 3A-3C) and 2008 (Trench 3D)*, 24-25. Report submitted in 2009 to the Office of the Advisor to Mr. Hassan Abdullah Aljaberi, Director of Land of Frankincense Sites, and to Dr. Said Nasser Alsalmi, Coordinator of Archaeological Work.

28. Zarins, *Land of Incense*, 128.

Islamic period.[29] This alternative suggestion is made more appealing by the presence of very similar "Indian Red Polished Wares" as well as incised and punctate decorations on the corpora from the Yemeni coastal sites of Sharma[30] and al-Shihr.[31] Clearly, the nature of settlement use by indigenous inhabitants in the region of Dhofar must be examined in detail before we can determine which ceramic forms and decorations are exclusively "pre-Islamic" versus "Islamic." Nevertheless, we can assert with confidence the presence of one imported pre-Islamic vessel type, the Shallow Carinate Bowl.

The Shallow Carinate Bowl (SCB): An Imported South Arabian Pottery Form

During the excavations conducted by Johnson at Trench 3C at Site 3, two potsherds stood out from all others. As we recorded in the pottery registry, two potsherds, KM 2007 3C3. 29 and KM 2007 3C3.30 (fig. 4), seemed to represent imported South Arabian wares. Upon reexamination and extensive post-field searches for parallels in the published literature, we can now assert that registered potsherd KM 2007 3C3.29 is the rim of a definite Shallow Carinate Bowl (SCB); KM 2007 3C3.30 is a body sherd that appears to come from a uniquely decorated carinate form, possibly from a bowl or jar. So far, potsherd KM 2007 3C3.29 stands alone, as no Iron Age

---

29. A similar argument exists for Zarins's type fossil for the first to second centuries AD, the bowl with "dot-in-circle" motif (Zarins, *Land of Incense*, 97), which is commonly encountered in all mixed deposits at Site 3 (see table 1, and W. D. Glanzman, *Initial Report on the Excavated Pottery from Khor Mughsayl, Sultanate of Oman: BYU Project 2007*; report submitted in 2008 to the Office of the Advisor to H.M. the Sultan for Cultural Affairs, and to Mr. Hassan Abdullah Aljaberi, Director of Land of Frankincense Sites, and to Dr. Said Nasser Alsalmi, Coordinator of Archaeological Work). A continuation into the Islamic period for this decorative device on various media including ceramics is certain, and it is still used today. M. C. Ziolkowski and A. S. Al-Sharqi, "Dot-in-Circle: An Ethnoarchaeological Approach to Soft-Stone Vessel Production," *Arabian Archaeology and Epigraphy* 17 (2006): 152–62.

30. Axelle Rougeulle, "Excavations at Sharma, Hadramawt: The 2001 and 2002 Seasons," *Proceedings of the Seminar for Arabian Studies* 33 (2003): 296, fig. 10.1–4.

31. Claire Hardy-Guilbert, "The Harbour of al-Shihr, Hadramawt, Yemen: Sources and Archaeological Data on Trade," *Proceedings of the Seminar for Arabian Studies* 35 (2005): 71, 78–81, figs. 4, 5.

Figure 4. Two photographs of Shallow Carinate Bowl, registry KM 2007 3C3.29 on left of each image and unique organic-tempered carinate vessel, registry KM 2007 3C3.30 on right; exterior views in left image; interior in right. Photographs by the author and Anne Woollam.

pottery imports from South Arabia have been illustrated from any other site in Oman. Its characteristics are largely comparable to the South Arabian repertoire.[32]

This potsherd comes from a vessel that was handmade, as were all of the "local" wares in the corpora from the trenches of Site 3. From hand specimen examination, it is composed of a very dense reduction-fired fabric that is different from the "local" pale brown wares, in that it lacks shell or limestone inclusions. Instead, it has only a minor quantity of organic temper and some small (less than 1 mm long) mica grains along with some rounded lithic inclusions, possibly of quartz.

Organic temper is a feature that characterizes the bulk of South Arabian pottery from sites within the hypothetical territories of the pre-Islamic kingdoms of Maʿin, Sabaʾ, Qataban and ʾAwsan. In the kingdom of Hadramawt, which generated the South Arabian colony that built up and controlled most, if not all, of the port complex

---

32. For a complete specimen from Hajar Surban in the Wadi Bayhan, see St John Simpson, *Queen of Sheba: Treasures from Ancient Yemen* (London: British Museum, 2002), 140–41; it belongs to the earlier first millennium BC. See also the organic-tempered wares from Hajar Ibn Humayd (ibid., 139–40).

facilities at Khor Rori,[33] the pottery of all pre-Islamic phases is not as well published as one might expect, given the intensity of excavation programs conducted there within the past four decades. The published corpus from Shabwa[34] and that from Gertrude Caton-Thompson's initial excavations of the "Moon Temple" in the Wadi 'Amd, within Hadramawt[35] reveal that many of the wares have organic temper added by the ancient potters to render their clay body workable and plastic.[36] As a result, the wares are seldom dense, in contrast to our specimen. In this respect, it is more similar to a few of the examples of the wares from Caton-Thompson's excavations.

On our potsherd there is no burnished slip; instead, it has a mottled slip that exhibits only a surface sheen (see fig. 4). Mottling occurs either in the firing stage of production, often from use, or even from post-depositional alteration such as exposure to some burning material in the soil matrix of the site. Sheen in ceramics may result from sintering of a fine slip, from polishing the surface before firing, or from use if it was reheated and handled repeatedly. Sheen, however, is not a common characteristic for the SCB, whereas burnishing is the rule.[37]

Our potsherd exhibits a shallow form with a slightly rounded carination and has a diameter of about 19.0 cm (fig. 5). The latter is fully within the range of the SCB rim diameters from Hajar ar-Rayhani in the Wadi al-Jubah, Hajar Ibn Humayd in the Wadi

---

33. Alessandra Avanzini, "The History of the Khor Rori Area: New Perspectives," in *Khor Rori Report 1*, ed. Alessandra Avanzini (Pisa: Edizioni Plus, Università de Pisa, 2002), 13–25.

34. Leila Badres, "Le sondage stratigraphique de Shabwa 1976-1981," *Syria* 67/1-4 (1991): 229–314.

35. Gertrude Caton-Thompson, *The Tombs and Moon Temple of Hureidha (Hadhramaut)* (London: The Society of Antiquaries, 1944); see William D. Glanzman, "Arts, Crafts, and Industries," in *Queen of Sheba: Treasures from Ancient Yemen*, 116, and vessel descriptions in the catalog, 189-90.

36. William D. Glanzman, "Toward a Classification and Chronology of Pottery from HR3 (Hajar ar-Rayhani), Wadi al-Jubah, Republic of Yemen" (PhD diss., University of Pennsylvania, 1994), 137-41.

37. Glanzman, "Classification and Chronology of Pottery," 140.

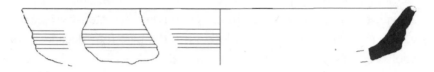

Figure 5. Pottery drawing of Shallow Carinate Bowl, registry KM 2007 3C3.29, drawn by the author.

Bayhan,[38] and elsewhere in South Arabia. Its thickness, varying between 5 and 8 mm, is a characteristic of the later production of the SCB in Saba' and Qataban.[39] Three incised grooves are extant above the carination; the rim is chipped, but does not exhibit any other grooves; this compares well with the SCB in general, which has between one and five incised grooves, although they are usually placed higher and closer toward the rim top.[40]

Taken together, the characteristics of our potsherd seem to derive from a slightly different—or merely a later—tradition of the SCB than exhibited by most of the South Arabian kingdoms. Like the Islamic period imports from the site, the vessel from which this potsherd derived may have entered Dhofar by camel caravan returning from the highland plateau or the Yemen, or even from al-Balid. Perhaps it was brought by caravaneers conducting commerce in aromatics or as a gift brought back by them; it also may have arrived by boat from either ports in Yemen or as near as al-Balid. We simply have no evidence to invoke for its transport.

Dating the SCB at Site 3

No independent dating is available for Trench 3C, nor for any deposit from the trenches on Site 3. Since there is only one potsherd in question here, we cannot invoke any suggestions for development through time. Hence, we must rely on our dated parallels to establish its chronology.

---

38. Glanzman, "Classification and Chronology of Pottery," 137-38.
39. Glanzman, "Classification and Chronology of Pottery," 595-620, table 3.2.
40. Glanzman, "Classification and Chronology of Pottery," 138, 140.

The form to which potsherd KM 2007 3C.29 belongs, the Shallow Carinate Bowl, is a classic South Arabian pottery form, one of the commonest encountered within the Yemen during the span of the late second millennium through to the fifth or fourth centuries BC.[41] The cumulative evidence sifted from the most detailed publications on South Arabian pottery[42] reveals that potsherd KM 2007 3C.29 is a late form. In the Yemen, the thicker variant appears later in the stratified sequence from Hajar ar-Rayhani.[43] The Shallow Carinate Bowl is eventually replaced by the Shallow Angled Bowl,[44] perhaps beginning around the sixth or fifth centuries BC.[45] This latter form continues in deposits that can be placed by calibrated radiocarbon dates within the late fourth to second centuries BC.[46] The date span for that replacement and for all aspects of the Shallow Angled Bowl, however, requires further study.

In reference to his Iron Age A of ca. 1300-300 BC, Zarins notes, "The ceramics, in contrast to the lithics, have little in common with the classical South Arabian sites in the west or North Oman to the east."[47] In reference to his stratified excavations at Shisur, belonging to his Iron Age B of ca. 300 BC-AD 650, however, he does suggest the presence of South Arabian imports into the region: "The earliest ceramics are most likely the simple, typically red, burnished bowls. These are well-known from the South Arabic tradition, and can be considered to date the earliest phase of the fortress. Contemporary to this repertoire may be the black, shiny, carinate ware resembling

41. See Glanzman, "Classification and Chronology of Pottery," 137-49, for a full discussion.
42. Caton-Thompson, *Tombs and Moon Temple*; Gus W. Van Beek, *Hajar Bin Humeid: Investigations at a Pre-Islamic Site in South Arabia* (Baltimore: Johns Hopkins Press, 1969); Badre, "Le sondage stratigraphique de Shabwa"; and Glanzman, "Classification and Chronology of Pottery."
43. Glanzman, "Classification and Chronology of Pottery," 140-41, table 3.2.
44. Glanzman, "Classification and Chronology of Pottery," 148, 257-61, table 3.22.
45. Glanzman, "Arts, Crafts, and Industries," 116.
46. Glanzman, "Classification and Chronology of Pottery," 528-31.
47. Zarins, *Land of Incense*, 87.

Attic ware and thus part of the Seleucid era."[48] His last comment about the presence of black, shiny carinate wares is very tempting for a possible parallel. Unfortunately, Zarins did not provide any citation for this supposed Seleucid (late Iron Age B) period parallel, nor did he illustrate any of these particular wares recovered from Shisur, so we have no comparable data for Oman or further afield.

The cumulative evidence, therefore, suggests that registered sherd KM 2007 3C.29 is the only candidate for an artifact whose date is close in time to the hypothesized sixth century BC arrival of migrants from the Levant. The questions of where it originated from and how it arrived are moot for the moment. Given the admixture of Islamic wares with "local" wares in Locus 003 of Trench 3C (see table 1), and the general developmental issues of its typological successor, we cannot assign the production or the use of this form exclusively to the sixth or even the fifth century BC.

Indeed, we have no publications of any stratified excavations for the entirety of Zarins's Iron Age A or B. In the region of Khor Rori, for instance, where both Zarins and the Italian Mission have conducted regional surveys, and at the archaeological site itself, where the Italian Mission is actively undertaking in-depth excavations, there have not yet been any occupational remains excavated that can be placed with certainty earlier than the fourth century BC. The dating obtained from the excavations is based upon comparisons of pottery assemblages to Raybun and other sites in the Wadi Hadramawt, and upon radiocarbon dates from those sites.[49] Even

---

48. Zarins, *Land of Incense*, 112.

49. Alessandra Avanzini and Alexander V. Sedov, "The Stratigraphy of Sumhuram: New Evidence," *Proceedings of the Seminar for Arabian Studies* 35 (2005): 11–17; "Khor Rori: History and Geography," at http://arabiantica.humnet.unipi.it/index.php?id=772 (accessed 8 January 2010). Unfortunately, the recently published volume on Khor Rori (Avanzini, *Port in Arabia*) has very little synthesis of the excavated remains; it is, instead, an interim report with numerous illustrations and descriptions for the trenches yielding pottery and other datable finds of interest to our chronology.

the Iron Age component of al-Balid, which is said to have the characteristic Iron Age B wares of Dhofar,[50] has yet to be published.[51]

Connections to the Book of Mormon?

As a search through the relevant contributions in the archives of the online *Journal of Book of Mormon Studies* reveals (e.g., "Lehi's trail," "Nahom," "Oman"), there are quite a few discussions concerning recent publications on Lehi's trail and the sites in Oman where locations for the end point of Lehi's migration have been suggested.[52] Some of these discussions were written by several of the team members of the BYU expeditions to Dhofar in the 1990s and the current BYU Dhofar project, with Kent Brown weighing in on several issues such as the location of Nahom (Semitic root *NHM*). The main contenders in the literature seem to be Khor Rori, al-Balid (modern Salalah), and Khor Kharfot in the Wadi Sayq. In all cases, the connections are to a time period of ca. 600 BC or the early sixth century BC. Here, too, it is tempting to draw support for Lehi's journey.

Archaeologists the world over are often tempted to draw equations to their research areas with the "earliest" example of some migration, artifact, or technology, as well as with historical events and characters. In the present case, as a cautious archaeologist and ceramic specialist, I would urge caution by all concerned who might want to suggest Site 3 has yielded evidence that can be linked to any particular group, indigenous or otherwise. Indeed, Kent most

---

50. Zarins, *Land of Incense*, 126.

51. Zarins (personal communications 2008, 2009) has noted there is a substantial Iron Age component at the site as well as an earlier Bronze Age component, and the tourist signage posted at the site and in the adjacent Land of Frankincense Museum note their presence, but the ongoing excavations for such a vast site suggest we will have to wait for quite a time before the publications will appear. In the meantime, we do have examples of various wares from the site, some of which seem to be pre-Islamic, published by Paul Yule and K. K. Mohammed, in *Report on Al-Baleed Pottery*, Reference Collection, Ruth-Aachen University (Muscat), Office of the Advisor to H.M. the Sultan for Cultural Affairs. The photographs are rather good, yet there is very little useful information contained in this brief report.

52. See Phillips, "Mughsayl," 49, for a review of the candidates.

admirably made it clear from the beginning that the Foundation for Ancient Research and Mormon Studies and the Neal A. Maxwell Institute for Religious Scholarship would never try to impose any interpretation on the archaeological data; rather, he stressed the data should always "speak for itself."

The data have spoken, and our caveat remains: the earliest occupation evidence we have recovered from Site 3 is the sole Shallow Carinate Bowl potsherd; it could date around the sixth century BC, although it may be a couple of centuries later, and we do not have any means of addressing where or when it was produced nor how it came to be at the site. Most importantly, we still have no way of addressing who may have been involved with its importation into Dhofar. Clearly, Site 3 and other sites in the area of Khor Mughsayl still have more to reveal about pre-Islamic times.

William D. Glanzman is associate professor of archaeology in the Department of Sociology and Anthropology at Mount Royal University in Calgary, Canada.

CHAPTER 8

✣

CYRILLONA'S *ON ZACCHAEUS*

Carl Griffin

E arly Syriac literature was the product of an eastern Christian tradition centered in greater Mesopotamia. Syriac is an Aramaic (i.e., Semitic) dialect, and early Syriac Christianity has been described as "essentially semitic in its outlook and thought patterns."[1] Like authors of the Hebrew Bible, early Syriac writers favored teaching theology through poetry that was extravagant in symbolism and lavish in trope, in stark contrast to the systematic and philosophical prose of the Greek East and Latin West. Because of this and other singular features, early Syriac Christianity has become of ever-increasing interest to church historians.

Unfortunately, little early Syriac literature survives that predates the Council of Chalcedon (451), when theological controversy precipitated the split of the Syriac church into eastern and western communions, each of which developed its own literary tradition. The post-Chalcedonian churches rapidly became hellenized, and

---

1. Sebastian P. Brock, "From Antagonism to Assimilation: Syriac Attitudes to Greek Learning," in *East of Byzantium: Syria and Armenia in the Formative Period*, ed. Nina G. Garsoïan, Thomas F. Mathews, and Robert W. Thomson (Washington, DC: Dumbarton Oaks, Center for Byzantine Studies, Trustees for Harvard University, 1982), 17. For an expansion of this idea, see Brock's *The Luminous Eye: The Spiritual World Vision of Saint Ephrem*, rev. ed. (Kalamazoo: Cistercian Publications, 1992), 14–15.

earlier works were often neglected. Most extant Syriac writings that predate Chalcedon "just happen to have been preserved, totally cut off from their original context, without any indication of when and where they originated. . . . There is no common denominator for this early literature: it consists of individual authors and anonymous works, each with its own characteristics, with very few connections between them. Much of this period soon must have fallen into oblivion."[2]

Cyrillona

One of the most noteworthy of these precious pre-Chalcedonian authors is Cyrillona, and he and his work certainly fit the description just given.[3] He is all but anonymous. His surviving works have been preserved by happenstance, severed from their original context, but with evident merits; however, their historical, literary, and theological antecedents are unclear. Cyrillona's writings are preserved in a single sixth-century manuscript in the British Library (BL Add. 14591).[4] This codex is a miscellany of hymns and homilies, some with named authors and others anonymous. One homily each is attributed to *Qurloka* and to *Quriloka*, clearly variants of the same name, regularized in English as Cyrillona.[5] On stylistic

---

2. Lucas Van Rompay, "Past and Present Perceptions of Syriac Literary Tradition," *Hugoye: Journal of Syriac Studies* 3/1 (2000): §§ 8-9 at http://syrcom.cua.edu/Hugoye/Vol3No1/HV3N1VanRompay.html (accessed 4 May 2009).

3. Detailed introductions to Cyrillona and his work may be found in Dominique Cerbelaud, *Cyrillonas. L'Agneau Véritable: Hymnes Cantiques et Homélies* (Chevetogne: Éditions de Chevetogne, 1984), 7-34; and Costantino Vona, *I carmi di Cirillona: Studio introduttivo, Traduzione, Commento* (Rome: Desclée and Editori Pontifici, 1963), 19-61. A published edition of the Syriac text may be found in Gustav Bickell, "Die Gedichte des Cyrillonas nebst einigen anderen syrischen Ineditis," *Zeitschrift der deutschen morgenländischen Gesellschaft* 27 (1873): 591-93; with corrections in Bickell, "Berichtigungen zur Cyrillonas," *Zeitschrift der deutschen morgenländischen Gesellschaft* 35 (1881): 531-32.

4. On the dating, see J. Josephus Overbeck, *S. Ephraemi Syri, Rabulae episcopi Edesseni, Balaei aliorumque Opera selecta* (Oxford: Clarendon, 1865), xx; and William Wright, *Catalogue of Syriac Manuscripts in the British Museum*, 3 vols. (London: Trustees of the British Museum, 1870-72), 2:669.

5. *Qurloka/Quriloka* is both unattested and inexplicable as a proper name. Cyrillona (*Qurilona*) is not an anciently attested name either, but would be the Syriac

and other internal grounds, three further anonymous works in this manuscript may confidently be ascribed to the same author.[6] The first editor of these texts praised Cyrillona as "the most important Syriac poet after Ephrem," who was the greatest poet of the patristic age.[7] He is certainly in the first rank of Syriac poets and one of the last masters of Syriac poetry's golden age.[8]

There survives no ancient testimony of Cyrillona or his work, and all attempts thus far to correlate him with a known historical figure must be judged unsuccessful. The inconsistent spelling of his name in the manuscript may indicate he was not even known to scribes working just two or three generations later. Based on his reference to a Hunnic invasion of 395,[9] Cyrillona must have been active in the late fourth century, and from the content of his writings we may assume he was a bishop or at least a priest. Three of his poems are based on the Last Supper, and more specifically the Last Supper and Last Discourse as found in the Gospel of John (John 13-17). A fourth poem, apparently a pastoral homily for a feast of all saints, concerns a plague of locusts, an invasion of the Huns, and other calamities. Associated in the manuscript with this homily *On the Scourges* is a short, untitled poem (*soghitha*) conventionally called *On Zacchaeus*.

---

diminutive form of the popular Christian name Cyril (*Qurilos*). Since Syriac *k* (*kaph*) and *n* (*nun*) are similar letterforms, and admittedly the names are badly written in the manuscript, scholars have concluded that the manuscript as it appears to be written is somehow in error. However conjectural, then, the naming of this author as Cyrillona has become a fixed convention.

6. The original editor ascribed to Cyrillona a sixth poem, *On the Wheat*, which I do not accept as genuine; see Cerbelaud, *Agneau*, 21.

7. "Ich halte ihn für den bedeutendsten syrischen Dichter nach Ephräm." Gustav Bickell, *Ausgewählte Gedichte der syrischen Kirchenväter Cyrillonas, Baläus, Isaak v. Antiochien und Jakob v. Sarug* (Kempten: Kösel, 1872), 14. This comment resonated with subsequent scholars, who at times have repeated it in substance or even verbatim, either with attribution to Bickell or simply as their own judgment.

8. So Robert Murray: "After Ephrem and Cyrillona, Syriac poetry falls into a facile and monotonous fluency which only a few writers of genius will transcend." *Symbols of Church and Kingdom*, rev. ed. (Piscataway, NJ: Gorgias, 2004), 340.

9. Cyrillona, *Scourges* 264-65, in Bickell, "Gedichte des Cyrillonas," 586.

I will dedicate the remainder of this paper to a discussion of *On Zacchaeus*, which is one of the earliest works based on the gospel story of Zacchaeus in all of Christian literature.[10] It is likewise one of the earliest Syriac texts devoted to the subject of repentance. Following an introduction, I will survey a number of important themes in this poem and contextualize them within the early Syriac tradition. Particular attention will be given to Ephrem the Syrian (ca. 306-73), Cyrillona's older contemporary and Syriac literature's greatest poet-theologian, whose writings and theology of symbols inform our understanding of Cyrillona on many points.[11] Familiarity with the poem will be helpful to the reader; reference may be made to the translation provided in the final section. All citations of it in my introduction and commentary are by line number. This is the first translation of *On Zacchaeus* into English, based on my own edition of the Syriac text.

Introduction to *On Zacchaeus*

In the manuscript, *On Zacchaeus* bears no title but rather the simple descriptor, "*soghitha* of the homily" (*sugita dileh dmimra*), apparently meaning the preceding homily *On the Scourges*. A *soghitha* is typically a kind of dialogue poem, which *On Zacchaeus* clearly is not, though it does exhibit some other standard features of *soghyatha*, such as 7+7 meter, brevity, stanzaic form, and acrostic structure.[12]

---

10. A hymn attributed to Ephrem, preserved only in Armenian, is devoted to the story of Zacchaeus and would predate Cyrillona if genuine (*Armenian Hymns* 25). A Greek homily on Zacchaeus attributed to Amphilochius of Iconium may also predate this poem (CPG 3239).

11. A basic introduction to Ephrem and his thought may be found in Brock, *Luminous Eye*. A useful anthology of Ephrem in English translation is Sebastian P. Brock and George A. Kiraz, *Ephrem the Syrian: Select Poems* (Provo, UT: Brigham Young University Press, 2006). My citations from Ephrem follow the standard editions conveniently listed, with available translations, in Brock and Kiraz, *Select Poems*, 259-62. Translations are my own unless otherwise noted. Some early writings that come down under Ephrem's name are of uncertain authenticity, which I denote, though their early date nevertheless makes them valuable for this study.

12. On this poetic genre, see Sebastian P. Brock, "Dramatic Dialogue Poems," in *IV Symposium Syriacum 1984: Literary Genres in Syriac Literature* (Groningen—Oosterhesselen 10-12 September), ed. H. J. W. Drijvers et al. (Rome: Pont. Institutum Studiorum

But because the use of the term *soghitha* only becomes well-attested at a much later date, its precise meaning as used here is unclear. This poem reads like a kind of short sermon (and early Syriac sermons were typically poems), but its original setting and use are unknown. Its relationship to *On the Scourges* is likewise not obvious. The two poems may have been composed separately and only later brought together.

The poem derives its modern title from its principal character, Zacchaeus (see Luke 19:1-10). It is not, however, a commentary on the gospel episode, but a discourse on salvation and the mercy of God toward sinners. In Syriac homiletic literature similar works often bear the title *On Repentance* (*datyabuta*). In its brief compass it invokes a number of the most potent and oft-used types and symbols of redemption in the Syriac tradition: the medicine of life, the garment of glory, the shepherd, the fisherman, the fruit of life, Eve and Mary, etc. Nevertheless, it is certainly not just a typological exercise, but a call to repentance and, even more so, a message of hope that presents Zacchaeus as an example of God's mercy toward penitent sinners.

Cyrillona, then, understands the story of Zacchaeus to be that of a penitent finding salvation. This was the story's traditional interpretation. Most interpreters of the Bible have assumed Zacchaeus was a sinner whom Jesus either called to repentance or who was moved to repent through their encounter. A contemporary Syriac biblical commentary portrayed Zacchaeus as, if not yet penitent, at least "praying in his heart" in the sycamore tree that he might entertain Jesus.[13] Cyrillona seems to take the more unusual, though not unique, position that Zacchaeus had repented before climbing the tree.[14] The gospel narrative does not in fact make Zacchaeus a sinner, former or current, except in the minds of a people who despised his profession as

---

Orientalium, 1987), 135-47, and Brock, "Syriac Dialogue Poems: Marginalia to a Recent Edition," *Le Muséon* 97 (1984): 29-58.

13. (Ps.) Ephrem, *Commentary on the Diatessaron* 15.20.

14. See similarly, e.g., Ps. Chrysostom, *De caeco et Zacchaeo* 3 (PG 59:603).

a tax collector. "For in the episode Jesus pronounces not forgiveness but the vindication of Zacchaeus: Jesus announces salvation to 'this house' because he sees that Zacchaeus is innocent, a true 'son of Abraham,' despite the post that he held, which branded him otherwise."[15]

Jesus's approbation of Zacchaeus was unappreciated or misunderstood by early Syriac exegetes, who regularly incorporated Zacchaeus into recitations on penitent sinners, associating him with others such as Rahab (Joshua 2 and 6), the adulterous Samaritan woman (John 4), and especially the "sinful woman" (prostitute) of Luke 7.[16] The collocation of Zacchaeus and the sinful woman was popular doubtless due to Jesus's (favorable) comparison of them both to the Pharisees.[17] Their professions were iconically sinful—in Ephrem's words, "Tax collectors and prostitutes are unclean snares"—making them potent icons of repentance.

> The sinful woman who had been a snare for men—
> he made her an example for penitents.
> The shriveled fig tree that had withheld its fruit
> offered Zacchaeus as fruit.[18]

---

15. Joseph A. Fitzmyer, *The Gospel according to Luke X-XXIV* (Garden City, NY: Doubleday, 1985), 1220-21. See Luke 19:9-10. The term *lost* in v. 10 does not mean Zacchaeus was necessarily a sinner. This verse is actually a fulfillment citation of Ezekiel 34:16, which describes Yahweh gathering scattered Israel as a shepherd. It summarizes the message of this story and is another affirmation that Zacchaeus "too is son of Abraham" (v. 9). In Luke, to the Pharisees, Jesus refers to both publicans and sinners equally as lost sheep, meaning, those outside the fold of the "righteous" who are nevertheless heirs of salvation (see Luke 15:1-7).

16. On the sinful woman in early Syriac literature, see Edmund Beck, "Der syrische Diatessaronkommentar zu der Perikope von der Sünderin, Luc. 7,36-50," *Oriens Christianus* 75 (1991): 1-15; Susan Ashbrook Harvey, *Scenting Salvation: Ancient Christianity and the Olfactory Imagination* (Berkeley: University of California Press, 2006), 148-55; and Hannah M. Hunt, "The Tears of the Sinful Woman: A Theology of Redemption in the Homilies of St. Ephraim and His Followers," *Hugoye: Journal of Syriac Studies* 1/2 (1998) at http://syrcom.cua.edu/Hugoye/Vol1No2/HV1N2Hunt.html (accessed 4 May 2009).

17. See Matthew 21:31 NRSV: "The tax-collectors and the prostitutes are going into the kingdom of God ahead of you."

18. Ephrem, *Hymns on the Nativity* 4.39-41, in Kathleen E. McVey, trans., *Ephrem the Syrian: Hymns* (New York: Paulist, 1989), 92-93, slightly revised. Compare Ephrem,

One of the best examples of this exegetical pairing is found in the introduction to another *soghitha*, one of two extant on the sinful woman:[19]

> The Compassionate Doctor turned aside;
>> towards sinners did He direct His path,
> showing humility towards them
>> so that they might come to Him without fear. . . .
>
> He caught Zacchaeus from the fig tree
>> and Zebedee's sons in the boat,
> likewise the Samaritan woman beside the well,
>> and the sinful one from Simon's house.
>
> The sinful woman heard the report
>> that He was dining in Simon's house;
> she said in her heart "I will go along,
>> and He will forgive me all I have done wrong.
>
> I am yearning actually to see
>> the Son of God who has clothed himself in a body.
> Just as he forgives Zacchaeus his sins,
>> so in his grace he will have compassion on me."[20]

Such depictions of Zacchaeus make him an unsurprising choice as the dramatic subject of this poem on repentance and divine mercy. More subtly, his very name (at least, its first letter) contributes to the poetic structure of this poem, which is an alphabetical acrostic, a

---

Nisibene Hymns 60.9 (Satan speaking): "I had made Zacchaeus the chief of usurers and her (the sinful woman) the chief of prostitutes—Jesus broke my two wings."

19. Both texts were published and translated in Sebastian P. Brock, "The Sinful Woman and Satan: Two Syriac Dialogue Poems," *Oriens Christianus* 72 (1988): 21-62. Brock dates the *soghitha* cited here to between the fifth and seventh century, and given certain parallels to a homily by Jacob of Serugh on the same topic, it is probable that the author knew Jacob's homily, or conversely, this poem was known to Jacob or even authored by him (Brock, "Sinful Woman," 25).

20. *On the Sinful Woman I* 2, 5-7 (trans. Brock, "Sinful Woman," 43-44, slightly revised). Other early Syriac texts on the sinful woman and Zacchaeus include (Ps.) Ephrem, *Commentary on the Diatessaron* 22.5; Ephrem, *Sermon on Our Lord* 42-48; Ephrem, *Nisibene Hymns* 60.1-10; and Ps. Ephrem, *Sermons I* 7.79-88.

popular device for *soghyatha*.[21] The first words of the poem's stanzas all begin with successive letters of the Syriac alphabet as follows: *zayn* (stanzas 1-4), *ḥeth* (stanzas 5-10), *ṭeth* (stanzas 11-14), *yod* (stanzas 15-18), *kaph* (stanzas 19-24), and *lamad* (stanzas 25-28). The varying number of stanzas for which each letter of the acrostic is employed (4 6 4 4 6 4) yields the chiastic structure A B A A B A.

The letters of this acrostic run from the seventh (*zayn*) to the twelfth (*lamad*) of twenty-two in the Syriac alphabet. Some scholars have speculated, based on this fact, that *On Zacchaeus* as we now have it may be incomplete, but I can see nothing in structure or content that would warrant such a thesis.[22] The fact that this alphabetical acrostic does not extend to all the letters of the alphabet indicates nothing in itself. Ephrem authored a large number of alphabetical acrostics (Palmer lists forty-one), and the majority do not extend to the full alphabet.[23] Ephrem's fourteenth *madrasha* of his *Hymns on Faith*, for example, covers the letters *zayn* through *nun*, very similarly to *On Zacchaeus*. In some cases Ephrem's reasons for selecting a certain range of letters is not entirely clear.[24] In this instance, Cyrillona's choice of *zayn* as the starting letter for his poem seems logical enough, given its central character—Zacchaeus (*Zakay*).

---

21. See the selection of such *soghyatha* published in Bruno Kirschner, "Alfabetische Akrosticha in der syrischen Kirchenpoesie," *Oriens Christianus* 6 (1906): 1-69; 7 (1907): 254-91.

22. See Vona, *Carmi*, 30, though he recognizes that nothing can be definitively concluded. Cerbelaud likewise states that *On Zacchaeus* is "certainly fragmentary," though he does not elaborate his reasoning (*Agneau*, 24).

23. See the useful tables in Andrew Palmer, "Akrostich Poems: Restoring Ephraim's *Madroshe*," *The Harp* 15 (2002): 283-85.

24. See the important studies of Andrew Palmer on this topic: "Akrostich Poems"; "The Merchant of Nisibis: Saint Ephrem and His Faithful Quest for Union in Numbers," in *Early Christian Poetry: A Collection of Essays*, ed. J. den Boeft and A. Hilhorst (Leiden: Brill, 1993), 167-233; "Restoring the ABC in Ephraim's Cycles on *Faith* and *Paradise*," *Journal of Eastern Christian Studies* 55 (2003): 147-94; "St Ephrem of Syria's Hymn on Faith 7: An Ode on His Own Name," *Sobornost / Eastern Churches Review* 17 (1995): 28-40; and "Words, Silences, and the Silent Word: Acrostics and Empty Columns in Saint Ephraem's *Hymns on Faith*," *Parole de l'Orient* 20 (1995): 129-200.

While less explicit, one might also discern a thematic structure to the poem that correlates with its acrostic and chiastic structure. *On Zacchaeus* may be divided into four main sections (four, ten, ten, and four stanzas), with the thematic structure A B B' A' and which I have titled:

A The Evil One and Zacchaeus (1-16 = *zayn* stanzas)
   B Fall and Redemption (17-56 = *ḥeth* and *ṭeth* stanzas)
   B' Christ, the Ocean of Mercies (57-96 = *yod* and *kaph* stanzas)
A' Zacchaeus and the Penitent (97-112 = *lamad* stanzas)

Cyrillona begins (A) with the story of a single penitent, a notable and even "chief" sinner. A seemingly incidental detail from Zacchaeus's story, the sycamore tree, becomes a typological point of departure for a meditation on the fall of man (B), in which the entire cosmic drama of sin and salvation is distilled into forty poetic lines. The climax of this drama is the incarnation of Christ and redemption of humanity. While salvation in Christ is a recurring theme throughout, it would seem quite deliberate that at the precise center of the poem "the serpent's bite (is) healed"—humanity is redeemed from the Fall (56).

But moving from the universal again to the specific, Cyrillona particularizes this act of redemption in the figure of Zacchaeus. He is introduced here a second time, now as an example of the patient solicitude of Jesus toward sinners, which Cyrillona elaborates upon at length (B'). But it is only in the final quaternary of stanzas (A') that Zacchaeus clearly becomes more than *an* example of God's redemptive grace. This poem begins with "Zacchaeus the chief," or first (*riša*)—chief or first among whom is left ambiguous (9).[25] But in the end Zacchaeus is clearly made an archetype of divine mercy. He is the chief among penitent sinners, through whom God calls out to all sinners (97), and the antitype of the first man, wrapped in mercy

---

25. See note 56 below.

and reclothed in Adam's lost glory (101-4). Zacchaeus is every sinner who repents and embraces the mystery of God (110).

Commentary

The Evil One and Zacchaeus (1-16)

The theme of Satan's defeat by Christ, and the decline of the devil's power with the rise of Christianity, is common in early Christian literature. It became a favorite theme of apologists, especially in the imperial era, when the rapid expansion of Christianity could be readily adduced as evidence of Christ's victory over Satan. The most notable example of this in the Syriac tradition may be a homily on the fall of the idols by Jacob of Serugh (ca. 451-521),[26] but this theme is found at least as early as Ephrem. Similar to Cyrillona (5-8), Ephrem dramatized the astonishment and dismay of Satan at the desertion of Zacchaeus and the sinful woman from his ranks, the beginning of his downfall:

> If Zacchaeus has become (Jesus's) disciple, and if (the
> sinful woman)
> has hearkened unto him, they have now put a halt
> to our craft.
> The idols are now a laughingstock; their artisans
> derided and their craftsmen ridiculed.[27]

While Ephrem described Satan's waning power among pagans and Jews,[28] Cyrillona celebrates his powerlessness among "the communities of those who have not sinned" (3). Opposing the Evil One is "the Son of Mary," to whom Satan's defecting minions turn for refuge (8) and of whom the chief is Zacchaeus.

---

26. See Paulin Martin, "Discours de Jacques de Saroug sur la chute des idoles," *Zeitschrift der deutschen morgenländischen Gesellschaft* 29 (1875): 107-47.

27. Ephrem, *Nisibene Hymns* 60.10-11; see also *Hymns on the Church* 40.1-4.

28. See *Nisibene Hymns* 60.14-16.

Early Syriac treatments of the story of Zacchaeus, as seen in Ephrem's *Armenian Hymns*,[29] often focus on Zacchaeus's reception of Jesus into his home and his remuneration of those he had defrauded. In contrast, this poem begins with Zacchaeus in the sycamore tree and focuses exclusively on his descent and cheerful greeting of Jesus. Only twenty-four lines are devoted directly to the figure of Zacchaeus, and Cyrillona's discussion of him is very narrowly circumscribed. And here his sycamore tree is as important as the recumbent Zacchaeus.

Early exegetes saw the sycamore tree from which Zacchaeus descends as a rich and multivalent symbol. Cyrillona identifies it first as Zacchaeus's refuge when he escaped from Satan: "the sycamore was a harbor on the path; / he came down from it weary and found rest" (11-12). The symbol of the haven or harbor (*lmina*) has rich typological potential in the Syriac tradition, often connected liturgically with baptism, but used as well in a number of other associations.[30] It was used as a metaphor for Christ as early as the *Acts of Thomas*, and in later liturgical usage (as also in the Manichaean psalms) Christ is called the "harbor of peace" and "harbor of life."[31] But while the sycamore certainly may be employed as a positive scriptural type,[32] here the tree seems to be called a *lmina* less for

---

29. See note 10 above and discussion below.

30. See Sebastian P. Brock, "The Scribe Reaches Harbour," *Byzantinische Forschungen* 21 (1995): 195-202 (esp. 195-96); E. R. Hambye, "The Symbol of the 'Coming to Harbour' in the Syriac Tradition," in *Symposium Syriacum 1972: célébré dans les jours 26-31 octobre 1972 à l'Institut pontifical oriental de Rome: rapports et communications* (Rome: Pont. Institutum Orientalium Studiorum, 1974), 401-11; and Murray, *Symbols*, 249-51.

31. See *Acts of Thomas* 37, 156; Hambye, "'Coming to Harbour,'" 403, 406; Murray, *Symbols*, 250-51, 362.

32. Ephrem alludes to a tradition, also found in Jewish Haggadah, that the tree which caused the fall of humanity also reached out in sympathy to Adam and Eve and even associates that tree with the sycamore of Zacchaeus (*Hymns on Virginity* 35.1-2). But in this particular case, Ephrem describes the tree as "worthy of curses," due to his association of it with the fig tree in Mark 11:12-14 and parallel passages, even if "the leaves of scorn stretched out to the guilty." See McVey, *Ephrem the Syrian: Hymns* (New York: Paulist, 1989), 417 n. 550, who also notes *Hymns on the Crucifixion* 5.15 and the discussion of Tryggve Kronholm, *Motifs from Genesis 1-11 in the Genuine Hymns of Ephrem the Syrian with Particular Reference to the Influence of Jewish Exegetical Tradition*

its function as a harbor or port than as a portal from the life of sin to life in Christ. Zacchaeus does not find rest or refuge in the sycamore, but rather in Christ upon his descent (12).

Zacchaeus descends from the tree weary because, as becomes clear from the narrative, it is a symbol of the fallen world. Cyrillona associates Zacchaeus's sycamore with the tree of knowledge in the Garden of Eden, since in Christ, the "barren fig" (sycamore) becomes fruitful—the tree of life.[33] This association is made explicit at the end of the text, when the penitent comes down from the tree, is planted again in paradise, and clothed in the "garment of mercy," which Adam lost (101-4). This typology is certainly not original to Cyrillona, but unique is his lyrical description of the very shade of the tree becoming luminous before Christ's splendor—a striking bit of poetic imagination (13-16). I think Vona rightly interprets this as a dramatic depiction of Christ dispelling the shadow cast upon the earth by the Fall.[34] A similar understanding is found in Ephrem, who said of Nathanael and his fig tree:

> Blessed are you whom they told among the trees,
> "We have found Him Who finds all,
> Who came to find Adam who was lost,
> and in the garment of light to return him to Eden."
> The world in the symbol of the shade of the fig tree

(Lund: LiberLäromedel/Gleerup, 1978), 219 (to which add 111 n. 66). Elsewhere Ephrem (or one of his school) portrays the sycamore as the antitype of the tree of knowledge: "The former fig tree of Adam will be forgotten, on account of the latter fig tree of the chief tax collector, and the name of the guilty Adam [will be forgotten] on account of the guiltless Zacchaeus." *Commentary on the Diatessaron* 15.20, in Carmel McCarthy, trans., *Saint Ephrem's Commentary on Tatian's Diatessaron* (Oxford: Oxford University Press on Behalf of the University of Manchester, 1933), 240.

33. Exegetes understood the tree of knowledge to be a fig tree—that is, the tree from which Adam and Eve took fig leaves to make garments (see Genesis 3:7). But both the Peshitta and Old Syriac gospels call Zacchaeus's tree a "barren fig tree" (*tita pakihta*; Gk. *sykomorea*), rather than a simple fig tree (*tita*) as found in Genesis. Of course this discrepancy was not prohibitive for exegetes, who found that discrepancy typologically useful (see the quotation from Ephrem cited just below). Cyrillona calls Zacchaeus's tree simply a *tita* (11).

34. Vona, *Carmi*, 29.

is belabored as if in a heavy shadow.
From beneath the fig tree as a symbol of the world,
     you emerged
to meet our Savior.[35]

When we understand the sycamore as a type of the tree of knowledge, the relationship between the call of Zacchaeus from that tree and the following discussion of the Fall becomes apparent.

Fall and Redemption (17-56)

This next section is cohesive even if, as is common in early Syriac poetry, it is more a rondo of symbolism than a linear narrative. Zacchaeus's tree, from which he descends and finds redemption from sin, points us to that tree through which sin came into the world. The tree of knowledge and its fruit are not directly named, but instead invoked through types. The tree was introduced in the image of a sycamore, and now a number of types corresponding to its fruit are introduced—sin, the blood of death, the salt of death, the leaven of death, and grief. Such images are prominent here, but employed in service to a narrative which is devoted to dramatic characters and their relationships: Eve and the serpent, Eve and Mary, Christ and Mary, Christ and Eve, Christ and the Evil One.

In Cyrillona's meditation on the Fall and redemption, the motif of fallen Eve (humanity) being restored to her paradisiacal state takes a central place. While fallen Adam is referenced at the end of the poem (103), the author may have been inspired to focus on Eve here, in part, for poetic reasons. As discussed above, this poem is an alphabetical acrostic, beginning with z (*zayn*) for Zacchaeus. The next letter in the Syriac alphabet and in the acrostic, beginning here, is ḥ (*ḥeth*)—the first letter of Eve's name (*Ḥawa*). While this connects Zacchaeus with the Fall poetically, also significant is the opportunity it provides to discuss Eve's antitype in the economy of salvation, the Virgin Mary.

---

35. Ephrem, *Hymns on Virginity* 16.9 (trans. McVey, *Ephrem the Syrian*, 331).

This section of *On Zacchaeus* has been much referenced in scholarly literature for its exploration of the Eve-Mary typology widely used in the early church.[36] This typology is touched upon in Justin Martyr (103-65), but the first full articulation is found in Irenaeus (d. ca. 202).[37] Irenaeus frames it within his elaboration of Pauline "recapitulation" (see Ephesians 1:10), whereby redemption in Christ comes through a second creation, restoring God's work to its original, paradisiacal form. So Christ the "last Adam" (1 Corinthians 15:45) recovers that which was lost by the first Adam in the Fall, destroying sin and death and restoring humanity to the image and likeness of God. Mary and Eve likewise are cast as antitypes in the drama of redemption:

> For Adam had necessarily to be restored (or, recapitulated) in Christ, that mortality be absorbed in immortality, and Eve in Mary, that a virgin, become the advocate of a virgin, should undo and destroy virginal disobedience by virginal obedience.[38]

---

36. For a general survey and bibliography on the Eve-Mary typology, see G. Söll, "Eva-Maria-Parallele," in *Marienlexikon*, ed. Remigius Bäumer and Leo Scheffczyk, 6 vols. (St. Ottilien: EOS, 1988-94), 2:420-21; on the early church specifically, see Lino Cignelli, *Maria nuova Eva nella Patristica greca (sec. II-V)* (Assisi: Porziuncola, 1966), and Hugo Koch, *Virgo Eva—Virgo Maria* (Berlin: de Gruyter, 1937); and for an incisive synthesis, Jaroslav Pelikan, *Mary through the Centuries: Her Place in the History of Culture* (New Haven: Yale University Press, 1996), 39-52. On the Syriac tradition, see esp. Sebastian P. Brock, *Bride of Light: Hymns on Mary from the Syriac Churches* (Keral, India: SEERI, 1994), 1-3 et passim; Brock, introduction to *Jacob of Serug, On the Mother of God*, trans. Mary Hansbury (Crestwood, NY: St. Vladimir's Seminary Press, 1988), 4-12; Brock, "Mary in Syriac Tradition," in *Mary's Place in Christian Dialogue*, ed. Alberic Stacpoole (Slough: St. Paul Publications, 1982), 182-91; Brock, "The Mysteries Hidden in the Side of Christ," *Sobornost* ser. 7, 6 (1978): 469-71; and Robert Murray, "Mary, the Second Eve in the Early Syriac Fathers," *Eastern Churches Review* 3/4 (1971): 372-84.

37. Justin Martyr, *Dialogue with Trypho* 100.5. On Irenaeus, see Cignelli, *Maria nuova Eva*, 32-39; Luigi Gambero, *Mary and the Fathers of the Church: The Blessed Virgin Mary in Patristic Thought*, trans. Thomas Buffer (San Francisco: Ignatius, 1999), 51-58; and Koch, *Virgo Eva—Virgo Maria*, 17-60.

38. Irenaeus, *Demonstration of the Apostolic Preaching* 33, in Joseph P. Smith, trans., *Proof of the Apostolic Preaching* (New York, NY: Newman, 1952), 69. Cf. Irenaeus, *Against Heresies* 3.22.4; 5.19.1.

We likewise find in Ephrem[39] and Cyrillona the idea of Mary becoming an "advocate" for Eve, in the fuller ancient sense.[40] In the tender image of Mary bearing up Mother Eve, Cyrillona depicts an act of both intercession and compassion:

> The crippled serpent crippled Eve;
>> Mary became feet for her mother.
> The maiden bore up the aged woman,
>> that she might draw life-breath in her
>>> former place. (33-36)

While he does not describe Mary as the feet of Eve, Ephrem invokes several anatomical images to relate Eve and Mary. So while Eve conceives sin through her ear, Mary conceives Jesus through hers, and while Eve is the blind left eye of humanity, Mary is the illuminated right.[41] Very striking is Ephrem's long description of Eve and Mary as two hands, sympathetic and synergistic: "as they move away from one another, they become weak; but when they are brought together, they dominate the world."[42]

---

39. Much has been published on Ephrem's development of the Eve-Mary motif. See, in addition to the general titles above (note 36): Edmund Beck, "Die Mariologie der echten Schriften Ephräms," *Oriens Christianus* 40 (1956): 22-39; P. J. Botha, "Original Sin and Sexism: St. Ephrem's Attitude towards Eve," in *Studia Patristica: Papers Presented at the Twelfth International Conference on Patristic Studies Held in Oxford, 1995*, ed. Elizabeth A. Livingstone, 5 vols. (Louvain: Peeters, 1997), 5:483-89; Paul Krüger, "Die somatische Virginität der Gottesmutter im Schrifttume Ephräms des Syrers," in *Alma Socia Christi V/I* (Rome: n.p., 1952), 77-83; Franz S. Mueller, "Die unbefleckte Empfängnis Marias in der syrischen und armenischen Überlieferung," *Scholastik* 9 (1934): 165-73; Ignacio Ortiz de Urbina, "Le Vergine Maria nella teologia di S. Ephrem," in *Symposium Syriacum 1972*, 89-96; Aristide Serra, *Miryam, figlia di Sion* (Milan: Paoline, 1997), 19-72; and Pierre Yousif, "Marie et les derniers temps chez saint Ephrem de Nisibe," *Études Mariales* 42 (1985): 48-55.

40. The Greek term *paraklētos* (*advocatus* in Latin) may mean "advocate," "helper," or "comforter."

41. See respectively Ephrem, *Hymns on the Church* 49.7 and 37. On Mary conceiving through her ear, see Alois Müller, *Ecclesia-Maria*, 2nd ed. (Freiburg: Universitätsverlag Freiburg, 1955), 150-51. Brock cites this as a "quaint idea" and example of the "purely 'mythological' elements" introduced by Syriac authors in developing the contrast between Eve and Mary (Brock, "Mary in Syriac Tradition," 188).

42. See Ephrem, *Hymns on the Church* 35.2-14 (quotation from 35.7).

But one of the most striking literary parallels to Cyrillona is a passage in a Pseudo-Ephremian hymn on Mary, of uncertain date, which is found in abbreviated form in later liturgical collections:

> (7) In Mary is Eve's bowed head raised up again,
> for she has carried the Child who seized hold
>   of the adder.
> Those fig leaves of shame have been swallowed
>   up in glory!
>
> (8) Two virgins have there been for humanity,
> one the source of life, the other the cause of death:
> in Eve death arose, but Life shone out through Mary.
>
> (9) The daughter gave support to her mother
>   who had fallen,
> and because she had clothed herself in fig
>   leaves of shame,
> her daughter wove and gave to her a garment of glory.[43]

Ephrem and Cyrillona both see in Mary not only the antitype of Eve, but a source of life who renews her mother through her Holy Child. So Cyrillona observes,

> Eve grew old and bent;
>   she begat Mary and was made young;
> and her daughter's child took it upon himself
>   to atone for the sins of his ancestor. (37-40)

Throughout this section Cyrillona interweaves and contrasts images of the Fall with the symbols of Christ the Redeemer, culminating with:

> The sweet maid bore the Good Fruit
>   and placed it with her hands in the manger.
> The nations ate it and, by its savor,
>   the serpent's bite was healed. (53-56)

---

43. Ps. Ephrem, *Hymnus de Beata Maria* 2.7-9 (Lamy 2:525; trans. Brock, *Bride of Light*, 36).

The contrast implicit here between the fruit of death and the fruit of life (the Body of Christ/Eucharist) is one of many Eucharistic typologies employed by Christians from a very early date and is first found in the Syriac tradition in Aphrahat and Ephrem.[44] Uniquely in Syriac, the fruit (*pi'ra*) of life even suggests homophonically the unleavened bread of the Eucharist (*paṭira*). Cyrillona here makes no distinction between the infant body of Christ laid by Mary in the manger, "the Good Fruit" of her womb (53-54), and the Eucharistic host which heals the nations with its savor (55-56). The Eucharistic fruit of life and Christ the Fruit of Life represent a single salvific reality.

Cyrillona employs a second familiar Eucharistic typology, this one looking not to the Garden but to pharmacology. Two verbs for mixing used here (*mzg* and *ḥlṭ*; 21-22, 24) were regularly employed by Ephrem in developing his typology of Christ as the Medicine of Life.[45] They are used of both the mixing of wine and the compounding of medicine. In theological usage, they may describe the hypostatic union of God and man in Christ. So Christ mingled divinity with humanity in the Incarnation and became the Medicine of Life. Likewise, when the Eucharistic wine is mixed and consecrated, it too becomes the medicine of life, the sanctifying blood of Christ. Typologically, Christ and the Eucharist are one Blood, one Medicine, and one Fruit of Life. Each of these symbols is implicit in the other, and may be freely interchanged in theological typology,

---

44. This broad and pervasive Eucharist imagery comprises an "intricate web of typology" (Brock) and "a very complex theological tradition" (Amar), which I just touch upon here. But for Aphrahat, Ephrem, and the early Syriac tradition, see the discussions in Joseph P. Amar, "Perspectives on the Eucharist in Ephrem the Syrian," *Worship* 61 (1987): 441-54; Edmund Beck, "Die Eucharistie bei Ephräm," *Oriens Christianus* 38 (1954): 41-67; Sebastian P. Brock, "Mary and the Eucharist: An Oriental Perspective," *Sobornost/Eastern Churches Review* 1/2 (1979): 50-59; François Graffin, "L'eucharistie chez saint Éphrem," *Parole de l'Orient* 4 (1973): 93-121; and the numerous studies of Pierre Yousif, culminating in his *L'Eucharistie chez Saint Éphrem de Nisibe* (Rome: Pontificium Institutum Orientale, 1984).

45. See Aho Shemunkasho, *Healing in the Theology of Saint Ephrem* (Piscataway, NJ: Gorgias, 2002), 150-51. A third "mixing" term employed here (*ptk*; 25) is more rare, and its use in this context seems unique to Cyrillona.

often assisted by their poetic assonance. So Cyrillona contrasts here, for example, the blood of death (*dma dmawta*) (22) with the Medicine of Life (*sama dhaye*) (26).

A third, related typology is implicit here as well: the Ephremian contrast between the poison of death (*sam mawta*) (poison of the serpent/fruit of death) and the Medicine of Life (*sam haye*).[46] Ephrem relates the poison and the Medicine, the fruit and the Fruit, in complex ways, since the Eucharist itself can be not only the remedy to the poison, but a poison itself if partaken by the unworthy:

> The Fruit came down and went up
> > to you in love—rejoice!
> Its sweetness should gladden you;
> > its exploration will not harm you.
> It is the Medicine of Life, which is able
> > also to become the poison of death.
> Take from it what it has produced—
> > also give to it that it might produce.[47]

While Cyrillona also contrasts the Medicine/Fruit with the venom of the serpent, he places his emphasis on the healing contained in its "sweet savor," which "overpowered the lethal salt of death" and healed the serpent's bite (27-28, 55-56).

Christ, the Ocean of Mercies (57-96)

Leaving the grand narratives of sin and redemption, Cyrillona returns to Zacchaeus. While Zacchaeus was introduced as a notable penitent (9-12), it is only now that his typological significance becomes fully clear. He is a vessel of mercy, a symbol of the serpent's

---

46. See Shemunkasho, *Healing*, 150-54, and further on this typology: 147-54, 236-37, 341-44, 381-82, 466. Since the same Syriac word (*sama*) is used for both poison or medicine (among other things), this trope is lost in translation.

47. Ephrem, *Hymns on Faith* 5.16. Elsewhere Judas is invoked as an example of one who received the Medicine unworthily and for whom it therefore became a poison (Ephrem, *Hymns on the Unleavened Bread* 18.16-17).

defeat, and proof that "compassion is greater than sin" (see Romans 5:20):

> The Ocean of Mercies flowed forth
> 	to wash away the impurity of Zacchaeus,
> and because compassion is greater than sin,
> 	the sinner arose without punishment. (57-60)

The floods hidden in Mary (45) now become the Ocean of Mercies that washes away Zacchaeus's sin. Here this is a reference to baptism, but in Cyrillona's sermon *On the Scourges*, a similar image is also invoked for the holy power vested in the relics of the saints and martyrs: "An Ocean without measure dwells in them, / which was conceived in the womb, / and was hung on the wood, / and was entombed in the sepulcher, / and worshipped on high."[48]

The typological employment of Zacchaeus as a symbol of God's mercy toward sinners is not unusual, but neither was it universal among early authors. His general employment as a notable penitent has been mentioned, but other lessons were drawn from his story as well. Ephrem notes, for example, the significance of his shortness of stature: "The example of Zacchaeus teaches me: because he reached out to you, / his shortness grew through you and, seeking, he came to you. / That word from you brought to you / him who had been far from you."[49]

Unlike Cyrillona, longer treatments of the story of Zacchaeus rarely focus on Zacchaeus coming down from the tree, but rather on his declaration: "Look, half of my possessions, Lord, I will give to the poor; and if I have defrauded anyone of anything, I will pay back four times as much" (Luke 19:8 NRSV). This is the focus of an Armenian hymn attributed to Ephrem, in which Zacchaeus becomes a model for the virtue and heavenly rewards of almsgiving:

---

48. *Scourges* 22-26 (Bickell, "Gedichte," 584). Cf. note 57 below on the baptismal imagery evoked in lines 45-48.

49. Ephrem, *Hymns on Faith* 25.14; cf. *Hymns against Heresies* 7.5, where Ephrem refers to "midgets" like Zacchaeus (*pelgut bnay 'naša*).

> First he satisfied his obligation, then thereafter
> > began to give alms.
> He paid first what he owed, and afterwards
> > gave for profit.
> When he restored all he had defrauded,
> > he paid his debts,
> And when he gave away half of his goods,
> > he gave to God with profit.
> O debtor who unexpectedly became a creditor![50]

But in Cyrillona there is no mention of almsgiving. Zacchaeus is used here solely as an example of penitence and of God's mercy.

This emphasis on mercy is in contrast to many similar texts on repentance which focus more on the divine punishments awaiting the unrepentant. That is, for example, the central theme of an early sermon on repentance attributed to Ephrem, a grueling recitation of the agonies that the sinful soul does now and, infinitely more so, will yet have to bear:

> Better is the grave without guilt / than the light
> > (of this world) full of sins.
> Whoever does sin here, / him will the
> > darkness overcome in the end.
> So what shall I do, my friends? / For both here
> > and there dwell I in grief,
> Here out of fear, because of my sins, / and there
> > because of punishment.[51]

---

50. (Ps.) Ephrem, *Armenian Hymns* 25.10-4. My translation is from the Latin version of Louis Mariès and Charles Mercier, *Hymnes de Saint Ephrem conservées en version arménienne* (Paris: Firmin-Didot, 1961), 139. Compare Ps. Ephrem, *Sermons on the Blessing of the Table* 10.8: "And when He was invited to the house of Zacchaeus, He showed there a sign: there He changed the plunderers and made them givers; Zacchaeus gave back the fourfold of all which he possessed," in Mary Hansbury, trans., *Hymns of Saint Ephrem the Syrian* (Oxford: SLG, 2006), 39.

51. Ps. Ephrem, *Sermons I* 5.119-26.

Beck has suggested that two other sermons, materially related to this one, were in fact intended as a tempering response to its "radicalism."[52] There is nothing to indicate that *On Zacchaeus* is a response to such oppressive rhetoric, but certainly Cyrillona is principally concerned with extolling the mercies of God, while not denying in any way his sure justice.

Cyrillona emphasizes divine justice with his repetition of the title "the Just One" (*ki'na*) (73, 85). But like any good pastor, he is also sure to remind of God's "stern and terrible rebuke" (77) and of his "bow (drawn) to terrify us" (79). God is an inquisitor who has prescribed a mournful judgment for transgressors (85-88) and whose "wrath has claim on those who refuse" to repent (96). Nevertheless, God is both "just *and* kind— / fear, O sinners, but also be confident" (93-94). Christ comes as the "Inquisitor who bears mercy" (88), who does not feel human anger toward sinners or take pleasure in their destruction (66). But instead, as the good shepherd, he seeks them out (61-64); "abundantly forgives" (77); "teaches the meaning" of salvation (74), and prepares the way to mercy (107-8), which he is eager to grant (92); and rejoices with the angels in the repentant sinner (67-68, 83). "Not a single day has he allowed / fury and wrath to remain upon us" (69-70; cf. Ephesians 4:26).

Zacchaeus's joyful countenance is scriptural (87; cf. Luke 19:6) but, given his sinful state, Cyrillona feels a need to temper that joy. He therefore ascribes to him a (nonscriptural) timidity and reticence which is proper for the penitent:

> How timid, nonetheless, was Zacchaeus—
>> he was afraid to seek mercy;
> but how forthright was our Lord—
>> he was eager to grant mercy. (89-92)

---

52. Edmund Beck, *Des heiligen Ephraem des Syrers Sermones I* (Louvain: Secrétariat du CorpusSCO, 1970), xx.

The impression conveyed is that Zacchaeus could not restrain his joy before such swift mercy, however much such a sinner should rightly feel to fear and mourn. This small expansion of the gospel narrative shows a pastor's concern to read into the biblical text the lived experience of the penitents in his care.

Zacchaeus and the Penitent (97-112)

In the preceding section Cyrillona develops Zacchaeus as an archetype of God's mercy to penitent sinners. He speaks of the body of sinners first as "they" (61-62, 65) and then, more personally, as "us" (70-74, 79). But it is only now in his closing exhortation that Cyrillona connects Zacchaeus directly with his audience:

> In Zacchaeus he calls out to you sinners,
>> that you may see his love, for how anxious is he!
> For he casts his nets like a fisherman,
>> that the leader of your cohort may rejoice in you.
>> (97-100)

The metaphor he invokes is of Jesus the fisherman as the Fisher of Men (cf. Matthew 4:18-22; Mark 1:16-20; Luke 5:1-11). The fact that birds, like fish, were caught in nets and snares underlies a more expansive typology to which Cyrillona tacitly refers. Zacchaeus the publican was a snare, yet himself was snared like a bird from the sycamore by Jesus's net, which saved him from the snares of the devil. While purely allusive here, these types were skillfully interwoven by Ephrem in an extended meditation on those caught by the Fisher:

> Into the stream from which fishermen come up,
> the Fisher of all plunged, and he came up from it.
> At the stream where Simon was catching his fish,
> the Fisher of men came up and caught him. . . .
> Tax collectors and prostitutes are unclean snares;
> the Holy One caught the snares of the Deceitful One.
> The sinful woman who had been a snare for men—
> He made her an example for penitents.

The shriveled fig tree that withheld its fruit
offered Zacchaeus as fruit.
Fruit of its own nature it had not given,
but it gave one rational fruit.[53]

Instead of "rational fruit," Cyrillona has the barren tree (the Fall) yielding a barren seed (fallen man) which God plants again in paradise and clothes with mercy (101-4). Cyrillona is moved to conclude, in the voice of Zacchaeus,

I have entered into your house instead of the sycamore;
I shall live in the mystery which I embrace,
for your cross is higher than the bough—
multiply the floods of your mercy upon me! (109-12)

The cross of Christ rises above that tree of sin, the shadow of the fall made luminous in the shadow of the cross (15-16), the sinner (Zacchaeus/Adam) again receiving a robe of light and glory (104).[54] For Cyrillona, the church ("your house") is the antitype of the tree, the paradise into which penitents enter as a refuge from the fallen world. The cross is a nest higher than any tree, to which the contrite sinner swiftly wings. His thoughts and joy are echoed in the verses of a contemporary homilist:

See, my Lord, how I have escaped from sin / like the bird
from the snare (Psalm 123:7).
I wish to flee to the nest of your cross, / which the
serpent cannot approach.

---

53. Ephrem, *Hymns on the Nativity* 4.35-36, 39-42 (trans. McVey, *Ephrem the Syrian*, 92-93, slightly revised). On Christ as the Fisher of Men, see also Murray, *Symbols*, 176-78. On the "shriveled fig," see note 33 above.

54. On the robe of glory, see the following studies by Sebastian Brock: "Clothing Metaphors as a Means of Theological Expression in Syriac Tradition," in *Typus, Symbol, Allegorie bei den östlichen Vätern und ihren Parallelen im Mittelalter: Internationales Kolloquium, Eichstätt 1981*, ed. Margot Schmidt and Carl-Friedrich Geyer (Regensburg: Pustet, 1982), 11-40; *Luminous Eye*, 85-97; "The Robe of Glory: A Biblical Image in the Syriac Tradition," *The Way* 39/3 [= *Spirituality and Clothing*] (1999): 247-59; and *St. Ephrem the Syrian, Hymns on Paradise* (Crestwood, NY: St. Vladimir's Seminary Press, 1990), 66-72.

See, my Lord, how I have flown away from my guilt / as
the dove from out of the nets (Psalm 55:6-7).
I wish to dwell in the heights of your cross, / where the
dragon cannot come.[55]

Translation

Cyrillona, *On Zacchaeus*

[*zayn*] The Accursed One has armed his blade against us,
and brandishes his sword to frighten us,
but among the hosts of those who have
not sinned,
among them it has melted like wax.

The Evil One trembles, for the companies of the just
have grown to be more than his band,
and his own troops are in revolt against him
and take refuge in the Son of Mary.

Zacchaeus the chief[56] escaped from him,
10   for his Lord met him and received him well.
The sycamore was a harbor on the path;
he came down from it weary and found rest.

The splendor of Jesus shone before him
who reclined on the tree in the path,
insomuch that the shadow cast upon the bough
became luminous in appearance!

---

55. Ps. Ephrem, *Sermons I* 7.554-61.

56. Syr. *riša*. Aside from its nominal usage ("head," "point"), *riša* is a widely used modifier to designate the first or principal example of *x*. Vona construes *riša* with the preceding couplet—"Zaccheo, capo dei peccatori" (Vona, *Carmi*, 28; cf. 1 Timothy 1:15)—that is, chief among Satan's rebellious troops. *Riša* may also refer more prosaically to his designation as a chief tax collector, shortened from *riš maksa*. While the Old Syriac gospels and the Peshitta render *rab maksa* for the Greek *architelōnēs* at Luke 19:2, Ephrem uses *riš maksa* (*Nisibene Hymns* 60.9), as does the later Harklean version.

[*ḥeth*]   Eve succumbed, besieged
        by counsel which made her an exile;
    Mary arose radiant—
20   she reclaimed the grace of the matriarch.

    The serpent mixed sin in secret
        and mingled (it) with the blood of death for Eve,
    and that she might not be loath to drink it,
        he filled her full of sins in the guise of a friend.

    Our Lord mixed wine with his blood;
        he confected the medicine of life 'till it
            brimmed over.
    His sweet savor descended and overpowered
        the lethal salt of death.

    Sins so beset Eve in Eden
30   that, succumbing, they drove her from the garden,
    and because she inclined her ear to the voice
            of the serpent,
        she became estranged from that garden.

    The crippled serpent crippled Eve;
        Mary became feet for her mother.
    The maiden bore up the aged woman,
        that she might draw life-breath in her former place.

    Eve grew old and bent;
        she begat Mary and was made young;
    and her daughter's child took it upon himself
40   to atone for the sins of his ancestor.

[*ṭeth*]   She had hidden there in our dough
        the leaven of death and grief;
    Mary strove to remove it,
        so that all creation would not be corrupted.

He hid his floods in the virgin,
    life flowed from the glorious maid;
his streams caught upon and climbed the mountains,
    and the depths and torrents climbed higher
        than them still![57]

This news about the Son brought low the Evil One,
50   whose soldiers too fell upon their faces.
He revealed himself (to them) when they
        questioned him,
    and they withered like straw, for they could not
        bear him.[58]

The sweet maid bore the Good Fruit
    and placed it with her hands in the manger.[59]
The nations ate it and, by its savor,
    the serpent's bite was healed.

[*yod*]   The Ocean of Mercies flowed forth
    to wash away the impurity of Zacchaeus,
and because compassion is greater than sin,[60]
60   the sinner arose without punishment.

Jesus, though smitten by adversaries,
    see how he was not angry with sinners;
in his mercy he was like a shepherd,
    and he went out and sought out that errant one.

---

57. The author's meaning here has not been clear to translators. It is the first instance of the recurring motif of Christ's vivifying mercy flowing out to us (cf. 57-58, 112), but the referent and meaning of the prepositional phrase *menhun* ("than them"; 48) is ambiguous. Perhaps the imagery is baptismal: Life (Christ) issues from Mary, flowing higher than the tops of the mountains, as did the cleansing Noachide floods, symbol of baptism (cf. Genesis 7:19-20; 1 Peter 3:18-22).

58. "The allusion remains obscure. Is it referring to an episode from the passion of Jesus (the soldiers falling backwards at Gethsemane: John 18:6; or those who guarded the tomb: Matthew 18:4?), or a more general reference to the fate of the impious?" (Cerbelaud, *Agneau*, 112 n. 90).

59. See Luke 2:7.

60. See Romans 5:20.

He swore this by himself,[61] that they[62] might
    have faith in him:
"I take no pleasure in those who perish;
in one sinner, if he repents,
    the Father rejoices with his angels."[63]

Not a single day has he allowed
70   fury and wrath to remain upon us;[64]
he has taken care that we might become like him,
    for he abundantly forgives those who go astray.

[kaph]   The Just One does not wish to destroy us,
    and he teaches the means (for salvation),
        that he might aid us;
the watchers on high revere him,
    but by those on earth, see how he is condemned!

His stern and terrible rebuke
    do tears appease and mollify;
he draws his bow to terrify us—
80   mercy opposes it and it goes slack!

When he was passing next to the sycamore,
    he saw the debtor, and regarded (him),
        and stopped;
just as with Simon (Peter),[65] so also he rejoiced
    in Zacchaeus, whom he brought down
        from the sycamore.

---

61. A biblical oath formula; cf. Isaiah 45:23; Jeremiah 22:5; 49:13; Hebrews 6:13.

62. Vona (*Carmi*, 129) translates this as 1 pl., but the form is clearly 3 m. pl. He was perhaps misled by the subject of the next stanza. The referent is the sinners just mentioned (see line 62).

63. Conflation of Ezekiel 33:11 and Luke 15:7, 10.

64. Cf. Ephesians 4:26.

65. This probably refers to the calling of Peter (Matthew 4:18-22; Mark 1:16-20; Luke 5:1-11) and would find a parallel in Ephrem, *Hymns on the Nativity* 4.34-35 (see note 53 above and quotation in text). It might also refer to Peter's confession of faith, blessing, and investiture (Matthew 16:16-19).

The Just One had commanded that, for the
    one who has gone astray,
  the Judgment should be mournful,
(but) his mien was merry[66] when he met
    that Inquisitor who bears mercy!

How timid, nonetheless, was Zacchaeus—
90   he was afraid to seek mercy;
but how forthright was our Lord—
    he was eager to grant mercy.

Your God is just and kind—
    fear, O sinners, but also be confident,
for he forgives the sins of those who repent,
    but wrath has claim on those who refuse.

[*lamad*] In Zacchaeus he calls out to you sinners,
    that you may see his love, for how anxious is he!
For he casts his nets like a fisherman,
100   that the leader of your cohort may rejoice in you.

He took the penitent from the sycamore
    and straightway planted him in the Garden;
he saw him stripped of glory, like Adam;
    he wove for him a garment of mercy
      and clothed him.[67]

Confess our Lord, who sought out and came
    to the debtor who was found owing,
and made a path on which we should go,
    that he might mete out (to us) the mercy
      which he bore.

I have entered into your house instead of
    the sycamore;

---

66. See Luke 19:6.
67. See Genesis 3:21.

110   I shall live in the mystery which I embrace,
   for your cross is higher than the bough—
    multiply the floods of your mercy upon me!

Carl Griffin is an assistant research fellow at the Neal A. Maxwell Institute for Religious Scholarship.

CHAPTER 9

❧

"IF . . . AND": A HEBREW CONSTRUCTION IN THE BOOK OF MOSES

Kent P. Jackson

The original text of Joseph Smith's New Translation of the Bible (JST) continues to reveal heretofore unrecognized information about the text's history and interesting new avenues for research.[1] The New Translation text that underlies the Book of Moses (Genesis 1:1–6:13) is particularly interesting because more than one Joseph Smith manuscript of it exists and because the Prophet made significant revisions to the text after his initial dictation.[2] Important questions regarding the New Translation of Genesis include "To what extent does the JST restore original text lost in antiquity?" and "What was the language of the original text?" I have argued elsewhere that evidence exists to suggest that at least part of the New Translation of Genesis is a restoration of an ancient Hebrew *Vorlage* because of the existence in the text of a grammatical construction that cannot be explained in English but represents good Hebrew.[3] To honor my former teacher and twenty-eight-year faculty colleague S. Kent

---

1. See Scott H. Faulring, Kent P. Jackson, and Robert J. Matthews, eds., *Joseph Smith's New Translation of the Bible—Original Manuscripts* (Provo, UT: BYU Religious Studies Center, 2004).

2. See Kent P. Jackson, *The Book of Moses and the Joseph Smith Translation Manuscripts* (Provo, UT: BYU Religious Studies Center, 2005).

3. Kent P. Jackson, "Behold I," *BYU Studies* 44/2 (2005): 169–75.

Brown, I would like to discuss another Hebrew grammatical construction found in the original manuscripts of the Book of Moses.

In English, conditional sentences are usually expressed with the use of an *if-then* formation. The protasis (the conditional clause) is preceded by *if*, and the apodosis (the consequence clause) typically is preceded by *then*. We see this formation in these examples, taken from the King James translation of the Old Testament: "*If* I find in Sodom fifty righteous within the city, *then* I will spare all the place for their sakes" (Genesis 18:26); and "Jacob vowed a vow, saying, *If* God will be with me, . . . *then* shall the Lord be my God" (Genesis 28:20-21). Often an English *if-then* clause lacks the *then* but communicates the message just as well, as in this example: "*If* ye shall still do wickedly, ye shall be consumed" (1 Samuel 12:25).

The examples presented above are good translations from the original Hebrew text. But in the two Genesis examples, the Hebrew uses *and* rather than *then* to introduce the consequence clauses. This is consistent with standard Hebrew usage that expresses the *if-then* idea with *'im* (*if*) to introduce the protasis, and *wĕ-* (*and*) to introduce the apodosis. Thus, more literal renderings of our two Genesis examples would yield, "*If* I find in Sodom fifty righteous within the city, *and* I will spare all the place for their sakes" (Genesis 18:26); and "Jacob vowed a vow, saying, *If* God will be with me, . . . *and* shall the Lord be my God" (Genesis 28:20-21). For all their literalness, these translations miscommunicate dramatically, so the translators wisely placed the phrases into more conventional English.

The *if-and* construction is evident in the earliest manuscripts of the Book of Mormon. Royal Skousen has discovered fourteen examples in the Original and Printer's Manuscripts, the presence of which argues strongly for a Hebrew-based text that underlies the 1829 English translation. But in preparation for the 1837 second edition, *and* was edited out of all of them to bring the wording into harmony with standard English usage.[4]

Only one example of the *if-and* construction is found in the original manuscripts of Joseph Smith's New Translation of Genesis.[5] The passage is now designated Moses 6:52 in the Pearl of Great Price. The first line of the passage was revealed to Joseph Smith, probably on 1 December 1830. The scribe for that line was his wife, Emma Smith, who wrote for her husband only for a short time, taking dictation for slightly more than two pages. Perhaps on that same day, and most likely by 10 December, John Whitmer took the dictation for the remainder of the passage. The dictated manuscript is called Old Testament Manuscript 1. The text of the conditional sentence in Moses 6:52 reads as follows, with the *if* and the *and* italicized:

> *If* thou wilt turn unto me, and hearken unto my voice, and believe, and repent of all their transgressions, and be baptized, even by water, in the name of mine Only Begotten Son, which is full of grace and truth, which is Jesus Christ, the only name which shall be given under heaven, whereby salvation shall come unto the children of men, *and* ye shall ask all things in his name, and whatsoever ye shall ask, it shall be given.[6]

---

4. Royal Skousen, "Critical Methodology and the Text of the Book of Mormon," *Review of Books on the Book of Mormon* 6/1 (1994): 132-33; "The Original Language of the Book of Mormon: Upstate New York Dialect, King James English, or Hebrew?" *Journal of Book of Mormon Studies* 3/1 (1994): 33-35.

5. In nonbiblical material in the Book of Moses, some other conditional sentences are found that do not have the *then/and*, for example, "If men do not repent, I will send in the floods upon them" (Moses 8:17; see also 5:29; 6:29; 8:24). In Genesis in Hebrew, forms without *then/and* are more common, outnumbering those with *then/and* by about 1.5 to 1.

6. For comparative purposes, capitalization, punctuation, and spelling have been made consistent with the text in the current (1981) edition of the Pearl of Great Price. Emma Smith's handwriting ends with the word *voice*.

The *if* and the *and* identify the protasis and apodosis of the conditional sentence; the *if*-clause lists the conditions of the promise, and the *then-* (in this case *and-*) clause identifies the consequences.[7]

Probably on 8 March 1831, John Whitmer began making a copy of the text of Old Testament Manuscript 1, which by that date had progressed to Genesis 24:41. On the resulting manuscript—Old Testament Manuscript 2—he faithfully (although not always flawlessly) copied the original, sometimes making needed spelling and grammatical corrections (for example, changing *their*, early in the above text, to *thy*). Old Testament Manuscript 2 was the document on which the Prophet continued the translation to the end of the Old Testament. And on Old Testament Manuscript 2, he made additional corrections to the text already recorded, editing and refining as he felt inspired to do so. With Sidney Rigdon serving as scribe, the Prophet made some important refinements to Moses 6:52. Following is Joseph Smith's final wording of Moses 6:52, with the *if* and the *and* italicized:

> *If* thou wilt turn unto me, and hearken unto my voice, and believe, and repent of all thy transgressions, and be baptized, even in water, in the name of mine Only Begotten Son, who is full of grace and truth, who is Jesus Christ, the only name which shall be given under heaven, whereby salvation shall come unto the children of men, *and* ye shall receive the gift of the Holy Ghost, asking all things in his name, and whatsoever ye shall ask, it shall be given you.[8]

---

7. I examined the possibility that the final *and* in the passage might introduce the apodosis. This seems less likely because "turn unto me," "hearken unto my voice," "believe," and "repent of all their transgressions" constitute a series of actions all governed by "thou wilt" in the first clause. The "and ye shall" forms a natural break, with a new subject, "ye," and a new governing verb, "shall."

8. Again, capitalization, punctuation, and spelling have been made consistent with the text in the current (1981) edition of the Pearl of Great Price.

Readers of the modern text of the Pearl of Great Price will note that the *and* that introduces the apodosis is no longer in the passage today. It was removed in the 1878 Pearl of Great Price. When Elder Orson Pratt was preparing the 1878 edition, he took the text of the Book of Moses directly from the *Inspired Version*, published by the Reorganized Church of Jesus Christ of Latter Day Saints in 1867. The *Inspired Version* is a printed edition of the New Translation with editing, punctuation, and chapter-and-verse divisions provided by a publication committee chaired by Joseph Smith III.[9] Because Elder Pratt and Latter-day Saints in Utah had no access to the original New Translation manuscripts, Elder Pratt drew the Book of Moses text from the best source available to him, the printed RLDS *Inspired Version*. For the first draft of the new Book of Moses, Elder Pratt edited a printed 1851 Pearl of Great Price against the *Inspired Version*, writing the corrections that needed to be made.[10] In the process, he made very few changes to the Book of Moses text,[11] and he wrote the corrections to Moses 6:52 precisely as the text reads in the 1867 *Inspired Version*. At some point after Elder Pratt wrote the needed corrections in his 1851 printing, the *and* of the apodosis at Moses 6:52 was removed. This probably took place in the proofreading process, removed either by Elder Pratt or by an editor in his employ. The reason seems clear. The *if-and* construction makes no sense in English. The *and* disguises the consequence clause and thus changes the intended thought. Removing the English *and* corrected the verse and expressed the passage in English with the meaning intended in the original.

---

9. The *Inspired Version* is a popular title for *The Holy Scriptures, Translated and Corrected by the Spirit of Revelation. By Joseph Smith, Jr., the Seer* (Plano, IL: The [Reorganized] Church of Jesus Christ of Latter Day Saints, 1867).

10. The 1851 Pearl of Great Price text was incomplete, out of order, and came from an inferior preliminary manuscript, so Elder Pratt was wise to replace it with the superior text of the RLDS *Inspired Version*. Elder Pratt's edited copy of the 1851 Pearl of Great Price is in the Church History Library, Church of Jesus Christ of Latter-day Saints, Salt Lake City, Utah.

11. See Jackson, *Book of Moses and Joseph Smith Translation Manuscripts*, 33–36.

The wording at Moses 6:52 has remained unchanged in the Pearl of Great Price since 1878.[12] The passage is a scriptural gem. It is a quotation of God's words when he taught the gospel to Adam and as such may be the earliest recital in human history of what we call the first principles and ordinances of the gospel. The *if-then* promise is both to Adam and to his children: *If* we turn to Christ, obey his voice, believe, repent, and are baptized, (*then*) we will receive the gift of the Holy Ghost, so that whatever we ask, we will receive.

The King James translators were thorough and consistent in rendering the Hebrew *if-and* formation as *if-then*. Thus there are no examples in the English Bible from which Joseph Smith could have modeled this Hebrew, non-English construction, just as it was not found in American spoken English. When added to evidence already published for the even more enigmatic "behold I" construction, we see a greater case being made for a Hebrew text behind the nonbiblical material in the Book of Moses.[13] These phrases are nonsense in English, are found nowhere in the English Bible, but are perfectly good Hebrew. Even in limited numbers, a Hebrew original seems to be the best way to explain their presence in the manuscripts. This is not to say that God spoke to Adam in Hebrew or that Enoch recorded God's words in Hebrew. But the evidence seems to suggest that the text of the early chapters of Genesis, revealed in English to Joseph Smith in 1830-31, came from an underlying Hebrew original.

Kent P. Jackson is professor of ancient scripture at Brigham Young University.

---

12. Readers will note one other difference between Joseph Smith's text of Moses 6:52 and the text in the current Pearl of Great Price. In the preparation of the 1867 *Inspired Version*, the RLDS publication committee did not use the Prophet's correction of the second *which* to *who*, probably due to simple oversight. Because Elder Pratt used the *Inspired Version* reading in the 1878 Pearl of Great Price, our current text includes the awkward, unintended sequence: "mine Only Begotten Son, *who* is full of grace and truth, *which* is Jesus Christ."

13. See Jackson, "Behold I."

CHAPTER 10

✺

JOHN PHILOPONUS: EGYPTIAN EXEGETE, ECCLESIASTICAL POLITICIAN

Leslie S. B. MacCoull

Egyptian Exegete

John Philoponus composed his work known as *De Opificio Mundi* (hereafter *Opif.*),[1] a commentary on Genesis written from the anti-Chalcedonian (Miaphysite) point of view, in the mid-sixth century either just before Justinian's Council of Constantinople (553) or shortly afterwards. He opened his text with the modesty topos, declaring that he was writing not of his own prompting but at that of his fellow Miaphysite, Sergius of Tella, patriarch of Antioch (r. 557/58–560/61)[2] and the first non-Chalcedonian holder of that see since the great

---

1. Throughout I use Johannes Philoponos, *Über die Erschaffung der Welt (De Opificio Mundi)*, ed. and trans. Clemens Scholten, 3 vols. (Freiburg: Herder, 1997), occasionally noting differences from the Teubner edition by Walter Reichardt (Leipzig, 1897), plus my own autoptic work on the Vienna manuscript (in 1993) and English translation (prepared in 1995). I have been greatly aided by *Jean Philopon: La Création du monde*, trans. Marie-Hélène Congourdeau and Marie-Claude Rosset (Paris: Migne, 2004), and thank the authors for kindly sending me a copy.

2. For Sergius, see Uwe M. Lang, "John Philoponus and the Fifth Ecumenical Council," *Annuarium Historiae Conciliorum* 37 (2005): 411-36, here 426. See also Leslie S. B. MacCoull, "The Historical Context of John Philoponus's *De Opificio Mundi* in the Culture of Byzantine-Coptic Egypt," *Zeitschrift für antikes Christentum* 9 (2006): 397-423, here 400, 409, 411; and cf. J. Schamp, "Photios et Jean Philopon: sur la date du *De opificio mundi*," *Byzantion* 70 (2000): 135-54.

Severus was deposed by Justin I in 518 and exiled to Egypt. Sergius himself, in the run-up to the Council of Constantinople, also urged Philoponus to write his Miaphysite treatise *The Arbiter*,[3] so this work was another one[4] inspired by the successor of Severus, the latter living on in Egypt as a Miaphysite hero until 538. This clearly witnesses to the transprovincial Miaphysite commonwealth of intellectuals all round the Mediterranean, thinkers who united classical and Christian *paideia*[5] in an epoch that saw the setting up of independent Miaphysite churches in both Egypt and Syria.

Philoponus in his *Opif.* prooemium addresses Sergius in the vocative as τιμιωτάτη μοι κεφαλή, a trope of official reverence simultaneously recalling the classical poetry (especially Homer) he knew, the government politesse he encountered in Egypt (the τιμιώτατος title for officeholders in sixth-century papyri), and epithets for Christ. In the next phrase he also calls him "the greatest adornment (ἐγκαλλώπισμα, "beautification") of those who are reckoned among the archpriests of God." This is deeply meaningful praise for someone named to fill a *sedes* long regarded as *vacans*. (Alexandria's own Miaphysite patriarch, Theodosius, was at the time being kept in detention in Constantinople;[6] and indeed Sergius himself also resided in the imperial capital.)[7] In this work, the *Opif.*, Philoponus is also honoring Sergius's predecessor Severus,

---

3. Uwe M. Lang, *John Philoponus and the Controversies over Chalcedon in the Sixth Century: A Study and Translation of the Arbiter* (Louvain, Belgium: Peeters, 2001); Edward J. Watts, *City and School in Late Antique Athens and Alexandria* (Berkeley: University of California Press, 2006), 249; also *The Crisis of the Oikoumene: The 'Three Chapters' and the Failed Quest for Unity in the Sixth-Century Mediterranean*, ed. Celia Chazelle and Catherine Cubitt (Turnhout, Belgium: Brepols, 2006).

4. A third had apparently been Philoponus's *On the Whole and Its Parts*, dedicated to Sergius before he became patriarch of Antioch (before 557/58); see Lang, "John Philoponus and the Fifth Ecumenical Council," 426-27.

5. See Leslie S. B. MacCoull, "Philosophy in Its Social Context," in *Egypt in the Byzantine World 400-700*, ed. Roger S. Bagnall (Cambridge: Cambridge University Press, 2007), 67-82.

6. Stephen J. Davis, *The Early Coptic Papacy* (Cairo: American University in Cairo Press, 2004), 101-7.

7. Lang, "John Philoponus and the Fifth Ecumenical Council," 426.

famously the first person to quote the author known as (the pseudo-) Dionysius the Areopagite,[8] by explicitly citing Dionysius—a writer new to the sixth-century world[9]—in his own exegesis of the work of creation.[10] These citations have been little noticed, and deserve scrutiny for both their content and their context.

Book 2 of the *Opif.* is an explanation of Genesis 1:2-5. After quoting verse 2 in the Septuagint, Aquila, Theodotion, and Symmachus text versions (as is his usual procedure), Philoponus immediately lets the reader know that Moses was being a good *physikos* in treating all the four elements—earth, air, fire, and water—partly explicitly and partly implicitly. He explains the following verses using both Basil's *Hexaemeron* and his own *De Aeternitate Mundi Contra Proclum*,[11] contradicting the Dyophysites Theodore of Mopsuestia and Theodoret by name and Cosmas "Indicopleustes" by implication. Finally he arrives at the first of the repeated Genesis formulations, "And there was evening and there was morning, one day." This sparks off a discussion of when a day begins and ends, along with the habit of reckoning a day from the preceding sundown. And

8. In his *Against the Apology of Julian* 25, citing *De Divinis Nominibus* 2.9, he also quotes Letter 4 (PG 3.1072C, with the to-be-famous formulation θεανδρικὴ ἐνέργεια); I thank Father U. M. Lang for verifying these references. The Julianist-controversy writings were composed while Severus was in Egypt (between 518 and 538).

9. I thank Dr. Marc D. Lauxtermann of Oxford for his e-mail comment that *Anthologia Palatina* 1.88, the three-line epigram on Dionysius that shows awareness of the *Celestial* and *Ecclesiastical Hierarchies*, is indeed probably sixth century. For parallels from just a bit later in Philoponus's Egypt, see Clement A. Kuehn, *Channels of Imperishable Fire: The Beginnings of Christian Mystical Poetry and Dioscorus of Aphrodito* (New York: Lang, 1995), 12-14, 176-82, 205-16, and elsewhere.

10. The Ps.-Dionysius's angelology also to some extent underlies Philoponus's treatment of angels in *Opif.* 1.8-12, 14-22; though he does not cite him by name, he clearly knew the *Celestial Hierarchy*; see Leslie S. B. MacCoull, "The Monophysite Angelology of John Philoponus," *Byzantion* 65 (1995): 388-95; Clemens Scholten, *Antike Naturphilosophie und christliche Kosmologie in der Schrift "De Opificio Mundi" des Johannes Philoponos* (Berlin: de Gruyter, 1996), 77, 174-76, 181.

11. Clemens Scholten, ed. and trans., *Johannes Philoponos, De aeternitate mundi / Über die Ewigkeit der Welt*, 2 vols. (Turnhout, Belgium: Brepols, 2009); *Against Proclus on the Eternity of the World*, trans. Michael Share and James Wilberding, 3 vols. (London: Duckworth, 2004-6).

this gets him into the question of just when Christ's resurrection and its preceding dark sky event (at the crucifixion; see Matthew 27:45; Mark 15:33; Luke 23:44-45) happened. He cites Phlegon of Tralles on the solar eclipse of the 202nd Olympiad (*Opif.* 2.21), probably taking it from Eusebius. And he specifies the nineteenth regnal year of Tiberius, "in which occurred the crucifixion of Christ that saved the world, and at the same time the astonishing (παράδοξος) solar eclipse, not customary in nature, took place in the manner which Dionysius the Areopagite described in his letter to Polycarp the hierarch" (2.21).[12] Book 3 explains Genesis 1:6-8, the firmament and the second day of creation. Philoponus adduces the same bit— both Phlegon and Dionysius—in *Opif.* 3.9 in the course of proving that the earth and the universe are spherical, refuting Cosmas and the Dyophysites. Solar eclipses, even the one at the crucifixion[13] that occurred paradoxically (and supernaturally) at the Paschal full moon,[14] take place, according to Philoponus, when the moon (the [backlit] lunar disk) comes perpendicularly (κατὰ κάθετον) in front of the sun, which does not permit our sightlines (ὄψεις) to coincide (ἐπιβάλλειν) with the sun's light (3.9).[15] What Philoponus is seeking to refute in this section of the *Opif.* is Cosmas's notion (held up to ridicule) that the ἄκρα of the heaven lie upon the "tabernacle"-shaped earth (Cosmas, *Top. Chr.* 2.17).[16] Solar eclipses, whenever

---

12. This is Ps.-Dionysius Letter 7 (PG 3.1081A). The observer supposedly could perceive the eclipse from as far away from Jerusalem as Heliopolis. See Scholten, *Antike Naturphilosophie und christliche Kosmologie*, 77 n. 273, pointing out that Philoponus is the first Christian author to cite this evidence; also 175 with n. 113.

13. Luke 23:45 has explicitly τοῦ ἡλίου ἐκλιπόντος; Philoponus (2.21) ἐκλείψαντος τοῦ ἡλίου.

14. "and also Dionysius the Areopagite narrates how it happened" (3.9).

15. Cf. Jean de Groot, *Aristotle and Philoponus on Light* (New York: Garland, 1991), 103, 109, 121.

16. On the anti-Cosmas point, cf. Anne Tihon, "Astrological Promenade in Byzantium in the Early Palaiologan Period," in *The Occult Sciences in Byzantium*, ed. Paul Magdalino and Maria Mavroudi (Geneva: La Pomme d'or, 2006), 265-90, here 270; also 289 n. 72. An interesting predecessor of Philoponus's arguments in *Opif.* 3.9-10 and elsewhere, also quoting and commenting on Isaiah 40:22b; Psalm 103:2; and Psalm 87:7 (as does Philoponus), is the fragmentary discourse of Shenoute beginning "Now

they may occur (even miraculously, since ordinarily they cannot take place at what earth-based observers see as full moon),[17] further manifest even to naked-eye perception earth's sphericity, and even an authority from the first century (as was thought) noticed that.[18]

Philoponus gives his highest praise for Dionysius in *Opif.* 3.13, a pro-patristic, anti-Dyophysite manifesto. Book 3, expounding the firmament, has been continuing the exegete's overall project of demonstrating that Moses's cosmogony both agrees with extant reality and underlies the classical astronomies of Hipparchus and Ptolemy. He has followed Basil in describing the spherical earth nested within the spherical heaven (3.6-7), openly deriding obtuse Dyophysites—uneducated "scripture fundamentalists" (clearly Cosmas, Theodore, et al.), equivalent to what we would today call "flat-earthers"—whose lack of understanding of even Christian scripture is making Christians look silly in the eyes of scientifically educated pagans.[19] But there are phenomena such as the movements of the constellations and of the Milky Way, the sun's yearly course, the stars' paths, for which these unhelpful dolts cannot even provide scriptural proof texts or traditional support even though they themselves could have had access to "Basil the Great and the holy Gregories [sc. of Nazianzus and of Nyssa] and Athanasius who

Many Words and Things I Said," in which he discusses this concept, the "measure" (ϭⲡⲓ) of heaven and earth, and the sun's course and the circumpolar stars; see Pierre du Bourguet, "Entretien de Chenouté sur des problèmes de discipline ecclésiastique et de cosmologie," *Bulletin de l'Institut français d'archéologie orientale* 57 (1958): 99-142, here 115-17 (Coptic text), 122-23 (French trans.); Stephen Emmel, *Shenoute's Literary Corpus*, 2 vols. (Louvain, Belgium: Peeters, 2004), 1:246-47, 249, 253-54; 2:522-623, 813.

17. Philoponus goes on with a discussion of lunar eclipses, which might fruitfully be compared with his commentary on the *Posterior Analytics* (Commentaria in Aristotelem Graeca 13.3; ed. Maximilian Wallies [Berlin: Reimer, 1909]), though that is concerned with reasoning, not with the natural phenomenon as such. Cf. Owen Goldin, *Explaining an Eclipse: Aristotle's* Posterior Analytics *2.1-10* (Ann Arbor: University of Michigan Press, 1996), 101-7, 110-11, 118-23.

18. See most recently Anne Tihon, "Numeracy and Science," in *The Oxford Handbook of Byzantine Studies*, ed. Elizabeth Jeffreys et al. (Oxford: Oxford University Press, 2008), 803-19, here 810.

19. Scholten, *Antike Naturphilosophie und christliche Kosmologie*, 385.

contended with them in apostolic struggles, and Dionysius, who with the highest degree of philosophy adorned [or "beautified"] in piety the see of the church of Athens."[20] What these "proto-orthodox" people—including Athanasius, Alexandria's pride, in the company of fathers who had studied ancient Greek wisdom—had to say agrees with the facts far better, and Christians (here properly educated Miaphysites) do not have to be ashamed of their *paideia* in any company.[21]

Note Philoponus's pan-Mediterranean stance on authorities, combining Cappadocian exegetes with an Egyptian one (always known by the epithet "the apostolic") and adding the figure thought to have been the first head of the see of Athens, a city famous for philosophy (where two of those Cappadocians, Basil and the elder Gregory, had studied) whose Christian Neoplatonic school had ceased to function in the same year (529) that Philoponus himself produced his refutation of the Athenian Proclus. Our author is showing that the supersession of the older wisdom by the new—actually itself older than the classical Greeks—has been going on for a long time. Thinkers on both shores of the sea have been participating in this process, one in which contemporary Egypt plays as active a role as other Byzantine lands in the past.[22] Above all, he concludes, "let nothing in any manner get in the way of the truth" (μηδὲν γὰρ ἔστω μηδενὶ τῆς ἀληθείας ἐπίπροσθεν, 3.17), recalling 3.13 where he proclaimed that "anyone honoring what is true, by whomever it may be found, honors Christ, the Truth" (τὸ γὰρ ἀληθές, ὑφ᾽ ὅτου ἂν εὑρεθείη, τιμῶν τις αὐτὴν τιμᾷ, Χριστὸν τὴν ἀλήθειαν).

One further text may help to interweave Philoponus into the tradition of Dionysian thought. A passage originally transmitted as part

---

20. καὶ τὸν μετὰ φιλοσοφίαν ἄκραν τῇ εὐσεβείᾳ τὸν Ἀθήνησι τῆς ἐκκλησίας θρόνον κοσμήσαντα Διονύσιον (3.13), using an epithet for Dionysius similar to the one he earlier used for Sergius the dedicatee himself. This sets Sergius (in the present) and Dionysius (in the apostolic past) on side-by-side thrones of prestige, as it were (with κοσμᾶν recalling the *kosmos*).

21. Scholten, *Antike Naturphilosophie und christliche Kosmologie*, 386.

22. See MacCoull, "Philosophy in Its Social Context," 67–82.

of Maximus the Confessor's scholia on the Dionysian corpus (PG 4.21D-24A) has recently been reattributed to the sixth century and specifically to Philoponus.[23] Interestingly, it repeats the Proclus connection, with a bit of a twist. "One must know that some of the 'outside' (ἔξω [i.e., non-Christian]) philosophers, and especially Proclus, often used observations (θεωρήματα) of the blessed Dionysius, even dry formulations (λέξεις), and from this it is possible to gather the suspicion (ὑπόνοια) that the more ancient of the philosophers in Athens made his matters (πραγματεῖαι) their own and concealed them, as is recorded in the present book, so that they might be seen as the fathers of his divine sayings (λόγια). And through God's dispensation (οἰκονομία) now the present matter (πραγματεία) has appeared (i.e., the Dionysian writings have become known)[24] so as to confute their vainglory and fakery (ῥᾳδιουργία [a word used of falsifying scriptural texts])." This comment continues with a quote of the old "Plato is Moses speaking Greek [lit. "Atticizing"]" topos and a reference to Eusebius of Caesarea to show that "those of the 'outside' (ἔξω) wisdom like to steal what is ours [i.e., Christians']."[25] This is a fine opposite to what we in the twenty-first century know to have been the actual temporal order, according to which the composer of the Dionysian texts made extensive use of Proclus! Whether or not this passage is really by Philoponus,[26] it would be just like him to claim that the

23. Beate R. Suchla, "Verteidigung eines platonischen Denkmodells einer christlichen Welt: Die philosophie- und theologiegeschichtliche Bedeutung des Scholienwerks des Johannes von Skythopolis zu den areopagitischen Traktaten," *Nachrichten der Akademie der Wissenschaften zu Göttingen, phil.-hist. Klasse* (1995): 1-28, at 12, 19-20.

24. As they were brought in evidence at the 532 Constantinopolitan council (*Acta Conciliorum Oecumenicorum* IV.2 [Berlin: de Gruyter, 1914], 172-73), though they were thought spurious by the council's Dyophysite presider, Hypatius of Ephesus (whom Sergius of Tella would have regarded as unqualified).

25. On the ἔξω formulation, see Katerina Ierodiakonou, "Introduction," in *Byzantine Philosophy and Its Ancient Sources*, ed. Ierodiakonou (Oxford: Clarendon, 2002), 1-13, esp. 9-10.

26. The main place where he seems to go in for the ἔξω label for non-Christian thought is right here in the *Opif.* prooemium, where he describes his own *Contra Proclum* as having been written in refutation (ἔλεγχον) of "outside discourses" (ἐξωτερικῶν λόγων). Cf. Michele Trizio, "Byzantine Philosophy as a Contemporary

pagan Athenian Proclus, whom he himself had refuted, had been "stealing" from Paul's Christian Athenian disciple Dionysius just as much as Plato took from Moses (*Opif.* 1.2).

Ecclesiastical Politician

Philoponus in his *Opif.* prooemium praises another individual besides Sergius of Tella: Athanasius, a "fellow-worker" (συνεργός) in Sergius's "zealous effort" (σπούδασμα), whom Philoponus describes as "famous in family" (γνώριμος τοῦ γένους) and no less so in piety toward God (θεοσέβεια). This was a young man of indeed imperial descent, Empress Theodora's nephew,[27] who had been Sergius's pupil and would be mentioned as a possible "short-list" candidate for non-Chalcedonian patriarch of Alexandria in 566. He would also in future support Philoponus in the latter's later-life controversies over "tritheism" and the resurrection. Here Philoponus nicknames Athanasius σκύμνος, a "lion cub" accompanying in the race (συμπαραθέων) the one who reared him for "excellence" (ἀρετή). This metaphorical label "lion cub" is an explicit Miaphysite marker: it is the favorite epithet in all of Coptic homiletic, hagiography, and hymnography (ⲘⲀⲤⲘⲞⲨⲒ) for Cyril of Alexandria, the authority most revered by the self-fashioning Egyptian church.[28] To be a "lion cub" was to be a second Cyril, an infallible touchstone

Historiographical Project," *Recherches de théologie et philosophie médiévales* 74 (2007): 247–94; and for more on "inside" and "outside," Anthony Kaldellis, "Byzantine Philosophy Inside and Out: Orthodoxy and Dissidence in Counterpoint" (forthcoming; I thank the author for a prepublication copy).

27. *Prosopography of the Later Roman Empire* (hereafter *PLRE*) 3A:147, Athanasius 5 (giving "grandson," but nephew seems more likely in the chronology); cf. *Opif.*, ed. Scholten, 1:75 n. 13. Theodora famously favored the Miaphysites.

28. Among many examples, see De Lacy O'Leary, *The Difnar (Antiphonarium) of the Coptic Church* (London: Luzac, 1926), 11a: "Truly I magnify the wonders and my mind is amazed; I seek words for your honor, Cyril the lion cub and our fathers the bishops who gathered in Ephesus"; 21b: "Athanasius the apostolic and Basil the teacher of piety; the second Gregory the true theologian . . . our father Cyril the strong lion cub who underwent troubles for orthodoxy"; and now Maria Cramer and Martin Krause, *Das koptische Antiphonar (M575 und P11967)* (Muenster: Aschendorff, 2008), 310–11, listing Mark, Dionysius, Peter the martyr, Athanasius, Cyril the lion cub, Dioscorus, Theodosius, and Benjamin, plus Severus of Antioch.

of orthodox (Miaphysite) belief[29]—which must have seemed quite a qualification for someone seeking to occupy Cyril's see! The epithet came of course originally from Genesis 49:9, "Judah is a lion's cub," and was applied to Cyril as being the nephew and successor of the respected Theophilus. By extension it came to denote Cyril as the victor at Ephesus and deposer of his opponents. In his prooemium Philoponus describes the teacher-pupil relationship of Sergius and Athanasius as "a gray-haired mind" (πολιὸς νοῦς) in the exercise of discourse creating "a venerable youth" (αἰδέσιμον νεότητα). So it is both the elder ecclesiastic and the *puer senex* nobleman who have prompted Philoponus to explain Genesis.

I would like to float the hypothesis that Philoponus's addressee Athanasius may further be identified with *PLRE*'s Athanasius 4, the *dux* of the Thebaid (in 567) praised in Dioscorus of Aphrodito's encomiastic poetry and target of his petitions. This Athanasius also, we now know (thanks to P.Vindob. G 16334), had in ca. 550–55 served as *dux* and *augustalis* of Alexandria and as *curator* (*phrontistês*) of the imperial estates (*domus divina*, θειοτάτη οἰκία)—that would have been Theodora's estates—in the Thebaid.[30] As a (pious) layman[31] there would have been in that period no impediment to his being mentioned in the 560s as a possible successor to Patriarch Theodosius—just the opposite. His blood kinship to the late, beloved empress who was such a friend to the Miaphysite church in its beginnings, a kinship that had qualified him to look after his late aunt's Upper

---

29. On the prestige of Cyril, see Daniel King, *The Syriac Versions of the Writings of Cyril of Alexandria* (Louvain, Belgium: Peeters, 2008), 7-15, 27-33, 44-46.

30. The identification of Athanasius the *dux* of the Thebaid with the Alexandrian *dux* and Theban *curator* is owed to the insight of Federico Morelli, "Zwischen Poesie und Geschichte: Die 'flagornerie' des Dioskoros und der dreifache Dux Athanasios," in *Les archives de Dioscore d'Aphrodité cent ans après leur découverte: Histoire et culture dans l'Égypte byzantine*, ed. Jean-Luc Fournet (Paris: de Boccard, 2008), 223-45. On 230-31 n. 27 Morelli mentions working conversations in Cairo, and since the honorand of this volume and the present writer were in 1978 the first two Fellows of the American Research Center in Egypt ever to have been appointed in Coptic studies, I hope he will recall similar interactions.

31. The word *monk* may have to be deleted from the *PLRE* entry for Athanasius 4.

Egyptian estates in an official capacity, would have been seen as an extra point in his favor along with his having been educated by the impeccably Miaphysite Sergius of Tella. At the time when Philoponus was composing his *Opif.* procemium, probably toward 560, he yoked together the elder Miaphysite prelate and his imperially born pupil, the Miaphysite official, in a bid for patronal support at the very highest level of the Byzantine state. Athanasius, who—if the identification is valid—had administered the very city of Alexandria in which Philoponus lived, lectured, and wrote, as well as being in charge of Upper Egyptian imperial lands, clearly had power at court thanks to his lineage and was to return to Egypt, this time also as a government official, not as a prelate in orders. He was to continue to support Philoponus even through times when their fellow Miaphysites stood against him. In the procemium to Philoponus's hexaemeral magnum opus we can see how our exegete was writing at a time when Egypt's Miaphysite church was beginning to build and decorate its own structures, compose its own liturgies, ordain its own clerics,[32] and interpret the Bible its own way. We can see this late antique polymath acting simultaneously as an Egyptian exegete and as an ecclesiastical politician doing his best to keep Constantinople aware of the validity of the position held by the majority of his countrymen and women. He and they were convinced that the Incarnation of the Word (rightly understood) was the fundamental mystery of creation.[33] This insight was unfolded in the Pseudo-Dionysian writings[34] of which Philoponus was aware. He was making it plain to his scriptural audience and his political supporters that only the Miaphysite understanding,

---

32. For example, Leslie S. B. MacCoull, "'Sleepers Awake': More Light on *PSI* I 65," *Le Muséon* 121 (2008): 1-10.

33. Cf. Bogdan G. Bucur, "Foreordained from All Eternity: The Mystery of the Incarnation according to Some Early Christian and Byzantine Writers," *Dumbarton Oaks Papers* 62 (2008): 199-215, esp. 200, 214 ("inscribed in the very design of creation").

34. Bucur, "Foreordained," 200-203.

their understanding, of who the incarnate Christ was could make sense of the universe.[35]

Leslie S. B. MacCoull is Senior Research Scholar of the Society for Coptic Archaeology (North America).

---

35. Also in loving memory of Mirrit Boutros Ghali (1908-92) (Pondus meum amor meus: eo feror quocumque feror, Augustine, *Confessions* 13.9).

RECONCILING THE IRRECONCILABLE: JOSEPH SMITH AND THE ENIGMA OF MORMONISM

Robert L. Millet

Because I spend a significant percentage of my time in outreach—attempting to establish friendships for the church and the university, to build bridges of understanding—I am often asked what it is that contributes to the growth of the Church of Jesus Christ of Latter-day Saints. There are, I suppose, a myriad of answers. In 1974 an article appeared in the popular magazine *Christianity Today* entitled "Why Your Neighbor Joined the Mormon Church." Five reasons were given:

1. The Latter-day Saints show genuine love and concern by taking care of their people.
2. They strive to build the family unit.
3. They provide for their young people.
4. Theirs is a layman's church.
5. They believe that divine revelation is the basis for their practices.

After a brief discussion of each of the above, the author of the article concluded: "In a day when many are hesitant to claim that God has said anything definitive, the Mormons stand out in contrast, and many people are ready to listen to what the Mormons think the voice of God says. It is tragic that their message is false, but it is nonetheless a lesson to us that people are many times ready to hear a voice of authority."[1] Well, so much for judging things by their fruits (see Matthew 7:15–20)!

Other reasons for church growth include the spirit of community among the Latter-day Saints; the industriousness of the people and their influence for good in society; the LDS adherence to time-honored moral values and a vigorous health code; and the church's doctrinal positions on timely but age-old issues. What I would like to suggest is another major factor that fascinates curious onlookers: an unusual kind of balance struck by the Latter-day Saints in which paradoxes or seeming contradictions—in doctrine and in practical living—are resolved. Let me suggest several as examples.

Wholly Other, Heavenly Father

Most people, even religious people, wrestle with who and what God is. Is he a force? Is he a *he*? A set of governing laws? The Unmoved Mover? The unknowable, unreachable, untouchable, unfathomable One? A person, a personality, or a being of some kind? Latter-day Saints teach a rather bold doctrine—that God is a man, an exalted and glorified man, a "Man of Holiness" (Moses 6:57). Joseph Smith stated in 1843: "The Father has a body of flesh and bones as tangible as man's; the Son also; but the Holy Ghost has not a body of flesh and bones, but is a personage of Spirit" (D&C 130:22). When we pray "Our Father which art in heaven," we mean just what we say. He is the Father of the spirits of all men and women (see Numbers 16:22; 27:16; Hebrews 12:9).

We believe that God possesses every godly attribute in perfection, meaning that there is no knowledge he does not possess nor any power he cannot exercise. He is "infinite and eternal, from everlasting to everlasting the same unchangeable God, the framer of

---

1. Donald P. Shoemaker, "Why Your Neighbor Joined the Mormon Church," *Christianity Today* 19 (11 October 1974): 11–13.

heaven and earth, and all things which are in them" (D&C 20:17). He embodies "glory, honor, power, majesty, might, dominion, truth, justice, judgment, mercy, and an infinity of fulness, from everlasting to everlasting" (D&C 109:77). At the same time, he is infinitely capable of being personal and available; his infinity precludes neither his immediacy nor his intimacy. Because he is a person, a personage, he is touched by the feeling of our infirmities, just as is his Beloved Son (see Hebrews 4:15).

Fallen Man, Eternal Man

What is the nature of man? Is he prone to choose the right, serve others, and make noble contributions to society? Or, on the other hand, is man a depraved creature, a sinful infidel who seeks only the gratification of the flesh? Which is it? To resolve this dilemma, we must first recognize that some statements from Latter-day Saint literature speak of man's *eternal* nature, while others speak of his *mortal* or fallen nature.

Joseph Smith taught that man is an eternal being. He declared that the intelligence of man "is not a created being; it existed from eternity, and will exist to eternity. Anything created cannot be eternal."[2] Subsequent church leaders have explained that the attributes, powers, and capacities possessed by our Father in Heaven reside in men and women in rudimentary and thus potential form. Thus there is a sense in which we might say that men and women, being spiritual heirs to godliness, are good by nature; that is, they are good because they are related to and products of the Highest Good. God is good, even the embodiment and personification of all that is noble, upright, and edifying, and we are from him. Such teachings would surely have stood in stark contrast to the more traditional belief in total depravity held by most Christians in the nineteenth century.

---

2. *Teachings of the Prophet Joseph Smith*, sel. Joseph Fielding Smith (Salt Lake City: Deseret Book, 1976), 158; see also 181, 352-54.

Because Latter-day Saints believe in a "fortunate fall," that the fall of our first parents was as much a part of the plan of God as the atonement—indeed, the atonement derives from the fall—they do not believe in the traditional doctrine of human depravity. "When our spirits took possession of these tabernacles," President Brigham Young observed, "they were as pure as the angels of God, wherefore total depravity cannot be a true doctrine."[3] Latter-day Saints tend to agree with C. S. Lewis on this matter of human depravity. For one thing, Lewis concluded that if people are truly depraved they cannot even decide between what is good and what is evil. "I disbelieve that doctrine [total depravity], partly on the logical ground that if our depravity were total we should not know ourselves to be depraved, and partly because experience shows us much goodness in human nature."[4]

On the other hand, LDS scripture, especially the Book of Mormon, is replete with references to the fallen nature of man—the affirmation that the fall of Adam and Eve was real; that it takes a measured toll on each of us, both physically and spiritually; and that unless one partakes of Christ's divine regenerating powers he or she remains in a fallen and unredeemed condition. Hence the debate between those who argue for man's nobility and those who argue for man's ignobility is resolved by asking the question, Which nature are we speaking of? Man is basically good, at least his eternal nature is. Man is basically fallen, at least his mortal nature is. Brigham Young summed up our position on the fall this way: "It requires all the atonement of Christ, the mercy of the Father, the pity of angels and the grace of the Lord Jesus Christ to be with us always, and then to do the very best we possibly can, to get rid of this sin within us, so that we may escape from this world into the celestial kingdom."[5]

---

3. *Journal of Discourses*, 26 vols. (Liverpool: Richards & Sons, 1851-86), 10:192.

4. C. S. Lewis, *The Problem of Pain* (New York: HarperCollins, 2001), 61; see *Christian Reunion and Other Essays* (London: William Collins Sons, 1990), 60.

5. *Journal of Discourses*, 11:301.

Elder Brother, Lord Omnipotent

In an eagerness to draw closer to Christ, some Christians have begun to cross a sacred line and go beyond that reverential barrier that must be observed by true followers of the Christ. They speak of Jesus as though he were their next-door neighbor, their buddy or chum, their pal. This is not the way to intimacy with the Savior. Oddly enough, strangely enough, it is not through humanizing Jesus, through trying to make him one of the boys, that we draw close to him and incorporate his saving powers. It is, rather, through recognizing his godhood, his divinity, his unspeakable power. In short, the more I sense his greatness, his infinity, his capacity to transform the human soul and my utter helplessness without him, the more I come unto him. It is through the recognition of our own nothingness and weakness that strength is derived (see Mosiah 2:20-21; 4:11-12, 26; Moses 1:10).

This is somewhat related to the LDS tendency to speak of Jesus as our elder brother. He is, of course, our elder brother in that he was what the scriptures call the firstborn of all creation (see Colossians 1:15). But it is of interest to me that the Book of Mormon prophets never speak of Jehovah as our elder brother. Rather, he is the Almighty God, the Eternal Judge, the Holy One of Israel, the Holy Messiah, the Everlasting Father, the Father of heaven and of earth, the God of nature, the Supreme Being, the keeper of the gate, the King of heaven, and the Lord God Omnipotent. One church leader, Elder M. Russell Ballard, explained to LDS students:

> We occasionally hear some members refer to Jesus as our Elder Brother, which is a true concept based on our understanding of the premortal life with our Father in Heaven. But like many points of gospel doctrine, that simple truth doesn't go far enough in terms of describing the Savior's role in our present lives and His great position as a member of the Godhead. Thus, some non-LDS Christians are uncomfortable with what they perceive as a secondary role

for Christ in our theology. They feel that we view Jesus as a spiritual peer. They believe that we view Christ as an implementor for God, if you will, but that we don't view Him as God to us and to all mankind, which, of course, is counter to biblical testimony about Christ's divinity.

Let me help us understand, with clarity and testimony, our belief about Jesus Christ. We declare He is the King of Kings, Lord of Lords, the Creator, the Savior, the Captain of our Salvation, the Bright and Morning Star. He has taught us that He is in all things, above all things, through all things and round about all things, that He is Alpha and Omega, the Lord of the Universe, the first and the last relative to our salvation, and that His name is above every name and is in fact the only name under heaven by which we can be saved. . . .

. . . [W]e can understand why some Latter-day Saints have tended to focus on Christ's Sonship as opposed to His Godhood. As members of earthly families, we can relate to Him as a child, as a Son, and as a Brother because we know how that feels. We can personalize that relationship because we ourselves are children, sons and daughters, brothers and sisters. For some it may be more difficult to relate to Him as a God. And so in an attempt to draw closer to Christ and to cultivate warm and personal feelings toward Him, some tend to humanize Him, sometimes at the expense of acknowledging His Divinity. So let us be very clear on this point: it is true that Jesus was our Elder Brother in the premortal life, but we believe that in this life it is crucial that we become "born again" as His sons and daughters in the gospel covenant.[6]

---

6. M. Russell Ballard, "Building Bridges of Understanding," *Ensign*, June 1998, 66–67.

Grace and Works

Various Christian churches wrestle with how much of the responsibility for salvation rests upon men and women and how much rests with God. Not long ago I heard an Evangelical speaker remark, "A Christ supplemented is a Christ supplanted." This bespeaks the notion of salvation by grace alone, the idea that nothing can be added to the finished work of Jesus Christ—including man's paltry and pitiful efforts to be good and do good. On the other hand, many others in the religious world speak as though human action is vital: we are to pray as if everything depended upon God and then act as if everything depended upon us. Roman Catholics believe that while men and women are saved by the grace of God—his unearned divine assistance, his unmerited favor—the seven sacraments are necessary in order to be accepted by and acceptable to God.

The Book of Mormon clearly states that "salvation is free" (2 Nephi 2:4). It cannot be purchased, bartered for, or, in the strictest sense, earned. Further, salvation or eternal life is "the greatest of all the gifts of God" (D&C 6:13; 14:7); it is only "through the merits, and mercy, and grace of the Holy Messiah" that people may be forgiven, renewed, and transformed spiritually (2 Nephi 2:8; see 31:19; Moroni 6:4; D&C 3:20). Now, having established that Latter-day Saints believe in the grace and mercy of God (and that we cannot, worlds without end, make it into heaven without divine assistance), I hasten to add that we have a strong religious work ethic. For us, works matter. They matter very much. Mormons are known as a hard-working bunch. We believe we have an obligation to go to church, pay tithes and offerings, visit the sick, minister to the poor, and in general live a life that would evidence our belief in Jesus Christ. In today's jargon, we believe that if we talk the talk we really ought to walk the walk. In short, more is expected of us than a verbal confession of faith.

And so how do we reconcile what would normally be two opposite ends of a theological spectrum? We answer that our good works, though a *necessary* condition for our salvation—in fact, they manifest our earnest desire to keep our covenant to love God and serve his children—are not *sufficient* for salvation. Another way of saying this is that there are not enough meetings to attend, prayers to offer, or selfless acts of service to assure our entry into the celestial kingdom. As the Book of Mormon puts it, we are saved by grace "after all we can do," meaning, above and beyond, notwithstanding, in spite of all we can do. As C. S. Lewis stated, "Christians have often disputed as to whether what leads the Christian home is good actions, or Faith in Christ. I have no right really to speak on such a difficult question, but it does seem to me like asking which blade in a pair of scissors is most necessary. . . . You see, we are now trying to understand, and to separate into water-tight compartments, what exactly God does and what man does when God and man are working together."[7]

Salvation Here and Hereafter

Whereas the ultimate blessings of salvation and glorification do not come until the next life, there is a sense in which people in this life may enjoy the assurance of salvation and the peace that accompanies that knowledge (see D&C 59:23). True faith in Christ produces hope in Christ—not worldly wishing but expectation, anticipation, assurance. As the apostle Paul wrote, the Holy Spirit provides the "earnest of our inheritance," the promise or evidence that we are on course, in covenant, and thus in line for full salvation in the world to come (Ephesians 1:13-14; see 2 Corinthians 1:21-22; 5:5). That is, the Spirit of God operating in our lives is like the Lord's "earnest money" on us—his sweet certification that he seriously intends to save us with an everlasting salvation. Thus if we are striving to cultivate the Holy Spirit in our lives, we are living in what might be called a "saved" condition.

---

7. C. S. Lewis, *Mere Christianity* (New York: HarperCollins, 1980), 148-49; see *Christian Reunion*, 18.

One of the most respected Evangelical theologians, John Stott, has written:

> Salvation is a big and comprehensive word. It embraces the totality of God's saving work, from beginning to end. In fact salvation has three tenses, past, present and future. . . . "I have been saved (in the past) from the penalty of sin by a crucified Saviour. I am being saved (in the present) from the power of sin by a living Saviour. And I shall be saved (in the future) from the very presence of sin by a coming Saviour." . . .
>
> If therefore you were to ask me, "Are you saved?" there is only one correct biblical answer which I could give you: "yes and no." Yes, in the sense that by the sheer grace and mercy of God through the death of Jesus Christ my Saviour he has forgiven my sins, justified me and reconciled me to himself. But no, in the sense that I still have a fallen nature and live in a fallen world and have a corruptible body, and I am longing for my salvation to be brought to its triumphant completion.[8]

Brigham Young taught:

> *It is present salvation and the present influence of the Holy Ghost that we need every day to keep us on saving ground. . . . I want present salvation.* I preach, comparatively, but little about the eternities and Gods, and their wonderful works in eternity; and do not tell who first made them, nor how they were made; for I know nothing about that. *Life is for us, and it for us to receive it to-day, and not wait for the millennium. Let us take a course to be saved to-day,* and, when evening comes, review the acts of the day, repent of our sins, if we have

---

8. *Authentic Christianity from the Writings of John Stott*, ed. Timothy Dudley-Smith (Downers Grove, IL: InterVarsity Press, 1995), 168.

any to repent of, and say our prayers; then we can lie down and sleep in peace until the morning, arise with gratitude to God, commence the labours of another day, and strive to live the whole day to God and nobody else.[9]

"I am in the hands of the Lord," Brother Brigham pointed out, "and never trouble myself about my salvation, or what the Lord will do with me hereafter."[10] As he said on another occasion, "our work is a work of the present. *The salvation we are seeking is for the present, and, sought correctly, it can be obtained, and be continually enjoyed.* If it continues to-day, it is upon the same principle that it will continue to-morrow, the next day, the next week, or the next year, and, we might say, the next eternity."[11]

David O. McKay, the ninth president of the church, likewise explained that "The gospel of Jesus Christ . . . is in very deed, in every way, the power of God unto salvation. It is salvation *here*—here and now. It gives to every man the perfect life, here and now, as well as hereafter."[12] In short, salvation is in Christ, and our covenant with Christ, our trust in his power to redeem us, should be demonstrated in how we live. The influence of the Holy Spirit in our lives is a sign to us that we are on course, "in Christ" (2 Corinthians 5:17), and thus in line for the fulness of salvation.

Static and Dynamic

To some extent, the growth and spread of the Church of Jesus Christ of Latter-day Saints may be attributed to what some would feel to be contradictory and irreconcilable processes: (1) constancy and adherence to "the ancient order of things"; and (2) development and change, according to needs and circumstances. Mormonism may thus be characterized as a religious culture with both static

---

9. *Journal of Discourses*, 8:124-25, emphasis added.
10. *Journal of Discourses*, 6:276.
11. *Journal of Discourses*, 1:131, emphasis added.
12. David O. McKay, *Gospel Ideals* (Salt Lake City: Improvement Era, 1953), 6.

and dynamic elements, a church acclimated to both conservative and progressive postures. The Saints have held tenaciously to and grounded themselves in what they perceive to be the particular beliefs and rites of both ancient Judaism and first-century Christianity. W. D. Davies, a respected New Testament scholar, once observed in an address at Brigham Young University that "Christianity has forgotten its Jewish roots." "Mormonism arose in a place and time," Davies continued, "when many utopian, populist, socialistic ideas were in the air. It gave these a disciplined, organized American outlet and form: what it did was to re-Judaize a Christianity that had been too much Hellenized." "Mormonism certainly injected, and I hope will continue to inject, into the American scene the realism of Judaism and thus challenged a too-Hellenized Christianity to renew its contact with its roots in Israel."[13]

At the same time, through a belief in modern and continuing revelation, Latter-day Saints have made shifts and developments in policies and procedures according to pressing needs and anticipated challenges. For example, much of the Judeo-Christian world would consider the Bible (particularly the parts they accept as scripture) as embodying the *canon*—the rule of faith and practice. As one of my professors in graduate school emphasized and reemphasized, if the word *canon*, the accepted books of scripture, means anything at all, it is then set, fixed, closed, and established. The LDS canon, on the other hand, is open, flexible, and (when church leaders feel divinely directed) expanding.

The sixth article of faith states: "We believe in the same organization that existed in the Primitive Church, namely, apostles, prophets, pastors, teachers, evangelists, and so forth." On the doorstep, a young LDS missionary might be asked, "What is it that you folks believe has been restored?" My guess is that often the missionary would respond something like this: "We believe that the church

---

13. W. D. Davies, "Israel, the Mormons and the Land," in *Reflections on Mormonism*, ed. Truman G. Madsen (Provo, UT: BYU Religious Studies Center, 1978), 91–92.

set up by Jesus in the first century has been reestablished." And, in general, the missionary would be correct. In point of fact, however, the answer is actually much broader than that, for Mormonism represents a restoration not only of New Testament Christianity but also the principles, doctrines, and divine authority enjoyed by prophets and righteous men and women in the Old Testament. In other words, while Latter-day Saints seek to live in harmony with the teachings of the Sermon on the Mount, they also participate in such matters as temple worship, a religious activity much more commonly associated with ancient Israel.[14]

Education and Religiosity

For some time now, studies have indicated that higher education tends to have a strong negative influence on religiosity. Various explanations have been offered, but perhaps the most popular is the secularizing effect of post-high school study on one's commitment to the faith. The British physicist Paul Davies observed: "If the [Christian] Church is largely ignored today it is not because science has finally won its age-old battle with religion, but because it has so radically reoriented our society that the biblical perspective of the world now seems largely irrelevant."[15] A related explanation posits that "higher education tends to both expand one's horizons and increase exposure to countercultural values. Such exposure works to erode the traditional plausibility structures which maintain the poorly understood religious convictions so typical of American religion. In other words, poorly grounded religious beliefs have simply been unable to stand in the face of challenges generated by modern science and higher education."[16]

---

14. See Jan Shipps, *Mormonism: The Story of a New Religious Tradition* (Urbana: University of Illinois Press, 1985), 46, 59, 68, 85.

15. Paul Davies, *God and the New Physics* (New York: Simon & Schuster, 1983), 2.

16. Stan L. Albrecht, "The Consequential Dimension to Mormon Religiosity," *BYU Studies* 29/2 (1989): 100.

Since their beginnings, the Latter-day Saints have placed tremendous stress on the value of education; it is a religious principle that men and women should strive to gain all of the education and training possible to better themselves and their circumstances in life. Thus for both males and females, the percentage of Latter-day Saints who have completed post-high school education or training is significantly higher than the nation as a whole. Research demonstrates that 53.5% of LDS males have some type of post-high school education, compared to 36.5% for the U.S. population. For females, 44.3% have received some post-high school education, 27.7% for the U.S. population. In addition, the Mormons defy the long-held thesis concerning higher education and religiosity. Weekly attendance at church for males works as follows: those with only a grade school education attended 34% of the time, while Mormon males with post-high school education attended 80% of the meetings. The same results followed in such other areas of religiosity as financial contributions, frequency of personal prayer, and regular personal scripture study. In short, the secularizing influence of higher education does not seem to hold for the Latter-day Saints.[17]

Empirical and Personal

It is not uncommon to hear comments about what some perceive to be an LDS overreliance upon feelings, sentiment, or emotion. Feelings do indeed play an important role in our faith and way of life, inasmuch as we believe that it is through the feelings (as well as through the mind) that Deity manifests divine truth to the sincere seeker. But so also is the mind a vital part of one's faith and commitment. I have heard people within the church say that they would live the life of a Latter-day Saint even if they should come to believe it is all untrue. I am not one of those kinds of persons. My religious convictions must be based, not alone upon what I feel but

---

17. See Stan L. Albrecht and Tim B. Heaton, "Secularization, Higher Education, and Religiosity," *Review of Religious Research* 26/1 (1984): 49–54.

also upon what I perceive and grasp and comprehend intellectually. My faith needs to be as satisfying to my mind as it is soothing and settling to my heart. There must be, to draw upon the words of the apostle Peter, a *reason* (meaning "a rational base") for the *hope* (meaning "the inner conviction") within me (see 1 Peter 3:15). I have chosen to be a practicing Latter-day Saint, not just because it makes me feel good inside but also because it makes good sense to me; the pieces fit together harmoniously. While there are still matters on the shelf, matters of faith in which tangible evidence is for the moment wanting, I refuse to allow my faith to be held hostage by what I do not know, or by what science has or has not uncovered to date, when in fact what I do know is so grand and mind-expanding. Thus for me Mormonism is "a rational theology."[18]

Professor Randall Balmer of Barnard College at Columbia, a respected historian of religion, undertook a gentle but straightforward critique of his own religious tradition:

> I believe because of the epiphanies, small and large, that have intersected my path—small, discrete moments of grace when I have sensed a kind of superintending presence outside of myself. I believe because these moments . . . are too precious to discard, and I choose not to trivialize them by reducing them to rational explanation. I believe because, for me, the alternative to belief is far too daunting. I believe because, at the turn of the twenty-first century, belief itself is an act of defiance in a society still enthralled by the blandishments of Enlightenment rationalism. . . .
>
> Let me lay my cards on the table. More than twenty years of personal reflection and a couple of decades studying evangelicalism in America have persuaded me that . . . evangelicalism stands to lose far more by surrendering its piety than it does by reexamining its theology. . . .

---

18. See John A. Widtsoe, *A Rational Theology* (Salt Lake City: Deseret News Press, 1915).

For roughly the last century we evangelicals have imbibed Enlightenment standards of rationality for our theological discourse. That is, we have taken the simple "good news" of the New Testament—the revolutionary notion that the grace of God rescues us from the ravages of our own depravity—and we have dissected it and bent it and crammed it into rationalistic categories that we think will be acceptable to the intellectual community.

One reading of evangelical theology in the twentieth century is that evangelicals were obsessed with fighting the battles they lost a century earlier. . . . Evangelical theologians have expended untold energies responding to the assaults of Enlightenment skeptics.

The evangelical response to . . . intellectual challenges has been, in my judgment, utterly misguided. To these arguments about religious belief, informed by Enlightenment rationalism, evangelicals mounted counterarguments, also informed by Enlightenment rationalism. . . .

Somehow, I don't think Jeffrey [who asks how he can know there is a God] wants me to rehearse the ontological, the teleological, and the cosmological arguments for the existence of God. . . . So instead of dusting off the teleological argument, I think I'll remind Jeffrey about Karl Barth, arguably the most important theologian of the twentieth century. Toward the end of his life, after he had written volume after volume on the transcendence of God and the centrality of Jesus, Barth was asked to sum up his work. The good doctor paused for a minute and no doubt looked out the window and played with the stubble on his chin before responding with the words of a Sunday school ditty: "Jesus loves me, this I know, for the Bible tells me so."[19]

---

19. Randall Balmer, *Growing Pains: Learning to Love my Father's Faith* (Grand Rapids: Brazos Press, 2001), 34, 42-43, 44-45, 61-62.

Individual vs. Community

The ideal society in Latter-day Saint theology, the holy city or City of God, is known as Zion. Mormons believe that the ancient prophet Enoch stands as the scriptural prototype of a success story—a story of a people who forsook their sins, emptied themselves of pride and arrogance, and looked to the good of their neighbors continually. They established Zion and were translated—taken into heaven without tasting death (see Hebrews 11:5; Moses 7:69). "And the Lord called his people Zion, because they were of one heart and one mind, and dwelt in righteousness; and there was no poor among them" (Moses 7:18).

Joseph Smith's vision of the kingdom of God was extremely broad and comprehensive. It consisted of more than preaching and study and Sabbath services; it entailed the entire renovation of the order of things on earth, the transformation of man and the elevation of society. And at the heart of that sublime vision was the doctrine of Zion, a doctrine and a worldview that would shape the early church and point the Saints of the twentieth and twenty-first centuries toward the eschatological ideal.

Joseph Smith seems to have first encountered the concept of Zion (in a sense other than the holy mount or holy city in Jerusalem) in his translation of the Book of Mormon. The Book of Mormon prophets spoke of Zion as a holy commonwealth, a *society* of the Saints, a *way of life* that was to be established or brought forth under God's direction. Among the earliest revelations given, now found in the Doctrine and Covenants, was the repeated command, "Now, as you have asked, behold, I say unto you, keep my commandments, and seek to bring forth and establish the cause of Zion" (D&C 6:6; also 11:6; 12:6; see 14:6). Zion thus came to be associated with the restored *church* and the grander work of the restoration, and the faithful could take heart in the midst of their troubles, for Zion was the city of God (see D&C 97:19). Indeed, in speaking of the sacred spot where the people of God congregated, the Lord said: "Behold, the land of Zion—I, the Lord, hold it in mine own hands" (D&C 63:25).

The idea that there was a specific location for the city of Zion within North and South America was taught very early. For a time it was Kirtland, Ohio, and then Joseph Smith received a revelation identifying the center place of Zion as Independence, Jackson County, Missouri (see D&C 57). In addition, Zion is spoken of in scripture as a banner or *ensign* around which a weary or beleaguered people may rally. It is also a *standard* against which the substance and quality of all things are to be evaluated. The Saints are expected to judge all things by a set of guidelines obtained from a source beyond that of unenlightened man (see D&C 64:37-38).

In addition, Zion was and is to be the focus, the convergence, and the concentration of all that is good, all that is ennobling, all that is instructive and inspirational. In short, according to Brigham Young, "every accomplishment, every polished grace, every useful attainment in mathematics, music, and in all science and art belong to the Saints."[20] The Saints "rapidly collect the intelligence that is bestowed upon the nations," President Young said on another occasion, "for all this intelligence belongs to Zion."[21] Zion is people, the people of God, those people who have come out of the world of Babylon into the marvelous light of Christ. In this vein the Lord encouraged his little flock: "Verily, thus saith the Lord, let Zion rejoice, for this is Zion—THE PURE IN HEART; therefore, let Zion rejoice, while all the wicked shall mourn" (D&C 97:21). Thus Zion is *a state of being*, a state of purity of heart that entitles one to be known as a member of the household of faith. Brigham Young therefore spoke of the Saints having Zion in their hearts: "Unless the people live before the Lord in the obedience of His commandments," he said, "they cannot have

---

20. *Journal of Discourses*, 10:224.
21. *Journal of Discourses*, 8:279.

Zion within them." Further, "As to the spirit of Zion, it is in the hearts of the Saints, of those who love and serve the Lord with all their might, mind, and strength."[22] On another occasion he affirmed: "Zion will be redeemed and built up, and the Saints will rejoice. This is the land of Zion; and *who are Zion? The pure in heart are Zion; they have Zion within them.* Purify yourselves, sanctify the Lord God in your hearts, and have the Zion of God within you."[23] *"Where is Zion? Where the organization of the Church of God is. And may it dwell spiritually in every heart*; and may we so live as to always enjoy the Spirit of Zion!"[24]

Zion is a place. Zion is a people. Zion is a holy state of being. It is the heritage of the Saints. "The building up of Zion," Joseph Smith taught,

> is a cause that has interested the people of God in every age; it is a theme upon which prophets, priests and kings have dwelt with peculiar delight; they have looked forward with joyful anticipation to the day in which we live; and fired with heavenly and joyful anticipations they have sung and written and prophesied of this our day; but they died without the sight; we are the favored people that God has made choice of to bring about the Latter-day glory.[25]

Zion is, as it were, heaven on earth.

The LDS doctrine of a divine plan—including that which deals with heaven and the hereafter—is especially appealing to those who encounter Mormonism. "Expressions of the eternal nature of love and the hope for heavenly reunion," Colleen McDannell and Bernhard Lang have written in their book, *Heaven: A History*, "persist in contemporary Christianity."

22. *Journal of Discourses*, 2:253.
23. *Journal of Discourses*, 8:198, emphasis added.
24. Brigham Young, in *Journal of Discourses*, 8:205, emphasis added.
25. *Teachings of the Prophet Joseph Smith*, 231.

Such sentiments, however, are not situated within a theological structure. Hoping to meet one's family after death is a wish and not a theological argument. While most Christian clergy would not deny that wish, contemporary theologians are not interested in articulating the motif of meeting again in theological terms. The motifs of the modern heaven—eternal progress, love, and fluidity between earth and the other world—while acknowledged by pastors in their funeral sermons, are not fundamental to contemporary Christianity. Priests and pastors might tell families that they will meet their loved ones in heaven as a means of consolation, but contemporary thought does not support that belief as it did in the nineteenth century. There is no longer a strong theological commitment.

They continue:

The major exception to this caveat is the teaching of The Church of Jesus Christ of Latter-day Saints, whose members are frequently referred to as the Mormons. The modern perspective on heaven—emphasizing the nearness and similarity of the other world to our own and arguing for the eternal nature of love, family, progress, and work—finds its greatest proponent in Latter-day Saint (LDS) understanding of the afterlife. While most contemporary Christian groups neglect afterlife beliefs, what happens to people after they die is crucial to LDS teachings and rituals. Heavenly theology is the result not of mere speculation, but of revelation given to past and present church leaders. . . .

There has been . . . no alteration of the LDS understanding of the afterlife since its articulation by Joseph Smith. If anything, the Latter-day Saints in the twentieth century have become even bolder in their assertion of the importance of their heavenly theology. In the light of what they perceive as a Christian world which has given up belief in heaven, many Latter-day Saints feel even more of a responsibility to define the meaning of death and eternal life.[26]

Unlike so many in the religious world, the Latter-day Saints anticipate celestial life on a material world. Orson Pratt, an early church leader, eloquently made this point as follows:

> A Saint who is one in deed and in truth, does not look for an immaterial heaven, but he expects a heaven with lands, houses, cities, vegetation, rivers, and animals; with thrones, temples, palaces, kings, princes, priests, and angels; with food, raiment, musical instruments, etc., all of which are material. Indeed, the Saints' heaven is a redeemed, glorified, celestial, material creation, inhabited by glorified material beings, male and female, organized into families, embracing all the relationships of husbands and wives, parents and children, where sorrow, crying, pain, and death will be known no more. Or to speak still more definitely, this earth, when glorified, is the Saints' eternal heaven. On it they expect to live, with body, parts, and holy passions; on it they expect to move and have their being; to eat, drink, converse, worship, sing, play on musical instruments, engage in joyful, innocent, social amusements, visit neighboring towns and neighboring worlds; indeed, matter and its qualities and properties are the only beings or things with which they expect to associate. . . .
>
> Materiality is indelibly stamped upon the very heaven of heavens, upon all the eternal creations; it is the very essence of all existence.[27]

---

26. Colleen McDannell and Bernhard Lang, *Heaven: A History* (New Haven: Yale University Press, 1988), 312–13, 322.
27. *Masterful Discourses and Writings of Orson Pratt* (Salt Lake City: Bookcraft, 1962), 62–63.

Christian, But Different

One of the frequently debated issues in the religious world today is whether Latter-day Saints are Christians. Some of our harsher critics even go so far as to suggest that we worship "a different Jesus." We resonate with the words of C. S. Lewis: "It is not for us to say who, in the deepest sense, is or is not close to the spirit of Christ. We do not see into men's hearts. We cannot judge, and are indeed forbidden to judge. It would be wicked arrogance for us to say that any man is, or is not, a Christian in this refined sense. . . . When a man who accepts the Christian doctrine lives unworthily of it, it is much clearer to say he is a bad Christian than to say he is not a Christian."[28]

Latter-day Saints are not Catholic. We are not Protestant. That is to say, we do not fall within the historical line of Christianity; genealogically speaking, we do not trace our authority to Roman Catholicism or to those who chose to protest against the abuses of the Mother church and sought for major reform. Because the Latter-day Saints believe in a period of apostasy or falling away in which divine authority and doctrinal truths were lost after the deaths of the original apostles, we do not accept the creeds of Christianity that grew out of the major church councils. Thus if the crucial criteria for Christian status is either an unbroken historical link with the Christian church or an acceptance of the creeds, then clearly we are not Christian.

On the other hand, Latter-day Saints believe in the divinity of Jesus Christ—that he taught, comforted, liberated, forgave sins, performed miracles (such as stilling the storms, healing the sick, and raising the dead), suffered and died as a substitutionary atonement, and rose from the dead three days after his crucifixion. We believe he came to earth as the Son of God with power to do what no mortal man or woman could ever do. Further, we believe his teachings provide a pattern for the abundant life and happiness here and

---

28. Lewis, *Mere Christianity*, xiv-xv.

eternal reward hereafter. In short, Latter-day Saints claim to be Christian, but different.

Conclusion

For Joseph Smith, spirituality was a state of being, a condition achieved through the merging of the temporal and the spiritual, the finite and the infinite. Spirituality was essentially the result of a righteous life coupled with heightened perspective, an increased sensitivity to the things of God. Spirituality consisted of tying the heavens to the earth, imbuing men and women with the powers of God, and thereby elevating society. Such a change in one's nature was to be undertaken in the world, amidst the throes of spiritual opposition; one need not resort to monasticism in order to come out of the world. It was to be accomplished by every person, not just priest or minister, "for God hath not revealed anything to Joseph, but what He will make known unto the Twelve [Apostles], and even the least Saint may know all things as fast as he is able to bear them."[29] Brigham Young spoke of Joseph Smith's ability to communicate spiritual matters:

> When I saw Joseph Smith, he took heaven, figuratively speaking, and brought it down to earth; and he took the earth, brought it up, and opened up, in plainness and simplicity, the things of God. . . .
>
> The excellency of the glory of the character of brother Joseph Smith was that he could reduce heavenly things to the understanding of the finite. When he preached to the people—revealed the things of God, the will of God, the plan of salvation, the purposes of Jehovah, the relation in which we stand to him and all the heavenly beings, he reduced his teachings to the capacity of every man, woman, and child, making them as plain as a well-defined pathway. . . .

---

29. *Teachings of the Prophet Joseph Smith*, 149.

When you hear a man pour out eternal things, how [good] you feel, to what a nearness you seem to be brought with God. What a delight it was to hear brother Joseph talk upon the great principles of eternity.[30]

In a very real sense, Mormonism seeks to put back together many dimensions of faith and religious practice that centuries of debate have chosen to separate. The restoration of the gospel entails a kind of de-Platonizing influence; an effort to deconstruct the "wholly other" deity; to reacquaint and rejoin mortal man with what has become the unknowable and unapproachable god of the philosophers. The following revelation came to Joseph Smith in September 1830: "Wherefore, verily I say unto you that *all things unto me are spiritual, and not at any time have I given unto you a law which was temporal*" (D&C 29:34; emphasis added). Thus the restoration set in motion by Joseph Smith is intended to be a major revolution. Less than two months before his death, Joseph stated boldly: "I calculate to be one of the instruments of setting up the kingdom of [God foreseen by] Daniel by the word of the Lord, and I intend to lay a foundation that will revolutionize the whole world. . . . It will not be by sword or gun that this kingdom will roll on: the power of truth is such that all nations will be under the necessity of obeying the Gospel."[31]

And so, Mormonism seeks to reconcile the irreconcilable, to show how Latter-day Saints are Christian, but different; how we can worship and look reverentially to a God who is an exalted Man; how we can be fallen beings with limitless eternal possibilities; how we can strike the delicate balance between the fathomless work of an infinite God and the earnest efforts of finite humankind; how Mormonism possesses both static and dynamic elements, how it is inextricably linked to the past but directed toward the future;

---

30. A combined expression of Brigham Young from three separate addresses in *Journal of Discourses*, 5:332; 8:206; 4:54.

31. *Teachings of the Prophet Joseph Smith*, 366.

how higher education has an almost sacramental dimension, that learning and study are a vital part of our faith and a somewhat unexpected contributor to sustained faithfulness in the church; and, finally, how the LDS heaven is anything but "pie in the sky in the great by and by"; Latter-day Saints rejoice in the fact that this earth will become the celestial kingdom, a tangible sphere on which glorified, pure, and refined men and women will live and enjoy eternal associations forever.

I have chosen to use the words "reconciling the irreconcilable" to refer to this process of synthesis that takes place within LDS culture. Generations have dissected and analyzed theology to the point that we have almost drained religious thought and practice of their dynamic features, created artificial distinctions when perhaps such were never intended, and thereby established opposites between concepts that are really quite similar or at least closely related. Joseph Smith spoke once of two poles of a doctrinal issue and then added "Truth takes a road between them both." [32] Or, as he stated on another occasion, "by proving contraries, truth is made manifest." [33]

Robert L. Millet is Abraham O. Smoot University Professor and professor of ancient scripture at Brigham Young University.

---

32. *Teachings of the Prophet Joseph Smith*, 338.

33. *History of the Church of Jesus Christ of Latter-day Saints*, 7 vols., ed. B. H. Roberts (Salt Lake City: Deseret Book, 1957), 6:428.

CHAPTER 12

ℑ⬤

FROM HISTORY TO HERMENEUTICS:
THE TALMUD AS A HISTORICAL SOURCE

Jacob Neusner

I met Kent Brown when I was teaching at Brown University and
he came as a graduate student. He was the second Mormon I ever
knew; the first ones, Richard and Claudia Bushman, predisposed
me to like and respect Mormons and to expect great things from
them. I was not disappointed. Kent's combination of intelligence
and erudition and high personal ideals quickly won for him a place
in the lives of everyone who knew him, and a lifelong friendship
between us followed. Many times I was drawn to BYU to renew my
acquaintance with that splendid community represented by Kent.

This paper solves a problem of historical knowledge deriving
from religious texts that occupies Latter-day Saints scholars and
scholars of Judaism: How are we to learn the historical lessons set
forth by the revealed documents of sacred scripture? What sort of
history can we derive?

How a culture organizes the social order forms a problem on
which the Talmud supplies absolutely dependable data. We can
reconstruct the hypothetical thought processes that produced the
rabbinic system for Israelite culture. Let me explain.

In the beginning is the chaos of data, vast clouds of information bearing no intelligible shape, deriving we know not whence,

traveling we know not whither. Out of chaos comes order, in the case of the halakhic sector of the rabbinic canon effected through sorting matters out by subject matter. The principal categories of a given cultural system organize all data in one structure rather than in some other, with one consequence for meaning, rather than another. The intrinsic, inherent traits of the facts then bring about their own ordering. These categories, fixed by the authoritative formulations of a culture, require interpretation. They demand an account of how the categories cohere, the components of which they are comprised, and the inner principles and rules of logic that permit the categories to be augmented and reconfigured. Then the interpretive process works through the traits of things—their common task or purpose or point of coherence—and appeals to their nature, their teleology. What is interpreted is the artifacts of culture, a vast corpus of established facts, some deriving from scripture, some from nature, some from logic. How these are to be interpreted—organized into intelligible constructions and compositions and recast, then, into structures and composites—forms the issue of hermeneutics. And it is to the hermeneutical task that the end of narrative history and the advent of cultural analysis in the past tense points us.

How to Identify the Category-Formations

We have first to describe and then to analyze the successive topical treatments of the Mishnah, Tosefta, Yerushalmi, and Bavli—all in dialogue with scripture. The Mishnah as a matter of fact forms the source of the fifty-nine category-formations of the norms of conduct that order the Halakha and that classify all of its data. The Mishnah's mode of organization governs the Tosefta's, Yerushalmi's, and Bavli's presentation of the same topics. When we understand how these category-formations work, we can make provision for fresh data and extend the system.

The Halakha of formative Rabbinic Judaism is organized by topical-analytical category-formations, roughly three score of them, corresponding in general terms to Mishnah-Tosefta-Yerushalmi-Bavli tractates. Nearly all the facts of the law are grouped by the subject that they treat. More important, these facts are rarely random. They are assembled not only to give episodic information about the topic, but also to conduct a systematic analysis of the topic or of entire problems that transcend topical limits. I call the hermeneutics of the former kind the particular hermeneutics of a category-formation, the latter, the generic hermeneutics of the Halakha.

By "particular hermeneutics of a category-formation," therefore, I mean the theory of interpretation—selection of data, interpretation thereof—that is generated by the distinctive traits of the topic of a given category-formation. The halakhic hermeneutics is formed within an encompassing theory of analogy and contrast that identifies, within a given subject, a question of special interest. That hermeneutics will be particular to the subject matter of the category-formation. It follows that the facts are not inert but respond, in organization and focus, to the requirements of the question about those facts that analogical-contrastive analysis has identified. So, in accord with the way that was taken, each of the category-formations of the Halakha undertakes a particular inquiry into the facts at hand with a distinctive question in mind, which I have characterized as a particular hermeneutics.

All of the topical-analytical category-formations, furthermore, are animated by a generic hermeneutics. By generic hermeneutics I mean the body of interpretative issues *common* to the halakhic category-formations viewed in the aggregate. Generic hermeneutics in the Halakha, by contrast, asks many topics to contribute to a limited analytical program that transcends the specifics of the topics. It thus selects data and interprets them so as to say the same thing about many things. It aims to show how abstract principles come to expression in concrete details. In the category-formations of the Halakha, the particularization of abstract questions addresses five specific issues of general intelligibility: (1) interstitiality, (2) mixture and (3) connection, (4) the rational resolution of problems of doubt, and (5) the demonstration of how many things come from one thing, how one thing encompasses many things.

Each type of hermeneutics undertakes its distinctive work, and the two types complement one another. The one particularizes the general, and the other generalizes the particular. Specifically, the hermeneutics particular to the several halakhic category-formations, respectively, transforms details of that topical category-formation into an account of a large and general matter. It treats the detail as exemplary in its quest for generalization. The particular hermeneutics, given pride of place in the category-formations, and the generic hermeneutics, framing in order the second and subsidiary range of questions within a given category-formation or its principal parts, account for most of the halakhic program of the category-formations; the remainder consists of facts that are necessary to a full account of matters, and these facts are inert and usually are given at the end of the intellectually active presentation. In these three exercises—particular hermeneutics, generic hermeneutics, and repertoire of facts—all of the compositions and composites of the several halakhic category-formations in our hands take their place.

I propose to extrapolate the rejected alternatives: theories of category-formation that can have served but were not utilized in the halakhic construction that defines the norm. Of a theoretically unlimited number of topics available for category-formations, the Halakha set forth in the Mishnah chose three score, and the successor documents added remarkably few to that number. To state matters simply, of topics available for a religious theory of the social order to address, there is in theory no necessary limit. But the halakhic category-formations actually number, at the end, not a great many more than at the outset.

Unrealized Theories of Category-Formation

Besides the Mishnah's normative theory of topical-analytical category-formation, I identify three other theories that account for anomalous composites. These turn out to form variations on the initial theory, and not very influential ones at that.

The Mishnah's Anomalous Tractates

- Organize halakhic materials by the names of cited authorities: *Eduyyot.*
- Organize halakhic materials topically, so that they cohere in a narrative of how things are done: *Tamid, Middot.*
- Organize halakhic materials circumstantially, for example, by the occasion on which rulings were adopted: *m. Yadayim* 4:1-4.

The topical-not-analytical tractates tell the story of the divine service of the temple and the building itself. What we learn in *Eduyyot* is how the preferred approach to category-formation would not be carried out; but the Talmuds, particularly the Bavli, would find useful the collection of composites around attributive formulas, whether or not limited to a particular halakhic topic or problem. The collection of halakhic compositions into composites identified by a common circumstance defined matters only episodically. Laws were not linked to events because the entire institutional foundation of the legal system—as it is portrayed by the documents themselves—did not frame the presentation of the law. Where a law was set forth mattered little, which authority sponsored it mattered still less. What made a law normative was the power of logic, not the legislative body behind it or the sponsorship of a prominent legal authority.

The Mishnah's Anomalous Composites

- Topical-not-analytical (narrative of how things are done): *m. Sheqalim* 3:1-4; *m. Yoma* 1:1-7:5; *m. Sukkah* 5:1-7; *m. Rosh Hashanah* 2:3-7; *m. Taʿanit* 2:1-4; *m. Nazir* 6:7-9; *m. Sotah* 1:4-2:5; *m. Negaʿim* 14:1-10; *m. Parah* 3:1-10.
- Analytical-not-topical (organize halakhic materials around an analytical problem, without a uniform topical core): *m. Pesahim* 4:4; *m. Megillah* 1:4-11; *m. Gittin* 4:1-5:9;

m. Menahot 10:3; *m. Hullin* 1:5-7; *m. Arakhin* 2:1-3:5; *m. Parah* 8:2-7.

The topical-not-analytical approach to category-formation in the Mishnah limited its interest to matters having to do with the cult; the use of narrative to convey the Halakha through a description of how things are done served for a particular subject. But no other rhetorical convention took over in presenting any other particular subject.

The Tosefta's Anomalous Composites

- Topical-not-analytical: *t. Berakhot* 4:8-11; 5:6; *t. Shabbat* 6:1-7:18; *t. Sanhedrin* 2:2-13.
- Analytical-not-topical: *t. Shevi'it* 7:2-8; *t. Bava Qamma* 6:29-31; *t. Shevu'ot* 4:1-5; *t. Shehitat Hullin* 1:12-25; *t. Menahot* 1:2-4; *t. Temurah* 1:18-22; *t. Zavim* 3:1-5:1; *t. Tevul Yom* 1:4-7.

The division of the topical-analytical method of category-formation into its components characterizes the Tosefta's anomalous composites.

The Yerushalmi's Anomalous Composites

- Topical-not-analytical: *y. Berakhot* 2:2-3 II:2-3; *y. Nazir* 9:2 I.3-7.
- Analytical-not-topical: *y. Shevi'it* 3:1 I-IV.

The Yerushalmi's contribution proves negligible.

The Bavli's Anomalous Composites

- Topical-not-analytical: *b. Berakhot* 2:1-2 I:2-11; [*b. Berakhot* 3:4 II:2-13;] *b. Berakhot* 7:1-2 I:16-24; *b. Berakhot* 7:1-2 XII:8-24; *b. Shabbat* 2:1 IX:6-36; *b. Shabbat* 2:1 X:3-6; *b. Pesahim* 3:7-8 I:3-17; *b. Yoma* 1:1 IV:3-7; *b. Rosh Hashanah* 1:1 II:2-9; *b. Megillah* 3:1-2 I:13-44; II:7-19, 20-49; *b. Ketubbot* 6:5 I:2-17; *b. Gittin* 4:4A-D I:8-24; *b. Bava Qamma* 7:7 I:12-55; *b. Bava Batra* 1:5 IV:4-48; *b. Sanhedrin* 7:5 I:2-22; *b. Zevahim*

2:1A–C VI:3–13; *b. Menahot* 3:7 II:5–52; *b. Menahot* 3:7 I:2–11, *b. Menahot* 3:7 III:2–39; *b. Menahot* 4:1 I:10–69.

- (Propositional or) analytical-not-topical: *b. Zevahim* 5:1 IV:2–14; *b. Menahot* 1:1 I:5–13.

The Bavli proves remarkably fecund in the presentation of topical-not-analytical composites, an observation that takes on meaning when we examine the topical program that the Bavli realizes.

The Four Plausible Theories of Category-Formation and the One that Was Chosen

The halakhic hermeneutics of comparison and contrast governed the definition of the fifty-nine topical-analytical category-formations set forth by the Mishnah, adopted by the Tosefta, and adapted by the two Talmuds. Four other theories episodically surfaced in the Mishnah and the Tosefta: (1) select and organize data topically, without imposing a purposeful set of questions upon the presentation of those data; (2) select and organize data to investigate an abstract theory or proposition of Halakha, without restriction as to the topics that instantiate that theory or proposition; (3) collect laws that cohere by reason of the authority behind them or the event that precipitated their promulgation (a given occasion or session, comparable to a given document!); (4) select laws of a common subject and order them in a narrative, with a beginning, middle, and end—a variation of the first option. The first, second, and fourth alternatives simply represent variations on the established theory of category-formation, the topical-analytical one. The third produced negligible results. The first with its variations accounts for the category-formations of an other-than topical-analytical character. It follows that the normative theory of category-formation is to choose data deemed to constitute a single subject, where possible forming the data into answers to theoretical questions, where necessary simply gathering data deemed to cohere as a topic.

The present mode of thought is so familiar as to obscure a perfectly plausible past. Scripture, in the Pentateuchal law, set forth alternative approaches to the selection and interpretation of established rules and the construction of those rules into compositions deemed to cohere. Other collections and arrangements of laws into large conglomerates were produced by other Israelite heirs of scripture, exemplified by the law codes of the Dead Sea Scrolls, Elephantine papyri, and the like. But in fact nothing comparable to the Mishnah-Tosefta-Yerushalmi-Bavli, either in analytical character or—all the more so—in sheer scope, volume, and coverage, emerges out of any other Judaic system and its writings. We look in vain to scripture, to the Dead Sea library, and to the writings of Philo for compositions of equivalent comprehensiveness. Let me state with appropriate emphasis: *in the Judaic corpus of antiquity, from Moses to Muhammad, the Mishnah-Tosefta-Yerushalmi-Bavli are unique, both severally and jointly.* The Halakha, the continuous statement of law formed by the foundation-documents of Judaism, is altogether unique; to its grandeur no other legal system among ancient Judaic writings aspires, to its comprehensive reformation of Israelite society none presents a counterpart, not the laws of the Dead Sea library read as a coherent composite, nor the adumbration of the laws set forth by Philo, nor, self-evidently, the lesser compilations.

The Halakha not only asks a set of questions that scripture does not address, but also follows its own familiar program, entirely outside of scripture's framework, which transforms scripture's facts into data for analysis along lines of inquiry pertinent to all manner of data. The particular is made exemplary, the case transformed and transcended. Thus questions of mixtures of types of materials or colors, cases of doubt as to the status of the fabric, the minimal measures, the point at which various fabrics are susceptible, changes in the status and condition of the cloth, the status of cloth of various classifications—all of these issues of an abstract character are investigated in the particular context at hand, vastly expanding the limits of scripture's account of the matter.

To state the point simply: here, even where the Halakha builds symmetrically upon scripture's own foundations, the Halakha brings to bear a set of analytical questions that vastly transcend scripture's factual account of matters. Where, dealing with the same topic—category-formation—scripture gives information particular to the subject at hand and insusceptible of translation into principles to animate other subjects, the Halakha has its own theory of the Halakha. The singular is made exemplary, the rule is turned into a case, and laws form data in the statement of transcendent, encompassing law. The Halakha brings to the topic a completely autonomous program of its own. It is possessed of its own integrity—and that means, in particular, the Mishnah.

The Halakha represents a labor not only of recapitulation and reformation of scripture's law, but also of reconstruction and systematization and renewal. The purpose of the sages, as revealed through the shape and structure of their work in the Halakha of the Mishnah-Tosefta-Yerushalmi-Bavli, is to translate the narratives, case law, stories, and sayings and rules of scripture into a coherent, cogent statement: a system meant to realize God's grand design for Israel's social order. Take the case before us, for instance. In the movement from scripture's statement of the uncleanness of garments to the Halakha's analysis of theoretical problems of mixtures, such as are embodied in this law as much as in any other, that transformation of cases into rules, of laws into jurisprudence, takes place.

Why the Topical-Analytical Theory of Category Formation?

If the intent of the Halakha, from the Mishnah forward, is to systematize and concretize the received laws of scripture and to transform them into a coherent design of the Israelite social order (whether in theory, whether in actuality), how were the sages to turn laws into jurisprudence and cases into rules—and effectively to present the results as a paradigm? Scripture offered no model, with its tight adherence to the mythic mode of presenting law.

Scripture's law cohered by reason of God's instruction to Moses. It was never recast into a coherent topical exposition. How, for example, someone can have turned the laws of Deuteronomy 12 through 26 into a design for the social architecture of Israel I cannot say. Scripture's heaviest emphasis lies in the origin of the laws with God, not in demonstrating the proportion, balance, coherence, and rationality of the laws. Moses left that task for his successors in the Oral Torah. His sole category-formation, the one thing that holds together many things and imparts to the whole coherence, lies in his language, "The Lord spoke to Moses saying, speak to the children of Israel and say to them," and the counterpart allegations, both formulaic and narrative, that altogether characterize the law of the Written Torah and endow it with cogency.

Moses left open the task undertaken by the sages who framed the Halakha by the theory of analogical-contrastive analysis yielding topical-analytical category-formations. Beyond the closure of scripture, once people determined to carry forward the halakhic enterprise, to provide Israel with God's plan for the social order of a kingdom of priests and a holy people, the design of God's dominion, what to do? At issue now was not the origin and authority of the law; those questions were settled by the Pentateuchal portrait. The question now was, how do the rules derive from cases, whence the logic and the order of the system seen as a whole? It was for the solution of precisely that problem, the sifting of discrete facts in quest of their proper position and proportion in the order of things, that natural history undertook its work of classification through comparison and contrast, through the identification of a genus and the species thereof.

The raw data—whether the facts of the natural world or the Torah's rules, commandments, and cases that altogether comprise an account of the social world—give way to that process of taxic ordering. Specifically it is through the identification of the variables that speciate data and form of the species a genus, a process to make its way, to bring order, as God brought order in creation, out of the chaos, the unformed void of discrete facts, across all of the categories and classifications of nature or of the social order. Then, as I said, cases turn exemplary, data fall into place, rules emerge, and laws accommodate actualities and impose order upon them. That is why the Halakha is recapitulated, reformed to make blatant the lines of structure and order that the category-formations indicate.

We see how the Halakha solved that problem of rendering scripture (and tradition) into a systematic statement from the very fundamental trait of the Halakha, its organization into its six divisions and fifty-nine topical-analytical subdivisions. Were we to ask the framers of such law codes as Exodus 20–23, Leviticus 1–15, or Deuteronomy 12–26, for a table of contents to their codes, the list of topics would show, for Exodus 20–23 and Deuteronomy 12–26, no accessible logic to account for the choice and sequence of subjects, just this and that and the other thing—in no apparent order. Considerations of narrative may play a role, but no logic intrinsic to the laws and attentive to their details enters in. The snippets of laws in the former, the wildly diverse program of the latter—these exercise no power of organization and effect no coherence among their data at all. And even Leviticus 1–15, which does produce a logical sequence of well-executed category-formations, proves truncated and insufficient to the task of yielding generalizations for the Israelite social order in all its dimensions. The Pentateuch provides the data for the social task undertaken by the sages but no model to guide them in their work. And from this perspective, we are able to answer the question, why this, not that: why the topical-analytical approach to halakhic category-formation?

The answer comes in response to the question, how then were they to proceed? Once we recognize their purpose, the question answers itself. If we wish to know the law that a case exemplifies, the rule that governs diverse cases, we have no choice but to ask the analytical questions of taxonomic logic: What species encompass the cases? What genus accommodates the species? Natural history defined the sole solution to the sages' assignment: a logical, not a mythic, re-presentation of the Halakha. The species embody the law for like things; the genus sets down the rule to hold together, to control for, the variables between and among the species thereof. Then the taxic indicators, the variables that we require, present themselves as signals of an inner order, a logic of the social order to be specific. In that context, the purpose of the halakhic enterprise dictates the available theories of the halakhic category-formation. For that labor of turning scripture's commandments, in their narrative setting, into a design for Israel's social order, such as the sages accomplished in the Halakha as we know it, only one theory of category-formation can have served. Analogical-contrastive analysis yielded the hermeneutics of selection and interpretation of data that produced these category-formations. The Mishnah recast the givens of scripture into its category-formations, working from the whole to the parts, because the framers of the category-formations that are realized in the Mishnah found in the logic of natural history the medium for accomplishing God's purpose in setting forth the Pentateuchal laws.

That logic—identify the data that constitute a topic, form of the data a species alike but unlike another (hypothetical) species to form a common genus, sustaining a process of analogy and contrast to set forth an analytical program of problems and their solution—produced what God's purpose required: the order, the rationality, that turned of the bits and pieces, the discrete parts, a transcendent whole. In secular language, when from two received bits of information, sages could generate a fresh point, when two cases produced a rule encompassing many more cases, sages accomplished their purpose. And the only way to accomplish that wonder of intellect lay through the topical-analytical path through the lush fields of Pentateuchal cases, laws, and commandments. Once we know *why this*, we realize there is *no that*.

The Rules of Choosing Topics

We can now answer our question about halakhic hermeneutics. A culture in theory may identify an unlimited range of category-formations, but in practice chooses to build with a finite number of building blocks. But these, then, are refined in a vast range of variations. This fact may be expressed in terms of food. A given culture selects from a long menu of possible sources of nourishment the few items it wishes to utilize, but then prepares those items in a singularly broad selection of pots and pans. A few types of grain yield bread, but bread comes in variations without limit. Once we realize that the entire corpus of new topics fits into the large divisions of the received ones, we recognize the primary position of the Mishnah's formulation of the halakhic category-formations. What we see is an item treated casually in the Mishnah may attract attention later on; rules for a familiar topic take shape and come together. But I cannot point to a single case of a new topic that falls entirely outside of the topical repertoire of the Mishnah. Not only so, but, as to the identification of a category-formation that selects data and interprets them in the way in which the Mishnah's category-formations do, the topics added beyond the Mishnah's program present exactly one instance. The Mishnah defined all the topical-analytical category-formations conventionally spun out, from the whole to the parts.

What about the new topical-not-analytical category-formations of the Bavli? Let us take up the formidable catalog and ask, where do we move beyond the limits of the Mishnah's topical program? In my catalog I specify in parentheses the tractate that encompasses the topic. We eliminate forthwith the following items, which simply develop topics treated in the Mishnah's category-formations in the context defined thereby. These all are matters to which the Mishnah makes casual reference but to which the continuator-documents, particularly the Bavli, supply a sizable body of laws:

> rules on the recitation of the Shema' (*Berakhot*);
> rules and regulations of a meal (*Berakhot*);

rules on saying grace (*Berakhot*);
improperly postponing the fulfillment of vows beyond the
passage of the year in which they are taken (*Nedarim/Rosh
Hashanah*);
the laws that govern the mourner (*Mo'ed Qatan*);
marrying off orphans (*Ketubbot*);
support of the poor (*Pe'ah*);
freeing slaves (*Gittin*);
rules on correct management of the land of Israel (*Bava
Qamma*);
the rules of philanthropy: Who contributes? Who receives
(*Pe'ah*)?
religious duty of sanctifying hands and feet by washing
(*Yadayim*);
the unlettered person and the disciple of the sage (*Horayot*).

Most of the new topics then find a place within an established
category-formation, and what the continuator-documents do, particularly the Bavli, is enrich the corpus of data, not recast its main
lines of structure and order. The hermeneutics of comparison
and contrast encompass these items within the larger exercise of
analogical-contrastive analysis. That reduces the list of genuinely
new items to a handful.

In all, I find these freestanding and essentially inert topics, each
of them autonomous and lacking counterparts:

the Torah scroll
the lampstand and candlestick
tefillin, sisit, mezuzah
Hanukkah

The first three are holy objects, each accorded a full halakhic
account. Hanukkah is the one holy day that the Mishnah's program
of category-formations omits but that requires attention in its own
terms. That is because it is unlike the pilgrim festivals, the Days of

Awe, the Sabbath, and so on; like Purim, it produces no occasion for temple offerings, but on other bases it is readily differentiated from Purim. So it is *sui generis*. And that provides a key to the other new topics of the Bavli.

Anyone can concur that the holy objects (or the holiday) demand legal definition and regularization. *But a second glance tells us that they all are* sui generis*, not species of a common genus. Each is unique in categorical context.*

What other species forms a common genus with the Torah scroll or tefillin or sisit or the mezuzah? None affords the opportunity hypothetically to designate a counterpart species for the formation of a common genus and a process of analogical-contrastive analysis. The Torah scroll stands for them all, and having said that, nothing more is needed. It is unique; the rules for writing and protecting it have no analogue. Tefillin, sisit, and the mezuzah bear no counterparts that sages would acknowledge, for example, among the ways of the Amorites!

The rules of choosing topics therefore are two: the new topic will be an established fact in Israel's holy life (1) that is not accommodated by the Mishnah's category-formations, and (2) that is *sui generis* and not accessible to analogical-contrastive analysis.

So we can answer the two critical questions that together frame the rule for selecting new topics. That is, we explain both *why not that*, meaning, (1) the omission of these items from the Mishnah's categorical foci, and *why this*, meaning, (2) their identification and inclusion later on.

And that yields these generalizations: (1) None of them can have generated a category-formation by the criteria that govern in the Mishnah: a topic bearing a counterpart-species of a common genus, therefore, susceptible of hermeneutical development through analogical-contrastive analysis. And none of them, as a matter of fact, does sustain analogical-contrastive analysis. But (2) all of them form components of the system, indeed of the holy objects of the system, data that are treated tangentially by the Mishnah's category-formations (for the reasons just now spelled out).

But they are then endowed with a rich factual amplification by the continuator-documents, particularly the Bavli. That explains why each of them is comprised by inert information, presented in random order, not focused on the solution of a theoretical problem, and not animated by an issue that transcends the facts and imparts consequence to them. The very character of the Bavli's representation of the new topics conforms to the rule: not coherent and logically well-ordered but merely miscellaneous laws, stories, precedents, exegeses, about a required topic.

Here is our answer to the question—*why this, not that*—both in particular and in general.

In general, those topics of scripture that invite speciation and analogical-contrastive analysis will yield category-formations through the hermeneutics now fully exposed; and those topics of the Pentateuch that do not will find their place within the Halakha, within the framework of those that generate category-formations.

Jacob Neusner is Distinguished Service Professor of the History and Theology of Judaism and senior fellow at the Institute of Advanced Theology, Bard College.

CHAPTER 13

JOSEPH SMITH'S INTERPRETATION OF THE NEW TESTAMENT PARABLES OF THE KINGDOM

Monte S. Nyman

During the second year of Jesus's ministry, as he toured the Galilee with his twelve apostles, a great multitude gathered on the seashore where Jesus sat. He entered a ship, and from the ship he taught them in parables (see Matthew 13:1-3). After the first parable, "when he was alone, they that were about him with the twelve, asked of him the parable" (Mark 4:10). After explaining why he spoke in parables, he gave the interpretation of the parable. He then gave three more parables to the multitude and sent them away (Matthew 13:11-36). After entering into a house, Jesus explained the second parable to his disciples and also gave them four additional parables (see Matthew 13:36-52). All eight of the parables that he gave on this occasion were on the same subject, the kingdom of heaven. All of these parables are well known among the Christian world, but have varied interpretations. The Prophet Joseph Smith gave members of the Church of Jesus Christ of Latter-day Saints his understanding of these eight parables, but before discussing his interpretation, I will first review his qualifications for expounding on scriptures.

About three months after the organization of the church, the Lord confirmed by revelation that Joseph was "called and chosen to write the Book of Mormon, and to my ministry" (D&C 24:1; July 1830). Thus the Lord's verification of the many things Joseph had done for him in these two callings was probably given as an incentive to keep the commandment that he was now given: "And thou shalt continue in calling upon God in my name, and writing the things which shall be given thee by the Comforter, and expounding all scriptures unto the church. And it shall be given thee in the very moment what thou shalt speak and write, and they shall hear it, or I will send unto them a cursing instead of a blessing" (D&C 24:5-6). The Lord then gave Joseph other admonitions and instructions, which included a conditional promise: "Attend to thy calling and thou shalt have wherewith to magnify thine office, and to expound all scriptures" (D&C 24:9). Joseph was certainly blessed at "the very moment" when he expounded the scriptures in word and in writing as he continued his ministry, and those who "shall hear it"—accept and follow his explanations of the scriptures—will also be blessed (D&C 24:6).

I will first give Joseph's explanation of the Savior's answer as to why he taught in parables and then his explanation of each of the eight parables. As we examine these eight parables, it will be shown that they begin with the earthly ministry of Jesus Christ through the dispensation of the fulness of times. His discussion of the parables comes from a letter, "To the Elders of the Church of Latter-Day Saints," written in September 1835.[1] I will use the text of the Inspired Version, or Joseph Smith Translation (hereafter JST), of the parables as another example of his commandment to expound the scriptures. The differences between the JST and the King James Version (hereafter KJV) will be delineated in boldface type.

---

1. I will use the version found in *Teachings of the Prophet Joseph Smith*, comp. Joseph Fielding Smith (Salt Lake City: Deseret Book, 1974), hereafter cited as *TPJS*. The letter appeared previously in *History of the Church*, 2:264-72.

Why Did Jesus Teach in Parables?

Some claim that Jesus taught in parables to simplify his teachings so people could understand them. However, quite the opposite was true—the Prophet Joseph's translation of Jesus's explanation of why he used parables clarifies that view.

8 **Then** the disciples came and said unto him, Why speakest thou unto them in parables?

9 He answered and said unto them, Because it is given unto you to know the mysteries of the kingdom of heaven, but to them it is not given.

10 For whosoever **receiveth,** to him shall be given, and he shall have more abundance;

11 But whosoever **continueth not to receive,** from him shall be taken away even that he hath.

12 Therefore speak I to them in parables; because they, seeing not, see not; and hearing not, they hear not; neither do they understand.

13 And in them is fulfilled the prophecy of Esaias **concerning them,** which saith, By hearing, ye shall hear and shall not understand; and seeing, ye shall see and shall not perceive.

14 For this people's heart is waxed gross, and their ears are dull of hearing, and their eyes they have closed, lest at any time they should see with their eyes and hear with their ears, and should understand with their hearts, and should be converted, and I should heal them.

15 But blessed are your eyes, for they see; and your ears, for they hear. **And blessed are you because these things are come unto you, that you might understand them.**

16 And verily, I say unto you, many **righteous** prophets have desired to see **these days** which **you** see, and have not seen them; and to hear **that** which **you** hear, and have not heard. (Matthew 13:8-16 JST)

The Prophet Joseph Smith commented on the Savior's answer to his disciples' question of why he spoke in parables (Matthew 13:10 KJV; 13:8 JST).

"[I would here remark, that the 'them' made use of in this interrogation, is a personal pronoun, and refers to the multitude.] He answered and said unto them, [that is, unto the disciples] because it is given unto you, to know the mysteries of the Kingdom of Heaven, but to them, [that is, unbelievers] it is not given; for whosoever hath, to him shall be given, and he shall have more abundance; but whosoever hath not, from him shall be taken away even that he hath."

We understand from this saying, that those who had been previously looking for a Messiah to come, according to the testimony of the prophets, and were then, at that time looking for a Messiah, but had not sufficient light, on account of their unbelief, to discern Him to be their Savior; and He being the true Messiah, consequently they must be disappointed, and lose even all the knowledge, or have taken away from them all the light, understanding, and faith which they had upon this subject; therefore he that will not receive the greater light, must have taken away from him all the light which he hath; and if the light which is in you become darkness, behold how great is that darkness! [quotes Matthew 13:13-14 KJV; 13:12-13 JST].

Now we discover that the very reason assigned by this prophet, why they would not receive the Messiah, was, because they did not or would not understand; and seeing, they did not perceive [quotes Matthew 13:15-17 KJV; 13:14-16 JST].

We again make remark here—for we find that the very principle upon which the disciples were accounted blessed, was because they were permitted to see with their eyes and hear with their ears—that the condemnation which rested upon the multitude that received not His saying, was because they were not willing to see with their eyes and hear with their ears; not because they could not, and were not privileged to see and hear, but because their hearts were full of iniquity and abominations; "as your fathers did, so do ye." The prophet, foreseeing that they would thus harden their hearts, plainly declared it; and herein is the condemnation of the world; that light hath come into the world. And men choose darkness rather than light, because their deeds are evil. This is so plainly taught by the Savior, that a wayfaring man need not mistake it.[2]

Parables of the Kingdom

The Gospel of Mark tells us that those who came to him after he had given the first parable were **"the twelve, and they that believed in him,** they that were about him with the twelve, asked of him the parable" (Mark 4:9 JST).[3] The Gospel of Luke tells us why he didn't give the interpretation to the multitude: "And he said, Unto you [the twelve] it is given to know the mysteries of the kingdom of God: but to others in parables; that seeing they might not see, and hearing they might not understand" (Luke 8:10). This reason is further clarified by the Prophet Joseph Smith's comments above.

Regarding the eight parables, the Prophet Joseph Smith remarked: "I shall now proceed to make some remarks from the sayings of the Savior, recorded in the 13th chapter of His Gospel according to St. Matthew, which, in my mind, afforded us as clear an understanding upon the important subject of the gathering, as anything recorded in the Bible."[4]

2. *TPJS*, 94–96; first two bracketed remarks are in the original.
3. The KJV of Mark gives the same information, but the JST text is clearer.
4. *TPJS*, 94.

The Parable of the Sower—the Earthly Ministry of Jesus Christ and His Apostles

The Savior gave the interpretation of this parable to the twelve and those who believed. The quotations of Joseph Smith, given below, are evidence of what God revealed to him as he spoke (see D&C 24:6 above). The JST verses are often numbered differently than the KJV.

3 Behold, a sower went forth to sow,

4 And when he sowed, some seeds fell by the wayside, and the fowls came and devoured them up:

5 Some fell upon stony places, where they had not much earth: and forthwith they sprung up; **and when the sun was up, they were scorched, because they had no deepness of earth** [the KJV reverses the sequence]; and because they had no root, they withered away.

6 And some fell among thorns, and the thorns sprung up and choked them.

7 But others fell into good ground, and brought forth fruit; some an hundred-fold, some sixty-fold, **and** some thirty-fold. Who hath ears to hear, let him hear. (Matthew 13:3-7 JST; 13:3-9 KJV)

The Savior's interpretation of the parable to the twelve and those who believed follows:

17 Hear ye therefore the parable of the sower.

18 When any one heareth the word of the kingdom, and understandeth [**it** deleted from KJV] not, then cometh the wicked one, and catcheth away that which was sown in his heart; this is he **who** received seed by the wayside.

19 But he that received the seed into stony places, the same is he that heareth the word and **readily** with joy receiveth it, yet **he hath** not root in himself, **and en**dureth

but for a while; for when tribulation or persecution ariseth because of the word, by and by he is offended.

20 He also **who** received seed among the thorns, is he that heareth the word; and the care of this world and the deceitfulness of riches, choke the word, and he becometh unfruitful.

21 But he that received seed into the good ground, is he that heareth the word and understandeth **and endureth** [**it** deleted from KJV]; which also beareth fruit, and bringeth forth, some an hundred-fold, some sixty, **and** some thirty. (Matthew 13:17-21 JST; 13:18-23 KJV)

The Gospel of Mark prefaces the above record of Matthew with a question that suggests this parable is the key to those that will follow. "And he said unto them, Know ye not this parable? And how then will ye know all parables?" (Mark 4:13). Whether the question refers to the parables that he will give in this setting or in future times is not clear, but for this setting it supports the sequential nature of the parables of the kingdom given at this time.

The Gospel of Luke identifies the seed that is sown as the "word of God" (Luke 8:11). This identification reminds us of the vision of the tree of life given to Lehi in the Book of Mormon (1 Nephi 8). I will not discuss it here, but the message in the two accounts is definitely parallel.

The Prophet Joseph gave us this interpretation of the parable of the sower.

> And again—hear ye the parable of the sower. Men are in the habit, when the truth is exhibited by the servants of God, of saying. All is mystery; they have spoken in parables, and, therefore are not to be understood. It is true they have eyes to see, and see not, but none are so blind as those who will not see; and, although the Savior spoke this to such characters, yet unto His disciples he expounded it plainly;

and we have reason to be truly humble before the God of our fathers, that He hath left these things on record for us, so plain, that notwithstanding the exertions and combined influence of the priests of Baal, they have not power to blind our eyes, and darken our understanding, if we will but open our eyes, and read with candor, for a moment.

But listen to the explanation of the parable of the Sower [quotes Matthew 13:19 KJV; see v. 18 JST above]. Now mark the expression—that which was sown in his heart. *This is he which receiveth seed by the wayside.* Men who have no principle of righteousness in themselves, and whose hearts are full of iniquity, and have no desire for the principles of truth, do not understand the word of truth when they hear it. The devil taketh away the word of truth out of their hearts, because there is no desire for righteousness in them [quotes Matthew 13:20-23 KJV; see vv. 19-21 JST above]. Thus the Savior Himself explains unto His disciples the parable which He put forth, and left no mystery or darkness upon the minds of those who firmly believe on His words.

We draw the conclusion, then, that the very reason why the multitude, or the world, as they were designated by the Savior, did not receive an explanation upon His parables, was because of unbelief. To you, He says (speaking to His disciples) it is given to know the mysteries of the Kingdom of God. And why? Because of the faith and confidence they had in Him. *This parable was spoken to demonstrate the effects that are produced by the preaching of the word; and we believe that it has an allusion directly, to the commencement, or the setting up of the Kingdom in that age; therefore we shall continue to trace His sayings concerning this Kingdom from that time forth, even unto the end of the world.*[5]

---

5. *TPJS*, 96-97, emphasis added.

The eight parables thus begin with the preaching of the gospel during the ministry of Christ upon the earth.

The Parable of the Wheat and Tares—the Apostasy

22 Another parable put he forth unto them, saying, The kingdom of heaven is likened unto a man who sowed good seed in his field;

23 But while **he** slept, his enemy came and sowed tares among the wheat, and went his way.

24 But when the blade [**was** deleted from KJV] sprung up, and brought forth fruit, then appeared the tares also.

25 So the servants of the house-holder came and said unto him, Sir, didst not thou sow good seed in thy field? [**from** deleted from KJV] whence then hath it tares?

26 He said unto them, An enemy hath done this.

27 **And** the servants said unto him, Wilt thou then that we go and gather them up?

28 But he said, Nay; lest while ye gather up the tares, ye root up also the wheat with them.

29 Let both grow together until the harvest, and in the time of harvest, I will say to the reapers, Gather ye together first the **wheat into my barn; and the tares are bound in bundles to be burned.** (Matthew 13:22-29 JST; the KJV reverses the sequence)

The Gospel of Mark gives an abbreviated version of the above parable (Mark 4:26-29), which some believe is a separate parable. Since Joseph Smith commented only on the Matthew account, I will not consider the Mark text. There is no account in Luke.

Jesus interpreted this second parable to his disciples, after he had "sent the multitude away, and went into the house" (Matthew 13:36).

36 He that soweth the good seed is the Son of man.

37 The field is the world; the good seed are the children of the kingdom; but the tares are the children of the wicked [**one** deleted from KJV].

38 The enemy that sowed them is the devil.

39 The harvest is the end of the world, **or the destruction of the wicked** [**and** deleted from KJV, and JST vv. 38-40 is one verse in KJV].

40 The reapers are the angels, **or the messengers sent of heaven.**

41 As, therefore, the tares are gathered and burned in the fire, so shall it be in the end of this world, **or the destruction of the wicked.**

42 **For in that day, before** the Son of man **shall come, he** shall send forth his angels **and messengers of heaven.**

43 And they shall gather out of his kingdom all things that offend, and them which do iniquity, **and shall cast them** [**into a furnace of fire** deleted from KJV] **out among the wicked; and** there shall be wailing and gnashing of teeth.

44 **For the world shall be burned with fire.**

45 Then shall the righteous shine forth as the sun, in the kingdom of their Father. Who hath ears to hear, let him hear. (Matthew 13:36-45 JST)

The Lord revealed a similar interpretation in December 1832, as the Prophet Joseph "was reviewing and editing the manuscript of the translation of the Bible" (D&C 86, section heading).

1 Verily, thus saith the Lord unto you my servants, concerning the parable of the wheat and of the tares:

2 Behold, verily I say, the field was the world, and the apostles were the sowers of the seed;

3 And after they have fallen asleep the great persecutor of the church, the apostate, the whore, even Babylon, that

maketh all nations to drink of her cup, in whose hearts the enemy, even Satan, sitteth to reign—behold he soweth the tares; wherefore, the tares choke the wheat and drive the church into the wilderness.

4 But behold, in the last days, even now while the Lord is beginning to bring forth the word, and the blade is springing up and is yet tender—

5 Behold, verily I say unto you, the angels are crying unto the Lord day and night, who are ready and waiting to be sent forth to reap down the fields;

6 But the Lord saith unto them, pluck not up the tares while the blade is yet tender (for verily your faith is weak), lest you destroy the wheat also.

7 Therefore, let the wheat and the tares grow together until the harvest is fully ripe; then ye shall first gather out the wheat from among the tares, and after the gathering of the wheat, behold and lo, the tares are bound in bundles, and the field remaineth to be burned. (D&C 86:1-7)

The KJV and the JST identify the sower of the good seed as the Son of man (Matthew 13:37 KJV; 13:36 JST), but the Doctrine and Covenants states that the apostles were the sowers of the seed (D&C 86:2). This is not a contradiction. Jesus began the sowing of the word of God, but after his resurrection, the apostles were commanded to "teach all nations" (Matthew 28:19; Mark 16:15).

The devil sowing the tares, which looked like wheat but were actually weeds, resulted in what is called the apostasy (Matthew 13:37-38 JST). The Doctrine and Covenants revelation describes how the apostasy did "drive the church into the wilderness" after the apostles had "fallen asleep" or had been killed or died (86:3; see Revelation 12:1-7 JST).

The Prophet Joseph gave this inspired interpretation:

Now we learn by this parable, not only the setting up of the Kingdom in the days of the Savior, *which is represented by the good seed,* which produced fruit, but also the *corruptions of the Church, which are represented by the tares,* which were sown by the enemy, which His disciples would fain have plucked up, or cleansed the Church of, if their views had been favored by the Savior. But He, knowing all things, says, Not so. As much as to say, your views are not correct, the Church is in its infancy, and if you take this rash step, you will destroy the wheat, or the Church, with the tares; therefore it is better to *let them grow together until the harvest, or the end of the world, which means the destruction of the wicked,* which is not yet fulfilled, as we shall show hereafter, in the Savior's explanation of the parable, which is so plain that there is no room left for dubiety upon the mind, notwithstanding the cry of the priests—"parables, parables! figures, figures! mystery, mystery! all is mystery!" But we will find no room for doubt here, as the parables were all plainly elucidated.[6]

That the time of the fulfillment of this parable extended to the latter days was confirmed by the Lord in Section 101 of the Doctrine and Covenants, given to the Prophet Joseph Smith on 16 December 1833, when "the saints who had gathered in Missouri were suffering great persecution" (section heading).

63 Again, verily I say unto you, I will show unto you wisdom in me concerning all the churches, inasmuch as they are willing to be guided in a right and proper way for their salvation—

64 That the work of the gathering together of my saints may continue, that I may build them up unto my name

---

6. *TPJS*, 97-98, emphasis added.

upon holy places; for the time of harvest is come, and my word must needs be fulfilled.

65 Therefore, I must gather together my people, *according to the parable of the wheat and the tares*, that the *wheat may be secured in the garners to possess eternal life*, and be crowned with celestial glory, when I shall come in the kingdom of my Father to reward every man according as his work shall be;

66 While *the tares shall be bound in bundles, and their bands made strong, that they may be burned with unquenchable fire.*

67 Therefore, a commandment I give unto all the churches, that they shall continue to gather together unto the places which I have appointed [stakes].

68 Nevertheless, as I have said unto you in a former commandment, let not your gathering be in haste, nor by flight; but let all things be prepared before you. (D&C 101:63-68)

After reading Matthew 13:33-38 (13:32-37 JST), the Prophet Joseph Smith inserted the following comments: "Now let our readers mark the expression—'the field is the world, the tares are the children of the wicked one, the enemy that sowed them is the devil, the harvest is the end of the world, (let them carefully mark this expression—the end of the world) and the reapers are the angels.'"[7] The Prophet Joseph then gave additional comments on the destruction of the tares (wicked) and the gathering of the wheat (members) in the last days.

Now men cannot have any possible grounds to say that this is figurative, or that it does not mean what it says: for He is now explaining what He had previously spoken in parables; and according to this language, *the end of the world is the destruction of the wicked, the harvest and the end of the*

---

7. *TPJS*, 100.

world have an allusion directly to the human family in the last days, instead of the earth, as many have imagined; and that which *shall precede the coming of the Son of Man, and the restitution of all things spoken of by the mouth of all the holy prophets since the world began*; and the *angels* are to have something to do in this great work, for they *are the reapers.* As, therefore, the tares are gathered and burned in the fire, so shall it be in the end of the world; that is, *as the servants of God go forth warning the nations,* both priests and people, and as they harden their hearts and reject the light of truth, these first being delivered over to the buffeting of Satan, and the law and the testimony being closed up, as it was in the case of the Jews, *they are left in darkness, and delivered over unto the day of burning*; thus being bound up by their creeds, and their bands being made strong by their priests, are prepared for the fulfilment of the saying of the Savior—[quotes Matthew 13:41-42 KJV; 13:42-43 JST]. We understand that *the work of gathering together of the wheat into barns, or garners, is to take place while the tares are to be bound over, and preparing for the day of burning*; that after the day of burnings, the righteous shall shine forth like the sun, in the Kingdom of their Father. Who hath ears to hear, let him hear.[8]

On a later occasion, 2 July 1839, the Prophet Joseph quoted Matthew 13:41 (13:42 JST) concerning angels coming down: "All these authoritative characters will come down and join hand in hand in bringing about this work."[9]

The second event, given in Jesus's parables of the kingdom (Matthew 13), is the apostasy from the true teachings of Jesus Christ given during his ministry on the earth. The influence of the apostasy will continue on through the time of the foretold restoration of the gospel in the latter days.

---

8. *TPJS*, 100-101, emphasis added.
9. *TPJS*, 159.

The Parable of the Mustard Seed—the Book of Mormon; Angels Restore Keys

> 30 **And** another parable put he forth unto them, saying, The kingdom of heaven is like to a grain of mustard seed, which a man took and sowed in his field;
>
> 31 Which indeed is the least of all seeds, but when it is grown, it is the greatest among herbs, and becometh a tree, so that the birds of the air come and lodge in the branches thereof. (Matthew 13:30–31 JST; 13:31–32 KJV)

The parable of the mustard seed is also recorded in the Gospels of both Mark and Luke. I will comment just on Mark's text, but will first acknowledge how Matthew's text was interpreted by the Prophet Joseph.

> And again, another parable put He forth unto them, having an allusion to the *Kingdom that should be set up, just previous to or at the time of the harvest* [quotes Matthew 13:31–32 KJV; 13:30–31 JST]. Now we can discover plainly that this figure is given to *represent the Church as it shall come forth in the last days.* Behold, the Kingdom of Heaven is likened unto it. Now, what is like unto it?
>
> Let us take *the Book of Mormon, which a man took and hid in his field, securing it by his faith, to spring up in the last days,* or in due time; let us behold it *coming forth out of the ground, which is indeed accounted the least of all seeds,* but behold it branching forth, yea, even towering, with lofty branches, and God-like majesty, until it, like the mustard seed, becomes the greatest of all herbs. And *it is truth, and it has sprouted and come forth out of the earth, and righteousness begins to look down from heaven,*[10] *and God is sending down His powers, gifts and angels, to lodge in the branches thereof.*

---

10. Joseph seems to be alluding to the Book of Mormon prophecies in Psalm 85:11; see Isaiah 45:8.

The Kingdom of Heaven is like unto a mustard seed. Behold, then is not this the Kingdom of Heaven that is raising its head in the last days in the majesty of its God, even the Church of the Latter-day Saints, like an impenetrable, immovable rock in the midst of the mighty deep, exposed to the storms and tempests of Satan, but has, thus far, remained steadfast, and is still braving the mountain waves of opposition, which are driven by the tempestuous winds of sinking crafts, which have [dashed] and are still dashing with tremendous foam across its triumphant brow; urged onward with redoubled fury by the enemy of righteousness, with his pitchfork of lies.[11]

The Gospel of Mark describes the "grain of mustard seed, which, when it is sown in the earth, is less than all the seeds that be in the earth" (Mark 4:31). There were many records kept by the Nephites and Jaredites who lived upon the American continent. Mormon, a prophet of the Lord there, abridged these many records upon the plates from which Joseph Smith translated the Book of Mormon (see D&C 17:6; 24:1). Mormon repeatedly states that he could not "write a hundredth part of the things of my people" (Words of Mormon 1:5; see Helaman 3:14; 3 Nephi 5:8; 26:6). Nephi, Jacob, and Moroni, the other major contributors to the Book of Mormon, make similar statements (see 1 Nephi 9:3-4; 19:3-4; Jacob 3:13; Ether 15:33). Certainly these statements of the Nephite writers verify Mark's description of the mustard seed symbolizing "less than all the seeds that be in the earth."

The third parable of the kingdom is that of the mustard seed (Book of Mormon) being brought from the earth, its being translated by the gift and power of God, its growing into a tree (the establishment of the Church of Jesus Christ in the last days), and the

---

11. *TPJS*, 98-99, emphasis added.

many angels who came and restored their keys and powers and the gifts of God again upon the earth.

The Parable of the Three Measures of Meal—Three Witnesses of the Book of Mormon

> 32 Another parable spake he unto them, The kingdom of heaven is like unto leaven, which a woman took and hid in three measures of meal, till the whole was leavened.
>
> 33 All these things spake Jesus unto the multitudes in parables; and without a parable spake he not unto them,
>
> 34 That it might be fulfilled which was spoken by the prophets, saying, I will open my mouth in parables; I will utter things which have been kept secret from the foundation of the world.[12] (Matthew 13:32-34 JST; 13:33-35 KJV)

The Prophet Joseph explained: "It may be understood that the Church of the Latter-day Saints has taken its rise from a little leaven that was put into three witnesses. Behold, how much this is like the parable! It is fast leavening the lump, and will soon leaven the whole."[13] The Prophet's interpretation is certainly one that is not even considered in the Christian world, but remember the Lord's promise to give him the words by the Comforter at "the very moment what thou shalt speak or write" as he expounded the scriptures to the church (D&C 24:5-6). This interpretation is consistent with both the New and the Old Testament teachings: "But if he will not hear thee, then take with thee one or two more, that in the mouth of two or three witnesses every word may be established" (Matthew 18:16; see Deuteronomy 17:6; 19:15). As

---

12. The quotation is from Psalm 78:2: "I will open my mouth in a parable: I will utter dark sayings of old," which is undoubtedly a poor translation, the Matthew quotation being correct. The Psalmist is probably quoting another prophet, which was the usual procedure in the Psalms.

13. *TPJS*, 100.

identified previously, the woman is symbolic of the church of God (see Revelation 12:1-7 JST).

The fourth parable of the kingdom foretells "The Testimony of Three Witnesses," which is given in the front of each copy of the Book of Mormon (see D&C 17).

The Parable of a Treasure Hid in a Field—the Gathering of the Saints

> Again, the kingdom of heaven is like unto **a** treasure hid in a field [**the which** deleted from KJV]. **And** when a man hath found **a treasure which is hid**, he [**hideth** deleted KJV] **secureth it,** and, **straightway,** for joy thereof, goeth and selleth all that he hath, and buyeth that field. (Matthew 13:46 JST; 13:44 KJV)

The Prophet Joseph Smith's interpretation was: "But to illustrate more clearly this gathering [of the wheat]: We have another parable—[quotes Matthew 13:44 KJV]. The Saints work after this pattern. See the Church of the Latter-day Saints, selling all that they have, and gathering themselves together unto a place that they may purchase for an inheritance, that they may be together and bear each other's afflictions in the day of calamity."[14] The fulfillment of this parable was the Saints gathering to New York, Kirtland, Missouri, Nauvoo, and finally Utah. After these gatherings, while the headquarters of the church remained in Salt Lake City, Utah, the converts continued to gather together in whatever area or location they were living.

The fifth parable of the kingdom portrays the Saints gathering together in groups or units throughout the world.

---

14. *TPJS*, 101.

The Parable of the Pearl of Great Price—Stakes Surround Zion

And again, the kingdom of heaven is like unto a merchantman, seeking goodly pearls, who, when he had found one pearl of great price, **he** went and sold all that he had and bought it. (Matthew 13:47 JST; 13:45-46 KJV)

The interpretation of this parable by the Prophet Joseph Smith was: "The Saints again work after this example. See men traveling to find places for Zion and her stakes or remnants, who, when they find the place for Zion, or the pearl of great price, straightway sell that they have, and buy it."[15] Although this parable may seem similar to the previous one, it is different. The place "for Zion" was revealed to Joseph on 20 July 1831, while the Saints were gathering to Missouri.

1 Hearken, O ye elders of my church, saith the Lord your God, who have assembled yourselves together, according to my commandments, in this land, which is the land of Missouri, which is the land which I have appointed and consecrated for the gathering of the saints.

2 Wherefore, this is the land of promise, and the place for the city of Zion.

3 And thus saith the Lord your God, if you will receive wisdom here is wisdom. Behold, the place which is now called Independence is the center place; and a spot for the temple is lying westward, upon a lot which is not far from the courthouse. (D&C 57:1-3)

The Saints attempted to establish the city of Zion during the next three years, but failed. The Lord described it this way:

3 they have not learned to be obedient to the things which I required at their hands, but are full of all manner

---

15. *TPJS*, 102.

of evil, and do not impart of their substance, as becometh saints, to the poor and afflicted among them;

4 And are not united according to the union required by the law of the celestial kingdom;

9 Therefore, in consequence of the transgressions of my people, it is expedient in me that mine elders should wait for a little season for the redemption of Zion—

10 That they themselves may be prepared, and that my people may be taught more perfectly, and have experience, and know more perfectly concerning their duty, and the things which I require at their hands.

11 And this cannot be brought to pass until mine elders are endowed with power from on high. (D&C 105:3-4, 9-11)

"The places for Zion" mentioned in Joseph Smith's interpretation of the parable were the stakes of Zion that were to be built up and surround the city of Zion. Other requirements to precede the building of the city of Zion were revealed in the remainder of the revelation quoted above (D&C 105). But Zion will be built:

17 Zion shall not be moved out of her place, notwithstanding her children are scattered.

18 They that remain, and are pure in heart, shall return, and come to their inheritances, they and their children, with songs of everlasting joy, to build up the waste places of Zion—

19 And all these things that the prophets might be fulfilled.

20 And, behold, there is none other place appointed than that which I have appointed; neither shall there be any other place appointed than that which I have appointed, for the work of the gathering of my saints. (D&C 101:17-20)

The sixth parable of the kingdom predicts the building up of the stakes of Zion to surround the city of Zion, and then those Saints designated by revelation selling all that they had and returning to build up the temple and the city of Zion.[16]

The Parable of the Net—the Cleansing of the Church

48 Again, the kingdom of heaven is like unto a net that was cast into the sea, and gathered of every kind, which, when it was full, they drew to shore, and sat down, and gathered the good into vessels, but cast the bad away.

49 So shall it be at the end of the world.

50 **And the world is the children of the wicked.**

51 The angels shall come forth, and sever the wicked from among the just, and shall cast them out into the [**furnace of fire** deleted from KJV] **world to be burned.** There shall be wailing and gnashing of teeth. (Matthew 13:48-51 JST; 13:47-50 KJV)

After quoting the above verses, the Prophet Joseph explained:

For the work of this pattern, behold the seed of Joseph, spreading forth the Gospel net upon the face of the earth, gathering of every kind, that the good may be saved in vessels prepared for that purpose, and the angels will take care of the bad. So shall it be at the end of the world—the angels shall come forth and sever the wicked from among the just, and cast them into the furnace of fire, and there shall be wailing and gnashing of teeth.[17]

The Lord revealed to Joseph Smith at Kirtland, Ohio, 23 July 1837:

16. For a more complete analysis of the building of Zion and her stakes, see Monte S. Nyman, "When Will Zion Be Redeemed?" in *The Doctrine and Covenants: A Book of Answers* (Salt Lake City: Deseret Book, 1996), 137-53.

17. *TPJS*, 102.

23 Verily, verily, I say unto you, darkness covereth the earth, and gross darkness the minds of the people, and all flesh has become corrupt before my face.

24 Behold, vengeance cometh speedily upon the inhabitants of the earth, a day of wrath, a day of burning, a day of desolation, of weeping, of mourning, and of lamentation; and as a whirlwind it shall come upon all the face of the earth, saith the Lord.

25 And upon my house shall it begin, and from my house shall it go forth, saith the Lord;

26 First among those among you, saith the Lord, who have professed to know my name and have not known me, and have blasphemed against me in the midst of my house, saith the Lord. (D&C 112:23-26)

Thus the end of the world, in the last days, will begin with the cleansing of the church. There will be wicked people among the members who have gathered, and they will be cast out of the church and burned among the wicked.

The fulfillment of the seventh parable of the kingdom will be the cleansing of the church before the wicked are burned at Christ's coming.

The Parable of the Householder—the Dispensation of the Fulness of Times

52 **Then** Jesus **said** [saith in KJV] unto them, Have ye understood all these things? They say unto him, Yea, Lord.

53 Then said he unto them, [**Therefore** deleted from KJV] Every scribe [**which is** deleted from KJV] **well** instructed [**unto** deleted from KJV] **in the things** of the kingdom of heaven, is like unto a [**man that is an** deleted from KJV] householder; **a man, therefore,** which bringeth forth out of his treasure [**things** deleted from KJV] **that which is** new and old.

54 And it came to pass, [**that** deleted from KJV] when Jesus had finished these parables, he departed thence. (Matthew 13:52–54 JST; 13:51–52 KJV)

The JST rewording of "*well* instructed *in the things* of the kingdom" (v. 53, emphasis added) differentiates between all who are instructed and those who are well instructed. It also distinguishes between worldly learning and the things learned of God. The mercy and justice of God are again illustrated.

Lastly, Joseph interpreted the eighth parable in his letter:

> For the works of this example, see the Book of Mormon coming forth out of the treasure of the heart. Also the covenants given to the Latter-day Saints, also the translation of the Bible—thus bringing forth out of the heart things new and old, thus answering to three measures of meal undergoing the purifying touch by a revelation of Jesus Christ, and the ministering of angels, who have already commenced this work in the last days, which will answer to the leaven which leavened the whole lump. Amen.[18]

Joseph commented on verse 52: "And we say, yea, Lord; and well might they say, yea, Lord; for these things are so plain and so glorious, that every Saint in the last days must respond with a hearty Amen to them."[19]

Finally, the last of the eight parables of the kingdom foretells the ushering in of the dispensation of the fulness of times, as prophesied by the apostle Paul: "That in the dispensation of the fulness of times he might gather together in one all things in Christ, both which are in heaven, and which are on earth; even in him" (Ephesians 1:10).

An understanding and acceptance of Joseph Smith's interpretation of these eight parables should bring a "hearty Amen" from the

---

18. *TPJS*, 102.
19. *TPJS*, 102.

readers of these parables. The Prophet Joseph Smith was blessed as he expounded on the parables of the kingdom of heaven.

Monte S. Nyman is emeritus professor of ancient scripture at Brigham Young University.

CHAPTER 14

Ꝫ☙

EXPLORATORY NOTES ON THE *FUTUWWA* AND ITS SEVERAL INCARNATIONS

Daniel C. Peterson

It is a privilege and a pleasure to participate in this volume in honor of Professor S. Kent Brown, who has been a major help to me at pivotal points in my career. I first went to the Middle East in a Jerusalem semester abroad group that he led during the first half of 1978. And then, when I returned to Egypt in the autumn of 1978 with my new bride, it was Kent Brown who met us at the Cairo airport and allowed us to stay with his family until we found housing of our own. He was also instrumental in setting the stage for my receiving a job offer at Brigham Young University and has remained a valued colleague, a friend, and a model of Christian living ever since.

These notes were first compiled in a 1981 graduate seminar at the American University in Cairo for Professor George Scanlan. Despite my intention of getting back to the subject, however, I had not. So, when I was invited to contribute to this volume in honor of a friend whom my wife and I will always associate with our time in Egypt, it seemed a good opportunity to resurrect something that I commenced there. My hope is either to pursue this topic further myself or, at least, to encourage some other researcher to look at it. Beyond minor mechanical changes (the paper was written on a typewriter), I have also made explicit some of the similarities that I perceive between the movements described here and the Gadianton robbers of the Book of Mormon—similarities that, for obvious reasons, I left unnoted in that first draft in Egypt.

A Connection to Mormon Studies

In her imaginative biography of Joseph Smith, *No Man Knows My History*, the late Fawn Brodie explained the Book of Mormon's Gadianton robbers as a fictional echo of nineteenth-century Freemasonry.[1] She has been followed in this by writers such as Robert Hullinger and Dan Vogel.[2] Along with other Latter-day Saint scholars, however, I have objected to the explanation as simplistic, inaccurate, historically provincial, and, of course, wrong.[3] There are, I contend, other parallels to the Gadianton robbers that are superior to the Freemasons and that pick up aspects of Gadiantonism—for example, its character as, first, ideologically motivated urban terrorism and then, frequently, as partisan or guerrilla warfare—that Freemasonry does not.[4] In these notes, I consider a premodern Middle Eastern group (or group of groups) that, in my judgment, offers several analogies to the Gadianton robbers.

---

1. Fawn M. Brodie, *No Man Knows My History: The Life of Joseph Smith*, 2nd ed. (New York: Knopf, 1975), 63–65.

2. Robert N. Hullinger, *Mormon Answer to Skepticism: Why Joseph Smith Wrote the Book of Mormon* (St. Louis: Clayton, 1980), 114 nn. 30–31; Dan Vogel, "Mormonism's 'Anti-Masonick Bible,'" *John Whitmer Historical Association Journal* 9 (1989): 17–30.

3. See, among other things, Daniel C. Peterson, "Notes on 'Gadianton Masonry,'" in *Warfare in the Book of Mormon*, ed. Stephen D. Ricks and William J. Hamblin (Salt Lake City: Deseret Book and FARMS, 1990), 174–224, which provides further references; Daniel C. Peterson, "'Secret Combinations' Revisited," *Journal of Book of Mormon Studies* 1/1 (1992): 184–88; reprinted in John W. Welch and Melvin J. Thorne, eds., *Pressing Forward with the Book of Mormon: The FARMS Updates of the 1990s* (Provo, UT: FARMS, 1999), 190–95; Paul Mouritsen, "Secret Combinations and Flaxen Cords: Anti-Masonic Rhetoric and the Book of Mormon," *Journal of Book of Mormon Studies* 12/1 (2003): 64–77; Nathan Oman, "Secret Combinations: A Legal Analysis," *FARMS Review* 16/1 (2004): 49–73.

4. See Daniel C. Peterson, "The Gadianton Robbers as Guerrilla Warriors," in *Warfare in the Book of Mormon*, 146–73.

The *Futuwwa* Complex(ity)

The study of the movements in the Muslim world known under the general name of *futuwwa* (the term is variously transliterated in the secondary literature) is made very difficult, as the late Claude Cahen noted, by the fact that they have assumed extremely diverse forms in the course of their history. Consequently, the documentary evidence relating to them "often appears . . . to be irreconcilable . . . and, despite the advance that has been made in our knowledge of them, it cannot be said that even now we really know exactly what they were."[5] The diversity appears in the very word itself: According to Hans Wehr's standard Arabic/English dictionary, the term *futuwwa* refers secondarily to "Islamic brotherhoods of the Middle Ages, governed by chivalrous precepts," but primarily to "youth" or "adolescence." (Adherents of the *futuwwa* are called *fityān* ["young people," "adolescents," "juveniles"], whatever their age.) Most puzzlingly, *futuwwa* denotes both "the totality of the noble, chivalrous qualities of a man, noble manliness, magnanimity, generosity, nobleheartedness, chivalry," and, in Egyptian colloquial, "bully, brawler, rowdy, tough; racketeer."[6]

Summarizing his findings on the situation in Nishapur between the fifth and eleventh centuries, Richard Bulliet concludes that "there is enough information to demonstrate the importance of the *futūwa* but not really enough to show what it was or what it did."[7] "The *futūwa* and related groups," laments Bulliet, "present a puzzle whenever and wherever they're encountered. Upon certain points there is agreement: the membership consisted of young men,

---

5. C. Cahen, "Futuwwa," in *Encyclopedia of Islam*, new ed., vol. 3 (Leiden: Brill, 1960), 961–65, esp. 961.

6. Hans Wehr, *A Dictionary of Modern Written Arabic*, ed. J. Milton Cowan (Wiesbaden: Harrassowitz, 1971), s.v. *futuwwa*. Curiously, the word is even etymologically connected with the legal term *fatwā*. On the latter, see Daniel C. Peterson, "Fatwā," in *Encyclopedia of Islam and the Muslim World*, ed. Richard C. Martin et al. (New York: Macmillan Reference USA, 2004), 1:255.

7. Richard W. Bulliet, *The Patricians of Nishapur: A Study in Medieval Islamic Social History* (Cambridge: Harvard University Press, 1972), 43–44, esp. 44.

usually celibate; special ritual and dress were involved; and there was some sort of connection with Ṣūfism. But beyond these points there is disagreement and mystery. Associations have been sought with banditry, chivalry, the upper class, the lower class, artisan guilds, police, and so forth."[8] "The term *futuwwa*," writes Sawsan El-Messiri, "may refer to groups with basically religious orientation as well as to groups with a criminal or outlaw orientation. Generally, it has been applied to the masses but occasionally to members of the elite as well. In all cases," she generalizes quite inaccurately, "the element of protection has been seminal to the role."[9] It is difficult for a student of the Book of Mormon not to think, when facing so ambiguous a phenomenon, of the Gadianton robbers, who are perceived by their opponents as violent thugs (see, for example, Helaman 6:18; 11:25-27) but who regard themselves as pursuing a "good" cause according to patterns "of ancient date" (3 Nephi 3:9).

Cahen sees two "incompatible" types of *fityān*—communal (bachelor) mystics on the one hand, and violent ruffians on the other—while Bulliet is able to distinguish patrician, mystic, and artisan/populist components in the *futuwwa*.[10] Elsewhere, Cahen has observed that the duality is so marked that "one might wonder whether it is one and the same organization that is being considered."[11] It truly seems, at first glance, that the manifestations of the *futuwwa* are connected only by a common name.[12]

I suspect, however, that Helmut Ritter may have been more perceptive in noting the analogies between *futuwwa* and

---

8. Bulliet, *Patricians of Nishapur*, 43. He overstates the agreement on celibacy.

9. Sawsan El-Messiri, "The Changing Role of the *Futuwwa* in the Social Structure of Cairo," in *Patrons and Clients in Mediterranean Societies*, ed. Ernest Gellner and John Waterbury (London: Duckworth, 1977), 239-53, esp. 239.

10. Cahen, "Futuwwa," 961; Bulliet, *Patricians of Nishapur*, 44; Paul Kahle, "Die Futuwwa-Bündnisse des Kalifen an-Nāṣir," in *Opera Minora* (Leiden: Brill, 1956), 215-46; see 242, which cites a *futuwwa* exhortation to shun violence.

11. Claude Cahen, *Pre-Ottoman Turkey*, trans. J. Jones-Williams (London: Sidgwick & Jackson, 1968), 339.

12. Thus Joseph Schacht, "Einige Kairiner Handschriften über *furusīja* und *futūwa*," *Der Islam* 19 (1931): 49-52, esp. 50.

Freemasonry[13]—analogies that merit further examination and that, as has already been alluded to, are comparable to those that have been confidently applied by some writers to the Gadianton robbers. To him, the fundamental characteristic of the *futuwwa* is the keeping of oaths and secrets.[14] I would go further and suggest that it is the shared *ritual* itself that forms the common basis of *futuwwa* phenomena and that *futuwwa* ideology is essentially epiphenomenal.[15] (I am influenced, in this suggestion, by "myth-and-ritual" theory, which sees in at least some ancient myths later explanations for ritual actions whose original signification had been lost.) It is, perhaps, significant that Christians, Jews, Muslims, and others have all participated, historically, in Masonic ritual because its theological content, while undeniably present, is sufficiently underdetermined as to allow adherents of quite different religious views to affirm it simultaneously. The opinions of scholars on the early *futuwwa* are various. The wonderful thing is that they may all be right.

Franz Taeschner, the doyen of *futuwwa* studies, views the *futuwwa* as having originated outside the realm of religion proper and as having adapted itself to Ṣūfism only later (albeit to such an extent that it was essentially *absorbed* by Ṣūfism).[16] Yet the writings of the *fityān* themselves never fail to present *futuwwa* as a kind of

---

13. Helmut Ritter, "Zur Futuwwa," *Der Islam* 10 (1920): 244-50. He is also reminded of medieval European student corporations; see 244.

14. Ritter, "Zur Futuwwa," 249.

15. This is not the place to go into my reasoning on the matter. El-Messiri seems to assume a similar notion without realizing it; see El-Messiri, "Changing Role of the *Futuwwa*," 240, when she posits a *"futuwwa* model" prior to the historical *futuwwa* itself, a kind of *Ur-futuwwa* or Platonic idea of *futuwwa* in which the *fityān* of the documents participate, to a greater or lesser degree. I take this seriously in historical terms. Nobody really knows the origin of the *futuwwa*: I am intrigued by the fact that the word *tekmīl*, which is used in connection with *futuwwa* initiation (Kahle, "Futuwwa-Bündnisse," 226-27), is precisely equivalent, in meaning and function, to the Greek *teleiosis*, a term connected with initiation into the famed Eleusinian mysteries.

16. Franz Taeschner, "Futuwwa-Studien: Die Futuwwabünde in der Turkei und ihre Literatur," *Islamica* 5 (1932): 285.

quasi-religion[17] passed down from prophet to prophet in the Bible—we might justly say that it claims to be "of ancient date" —and arriving finally in the hands of Muḥammad.[18] Corporate *futuwwa* identity was preserved and shared by means of rites that had been passed down, allegedly, from the founding of the order in earliest biblical times.[19] It is, however, far beyond the scope of this paper to enter into a discussion of these fascinating rituals.[20]

In a somewhat comparable manner, Latter-day Saint scripture, too, assigns a very ancient origin to the Gadianton robbers and related "secret combinations": "And behold, I am Giddianhi," says one of the group's leaders in the Book of Mormon, "and I am the governor of this the secret society of Gadianton; which society and the works thereof I know to be good; and they are of ancient date and they have been handed down unto us" (3 Nephi 3:9).

But the scriptural authors judge that origin and the movement itself to be evil, rather than good. "These abominations were had from Cain," says the Book of Moses in the Pearl of Great Price, "for he rejected the greater counsel which was had from God."

> And Cain was wroth, and listened not any more to the voice of the Lord, neither to Abel, his brother, who walked in holiness before the Lord.
>
> And Adam and his wife mourned before the Lord, because of Cain and his brethren.
>
> And it came to pass that Cain took one of his brothers' daughters to wife, and they loved Satan more than God.

---

17. For example, Kahle, "Futuwwa-Bündnisse," 244-45; see Bertold Spuler, *Geschichte der islamischen Länder*, part 1 (Leiden: Brill, 1952), 131.

18. Taeschner, "Futuwwa-Studien," 298; Franz Taeschner, "Eine Schrift des Šihābaddīn Suhrawardī über die Futūwa," *Oriens* 15 (1962): 277-80, esp. 277-79; Ritter, "Zur Futuwwa," 245. It was, however, possible for a non-Muslim to be a *fatā*. See Kahle, "Futuwwa-Bündnisse," 231.

19. Taeschner, "Futuwwa-Studien," 299-300.

20. Some notes on these can be found in Ritter, "Zur Futuwwa," 246; Ziadeh, *Urban Life in Syria*, 167; Kahle, "Futuwwa-Bündnisse," 226-27, 239-40; Taeschner, "Futuwwa-Studien," 328 (and n. 2). This listing is far, far from exhaustive.

And Satan said unto Cain: Swear unto me by thy throat, and if thou tell it thou shalt die; and swear thy brethren by their heads, and by the living God, that they tell it not; for if they tell it, they shall surely die; and this that thy father may not know it; and this day I will deliver thy brother Abel into thine hands.

And Satan sware unto Cain that he would do according to his commands. And all these things were done in secret.

And Cain said: Truly I am Mahan, the master of this great secret, that I may murder and get gain. Wherefore Cain was called Master Mahan, and he gloried in his wickedness. (Moses 5:25–31)

According to the Book of Mormon, such "secret combinations" took root in the Old World, but were brought from there into the New World via records carried across the sea by the earliest Jaredites. And, very early on, these strangely religious oath-bound conspiracies became intertwined with politics. The account of Ether, for example, tells of an overly ambitious prince, Jared, whose too-long wait for the throne had plunged him into dark depression. "Now the daughter of Jared was exceedingly fair. And it came to pass that she did talk with her father, and said unto him: Whereby hath my father so much sorrow? Hath he not read the record which our fathers brought across the great deep? Behold, is there not an account concerning them of old, that they by their secret plans did obtain kingdoms and great glory?" (Ether 8:9). Plotting together, Jared had his daughter dance for Akish, who then desired her for his wife. The condition Jared laid on that proposal was that Akish bring him the head of his father.

And it came to pass that Akish gathered in unto the house of Jared all his kinsfolk, and said unto them: Will ye swear unto me that ye will be faithful unto me in the thing which I shall desire of you?

And it came to pass that they all sware unto him, by the God of heaven, and also by the heavens, and also by the earth, and by their heads, that whoso should vary from the assistance which Akish desired should lose his head; and whoso should divulge whatsoever thing Akish made known unto them, the same should lose his life.

And it came to pass that thus they did agree with Akish. And Akish did administer unto them the oaths which were given by them of old who also sought power, which had been handed down even from Cain, who was a murderer from the beginning.

And they were kept up by the power of the devil to administer these oaths unto the people, to keep them in darkness, to help such as sought power to gain power, and to murder, and to plunder, and to lie, and to commit all manner of wickedness and whoredoms.

And it was the daughter of Jared who put it into his heart to search up these things of old; and Jared put it into the heart of Akish; wherefore, Akish administered it unto his kindred and friends, leading them away by fair promises to do whatsoever thing he desired.

And it came to pass that they formed a secret combination, even as they of old; which combination is most abominable and wicked above all, in the sight of God;

For the Lord worketh not in secret combinations, neither doth he will that man should shed blood, but in all things hath forbidden it, from the beginning of man.

And now I, Moroni, do not write the manner of their oaths and combinations, for it hath been made known unto me that they are had among all people, and they are had among the Lamanites.

> And they have caused the destruction of this people of
> whom I am now speaking, and also the destruction of the
> people of Nephi. (Ether 8:13-21)

The Ideology of the Futuwwa

While Muḥammad appeared in the *futuwwa* genealogy, it is
nonetheless true that ʿAlī is the actual patron of the movement,
and ʿAlī is viewed by the *fityān* as the initiator of their traditions.[21]
ʿAlī is also, of course, the pivotal figure in Shiʿite Islam; the term
Shiʿite derives from the Arabic phrase *shiʿat ʿAlī*, or "faction of ʿAlī."
Futuwwa handbooks—which date, admittedly, from generally later
periods—invariably consist of page after page of quotations from,
in this order, the Qurʾan, the hadith or authoritative sayings and
precedents of Muḥammad and his "companions," sayings of ʿAlī,
and sayings of famous Ṣūfis.[22]

The *fityān* uniformly revere ʿAlī and invoke blessings upon him
and upon his sons Ḥasan and the martyr Ḥusayn—which would
ordinarily be taken as a sign of Shiʿi orientation. But they also call
down blessings upon Abū Bakr amd ʿUmar, the first two of what
Sunnis often call the "orthodox caliphs," whom Shiʿis typically reject and often revile.[23] ʿUthmān, the third of the four "orthodox
caliphs" (ʿAlī is accepted by Sunnis as the fourth), is conspicu-
ously absent from the list, which makes it no less puzzling. ʿAlī
is said to have initiated the early Iranian Muslim Salmān al-Fārisī
into the *futuwwa*—that is, to have "girded" him; the ritual involves
special clothing—and the latter follows ʿAlī in the *silsila* (or chain

---

21. Cahen, *Pre-Ottoman Turkey*, 260; Taeschner, "Futuwwa-Studien," 309.

22. Taeschner, "Futuwwa-Studien," 292, 296.

23. See Kahle, "Futuwwa-Bündnisse," 240-42. The Zaydi Shiʿites, a small minority
faction now largely restricted to the northern mountains of remote Yemen, are the
exception; though there are exceptions, they tend to respect Abū Bakr and ʿUmar.
For information on the Zaydis, see the annotated online guide by Daniel C. Peterson,
"Zaydi Bibliography" (Oxford University Press, forthcoming). Nicola A. Ziadeh, *Urban
Life in Syria under the Early Mamluks* (Beirut: American Press, 1953), 253 n. 151, citing
Al-Fakhri, Cairo, 1317: 287, likewise seems to link the *futuwwa* with Shiʿi Islam.

of authorities) of the movement.[24] Interestingly, Cahen describes Salmān as "the patron of Irano-Mesopotamian artisans."[25] (In this context, one thinks of the less than obvious connection between "speculative Freemasonry," a quasi-religious fraternal movement, and "practical Freemasonry," a building trade.) It is difficult to know how seriously to take such *isnāds* or chains of transmitters, of course, and it is certainly easy to doubt them. Very likely, the construction of such exalted genealogies began only after the career of the Caliph al-Nāṣir, to whom we shall come presently.[26]

The term *futuwwa* seems to have been invented for the movements under discussion here in about the eighth century.[27] Gustave von Grunebaum sees the *futuwwa* amalgamating with lower-class thugs known as ʿ*ayyarūn* by the ninth century.[28] Yet by the eleventh century, in the view of Professor Cahen, the *futuwwa* is moving away from violence and the rabble toward a corporate, initiatory mysticism. It is at this point, he says, that intellectuals and the upper classes begin to join up.[29] Marshall Hodgson, on the other hand, views the evolution of the *futuwwa* in a completely different manner. To him, the phenomenon is originally an upper-class one. After all, it was the upper class that first became Arabized in conquered lands, and we must initially look for the origin of the term *futuwwa* among the elite rather than among the inert peasant mass. Only

---

24. Taeschner, "Futuwwa-Studien," 307 (and n. 3), 309.
25. Cahen, "Futuwwa," 964.
26. Cahen, "Futuwwa," 964.
27. Cahen, "Futuwwa," 964.
28. G. E. von Grunebaum, *Classical Islam: A History 600-1258* (London: Allen and Unwin, 1970), esp. 104-5, 196. Cf. Cahen, "Futuwwa," 962, and Ernst Werner, *Die Geburt einer Grossmacht—Die Osmanen (1300-1481)*, 2nd ed. (Vienna: Böhlaus Nachfolger, 1972), 76. The philosopher Al-Fārābī was killed by a gang of *fityān* in December of 950. See D. M. Dunlop, *The Fuṣūl al-Madanī of al-Fārābī* (Cambridge: Cambridge University Press, 1961), 14-15. Von Grunebaum suggests the German term *Junker* as an equivalent to *fatā*; see his *Classical Islam*, 104. A *Junker* was a member of the landed nobility of Prussia and eastern Germany, mostly associated with the old feudal aristocracy of the region, the *Uradel*.
29. Cahen, "Futuwwa," 963.

later, in his opinion, does the *futuwwa* begin to gain acceptance among the lower classes.[30]

We do have one small area and one small fact on the earlier *futuwwa* that seems secure, although of uncertain significance: In his survey of eleventh-century Nishapur, Bulliet finds the *fityān* invariably belonging to the Shafi'i *madhab* (or "school") of Sunni Islamic law, never to the rival Hanafi *madhab*.[31] Because of their veneration of 'Alī, as described above, the *fityān* have frequently been viewed as Shi'ites—a fact that would not appear to tally with Bulliet's identification of the Nishapuri *fityān* as devout Shafi'is. They seem, in fact, to have adopted the efficient organization of the Isma'ili Shi'ites. But this need not imply doctrinal borrowings. Indeed, we have at least one example (from Ibn Jubayr) of a violently anti-Isma'ili group of Sunni *fityān*.[32]

Certainly the most famous phase of the *futuwwa* is that associated with its reform at the hands of the 'Abbasid caliph al-Nāṣir li-Din Allah, who reigned in Baghdad from 1180 to 1225.[33] In Cahen's theory, as we have previously noted, the *futuwwa* had been considered "a popular oppositional organization";[34] under al-Nāṣir it definitely ceased to be such, if it ever really was.[35] What the caliph seems to have done was to consolidate divergent sects of *futuwwa* by systematizing their ritual and dusting off their rules.[36] And, true to the nature of al-Nāṣir's entire enterprise—which was intended to

---

30. Marshall G. S. Hodgson, *The Venture of Islam*, vol. 2 (Chicago: University of Chicago Press, 1974), 126.

31. Bulliet, *Patricians of Nishapur*, 45.

32. Taeschner, "Futuwwa-Studien," 311; von Grunebaum, *Classical Islam*, 196.

33. See Taeschner, "Schrift des Šihābaddīn Suhrawardī," 277.

34. According to El-Messiri, "Changing Role of the *Futuwwa*," 249, this is essentially its role today. I don't know that anyone has yet investigated what relationship, if any, obtains between the *futuwwa* and the *Iuvenes*, the semimilitary or athletic youth clubs of the early Roman Empire. On these, see E. Norman Gardiner, *Athletics of the Ancient World* (Oxford: Oxford University Press, 1930), 124-27.

35. C. Cahen, "The Body Politic," in *Unity and Variety in Muslim Civilization*, ed. G. E. von Grunebaum (Chicago: University of Chicago Press, 1955), 132-63, esp. 153.

36. Kahle, "Futuwwa-Bündnisse," 217.

restore real power to the caliphate—the Grand Master of his New *Futuwwa* was the caliph himself.[37] Also in the circle of al-Nāṣir, promoting *futuwwa* and seeming to act the role of court theologian, was the mystic and eventual martyr Suhrawardī (d. 1191).[38] When one comes to study the essential nature of *futuwwa* itself, one is not surprised to learn that a caliph who was bent on strengthening the social fabric under his own patronage would support it.

Among the major aspects of the movement was the ideal of the absolute obedience of the *futuwwa* disciple, or *ṣaghīr* (the Arabic word means "small" or, derivatively, "young"), to his superior, who was, not unexpectedly, called the *kabīr* (the Arabic word means "large," or derivatively, "old[er]"). The *ṣaghīr* was to be more obedient to his *kabīr* than the *kabīr*'s shoe, and a better follower than the *kabīr*'s shadow.[39] Further, the *fityān* had an obligation to avenge one another.[40] *Futuwwa* could even be called a cult of friendship, for the duty of the *fityān* to one another was held to be valid even in matters offensive to morality and ethics.[41]

Here again, the Book of Mormon offers a parallel. The Gadianton robbers, it says disapprovingly, had "covenants and . . . oaths, that they would protect and preserve one another in whatsoever difficult circumstances they should be placed, that they should not suffer for their murders, and their plunderings, and their stealings. And it came to pass that they did have their signs, yea, their secret signs, and their secret words; and this that they might distinguish a brother who had entered into the covenant, that whatsoever wickedness his brother should do he should not be injured by his brother,

---

37. Cahen, "Futuwwa," 964.

38. Taeschner, "Schrift des Šihābaddīn Suhrawardī," 15. For Suhrawardī's thought, see Yaḥyā b. Ḥabash al-Suhrawardī, *The Philosophy of Illumination: A New Critical Edition of the Text of Ḥikmat al-ishrāq*, with English translation, notes, commentary, and introduction by John Walbridge and Hossein Ziai (Provo, UT: Brigham Young University Press, 1999).

39. Kahle, "Futuwwa-Bündnisse," 221; cf. 231.

40. Kahle, "Futuwwa-Bündnisse," 221.

41. Ritter, "Zur Futuwwa," 245.

nor by those who did belong to his band, who had taken this covenant" (Helaman 6:21-22). Advocates of the identity of the Gadianton robbers with nineteenth-century American Freemasonry have tended to see such obligations of mutual assistance as plain and unique pointers to the Masons, but, manifestly, such things are not peculiar to the early American republic.

Moreover, the mixture of good (or purported good) and bad (or reputed bad) that is so characteristic of the Book of Mormon's Gadianton robbers characterizes the *futuwwa* movement(s), as well. The chief *futuwwa* virtue was generosity, which included charity to the poor.[42] This may be an echo of the *Jāhilī fatā*, the noble and generous youth of pre-Islamic or *jāhiliyya* Arabia famously celebrated in the figure of Ḥātim al-Ṭā'ī.[43] In fact, the ideal of the *fityān*—which seems only fitfully attained in the historical records—was a kind of avowed poverty, a style of life that avoided contamination by riches and by association with the wealthy.[44]

Futuwwa and Government Power

If we are speaking in terms of the *futuwwa* of the proletariat, the *futuwwa* flourished in caliphal times during periods when the central government was weak.[45] Likewise, with the decline of the Seljuqs during the thirteenth century in Anatolia, the *fityān* reappeared.[46] The same was true of the so-called *akhis*, who, as we shall see, seem to represent an Irano-Anatolian variant of the popular *futuwwa*. In Iran, at the last of the thirteenth and the beginning of

---

42. Taeschner, "Schrift des Šihābaddīn Suhrawardī," 279; El-Messiri, "Changing Role of the *Futuwwa*," 244-45.

43. El-Messiri, "Changing Role of the *Futuwwa*," 240. On Ḥātim al-Ṭā'ī, see Reynolds Nicholson, *A Literary History of the Arabs*, and, even, Edward Fitzgerald's "Rubaiyat of Omar Khayyam."

44. Franz Taeschner, "Beiträge zur Geschichte der Achis in Anatolien (14.-15. Jht.)," *Islamica* 4/9 (1931): 1-47; R. M. Savory, "Communication," *Der Islam* 38 (1962): 161-65; esp. 162.

45. El-Messiri, "Changing Role of the *Futuwwa*," 240-41; Cahen, "Futuwwa," 961-65.

46. Cahen, *Pre-Ottoman Turkey*, 49.

the fourteenth century, fully one-third of the government's budget was devoted to maintaining religious institutions—among them *akhi* lodges (*zawiyas*).[47]

This was the Golden Age of *akhidom*. The quasi-anarchic condition of pre-Ottoman Anatolia allowed the strict organization and rigid discipline of the *akhis* to show itself to full advantage. In fact, the "organization of the towns was . . . bound up with the organization of the *akhis*."[48] Leaders of the movement, tending to disregard the admonitions to simplicity of life issuing incessantly from the *futuwwa*-theorists, came to form "a kind of bourgeois patrician class." Indeed, in later writers the term *akhi* becomes synonymous with "patrician."[49] They sometimes held actual political power, most notably in Ankara.[50] On the other hand, when the rising power of the Ottoman dynasty reached Ankara (in the person of Murad I), *akhi* control there ceased,[51] and the same was eventually true of all of Anatolia. In the reign of Murad II, we hear for the last time of any important political role being played by the *akhis*.[52]

In summary, Anatolian *akhi* lodges blossomed in the thirteenth and fourteenth centuries and were still to be found in the fifteenth century. Significantly, Turkish guilds, called *futuvvet*, begin to appear in the fifteenth century and then to bloom in the two centuries thereafter.[53] In Syria, under the comparatively strong control of the Mamluks in the fourteenth and fifteenth centuries, *futuwwa* of the popular kind never developed at all.[54]

Similarly, in the Book of Mormon, the Gadianton robbers tend to rise and fall in inverse relation to the vigor and effectiveness of the central government. Moreover, the robbers seem to have been

---

47. Bertold Spuler, *Die Mongolen in Iran* (Berlin: Akademie Verlag, 1968), 163 (and n. 2).
48. Cahen, *Pre-Ottoman Turkey*, 195.
49. Taeschner, "Beiträge zur Geschichte," 10.
50. Taeschner, "Beiträge zur Geschichte," 3, 28; Cahen, *Pre-Ottoman Turkey*, 340.
51. Taeschner, "Beiträge zur Geschichte," 3.
52. Taeschner, "Beiträge zur Geschichte," 28.
53. Taeschner, "Futuwwa-Studien," 289.
54. Ziadeh, *Urban Life in Syria*, 168.

plainly aware of that fact, sometimes deliberately acting to weaken the government in order to secure freedom of action for themselves. The Gadianton movement first emerges among the Nephites with a political assassination, committed in roughly 52 BC during a time of division among the people and instability in the Nephite chief judgeship. Strong government actions, however, drive them from their original urban base into the wilderness, rendering them relatively invisible and ineffective (Helaman 1:1-12; 2:1-11). Roughly a quarter of a century later, however, their numbers surge in the wake of another pair of successful political assassinations, but, while they prosper among the Nephites, a vigorous Lamanite response eliminates them from Lamanite territory within a few years (Helaman 6:15-41). Again, around AD 15, social decay, contention, and political dissent again provide an opportunity for the Gadianton movement to rise to prominence (3 Nephi 2:11, 18). In AD 29-30, a Gadianton-style secret combination renders the central government impotent and eventually destroys it altogether, leaving Nephite society in a state of tribal anarchy that allows the conspirators to establish an independent kingdom of their own (3 Nephi 6:27-7:14). The Gadianton movement is invisible during the decades of stability and peace that follow the transformative visit of the resurrected Christ to the New World, but when, about AD 231, "there [is] a great division among the people," they "spread over all the face of the land" (4 Nephi 1:35, 46). Thereafter, for the next century and a half, they play a crucial role in the decline and eventual death of Nephite civilization. "This Gadianton," writes the prophet-chronicler Mormon, "did prove the overthrow, yea, almost the entire destruction of the people of Nephi" (Helaman 2:13).

The Akhis

It is quite possible, as we have seen above, to distinguish two distinct strains of *futuwwa*, if not more. Taeschner calls these the "courtly" (*höfische*) and the "bourgeois" (*bürgerliche*).[55] In view of what we have seen above, and other evidence too vast to enumerate, we might actually be tempted to call the latter a "proletarian" *futuwwa*.

When the Mongol invasion obliterated the caliphate in Baghdad, the *futuwwa* experiment of al-Nāṣir was obliterated with it. Nevertheless, the courtly *futuwwa* was carried on in Cairo, where the Mamluk elite aspired to fill the vacancy created by the fall of the caliphate and even appointed a series of powerless puppet caliphs to give themselves credibility.[56] What occurred there under the Mamluk sultan Baybars was very much an "official revival."[57] This took place in 1261, and we know that the Mamluk rulers were still granting *futuwwa*-investment to prominent allies as late as 1293. But courtly *futuwwa* wanes in Egypt in the fourteenth century, lingering at the very latest into the fifteenth.[58]

This phenomenon is probably to be explained by the same reasoning with which we account for Baybars's eagerness to have an 'Abbasid caliph in Cairo: It gave him badly needed legitimacy. And, after all, *futuwwa* had been an important component in the caliphate of the prestigious al-Nāṣir, whose career was not so long before. It may have seemed to Baybars and his contemporaries that *futuwwa* was a part of the caliphate and that a claim by the new puppet caliph to *futuwwa*-lineage would go a long way toward validating his claim to the caliphal office as well.

Cahen asserts that al-Nāṣir's *futuwwa* also found its continuation among the *akhis* of Anatolia.[59] Taeschner, by contrast, claims that courtly *futuwwa* had existed in Anatolia under the Saljuqs of Rum,

---

55. Taeschner, "Schrift des Šihābaddīn Suhrawardī," 279.

56. Franz Taeschner, "Futuwwa," in *Encyclopaedia of Islam*, 3:966–69, esp. 966.

57. Ziadeh, *Urban Life in Syria*, 167–68. Syedah F. Sadeque, *Baybars I of Egypt and Syria* (New York: AMS, 1980), 133, 163, 190, 197, offers several examples of *futuwwa* rites practiced under Baybars I.

58. Taeschner, "Futuwwa," 966.

59. Cahen, "Futuwwa," 964.

but denies any connection between it and the *akhis*.[60] "The question of the origin of *akhidom* in Anatolia," writes Taeschner with sublime understatement, "is a very complicated one."[61] He suggests that the *akhis* were foreigners and notes that the word *akhi* is an East Turkic one whose connection with the Arabic Ṣūfi term *akhi* ("my brother") is fortunate but, otherwise, purely fortuitous. Elsewhere, he posits an origin in ʿAyyubid Egypt (that is, circa the mid-twelfth to mid-thirteenth century).[62] Bertold Spuler thinks it obvious that the *futuwwa* itself began along the Islamic frontier with the Byzantine Empire, among the "march warriors (*Grenzkriegern*), with their various Shiʿite tendencies."[63] Analogously, the military character of the Gadianton robbers is obvious in the Book of Mormon, where they hide out in inaccessible areas and are frequently confronted by Nephite and even Lamanite armies. (The Book of Mormon implicitly recognizes them as a military rather than a merely criminal threat and expresses that recognition in a manner that, strikingly, appears to accord with ancient law.)[64]

In still another place, Taeschner notes that *akhidom* can be traced earlier in Iran than in Anatolia, and, accordingly, that it probably traveled from the former to the latter.[65] Ernst Werner is still more positive and informs us that the leader of the *akhis* entered Anatolia from Iran at the beginning of the thirteenth century.[66] If we can accept Werner's theory, we notice that it accords—just barely—with Cahen's notion that "the organization of the akhis . . . was not clearly revealed in its full vigour until the Mongol regime and later,

60. Taeschner, "Futuwwa," 964.
61. Taeschner, "Beiträge zur Geschichte," 14-15.
62. Taeschner, "Beiträge zur Geschichte," 19 (and n. 3); Taeschner, "Futuwwa-Studien," 308-9.
63. Spuler, *Geschichte der islamischen Länder*, 103.
64. See John W. Welch and Kelly Ward, "Thieves and Robbers," in *Reexploring the Book of Mormon*, ed. John W. Welch (Salt Lake City: Deseret Book and FARMS, 1992), 248-49.
65. Taeschner, "Futuwwa," 966-69.
66. Werner, *Geburt einer Grossmacht*, 77.

but . . . nevertheless was in existence before it."[67] If Werner is correct, his *akhi* leaders arrived just in time. In fact, the first mention of the term *akhi* dates from 1068 to 1069 in Iran.[68] And a number of *akhis* were prominent among the companions and disciples of Shaykh Ṣafī al-Dīn Ardabīlī (1252–1334), the ancestor of the Safavid shahs who ruled Iran or Persia from AD 1501 to 1722.[69] Further evidence of Iranian origins is the fact that the Anatolian *akhis* of the fourteenth century adopted as their companion the figure of Abū Muslim, the Persian patriot.[70]

Still, there is the possibility—not to be entirely discounted—of a relationship between the *akhis* (*ukhuwwa*) and the famous "Brethren of Purity" or *Ikhwan as-Safa*, who flourished in Basra, in southern Mesopotamia, during the tenth century. The groups share the same tight organization. But no line of connection has been demonstrated, and the doctrine of the "Brethren" is distinctly lacking among the *akhis*.[71]

"This institution is of great interest," writes Cahen of the *akhis*, "but also raises many problems."[72] At least, says Taeschner, among all the confusion surrounding the *akhis*, there is no question that they belong to the phenomenon known generally as *futuwwa*.[73] But whether *fityān* and *akhis* are identical is quite another matter.[74] At one point, Taeschner confidently places the *akhis* among the *futuwwa* movements "decisively influenced" by al-Nāṣir.[75] Yet elsewhere he

---

67. Cahen, *Pre-Ottoman Turkey*, 195.
68. Werner, *Geburt einer Grossmacht*, 72.
69. Taeschner, "Futuwwa," 967.
70. Cahen, *Pre-Ottoman Turkey*, 340.
71. Taeschner, "Beiträge zur Geschichte," 15, and Taeschner, "Futuwwa-Studien," 292 n. 5; 311 n. 1. See Taeschner "Beiträge zur Geschichte," 5-6, for data demonstrating that the *Akhis* were, in fact, an organization rather than an amorphous mass.
72. Cahen, *Pre-Ottoman Turkey*, 195.
73. *Taeschner,* "Beiträge zur Geschichte," 27, and Taeschner, "Futuwwa-Studien," 289. The phrase *akhiyyat al-fityān* occurs in Ibn Baṭṭūta. See Taeschner, "Beiträge zur Geschichte," 2.
74. Taeschner, "Futuwwa-Studien," 292.
75. Taeschner, "Futuwwa-Studien," 308.

is careful to distinguish between the courtly *futuwwa* of the caliph and the *futuwwa* of the court theologian (and *futuwwa*-promoter) Suhrawardī. And, in Taeschner's view, the *akhis* are clearly to be associated with the theologian and not with the caliph.[76]

One characteristic of the *akhi* movement that undoubtedly adds to the difficulty of studying it today is the secrecy in which it functioned. The ideal was that nobody else would know that one was an *akhi*, and we have at least one example of an Anatolian *Futüvvetnāme* (or "*futuwwa* book") that closes with the strict admonition that it not be shown to the uninitiated.[77] Similarly, the Book of Mormon says, the practice of the Gadianton robbers was that "whosoever of those who belonged to their band should reveal unto the world of their wickedness and their abominations, should be tried, not according to the laws of their country, but according to the laws of their wickedness, which had been given by Gadianton and Kishkumen" (Helaman 6:24). Thus, at one point, when the Gadianton robbers were under intense military pressure, they "concealed their secret plans in the earth" (Helaman 11:10). (The reference here is, quite plainly, to written materials, perhaps even to secret books.) Unfortunately, only a few years later, when they had regained their strength and self-confidence, "they did search out all the secret plans of Gadianton" once again (Helaman 11:26).

If there is a difference between the *akhis* and the ordinary *fityān*, it is perhaps to be found in an increasingly craft-and-trade-centered focus among the former. Indisputably, though, in early modern history, the first craft guilds and trade unions in the Arab world referred to themselves as *futuwwa*. (One thinks, yet again, of the peculiar use of the construction term *masonry* to refer to a fraternal/ritual organization.) This is, however, otherwise an area of great controversy.[78] But when we begin to examine the *akhis* closely, we

---

76. Taeschner, "Schrift des Šihābaddīn Suhrawardī," 279-80.
77. Taeschner, "Beiträge zur Geschichte," 9.
78. Compare Ziadeh, *Urban Life in Syria*, 168, and Werner, *Geburt einer Grossmacht*, 72, to Cahen, "Futuwwa," 961.

are immediately aware of certain very familiar traits. The chief virtue of the *akhis* is said, for example, to be their hospitality.[79] They
venerate ʿAlī, but they also venerate Abū Bakr.[80] Finally, their ritual
and their hierarchy are virtually identical to those we have encountered earlier among the *fityān*. (The former includes, curiously, the
shaving of a tonsure on the head of the initiate, which may well be
a relic of Christian monasticism.)[81]

Futuwwa and Mysticism

It is of interest to note that Šihābaddīn Suhrawardī, whom we
have briefly met as a promoter and theorist of *futuwwa* with special
ties to the *akhis* of Anatolia, was also a Ṣūfi.[82] Thus we are not particularly surprised to learn that the treatises on the *futuwwa*—secret
books, in at least some cases—written after Suhrawardī are themselves "semi-mystical."[83] And, carrying further with our essential
identification of *fityān* and *akhis*, we find, not unexpectedly, that
the *akhi* movement is itself considered to be a part of the greater
Ṣūfi phenomenon.[84] Indeed, in Taeschner's view, *futuwwa* and its
related movements represent the vehicle by which Ṣūfism gained
access to the bourgeois strata of Islamicate society.[85]

Interestingly, this seems to be the view of many of the *akhi*
sources themselves, which explicitly link—and sometimes equate—
futuwwa and *taṣawwuf* (Ṣūfism).[86] One source relates that *futuwwa*
and mysticism were originally synonymous at the time of their

---

79. Taeschner, "Beiträge zur Geschichte," 8.

80. Taeschner, "Beiträge zur Geschichte," 7, 19.

81. Taeschner, "Beiträge zur Geschichte," 6-9.

82. He is not, however, to be confused with his fellow countryman and rough
contemporary, ʿUmar Suhrawardī, the eponymous founder of an order of Ṣūfis. See
Cahen, *Pre-Ottoman Turkey*, 256.

83. Cahen, *Pre-Ottoman Turkey*, 350.

84. Taeschner, "Beiträge zur Geschichte," 10.

85. Taeschner, "Futuwwa-Studien," 285. Cf. the opinion of ʿAbbās Iqbāl, quoted in
Savory, "Communication," 161-62.

86. See, for example, Savory, "Communication," 162-63; Kahle, "Futuwwa-
Bündnisse," 229, 238; Taeschner, "Futuwwa-Studien," 291 (and n. 1).

founding by Seth; it was only at the time of Abraham that *futuwwa* was distinguished as a mysticism for the weak.[87]

The most important literary source to come to us out of *akhi* circles, according to Taeschner, is a late fourteenth-century *Futüvvetnāme* by a certain Yaḥyā b. Khalīlī b. Jubān al-Burghāzī.[88] Significantly, "the ethic which it portrays is a wholly normal mystic one, with the usual requirements of the moderate Ṣūfi ethics, without any kind of extravagance."[89] Thus we are prepared when Taeschner suggests that *akhidom* survived, after its death among the dervishes, with a kind of bourgeois moderation.[90] (Ritter attempts to counter such a suggestion by noting that, "among the mystics, it is *sunna* to shave the head, but this is not the case among the *fityān*."[91] However, on the basis of evidence alluded to earlier, we know that he is quite simply wrong.)

Even in terms of its ritual, *futuwwa* can be recognized in later dervish practices. The *futuwwa* rank of *naqīb*, responsible for the *shedd* initiation ceremony, reappears with the same title and the same function in more than one dervish order to this day.[92] And during that ceremony, the initiate makes a familiar promise to "dedicate [himself] zealously to the service of the poor and needy, to the extent of [his] ability."[93]

---

87. Taeschner, "Schrift des Šihābaddīn Suhrawardī," 278. Seth is a very curious figure in biblical pseudepigrapha and gnostic literature, and his role here fairly cries out for study. Also significant in this religious view of *futuwwa* is the fact that at least one *akhi* rank bears as title an Uighur word signifying, elsewhere, a Buddhist priest. See Taeschner, "Schrift des Šihābaddīn Suhrawardī," 292–94 (and 294 n. 2). Curiouser and curiouser.

88. Taeschner, "Beiträge zur Geschichte," 4–5, 40, and Taeschner, "Futuwwa-Studien," 300 n. 1. It betrays, incidentally, not a trace of Shiʿism. And, since the book was intended to be secret, this cannot be rationalized as *taqiyya*-dissimulation. See Taeschner, "Beiträge zur Geschichte," 18.

89. Taeschner "Beiträge zur Geschichte," 9.

90. Taeschner, "Beiträge zur Geschichte," 21–22.

91. Ritter, "Zur Futuwwa," 247.

92. Paul Kahle, "Zur Organisation der Derwisch-orden in Egypten," *Der Islam* 6 (1916): 149–69, esp. 164–66; Taeschner, "Beiträge zur Geschichte," 8; and Taeschner, "Futuwwa-Studien," 296, 326–35.

93. Kahle, "Zur Organisation der Derwisch-orden," 162.

Akhis and Mevlevīs

In the second half of the thirteenth century, after the death of Zarkūb, the preeminent disciple of the great Persian mystic Jalāl al-Dīn Rūmī was Ḥusām al-Dīn Çelebi, one of the principal *akhi* leaders in Konya. On Rūmī's death, Çelebi became his successor (*khalīfa*).[94] Taeschner argues that, by the beginning of the fourteenth century, the Mevleviyya—the mystical order of the disciples of Rūmī —was still concentrated in and about Konya and that the *akhis* elsewhere constituted a group of what we might term "fellow-travelers." We know that the *akhis* danced at their meetings, and Taeschner is certain that we must here understand this to be the same as the famed cultic dance practiced by the Mevlevīs, the so-called "whirling dervishes."[95] Taeschner further notes a certain *baṭinī* (or esoteric) character—secret doctrine, reserved for initiates—that he sees shared by both *akhis* and Mevlevīs. And, finally, he reminds us that Rūmī traced his genealogy back to Abū Bakr, a fact that would conceivably explain the *akhis*' notorious invocation of the first caliph as a saint along with the predictable 'Alī.[96]

But there are problems with this connection. We know, for example, that the *akhi* leader Ahmad of Konya was disliked by Aflākī, the hagiographer of the Mevlevīs, as being insufficiently aristocratic and an enemy of Jalāl al-Dīn Rūmī.[97] And the feelings seem to have been mutual: Werner is able to detect hostility on the part of the lower- and middle-class *akhis* toward the "feudal aristocratic" Mevlevīs.[98]

Akhis and Bektāshīs

The well-known Turkish scholar M. F. Köprülüzade considered the *akhis* to be identical with the Bektāshī order of dervishes;

---

94. Cahen, *Pre-Ottoman Turkey*, 351.
95. Taeschner, "Beiträge zur Geschichte," 16-17.
96. Taeschner, "Beiträge zur Geschichte," 15-17 (and 17 n. 4).
97. Cahen, *Pre-Ottoman Turkey*, 351.
98. Werner, *Geburt einer Grossmacht*, 75. Werner is a Marxist.

he alleged that the term *akhi* died out at the coming of the title *bektāshiyya*.[99] While Taeschner does not entirely agree with Köprülüzade on this point, he does permit substantial identification, noting that the founding fathers of the *bektāshiyya* included several prominent *akhis*.[100] And again, the familiar ambiguity is present, for R. Tschudi comments of the Bektāshīs that, "in their secret doctrines, they are Shiʿis."[101] One "Great Futuwwetname" of a decidedly Twelver Shiʿi character, written in the sixteenth century, is quoted in Bektāshī ceremonies.[102] And the Bektāshīs, like the *akhis*, are secretive, a fact that has brought upon them accusations of all manner of immorality.[103] Ironically, though, a small group of the Bektāshīs vow themselves to celibacy[104]—as did a similar percentage of the *akhis*.[105]

We know that the Bektāshīs had acquired exclusive spiritual authority among the elite Ottoman military order of the Janissaries, the *Yeniçeri*, by the second half of the fifteenth century,[106] and it is important in this regard to recall that the *akhi*-cap was identical to the headdress of the *Yeniçeri*.[107] It seems, in fact, that the *akhis* were involved militarily on the side of the Ottoman dynasty from its very first days; there is some evidence that Murad I—the third of the thirty-six Ottoman sultans, who reigned from roughly 1360 to his death at the Battle of Kosovo in 1389—was a Grand Master of the *akhis*.[108]

---

99. Taeschner, "Beiträge zur Geschichte," 20, 24, 25.

100. Taeschner, "Beiträge zur Geschichte," 23-24.

101. R. Tschudi "Bektashiyya," in *Encyclopaedia of Islam*, new ed. (Leiden: Brill, 1960), 1:1161-63, esp. 11622.

102. Taeschner, "Futuwwa," 967-68.

103. Hans Joachim Kissling, "Zur Frage der Anfänge des Bektašitums in Albanien," *Oriens* 15 (1962): 281-86, esp. 285 n. 1. Compare the experiences of the Masons, the Mormons, the early Christians, etc.

104. Tschudi, "Bektashiyya," 1162.

105. Taeschner "Beiträge zur Geschichte," 19 n. 4. See Kissling, "Zur Frage der Anfänge," 286, on what he calls "Kryptochristianismus."

106. Tschudi "Bektashiyya," 1162.

107. Taeschner, "Beiträge zur Geschichte," 25-26.

108. Taeschner, "Beiträge zur Geschichte," 25-26; Werner, *Geburt einer Grossmacht*, 99-102, 88.

However, there are problems in associating the *akhis* and the *bektāshiyya*, as one could, by now, have predicted that there would be. Ḥājī Bektāsh "was probably a disciple of Bābā Isḥāq. . . . The aristocratic entourage of the rival Mawlawiyya order later laid emphasis on this."[109] (Werner, by the way, views the Bābā'ī revolt as "an expression of the weakness of the central authority and the incipient feudal shattering of the sultanate"[110]—familiar conditions.) But we know that the *akhis* of Sivas defended that city *against* Bābā Isḥāq's siege.[111]

A final candidate for Dervish Continuator of the *futuwwa* is the order of the Naqshbandiyya. They too are known for esoterica and secrecy.[112] They too trace their *silsila* back to both ʿAlī and Abū Bakr.[113]

Conclusion

It is widely agreed that at least some of the *akhi* tradition continued in the guilds of the Middle East,[114] although the error of supposing that all *futuwwa* organizations were guilds from the very start should be avoided.[115] Werner is reminded, in thinking of this question, of the two broad divisions of *futuwwa* to which we have repeatedly alluded. The quietistic mystics he sees represented in

---

109. Tschudi, "Bektashiyya," 1161-62, notes that the rituals characteristic of the later *bektāshiyya* are not to be found in the writings of Ḥājī Bektāsh himself. My bet is that they are a later contribution, at least in part, of the *akhis*. Incidentally, adepts of the *rasūl*, Bābā Isḥāq, wore a cap like that of the illustrious Qizilbāsh. A special relationship exists, in fact, between the *bektāshiyya* and the Qizilbāsh (Tschudi, "Bektashiyya," 1162).

110. Werner, *Geburt einer Grossmacht*.

111. Werner, *Geburt einer Grossmacht*.

112. Madelain Habib, "Some Notes on the Naqshbandi Order," *Muslim World* 59/1 (1969): 40-49, esp. 45 (and n. 28), 47-48.

113. Habib, "Some Notes on the Naqshbandi Order," 40-41; Taeschner, "Beiträge zur Geschichte," 17.

114. Taeschner, "Beiträge zur Geschichte," 20; Taeschner, "Futuwwa-Studien," 301; Raphaela Lewis, *Everyday Life in Ottoman Turkey* (London: Batsford, 1971), 145.

115. Gabriel Baer, "Guilds in Middle Eastern History," in *Studies in the Economic History of the Middle East*, ed. M. A. Cook (London: Oxford University Press, 1970), 11- 30, esp. 11.

more recent times by the Ṣūfī orders, whereas the political activists find their more modern counterparts in the guilds.[116]

In fact, "the rise of the guilds was closely connected with the decline of the free *futuwwa* and *akhi* associations," which took place in the fifteenth and sixteenth centuries.[117] As the government came more and more to control the nascent trade associations, the *futuwwa* simply died out[118]—central authority being, as ever, its nemesis. This occurred, at the latest, by the seventeenth century. The guild of tanners retained its *akhi* associations longest and in greatest purity, and was able thereby to achieve a remarkable ascendancy over the other guilds that lasted for a considerable length of time.[119] However, by 1914 Paul Kahle was able to find only twenty-year old memories of the *futuwwa shedd*-initiation in the Cairo guild,[120] and by 1927 "almost none of the traditional ceremonies remained" in the guilds of Damascus.[121]

Still, the *futuwwa* associations of the early guilds are instructive. They teach us, for example, to be wary of the provincial, twentieth-century secularism implicit in such statements as Raphaela Lewis's remark that "throughout Ottoman Turkey, a man's allegiances were, in order of priority, to his guild, to his religion and to the Sultan."[122] It is doubtful that a medieval *akhi* or a later premodern guildsman would have distinguished between guild and religion.[123]

---

116. Werner, *Geburt einer Grossmacht*, 75; El-Messiri, "Changing Role of the *Futuwwa*," 240, is confused by the relationship of the two strands, as in Kahle ("Zur Organisation der Derwisch-orden," 149), who ought to know better.

117. Baer, "Guilds in Middle Eastern History," 29.

118. Baer, "Guilds in Middle Eastern History," 18, 20.

119. Taeschner, "Futuwwa-Studien," 301; Kahle, "Zur Organisation der Derwisch-orden," 149 (and n. 2); Taeschner, "Futuwwa," 968; Lewis, *Everyday Life in Ottoman Turkey*, 145.

120. Kahle, "Zur Organisation der Derwisch-orden," 149 (and n. 2).

121. Baer, "Guilds in Middle Eastern History," 23.

122. Lewis, *Everyday Life in Ottoman Turkey*, 145.

123. See Franz Taeschner, "Aufnahme in eine Zunft, dargestellt auf einer türkischen Miniatur," *Der Islam* 6 (1916): 169-72. The article features a Turkish miniature which distinctly illustrates the *futuwwa*-religious character of reception into a guild.

Likewise, as I have argued elsewhere, although the authors and editors of the Book of Mormon clearly suppress the religious character of the Gadianton robbers (as at Alma 37:27-32 and Ether 8:20), it is unlikely that the Gadiantons saw their efforts as purely secular, let alone as criminal murder and robbery. Although, at this late date and given the nature of our source materials, we can't tell precisely what it was—in which respect, again, the *futuwwa* movements offer a kind of analogy—they were fighting for an alternate religious vision, one that many of the peoples of the Book of Mormon plainly saw, at various times, as quite attractive.[124]

Brodie, Hullinger, Vogel, and others who equate the secret combinations described in the Book of Mormon with the Masons of nineteenth-century America simply haven't read widely enough. The similarities they adduce are neither unique to Freemasonry nor, sometimes, as compelling as are those in other movements. Parallels to the Gadianton robbers are easy to find, from antiquity through the medieval Near East to the mountains of today's Tora Bora. "They are," as the prophet Moroni wrote more than a millennium and a half ago, "had among all people" (Ether 8:20).

Daniel C. Peterson is professor of Islamic studies and Arabic at Brigham Young University

---

124. Peterson, "Notes on 'Gadianton Masonry.'"

CHAPTER 15

ᴣ⟶

EXPLORING THE BIBLICAL PHRASE "GOD OF THE SPIRITS OF ALL FLESH"

Dana M. Pike

It is a pleasure to dedicate this study to S. Kent Brown, who has been a colleague and friend to me at BYU. I have learned much from Kent. I appreciate and have enjoyed the opportunities I have had to work and travel with him.

Various biblical passages indicate that ancient Israelites believed in the existence of a person's "spirit," a spirit personage, which lived on *after* human death. Biblical prohibitions against necromancy—consulting the spirits of the dead for information and protection—certainly testify to this (e.g., Leviticus 19:31; 20:6).[1] And there is the classic narrative about the medium of Endor who reportedly called up the spirit of dead Samuel at Saul's request (1 Samuel 28:5-20). However, what is never discussed in the Old Testament is when, where, or how such spirits originated.

This article represents the revised form of a presentation I gave in the "Latter-day Saints and the Bible" section at the national meeting of the Society of Biblical Literature, 19 November 2007 in San Diego, California. I thank Jacob Rennaker and Trevan Hatch for assisting with gathering materials for this study.

1. See the discussion, for example, by J. Tropper, "Spirit of the Dead," in *Dictionary of Deities and Demons in the Bible*, ed. Karel van der Toorn, Bob Becking, and Pieter W. van der Horst, 2nd ed. (Boston: Brill, 1999), 806-9.

Modern scholars generally consider the claim in Jeremiah 1:5—that the Lord "knew" Jeremiah *before* he was conceived in the womb—to be figurative. In reviewing this concept—"figurative preexistence"—I have wondered about this question: does the Hebrew Bible (the Christian Old Testament) contain any persuasive indication that at least some Israelites believed in the premortal existence of spirits that inhabit human bodies?

Because of the restoration of Christ's gospel through the Prophet Joseph Smith, Latter-day Saints understand and accept the premortal existence of all humans.[2] This doctrine is not based on clear exposition in the Old or New Testaments. But Latter-day Saints claim some biblical passages do attest to and presuppose this doctrine. This article does not seek to "prove" the doctrine of premortal existence by using the Hebrew Bible. Rather, it explores the biblical language of the phrase *'ĕlohê hārûḥōt lĕkol-bāśār*,[3] "God of the spirits of all flesh," which is found only in Numbers 16:22 and 27:16, to determine whether this phrase can plausibly be read as presupposing the idea of premortal existence even if a person does not accept the Restoration. I have elsewhere examined Jeremiah 1:5, the best Old Testament passage preserving this concept.[4] The present study is another test case, an additional stone in a larger mosaic of studies.[5]

---

2. See, for example, "The Family: A Proclamation to the World," *Ensign*, November 1995, 102; and Gayle O. Brown, "Premortal Life," in *Encyclopedia of Mormonism*, 1123-25.

3. The transliteration scheme used in this article follows the academic style provided in *The SBL Handbook of Style*, ed. Patrick H. Alexander et al. (Peabody, MA: Hendrickson, 1999), 26-27.

4. I analyzed the content of this verse in a presentation entitled "Figurative Preexistence?—The Case of Jeremiah 1:5" at the national meeting of the Society of Biblical Literature, 24 November 2008, in Boston, Massachusetts. This presentation will soon be published elsewhere.

5. It is a happy coincidence that the entry, "Souls, Preexistence of," in the academic *Anchor Bible Dictionary*, ed. David Noel Freedman (New York: Doubleday, 1992), 6:161, was written by S. Kent Brown, the Latter-day Saint scholar honored by this article and this volume!

Academic discussions of the concept of premortal existence in the Old Testament deal only with the female personification of Wisdom. An important passage in Proverbs 8 reads: "I wisdom dwell with prudence. . . . The LORD possessed me in the beginning of his way, before his works of old. I was set up from everlasting, from the beginning, or ever the earth was . . . when he appointed the foundations of the earth: Then I was by him, as one brought up with him: and I was daily his delight, rejoicing always before him" (Proverbs 8:12, 22-23, 29-30).[6] Thus Wisdom, personified as a woman, existed before the creation of the earth.[7]

Christ's premortal existence, however different Christians interpret this concept, is well attested in the New Testament.[8] The concept of individual premortal existence of humans is not clearly attested in texts in the biblical tradition until the last few centuries BC on into the early Christian centuries. Examples found in some early Jewish and Christian documents include:

> As a child I was naturally gifted, and a good soul fell to my lot; or rather, being good, I entered an undefiled body. (Wisdom of Solomon 8:19-20)[9]

> But he [God] did design and devise me [Moses], who (was) prepared from the beginning of the world, to be the mediator of his covenant. (*Testament of Moses* 1:14)[10]

---

6. Biblical quotations are taken from the King James Version (KJV) unless otherwise indicated. NRSV is the abbreviation for the New Revised Standard Version.

7. Speaking of personified wisdom, Roland E. Murphy, "Wisdom in the OT," in *Anchor Bible Dictionary*, 6:927, states: she "seems to be something of God, born of God, in God. Usually she is said to be a divine attribute, a personification of the wisdom with which God created the world."

8. See the LDS Topical Guide, s.v. "Jesus Christ, Antemortal Existence of." See also, for example, Douglas McCready, *He Came Down from Heaven: The Preexistence of Christ and the Christian Faith* (Downers Grove, IL: InterVarsity, 2005).

9. NRSV Apocrypha, as found in *The New Oxford Annotated Bible with Apocryphal/ Deuterocanonical Books*, ed. Bruce M. Metzger and Roland E. Murphy (New York: Oxford, 1994), AP 68.

10. As found in James H. Charlesworth, ed., *The Old Testament Pseudepigrapha* (New York: Doubleday, 1983, 1985), 1:927; hereafter abbreviated *OTP*.

Enoch was instructed that "all the souls are prepared for eternity, before the composition of the earth." (*2 Enoch* 23:5; see further *1 Enoch* 48:2-3)[11]

Such attestations of this concept in early Jewish and Christian texts are regularly cited as dependent on Greek influence, especially Platonic thought. For example, "the Platonic view of the soul as pre-existent seems to be reflected here [in Wisdom of Solomon 8:19-20], but unlike Plato's view, there is union with an *undefiled body*."[12]

Numbers 16:22 and Numbers 27:16 in Context

The phrase *ʾĕlohê hārûḥōt lĕkol-bāśār*, "God of the spirits of all flesh," occurs only twice in the Masoretic Text, the traditional text of the Hebrew Bible: Numbers 16:22 and Numbers 27:16. Both of these passages occur in what scholars refer to as Priestly texts, due to the priestly perspectives and concerns in this material. And both of these passages occur in expressions of intercession, attributed to Moses and Aaron in the first passage and to Moses alone in the second.

Numbers 16 recounts the rebellion of Korah and his followers against Moses and Aaron. In the dramatic showdown, "Korah gathered all the congregation against them unto the door of the tabernacle of the congregation: and the glory of the LORD appeared unto all the congregation. And the LORD spake unto Moses and unto Aaron, saying, Separate yourselves from among this congregation, that I may consume them in a moment. And they [Moses and Aaron] fell upon their faces, and said, O God, the God of the spirits of all flesh, shall one man sin, and wilt thou be wroth with all the congregation?" (Numbers 16:19-22). Rather than destroy all the Israelites, the earth opened and only swallowed up those who rebelled against Moses and his brother (16:23-35).

---

11. As found in *OTP*, 1:140.

12. Note on Wisdom of Solomon 8:19-20, in *New Annotated Oxford Bible*, AP 68, emphasis in the original.

According to Numbers 27:12-23, "the LORD"—the conventional way of rendering Hebrew *yhwh*/YHWH, also known in English as Jehovah—informed Moses that he (Moses) would not enter the promised land because of his rebellion against YWHW/Jehovah at the waters of Meribah.[13] At that point Moses, concerned for his people, pled, "Let the LORD, the God of the spirits of all flesh, set a man over the congregation . . . that the congregation of the LORD be not as sheep which have no shepherd" (Numbers 27:16-17).[14] The Lord instructed Moses to set Joshua apart as his divinely sanctioned successor (27:18-23).

Neither of these two passages occurs in the context of a theological discussion or sermon on creation or some other aspect of the plan of salvation. Nor is it immediately clear why this particular title was employed when YWHW/Jehovah was invoked in both of these passages. While Numbers 16 narrates that the power of God, who is the giver of life, was employed to put to death the rebellious Israelites, the death of people by God's power is narrated elsewhere in the Old Testament without the use of this phrase in reference to God.

The Components of the Phrase "God of the spirits of all flesh"

The following comments discuss the major components of the phrase "God of the spirits of all flesh" in order to illustrate challenges to accurately translating and understanding it.

---

13. For a discussion of why the divine name *yhwh* is rendered "the LORD," and how the form "Jehovah" originated, see Dana M. Pike, "Biblical Hebrew Words You Already Know, and Why They Are Important," *Religious Educator* 7/3 (2006): 97-114, especially 106-9.

14. Interestingly, the first eleven verses of Numbers 27 recount that the daughters of Zelophehad, of the tribe of Manasseh, approached Moses at the "entrance to the tent of meeting," requesting that they receive their father's inheritance since he had died with no sons. Included in their request is the claim that "our father died in the wilderness; he was not among the company of those who gathered themselves together against the LORD [*yhwh*] in the company of Korah" (Numbers 27:3). This suggests a literary connection between this passage and Numbers 16, in which appears the only other biblical attestation of the phrase "God of the spirits of all flesh." The Lord revealed that Moses should honor their request (27:6-7).

God. In Numbers 27:16, Moses invoked "the LORD" [*yhwh*/Je-hovah], the God [*ʾĕlohê*] of the spirits of all flesh." Numbers 16:22 reads, "O God [*ʾēl*], the God [*ʾĕlohê*] of the spirits of all flesh." In the context of Numbers 16 as it now exists, YHWH/Jehovah is clearly the *ʾēl*, or God, intended (see verses 19, 20, 23). The term translated "God" in the phrase "God of the spirits of all flesh" in Numbers 16:22 and 27:16 is the noun *ʾĕlohê*, a grammatically altered form of *ʾĕlohîm*. Throughout the Hebrew Bible the title *ʾĕlohîm*, "God," is used interchangeably with *yhwh*/Jehovah, Israel's God, as it is here.[15] Thus, YHWH/Jehovah is titled "the God [*ʾĕlohê*] of the spirits of all flesh." This could be viewed as problematic for Latter-day Saints, who teach that God the Father, not Jehovah—God the Son—created the premortal spirits of all humans. However, creation of spirits is not the issue here. The issue is who presides over and judges "the spirits of all flesh," and that was YHWH/Jehovah, as far as the ancient Israelites were concerned.

The spirits. The most important factor for interpreting this phrase is determining what *hārûḥōt*, "the spirits," designates. The singular form of this noun, *rûaḥ*, has a broad semantic range in biblical Hebrew, signifying "moving air, breeze, wind, breathe, life-breath, and spirit," with "spirit" designating a person's life force and internal power, as well as the "spirit of the LORD," the "spirit of God," the "holy Spirit," an evil spirit, and a spirit personage. One example of the challenge facing translators when rendering the noun *rûaḥ* into English is found in Ezekiel 37:9-10.[16] In this passage

---

15. For a discussion of the titles *ʾēl* and *ʾĕlohîm* (of which *ʾĕlohê* in this phrase is a grammatical variant) in the Hebrew Bible and how they are used in relation to YHWH/Jehovah, see Dana M. Pike, "The Name and Titles of God in the Old Testament," *Religious Educator* 11/1 (2010): 17-31, especially 21-25. See also the study elsewhere in this volume by Ryan Conrad Davis and Paul Y. Hoskisson, "The Usage of the Title *elohim* in the Hebrew Bible and Early Latter-day Saint Literature," pages 113-35, that demonstrates how early Latter-day Saint church leaders were not always so consistent with their use of the term Elohim.

16. While Latter-day Saints often consider Ezekiel 37:1-14 to be about resurrection, this passage actually utilizes resurrection imagery to depict the future restoration of

Ezekiel learns that the future gathering of Israel will be as a great army of dead soldiers coming back to life.

> KJV: Then said he unto me [Ezekiel], Prophesy unto the wind [hārûaḥ], prophesy, son of man, and say to the wind [hārûaḥ], Thus saith the Lord God; Come from the four winds [rûḥôt], O breath [hārûaḥ] and breathe [pĕḥî] upon these slain, that they may live. So I prophesied . . . and the breath [hārûaḥ] came into them, and they lived.

> NRSV: Then he said to me, "Prophesy to the breath, prophesy, mortal, and say to the breath: Thus says the Lord God: Come from the four winds, O breath, and breathe upon these slain, that they may live." I prophesied . . . and the breath came into them.[17]

The variety of interpretive possibilities and the ambiguity inherent in certain attestations of rûaḥ thus create a challenge to understanding the intent of the phrase ʾĕlohê hārûḥōt lĕkol-bāśār, often translated "God of the spirits of all flesh" but occasionally translated "the breath of all flesh" (see below).

Curiously, the feminine plural suffix -ôt on hārûḥōt in both Numbers 16:22 and 27:16 is written defectively: -ōt. These are the only two times the plural of rûaḥ (always feminine) is written this way in the Hebrew Masoretic Text. The significance of this defective orthography in the plural ending—rûḥōt—is not readily apparent. There are examples of the nominal feminine plural suffix written defectively in other words in the Masoretic Text. For example, the Hebrew word translated "fire-pan" is written maḥtôt in Numbers 16:6, but maḥtōt in Numbers 16:17. So, defective feminine plural suffixes do

---

Israelites to their land. It is not a passage about the resurrection per se.

17. There are other interesting examples of passages in which rûaḥ is rendered differently in different translations, including Psalm 104:4, in which the KJV reads: "Who maketh his angels spirits [rûḥôt]; his ministers a flaming fire," but the NRSV reads: "you make the winds [rûḥôt] your messengers, fire and flame your ministers."

occur, but the only defective plural forms of *rûaḥ* are in Numbers 16:22 and 27:16.[18]

Forms of the noun *rûaḥ* occur 378 times in the Masoretic Text; feminine plural forms constitute only thirteen of those occurrences. Complete *plene* orthography, *rûḥôt*, is attested nine times, in passages that contextually assure the translation "[four] winds" (e.g., Jeremiah 49:36; Ezekiel 37:9). The exception is Proverbs 16:2, in which this *plene* plural form is translated "spirits" in the KJV. The more likely rendition, based on the context (16:1-3), is "intentions, motives," as is found in some modern translations. The medially defective form *rūḥôt* occurs twice and can be confidently rendered "winds" both times (Jeremiah 49:36; Zechariah 6:5). The remaining two occurrences of the plural are in the two verses examined herein. Thus, the feminine plural form of *rûaḥ*, no matter what the orthography, typically designates something specific, although intangible (winds, spirits, intentions); it is not used to represent an abstract phenomenon such as "life force."

All flesh. In the Hebrew Bible the noun *bāśār* designates human as well as animal "flesh." The expression *lĕkol-bāśār*, "(belonging to) all flesh," occurs eight times in the Masoretic Text, including the two verses under discussion. Given the context of Numbers 16:22 and 27:16, the term *bāśār* in these verses clearly refers to humans. Thus, in these two verses YHWH/Jehovah is described as the God of the spirits of all humanity, or of human flesh (according to the common translation). This suggests that the term *hārûḥōt*, "the spirits," is not simply referring to the heavenly host located in YHWH/Jehovah's presence. That spirits were part of this host is attested in 1 Kings 22, where the adventures of a prophet named Micaiah are narrated. At one point Micaiah proclaimed: "Hear thou therefore the word of the LORD: I saw the LORD sitting on his throne, and

---

18. Given this limited data, and the fact that *rûḥôt* and *rūḥôt* also occur, it is not possible to confidently claim that a literary "signal" was intended by the use of defectively written *rûḥōt* in the phrase "God of the spirits of all flesh," but it is possible.

all the host of heaven standing by him on his right hand and on his left. And the LORD said, Who shall persuade [king] Ahab, that he may go up and fall [in battle] at Ramoth-gilead? . . . And there came forth a spirit [*hārûaḥ*] and stood before the LORD, and said, I will persuade him" (1 Kings 22:19-21 // 2 Chronicles 18:20). There is nothing in this passage, however, suggesting that such spirits—spirit personages—would inhabit human "flesh," or even that God created such spirits (although this latter point could be assumed).

Other Textual Witnesses

The phrase *ʾĕlohê hārûḥōt lĕkol-bāśār*, "God of the spirits of all flesh," is not attested in any Israelite or other ancient Semitic inscriptions, so only versions of the biblical text are available for this study. The remains of eight copies of the book of Numbers were found at Qumran among the Dead Sea Scrolls. The remains of three other copies were found elsewhere in the Judean Desert. However, none of these preserves the text of Numbers 16:22 or 27:16.[19] The text of the Hebrew phrase in question is essentially the same in the Samaritan Pentateuch as in the Masoretic Text, with the exception that the feminine plural ending on *rûḥōt* is written *plene* in both verses: *rûḥôt*.[20]

In the Septuagint, the early Greek translation of the Hebrew scriptures, the phrase in Numbers 16:22 and 27:16 reads: *theos tōn pneumatōn kai pasēs sarkos*, "God of the spirits [*pneumatōn*] and of all flesh."[21] The occurrence of *kai*, "and," in the Greek version of this phrase disassociates the "spirits" and the "flesh," possibly suggesting two separate entities: (heavenly?) spirits and human flesh.

---

19. See, for example, David L. Washburn, *A Catalog of Biblical Passages in the Dead Sea Scrolls* (Atlanta: Society of Biblical Literature, 2002), 50-52, and Eugene Ulrich, ed., *The Biblical Qumran Scrolls: Transcriptions and Textual Variants* (Boston: Brill, 2010).

20. A. F. von Gall, *Der hebräische Pentateuch der Samaritaner*, 4 vols. (Giessen: Töpelmann, 1916).

21. So translated by Peter W. Flint in *A New English Translation of the Septuagint*, ed. Albert Pietersma and Benjamin G. Wright (New York: Oxford, 2007). For the Greek text, see John William Wevers, *Numeri* (Göttingen: Vandenhoeck & Ruprecht, 1982).

Alternatively, one commentator suggests "the spirits refer to the breath of life for all flesh."[22]

There is quite a bit of variation from the phrase *'ĕlohê hārûḥōt lĕkol-bāśār* in the Targumim (or Targums), the Aramaic versions of the Hebrew scriptures. The phrase in *Targum Onqelos* essentially parallels the Masoretic Text of Numbers 16:22 and 27:16: *'ylh rwḥy' lkl-bysr'*.[23] Inexplicably, one translator renders this, "God of the breath of all flesh" in Numbers 16:22, but as "God of the spirits of all flesh" in 27:16.[24] Numbers 16:22 in the *Jerusalem Targum (Pseudo-Jonathan)* is rather expansive: "O God, who put the spirit [*rwḥ*] of life in the bodies of mankind and from whom is given the spirit [*rwḥ'*, singular] to all flesh." Numbers 27:16 in the same Targum reads: "Let the Memra [utterance] of the Lord, which rules over the soul [*nšmh*] of man and from whom has been given the breath [*rwḥ*, singular] of life to all flesh."[25] Finally, Numbers 16:22 in *Targum Vatican Neophyti* (or, *Neofiti*) reads: "O God, you who rule the breath [or, spirit; *nšmh*] of all flesh"; and 27:16 reads: "God who rules the spirits [*nšmh*] of all flesh."[26] Thus, the word *nšmh* has replaced *rwḥ* in both of these verses in *Targum Neofiti*. This is not too surprising, since even in the Hebrew Masoretic Text *nĕšāmâ*, "breath," and *rûaḥ* sometimes occur combined or in parallel. For example, "All [on dry land] in

---

22. John William Wevers, *Notes on the Greek Text of Numbers* (Atlanta: Society of Biblical Literature, 1998), 270.

23. Israel Drazin, ed., *Targum Onkelos to Numbers* (Hoboken, NJ: Ktav, 1987), 181. The Targumim are not vocalized as the Masoretic Text is, so the transliteration only represents the consonantal text.

24. Drazin, *Targum Onkelos to Numbers*, 180. Again highlighting the ambiguity of the term *rûaḥ*, Bernard Grossfeld, *The Targum Onqelos to Leviticus and the Targum Onqelos to Numbers* (Wilmington, DL: Glazier, 1987), 115, translates Numbers 16:22 as "God of the spirits of all mankind," similar to how the Hebrew is often rendered.

25. Ernest G. Clarke, trans. and ed., *Targum Pseudo-Jonathan: Numbers* (Collegeville, MN: Liturgical/Glazier, 1987), 270, emphasis deleted. For the Aramaic text, see Ernest G. Clarke, *Targum Pseudo-Jonathan of the Pentateuch: Text and Concordance* (Hoboken, NJ: Ktav, 1984), 193.

26. Martin McNamara, trans. and ed., *Targum Neofiti 1: Numbers* (Collegeville, MN: Liturgical/Glazier, 1987), 97, 150, emphasis deleted. The Aramaic text is available in Alejandro Díez Macho, ed., *Neophyti 1*, vol. 4 (Madrid: Consejo Superior de Investigaciones Científicas, 1974), 155, 261.

whose nostrils was the breath of life [*nišmat-rûaḥ ḥayyîm*] . . . died"
(Genesis 7:22); and "By the blast [*nišmat*] of God they perish, and by
the breath [*rûaḥ*] of his nostrils are they consumed" (Job 4:9).

While theological motivation may well lie behind how this
phrase is represented in these expanded and altered renditions in
some of the Targumim, and perhaps also in the Septuagint, they
conceptually hark back to the expression "breath/spirit of life" in
Genesis 2:7: "the LORD God formed man of the dust of the ground,
and breathed [*yippah*] into his nostrils the breath of life [*nišmat
ḥayyîm*]; and man became a living soul." This concept appears to
also lie behind Ezekiel 37:9-10 (quoted above), in which "breath
[*hārûaḥ*]" enlivened the dead who were coming back to life. Thus,
those who employed the singular *rwḥ* or *nšmh* when rendering the
Hebrew plural *hārûḥōt* into Aramaic did not have to alter much to
build what for them was a biblically based interpretation into their
translation.

Numbers 16:22 and 27:16 in Various English Translations and Commentaries

It is instructive to see how the Hebrew phrase *ʾēl ʾĕlohê hārûḥōt
lĕkol-bāśār* (Numbers 16:22) has been rendered in some of the leading English translations of the Old Testament:[27]

> KJV: O God, the God of the spirits of all flesh
> NRSV: O God, the God of the spirits of all flesh
> NET: O God, the God of the spirits of all people
> NJPSV: O God, Source of the breath of all flesh

As illustrated in this sample, many English translations render
hārûḥōt in Numbers 16:22 and 27:16 as "the spirits." The NJPSV
translates it as "breath," presumably drawing on the sense conveyed in Genesis 2:7 (quoted just above).

---

27. KJV = King James Version; NRSV = New Revised Standard Version; NET = New
English Translation; and NJPSV = New Jewish Publication Society Version.

Even when *hārûḥōt* in this phrase is translated "the spirits," most readers and commentators understand the sense of this term differently than do Latter-day Saints. Unfortunately, some commentators provide no explanation at all of *hārûḥōt*, "the spirits." Some commentators observe that the phrase conveys God's power to create, enliven, and sustain life, conveying the understanding behind the NJPSV translation "the [life-]breath of all flesh."[28] Others indicate this phrase is similar to expressions in "postbiblical literature," meaning post-Hebrew Bible or Old Testament, but provide no further comment.[29] Obvious similarities with later Jewish and Christian texts include:

In *Jubilees* 10:3 Noah addressed the "God of the spirits which are in all flesh."[30]

2 Maccabees 3:24 refers to God as "the Sovereign of spirits and of all authority."[31]

1 Enoch 37-71, the so-called "Book of Parables (or, Similitudes)," often refers to God as "the Lord of the Spirits" (e.g., 37:2, 4; 38:2, 4, 6; 40:1-10).[32]

Hebrews 12:9: "Furthermore we have had fathers of our flesh which corrected us, and we gave them reverence: shall we not much rather be in subjection unto the Father of spirits [*pneumatōn*], and live?"

---

28. See, for example, Martin Noth, *Numbers: A Commentary* (Philadelphia: Westminster, 1968), 127, who comments, "God is addressed as the creator of life (*rûaḥ*, in the plural here, is to be understood in this sense)"; and Jacob Milgrom, *The JPS Torah Commentary, Numbers* (Philadelphia: Jewish Publication Society, 1990), 135, who states, "The implication of this divine epithet is that since God is the creator of all life, He alone determines who is to live and who is to die."

29. See, for example, Timothy R. Ashley, *The Book of Numbers* (Grand Rapids, MI: Eerdmans, 1995), 313.

30. *OTP*, 2:75.

31. Translation from *New Annotated Oxford Bible*, AP 234. 2 Maccabees 14:46, which refers to God as "the Lord of life and spirit," is sometimes cited in this regard as well (translation from *New Annotated Oxford Bible*, AP 256).

32. *OTP*, 1:30-32.

Such similarities are helpful in supporting a translation of the phrase "God of the spirits of all flesh" in Numbers 16:22 and 27:16 and in providing an understanding of "the spirits" that appears to be in harmony with a Latter-day Saint perspective. However, since these later texts postdate the Greek Platonic view of the premortality of souls—individual spirits—their value for determining whether at least some ancient Israelites believed in the premortal existence of spirits that entered physical bodies is limited.

Conclusion

Latter-day Saints bring a full-blown doctrinal position—belief in the premortal existence of spirits that inhabit human bodies—to bear in interpreting certain texts in the Hebrew Bible (e.g., Numbers 16:22 and 27:16; Jeremiah 1:5; plus John 9:2). In this regard, they have the benefit of Restoration scripture that is related to the Old Testament. Both the Book of Abraham and the Book of Moses contain specific references to the premortal existence of spirits that would inhabit human bodies (e.g., Abraham 3:22-28; 5:7; Moses 4:1-4; 5:24). Abraham 5:7, for example, delineates between the "man's spirit" that was put into Adam's body and the "breath of life" that was "breathed into his nostrils," something that is not clearly recounted in the received text of Genesis. This reinforces the idea that ancient saints did understand this doctrine, despite its general absence in the text of the Old Testament as it has come down to us.

Most biblical scholars would say that the Latter-day Saint doctrine of premortal spirits is not expounded in nor substantiated by the received text of the Hebrew Bible. Since they do not accept the notion of premortal existence, most modern Jews and Christians do not "see" any such thing in the Hebrew Bible (other than the preexistence of "Wisdom" personified). This is partly because they are not looking for it and partly because of the ambiguous nature of the Hebrew term *rûaḥ*, as reviewed above. And as emphasized herein, the primary challenge is how to understand the plural form *hārûḥōt*, "the spirits," in Numbers 16:22 and 27:16.

To summarize the points made above about the phrase *ʾĕlohê hārûḥōt lĕkol-bāśār,* "God of the spirits of all flesh":

- occurrences of the plural form *rûḥôt* in the Masoretic Text are best rendered as plurals (e.g., "winds"), not abstracts, so "the spirits" seems to be the most likely translation of *hārûḥōt* in the phrase in question (and so it is usually translated);
- the plural *rûḥôt* (or *rûḥōt,* as in the phrase under review), "winds, spirits," is not used in the Masoretic Text to refer to God's "breath of life"; rather, the singular *rûaḥ* is;
- with the exception of the less preferable KJV translation of Proverbs 16:2, there is no other passage besides Numbers 16:22 and 27:16 in the Masoretic Text in which *rûḥôt* or *rûḥōt* is rendered "spirits," thus making its use in those verses unique (neither "winds" nor "intentions" makes sense in them);
- the qualifying expression, *lĕkol-bāśār,* "of all flesh," in the Hebrew text indicates these "spirits" do not function merely as part of the heavenly host, but somehow belong to "(human) flesh";
- most non-Hebrew versions of this phrase exhibit a tendency to distance themselves from the plain reading of the Masoretic Text, which appears to preserve the oldest form of this passage;
- most commentators favor explaining the plural *rûḥōt* as if it were the singular *rûaḥ,* rendering this phrase in harmony with the concept that God creates and sustains life.

These points combine to indicate that there is something preserved in the phrase "God of the spirits of all flesh" in Numbers 16:22 and 27:16 that is different from the occurrences of *rûḥôt* in the Bible (why translate *rûḥôt* as "spirits," but explain away the plain sense of the term in this context?). It is thus my assertion that certain passages in the received text of the Hebrew Bible, including Numbers 16:22 and 27:16, do plausibly support the idea that some ancient Israelites believed in premortal existence. The concept of premortal existence is not as clear-cut and conclusive in the Old Testament as many Latter-day Saints think it is, but it is attested there.

Dana M. Pike is professor of ancient scripture and coordinator of Ancient Near Eastern Studies at Brigham Young University.

CHAPTER 16

ALMA THE YOUNGER'S SEMINAL SERMON AT ZARAHEMLA

Robert A. Rees

The book of Alma is a microcosm of the cosmic conflict between the forces of good and evil. The stage for this conflict is set in the very first chapter when two men on opposite sides claim to preach the word of God. Nehor, inspired by Satan, introduces priestcraft for the first time among the Nephites, preaching "that which he termed to be the word of God" (Alma 1:3) and testifying that "all men should have eternal life" (v. 4). Immediately, Nehor is confronted by Gideon, a righteous teacher and former military leader. "Because Gideon withstood him with the words of God" (v. 9), Nehor killed him with his sword. The conflict in Alma between word and sword thus commences. And while in the beginning the victor in this conflict may seem in doubt, Alma later assures us that "the preaching of the word had a . . . more powerful effect upon the minds of the people than the sword" (Alma 31:5).

The contest for the souls of the people ensues over the entire sixty-three chapters of Alma, with Alma the Younger and his sons, the sons of Mosiah, and their companions "bearing down in pure testimony" (Alma 4:19) against the Nephites, Lamanites, Amulonites, Amalekites, and Zoramites, and with such figures as Nehor, Amlici, Korihor, and Zeezrom attempting to undermine their work at every step. The dramatic struggle plays out as powerful men fight one another with words and with weapons of war.

It is fascinating to note the degree to which the archetypal conflict in Alma is a contest of words. Alma, who might be considered the great intellectual in the Book of Mormon, has impressive persuasive power, as do the sons of Mosiah. They are all adept in using language to call members of the church to repentance or to convert the Lamanites and other nonbelievers. Those who oppose these preachers of the word are also sophisticated in the use of language. One after another they lead people astray by their sophistry. These language merchants "were learned in all the arts and cunning of the people; and this was to enable them that they might be skilful in their profession" (Alma 10:15). By the use of intellectual argument, cross-examination, contradiction, and verbal deception, these men try to undermine the work of the Lord's servants. For example, when Korihor appears before Alma, we are told "he did rise up in great swelling words" (Alma 30:31).

That the contest between good and evil is waged with words is seen in the way *word* is used in Alma's narrative. Nearly half the instances of *word* in the Book of Mormon are found in this one book, including such phrases as *the word, the word(s) of God, the word of the Lord* (Alma 9:14), *the word(s) of Christ* (Alma 37:44-45), and so forth. Together, they constitute a leitmotif running throughout the narrative. *The word* is used so frequently and in such a variety of ways and contexts that it begins to take on powerful symbolic significance. By the end of the book the accumulated associations of *the word* with Christ (see, for example, Alma 37:44-45 and Alma 44:5) may remind us of John's opening declaration, "In the beginning was the Word, and the Word was with God, and the Word was God" (John 1:1). Both testaments of Christ confirm that he is the embodiment of God's power and love.

Central to understanding the conflict between good and evil are the five sermons of Alma the Younger directed to (1) the members of the church and potential converts at Zarahemla (Alma 5); (2) the people in Gideon (Alma 7); (3) those in Ammonihah (Alma 9:8-30); (4) Zeezrom and "the people round about; for the multitude was great" (Alma 12:2, 12:3-13:30); and (5) the Zoramites (Alma 32:8-33:23). This paper examines in detail the first of these, Alma's great sermon at Zarahemla.

It is important to establish the context for this sermon. The Nephites had recently passed through a crisis that nearly destroyed their civilization. The wickedness of King Noah and his corrupt priests resulted in a cultural crisis of such dimensions that had it not been for Alma's father rescuing the church, the society might have disintegrated into the kind of mutual annihilation that destroyed the Jaredites.

At the waters of Mormon, Alma the Elder began a small but ultimately triumphant reformation that transformed Nephite society by reestablishing ecclesiastical primacy and social coherence. While Alma the Younger was blessed to come of age during this period of peace and stability, he and the sons of Mosiah rebelled against their fathers and "went about . . . seeking to destroy the church of God" (Alma 36:6). As the formerly sinful son of a prophet, Alma, addressing the people at Zarahemla, knows the societal dangers of discord. More significantly, he knows the personal price that must be paid by those who rebel against God, for as he later recalls to his own son Helaman, "I [was] racked with eternal torment, for my soul was harrowed up to the greatest degree and racked with all my sin. . . . I was racked, even with the pains of a damned soul" (Alma 36:12, 16).

A repentant Alma becomes the high priest upon the death of his father, which puts him in "charge concerning all the affairs of the church" (Mosiah 29:42). He is also appointed chief judge and thus inaugurates the reign of the judges. Immediately, Alma has to deal with political dissent, treason, social unrest, ecclesiastical divisiveness, and armed conflict with the rebellious Amlicites, who have joined forces with the Lamanites. Although Alma is successful in defeating his enemies, the war exacts a great cost to the Nephites: "Now the number of the slain were not numbered, because of the greatness of their number. . . . Now many women and children had been slain with the sword, . . . and also many of their fields of grain were destroyed" (Alma 3:1-2). These losses produce a brief period of retrenchment during which thousands join the church, a condition that creates social stability. This stability, however, quickly starts to erode when the wealthier members of the church begin setting themselves above their poorer brothers and sisters and persecuting them. These prideful members infect not only the church, but also "lead those who were unbelievers on from one piece of iniquity to another, thus bringing on the destruction of the people" (Alma 4:11).

It is against this backdrop of external threat and internal discord that Alma surrenders his position as chief judge and, retaining his office of high priest, goes "forth among his people . . . that he might preach *the word of God* unto them, to stir them up to remembrance of their duty, and that he might pull down, by *the word of God*, all the pride and craftiness and all the contentions which were among his people, seeing no way that he might reclaim them save it were in bearing down in pure testimony against them" (Alma 4:19). The repetition of the phrase *the word of God* foreshadows the importance of this expression in the narrative that ensues.

Alma's sermon to the unrepentant church members in Zarahemla as recounted in Alma 5 is a verbal symphonic composition of complexity and elegance. Its skillful blending of various rhetorical devices makes it a virtual sermonic tour de force. These devices include parallelism, allusion, repetition, imagery, symbolism, contrasting pairs, rhetorical questions, and so forth. Suggesting his skill and power with language, Alma is described earlier in the narrative as "a man of many words" (Mosiah 27:8).

Alma begins his sermon with a clear statement of his identity and authority. He echoes Nephi's words at the very beginning of the Book of Mormon when he declares: "I, Alma, having been consecrated by my father, Alma" (Alma 1:3). By echoing Nephi, he reminds his hearers of the deliverance of their ancestors from the destruction at Jerusalem and their blessings in being brought to a land of promise. By invoking his father, he reminds them of the dramatic turn in Nephite history brought about by his father's faith and courage: "He [Alma the Elder] having power and authority from God to do these things, behold, I say unto you that he began to establish a church in the land which was in the borders of Nephi; . . . yea, and he did baptize his brethren in the waters of Mormon" (Alma 5:3). By alluding to the rebaptism of lapsed members at the waters of Mormon, Alma is hoping his hearers remember the dramatic contrast between life under the wicked King Noah and that under King Mosiah and his father. He skillfully brackets his sermon by invoking the baptismal renewal at the waters of Mormon at the beginning of his sermon and returning to it at the end when, alluding also to Lehi's powerful dream, he invites his hearers to "Come and be baptized unto repentance, that ye also may be partakers of the fruit of the tree of life" (v. 62).

To emphasize the significance of his father's restoration of the church after the wickedness of King Noah and his own personal rescue from "the pains of hell" (Alma 36:13), Alma introduces the first of his themes and one of the central themes of the Book of Mormon and of Hebrew history—the contrast between captivity/bondage and deliverance/liberation. He reminds his listeners of the social and political bondage their people suffered under King Noah and the physical bondage and captivity they suffered at the hands of the Lamanites: "Behold, I say unto you, they were delivered out of the hands of the people of king Noah, by the mercy and power of God. . . . They were brought into bondage by the hands of the Lamanites; . . . yea, . . . they were in captivity, and again the Lord did deliver them out of bondage" (Alma 5:4-5). Here Alma is echoing Mosiah, who, just before Alma was chosen as leader, told the people: "Yea, remember king Noah. . . . Behold what great destruction did come upon them [the people]; and also because of their iniquities they were brought into bondage" (Mosiah 29:18).

Just as Jews traditionally have been admonished to remember the captivity and subsequent deliverance of their forebears in Egypt, so Alma asks his fellow Nephites, "Have you sufficiently retained in remembrance the captivity of your fathers? Yea, and have you sufficiently retained in remembrance his mercy and long-suffering towards them? And moreover, have ye sufficiently retained in remembrance that he has delivered their souls from hell?" (Alma 5:6). Captivity and deliverance is just one of the themes Alma continues to weave throughout his narrative. He uses powerful images to dramatize the difference between bondage and freedom, including "bands of death" and "chains of hell," both of which can be loosed as people repent and turn to God (v. 9). His use of such imagery undoubtedly is related to his own personal spiritual captivity, for he speaks of being bound himself by the chains of iniquity.

In this sermon, Alma presents his hearers with a series of contrasting pairs that throw into bold relief the choice before them of choosing salvation or damnation, life or death. These include God or the devil; birth/life or death; light or dark; white or stained; pure or filthy; truth or lies; awake or asleep; saved or damned/destroyed; rejoice or mourn/wail; accept or deny; righteous or wicked; faithful or unfaithful; faith/belief or doubt/unbelief; remember or forget; hearken or ignore (not listen); humility or pride; rich or poor; guilty or guiltless; good shepherd or bad shepherd; sheep or wolves; and tree of life or tree of death. Alma uses such a long catalogue of opposites not only to demonstrate that his listeners have been making the wrong choices at the peril of their souls, but also to remind them that they have the agency and the power to choose which way they will live on the very day he addresses them: "Can ye feel so *now*?" (Alma 5:26).

One of Alma's chief rhetorical devices is repetition. Not only does he repeatedly present contrasting choices, but he continually repeats words and phrases for emphasis. In fact, one gets the impression that nearly every word or phrase is repeated at least once in the sermon. One of the most important of these repeated phrases is "I say unto you." This phrase is found an amazing thirty-five times in this sermon (along with one variant, "I can tell you," at Alma 5:11). The effect of such repetition is not only the affirmation of Alma's authority but also the depth of his personal witness. That is, he is speaking to them not only as high priest and leader of the church but also as a reformed sinner ("a very wicked and an idolatrous man," Mosiah 27:8). He thus speaks out of ecclesiastical as well as personal authority. Toward the end of the sermon as he continues to use this phrase, Alma cleverly expands it from "I say unto you" to "thus saith the Spirit" (Alma 5:50), "the Spirit saith unto me" (v. 51), and "the Spirit saith" (v. 52), extending the authority of his words to that of the Holy Spirit and ultimately to Christ: "I say unto you, can you imagine to yourselves that ye hear the voice of the Lord?" (v. 16) and, "I say unto you, all you that are desirous to follow the voice of the good shepherd" (v. 57). Then, cleverly altering his phraseology, he shifts the burden to them: "What have ye to say against this?" (v. 58). The accumulated force of his multiple uses of "I say unto you" and his one "What have ye to say?" would, one would guess, leave his hearers speechless. What could they say against such a fortress of logic and testimony?

Counterbalanced by the rhetorical declarative "I say unto you" are a series of thirty-five rhetorical questions, most at the beginning of his sermon. The majority of these questions take the form, "I ask" or "I ask of you." These are often interwoven with "I say unto you," as in the following example:

And now *I ask of you*, my brethren, were they destroyed? Behold, *I say unto you*, Nay, they were not. And again *I ask*, were the bands of death broken, and the chains of hell which encircled them about, were they loosed? *I say unto you*, Yea, they were loosed, and their souls did expand, and they did sing redeeming love. And *I say unto you* that they are saved. (Alma 5:8–9)

Most instances of Alma's use of "I say unto you" are followed by a question, as in the following example: "I say unto you, can you imagine to yourselves that ye hear the voice of the Lord?" (Alma 5:16). This constant saying and questioning creates a powerful accumulation of emotional logic, especially as Alma brings it to the present moment. He knows he is speaking to members of the church who are aware of the teachings and practices that once were but no longer are a part of their spiritual observances. Thus, as pointed out above, he asks, "If ye have experienced a change of heart, . . . can ye feel so now?" (v. 26).

Not satisfied with a general call to repentance ("Have ye spiritually been born of God?" Alma 5:14), which might allow his hearers to excuse certain sinful behaviors, Alma zeroes in on their specific transgressions: "Have [ye] been sufficiently humble?" (v. 27), "Are ye stripped of pride?" (v. 28), "Is there one among you who is not stripped of envy?" (v. 29), "Is there one among you that doth make a mock of his brother, or that heapeth upon him persecutions?" (v. 30). Such questions bridge the old and new laws.

That Alma is concerned with an inner sanctification and not just an outward show of obedience can be seen in his most penetrating question, one that cuts to the heart of his listeners: "And now behold, I ask of you, my brethren of the church, have ye spiritually been born of God? Have ye received his image in your countenances? Have ye experienced this mighty change in your hearts?" (Alma 5:14). Alma here is suggesting that evidence of one's spiritual repentance and renewal is visible. And Alma is suggesting as well the idea of "Christogenesis" articulated by the Catholic theologian Teilhard de Chardin: in Christ is the power for us to radically change our lives, to transform them through his loving atonement and thereby to transform the world itself.[1] Alma asks his hearers not simply to consider or think about their repentance ("Can ye *think* of being saved when you have yielded yourselves to become subjects to the devil?" v. 20), but to use their imaginations as well: "Can you *imagine* to yourselves that ye hear the voice of the Lord?" "Do ye *imagine* to yourselves that ye can lie unto the Lord?" "Can ye *imagine* yourselves brought before the tribunal of God?" (vv. 16-18). This constitutes an invitation to be wholly engaged in an examination of their lives in relation to the standards of gospel adherence—feeling, doing, and thinking: "Can ye look up to God at that day with a *pure heart* and *clean hands*? . . . can ye *think* of being saved?" (vv. 19-20).

Another clever strategy Alma employs to call his hearers to repentance is to invoke the fathers—that is, the ancient prophets and patriarchs—but he does so by moving from the personal "my father" and "your fathers," to the collective "our fathers" (Alma 5:21), to specifically naming the three great fathers of Israel: "Behold, my brethren, do ye suppose that such an one [i.e., an unrepentant sinner], can have a place to sit down in the kingdom of God, with Abraham, with Isaac, and with Jacob?" (v. 24). Nothing in the history of Israel is more calculated to get people's attention than to remind them of the great figures with whom God established Israel through covenant. Even though this is a pre-Christian-era Christian community, recognizing that they have refused to abide by the new law of Christ, Alma points them to the old law, the one closer to the literalistic gospel that seems to be governing their lives. Later, he says, "I am commanded to stand and testify unto this people the things which have been spoken by our fathers concerning the

---

1. "Teilhard's aim has been to reformulate the theology of creation in terms of a genesis, a 'becoming' of the universe, in Christ. The word he finally makes up after years of reflection is 'Christogenesis,' an awkward word perhaps, but a word that sums up the evolutive structure of the universe as Teilhard sees it: a dynamic movement directed to the final unity of all things in Christ, directed to Christ in the fullness of the Pleroma." Robert L. Faricy, "Teilhard De Chardin on Creation and the Christian Life," *Theology Today* 23/4 (1967): 516.

things which are to come" (v. 44); "And moreover, I say unto you that it has thus been revealed unto me, that the words which have been spoken by our fathers are true" (v. 47).

This invocation of the fathers was deeply ingrained in the consciousness of every father in Israel, who was expected to teach his children to remember these first patriarchs. Later in speaking to his son Helaman, Alma says, "I would that ye should do as I have done, in remembering the captivity of our fathers; for they were in bondage, and none could deliver them except it was the God of Abraham, and the God of Isaac, and the God of Jacob" (Alma 36:2).

Alma also invokes the first fathers of the Book of Mormon, Lehi and Nephi, by using the central image of their remarkable shared vision—the tree of life: "Yea, he [the Lord God] saith: Come unto me and ye shall partake of the fruit of the tree of life; yea, ye shall eat and drink of the bread and waters of life freely" (Alma 5:34). By invoking this central Book of Mormon story, Alma is reminding his hearers of the dramatically contrasting choices made by Lehi's sons—those who chose righteousness and those who chose wickedness—and of the unfolding of their respective histories from these seminal decisions. Alma's hearers have just suffered the consequences of the kinds of choices made by Lehi's sons Laman and Lemuel.

Alma expands his reference to the tree by alluding to ancient tree imagery, including the central tree at the heart of Eden and Jesus's parable of the tree, as recounted in Matthew 3:10. Thus he includes two contrasting tree images: the tree of life from Genesis (which alludes to the primal gift of agency) and the tree of death: "Behold, the ax is laid at the root of the tree; therefore every tree that bringeth not forth good fruit shall be hewn down and cast into the fire, yea, a fire which cannot be consumed, even an unquenchable fire" (Alma 5:52).

As noted earlier, to signify their spiritual captivity, Alma employs images of bondage: "They were encircled about by the bands of death, and the chains of hell" (Alma 5:7). In fact, Alma increases the force of these images through repetition. Having introduced them in verse 7, he asks, "Were the bands of death broken, and the chains of hell which encircled them about, were they loosed?" (v. 9). He then asks how they could have been loosed: "What is the cause of their being loosed from the bands of death, and also the chains of hell?" (v. 10).

Alma next introduces images having to do with purity and impurity: "Can ye look up to God at that day with a pure heart and clean hands?" (Alma 5:19); "How will any of you feel, if ye shall stand before the bar of God, having your garments stained with blood and all manner of filthiness?" (v. 22). Contrasted with the blood that stains is the cleansing and purification that come through the blood of Christ: "For there can no man be saved except his garments are washed white; yea, his garments must be purified until they are cleansed from all stain, through the blood of him of whom it has been spoken by our fathers, who should come to redeem his people from their sins" (v. 21). The unclean to whom Alma addresses his remarks are set against "all the holy prophets, whose garments are cleansed and are spotless, pure and white" (v. 24).

Another archetypal image used by Alma in this sermon is that of the shepherd and his sheep. Emphasizing the role of the caring and beneficent shepherd, Alma uses the term *good shepherd* seven times, most instances coming at the end of his sermon.

Echoing both Isaiah 53:6 and Matthew 9:36, he speaks to those who "are not the sheep of the good shepherd" (Alma 5:38) but rather "sheep having no shepherd, notwithstanding a shepherd hath called after [them] and is still calling after [them], but [they] will not hearken unto his voice!" (v. 37). Instead of listening to the voice of the Good Shepherd, these Nephites have chosen "the devil [as their] shepherd" (v. 39). Not only is the devil seen as a bad shepherd, his undershepherds are seen as "wolves [that] enter . . . and devour his flock" (v. 59).

Alma's attitude toward his hearers is seen in his frequent reference to them as "my brethren," an appellation which occurs seven times in the beginning and middle of the sermon. At the end of the sermon when the logic of his argument reaches its climax—that is, when he hopes that the accumulated pleas and threats will bring his hearers to true repentance, Alma shifts to the more endearing "My beloved brethren," which he repeats three times. This is similar to the way Alma ends his second sermon, delivered not long after this one: "And now, my beloved brethren, for ye are my brethren, and ye ought to be beloved" (Alma 9:30). Thus, not only does Alma remind his hearers of their kinship and spiritual relationship, he reveals the charity he feels toward them in spite of his strong language condemning their recalcitrant wickedness.

There is a definite shift in the middle of the sermon when Alma begins to modulate his more accusatory and condemnatory language with the softer invitation to accept Christ: "Behold, he sendeth an invitation unto all men, for the arms of his mercy are extended towards them, and he saith: Repent, and I will receive you. Yea, he saith, Come unto me" (Alma 5:33-34). Christ is the "good shepherd [who] doth call you; yea, and in his own name he doth call you" (v. 38).

Alma's language continues to be strong, undoubtedly motivated by what he must sense is the reluctance of some of his hearers to respond to his message. "O ye workers of iniquity; ye that are puffed up in the vain things of the world" (Alma 5:37). He accuses them of being "liar[s] and . . . child[ren] of the devil" (v. 40).

His words indicate that he senses the pride and stubbornness of his hearers, especially evident in his repetition of "persist": "*Will ye still persist* in the wearing of costly apparel and setting your hearts upon the vain things of the world, upon your riches? Yea, *will ye persist* in supposing that ye are better one than another; yea, *will ye persist* in the persecution of your brethren. . . . Yea, and *will you persist* in turning your backs upon the poor, and the needy, and in withholding your substance from them?" Perhaps sensing that his hearers are inclined to answer in the affirmative, Alma shifts from rhetorical questions to an affirmative statement: "And finally, all *ye that will persist* in your wickedness, I say unto you that these are they who shall be hewn down and cast into the fire except they speedily repent" (Alma 5:53–56) .

Perhaps anticipating that his hearers are forming arguments against his words, Alma makes an attempt to disarm them when he says, "I have spoken unto you plainly that ye cannot err" (Alma 5:43). And, as did Abinadi before him, he makes sure his hearers know the ultimate authority behind his words: "I am called to speak after this manner, according to the holy order of God, which is in Christ Jesus; yea, I am commanded to stand and testify unto this people" (v. 44).

The ultimate strength of Alma's sermon is seen not in the logic of his argument, not in his many rhetorical devices, but in the emotional power of his personal witness. He reveals this in a number of instances: First, as emphasized at the beginning of this paper, by establishing the authority he has received at the hands of his father; second, by indicating that these things have been revealed to him: "Behold, I say unto you they [the things he has told them] are made known unto me by the Holy Spirit of God" (Alma 5:46); and by divine commission: "I speak by way of command unto you that belong to the church" (v. 62). Alma seals all of this with his personal witness ("I speak in the energy of my soul," v. 43): "Do ye not suppose that I know of these things myself? Behold, I testify unto you that I do know that these things whereof I have spoken are true" (v. 45). To dramatize the difference between the apparent indifference of his listeners and his own willingness to sacrifice for the knowledge he has gained, he tells them exactly how he knows: "Behold, I have fasted and prayed many days that I might know these things of myself. And now I do know of myself that they are true; for the Lord God hath made them manifest unto me by his Holy Spirit; and this is the spirit of revelation which is in me" (v. 46).

Of course, Alma's hearers would know the spiritual trajectory of his life. As the notorious son of a famous father, his story would be familiar to everyone in the culture. His life is a dramatic example of someone who sank to the lowest depths and rose through the mercy of Christ to the preeminent position in his society. They likely would have heard him testify on previous occasions that "after wading through much tribulation, repenting nigh unto death, the Lord in mercy saw fit to snatch me out of an everlasting burning, and I am born of God. . . . I was in the darkest abyss; but now I behold the marvelous light of God" (Mosiah 27:28-29).

Everything in Alma's sermon at Zarahemla—his invitation to his hearers to repent of their sins, to break their bonds of iniquity, to cleanse their garments, to remember God's long-suffering and mercy toward them—is designed to bring his hearers to Christ so that they might repent of their sins and gain salvation. This includes the rhetorical devices he uses—the multiplication of images, the repetition of words and phrases, the allusions to past Israelite and Nephite history, the rhetorical questions and declarative statements, the references to scripture, the symbolism, and the invocation (by direct reference or by implication) of Lehi, Nephi, Abinadi, Mosiah, and Alma the Elder, as well as Abraham, Isaac, and Jacob. The language he uses indicates that he sees this as an ultimate decision. That is, he expects his hearers not merely to make an outward show of their devotion or even a half-hearted commitment, but rather to undergo a total conversion, one involving "a mighty change" of their hearts (Alma 5:12-14) that would result in God's image being engraved on their countenances and cause them "to sing the song of redeeming love" (v. 26).

Alma ends his sermon at Zarahemla by making a distinction between those who are members of the church and those who are not. To the former he says, "I speak by way of command," and to the latter he says, "I speak by way of invitation, saying: Come and be baptized unto repentance, that ye also may be partakers of the fruit of the tree of life" (Alma 5:62). The effect of Alma's sermon is immediate, both for those who accept his message and for those who reject it. As soon as he finished his address, "he ordained priests and elders, by laying on his hands according to the order of God, to preside and watch over the church. . . . And thus they began to establish the order of the church in the city of Zarahemla" (Alma 6:1, 4). Those who refused to repent "were rejected, and their names were blotted out, that their names were not numbered among those of the righteous" (Alma 6:3). Having fully succeeded in cleansing and reforming the church, Alma relinquishes his ecclesiastical responsibilities at Zarahemla and departs for Gideon to continue his mission.

In his subsequent sermons, Alma uses many of the devices he employed in his great sermon at Zarahemla, but in none as extensively or as impressively as in his first sermon, and none reflects the intellect, learning, complexity, and rhetorical sophistication of this one. It is as if Alma, sensing the pivotal role he will play in Nephite history for the next two decades, wants to make as certain and as strong a statement as possible, to nail, as it were, his theses to the door. In a way, this sermon can be seen as his inaugural address. And it can be seen as defining his ministry. The themes he introduces here will continue to be emphasized throughout his ministry, and the language he uses with such skill and sophistication will continue to echo in his role as chief priest. All in all, it is one of the most brilliant sermons in sacred literature.

Robert A. Rees is professor of Mormon studies at Graduate Theological Union in Berkeley, California.

CHAPTER 17

"With Her Gauzy Veil before Her Face": The Veiling of Women in Antiquity

Stephen D. Ricks and Shirley S. Ricks

A charm invests a face
Imperfectly beheld.
The lady dare not lift her veil
For fear it be dispelled.

But peers beyond her mesh,
And wishes and denies,
'Lest interview annul a want
That image satisfies.[1]

The Ricks family has been acquainted with Kent Brown for well over four decades. In the mid-sixties when Kent was an undergraduate student at the University of California, Stephen was an energetic schoolboy in Berkeley. After marriage, Stephen and Shirley maintained that acquaintance and friendship with Kent while at Brigham Young University and, years later, as accompanying faculty at the BYU Jerusalem Center for Near Eastern Studies. We

---

1. Emily Dickinson, "A Charm Invests a Face."

honor Kent for his dedicated scholarship and for his devotion to the university and the church.

Face veiling in public, occasional or ongoing, was expected of women of higher social status in the ancient world. The first mention of face veiling of women is recorded in an Assyrian text from the thirteenth century BC that restricted its use to noble women: "Women, whether married or [widows] or [Assyrians] who go out into a (public) street [must not have] their heads [uncovered]. Ladies by birth . . . whether (it is) a veil(?) or robe or [mantle?], must be veiled; [they must not have] their heads [uncovered]."[2] "Women of the upper classes, whether married or not," observe G. R. Driver and John C. Miles, "must be veiled in public."[3] Further, prostitutes and common women were prohibited from assuming the veil, the sanction for which was a fearsome penalty: "A hierodule, . . . whom a husband has not married, must have her head uncovered in the (public) street; she shall not be veiled. A harlot shall not be veiled; her head must be uncovered. He who sees a veiled harlot shall arrest(?) her; he shall produce (free) men (as) witnesses (and) . . . she shall be beaten 50 stripes with rods, (and) pitch shall be poured on her head."[4] Free married women and widows as well as women who were "captive maids" or "concubines"[5] (Assyrian *esirtu*)—who were, in the view of Jeremias, in the "middle stage between free woman and a slave woman"[6]—were obliged to be veiled.

---

2. G. R. Driver and John C. Miles, *The Assyrian Laws* (Oxford: Clarendon, 1935), 407.

3. Driver and Miles, *Assyrian Laws*, 127; cf. Karel van der Toorn, "The Significance of the Veil in the Ancient Near East," in *Pomegranates and Golden Bells: Studies in Biblical, Jewish, and Near Eastern Ritual, Law, and Literature in Honor of Jacob Milgrom*, ed. David P. Wright, David Noel Freedman, and Avi Hurvitz (Winona Lake, IN: Eisenbrauns, 1995), 329–30.

4. Driver and Miles, *Assyrian Laws*, 407, 409.

5. Driver and Miles, *Assyrian Laws*, 127.

6. Alfred Jeremias, *Der Schleier von Sumer bis heute* (Leipzig: Hinrichs, 1931), 14; in the view of Theophile J. Meeks, "The Middle Assyrian Laws," in *Ancient Near Eastern Texts relating to the Old Testament*, ed. James B. Pritchard, 3rd ed. (Princeton: Princeton University Press, 1969), 183 n. 21, the fate of the "'captive woman . . . was to become a concubine or secondary wife." The translation of the text itself is "concubine."

Two basic interpretations of face veiling have been offered: veiling, according to Morris Jastrow, "was originally designed to mark a woman as the property of a man."[7] Emile Marmorstein, on the other hand, observes more favorably that veiling was "the mark of the well-born women, a symbol of privilege, and that it was imitated by all women in the towns" and that even "the ruling class of Ancient Greece adopted it."[8] In the Israelite and early Christian traditions, however, reflected in the Old and New Testaments, face veiling was practiced in order for the woman to disguise herself (or to be disguised) and as a sign of modesty and purity. Incidentally, the veiling of men, as well as sacred parts of the temple, also occurs in the biblical tradition.[9]

Veiling in Ancient Near Eastern Mythology

As art imitates life, so in the ancient Near East, facets of daily life such as the wearing of the veil found their way into legend and myth. In the Mesopotamian *Epic of Gilgamesh*, Siduri, the divine barmaid who lives by the sea at the edge of the world and guards the vine in order to make sacred wine, wears a veil.[10] Ishtar (Inanna in the Sumerian tradition) descends to the underworld to the presence of her sister, Ereshkigal, queen of the underworld.[11] At each of seven gates Ishtar is deprived of her garments, "vom Kopftuch bis

---

7. Morris Jastrow, "Veiling in Ancient Assyria," *Revue archéologique* 14 (1921): 215.

8. Emile Marmorstein, "The Veil in Judaism and Islam," *Journal of Jewish Studies* 5/1 (1954): 11.

9. After coming down from Sinai, Moses's face shown with such brightness that it had to be veiled: "When [Moses] entered the Lord's presence to speak with him he removed the veil until he came out. And when he came out and told the Israelites what he had been commanded, they saw that his face was radiant. Then Moses would put the veil over his face until he went in to speak with the Lord" (Exodus 34:33–35). It appears that Moses veiled his face after speaking with the Lord so that the brightness of his countenance would not harm those who viewed him.

10. E. A. Speiser, "The Epic of Gilgamesh," Tablet IX, in Pritchard, *Ancient Near Eastern Texts*, 90; further, see van der Toorn, "Significance of the Veil," 331.

11. E. A. Speiser, "Descent of Ishtar to the Nether World," in Pritchard, *Ancient Near Eastern Texts*, 108.

zum Schamtuch" ("from veil to undergarments"), until she stands completely naked in the presence of Ereshkigal.[12]

Face Veiling in the Bible

The customary practice of prohibiting prostitutes from veiling themselves may also have prevailed in the ancient eastern Mediterranean, although the story of Tamar veiling herself before encountering Judah as a prostitute in order to disguise herself from him (Genesis 38:14) appears to be an exception. That she was to be understood as a harlot is indicated, not by her veiling or special dress, but instead by her sitting at the highroad (cf. Ezekiel 16:25).[13]

When Rebekah was returning with Abraham's servant to meet Isaac, her husband-to-be, she saw a man in the distance walking toward them in the field. She inquired of the servant who it was, and when told it was Isaac, "she took a vail, and covered herself" (Genesis 24:65). Indicating "principles of modesty and humility" before God, the veil seems to be a "symbolic connection between clothing and faith."[14]

Brides' faces were also veiled: Leah's face was veiled at the time of her marriage to Jacob—hence Jacob's consternation at being deceived by Laban, who coolly informed him that it was the custom in his land for the elder daughter to be married before the younger (Genesis 29:26-27).[15] Mercifully, Laban allowed Jacob to marry Ra-

---

12. Josef Kroll, *Gott und Hölle: Der Mythos vom Descensuskampfe* (Leipzig: Teubner, 1932), 208. The dance of the seven veils—said to be performed by Salome to inflame King Herod with desire—is thought to have originated with the myth of the goddess Ishtar.

13. See Jastrow, "Veiling," 225-26.

14. Jennifer Heath, introduction to *The Veil: Women Writers on Its History, Lore, and Politics* (Berkeley: University of California Press, 2008), 7.

15. The most ancient representation of Jacob's marriage to Rachel, found in the church of Santa Maria Maggiore in Rome, is obscured by damage to the mosaics sufficient to make it unclear whether Rachel's face is veiled or not. "In this scene, Laban performs the marriage and, like Juno Pronuba or Concordia, stands behind the bridal pair and with his arm leads Rachel to Jacob. He wears an orange-red pallium pulled over his shoulder and is looking at Rachel. Rachel herself is dressed in a golden gown with her neck decked with precious stones. Above her brow two diamonds are

chel following the week-long wedding celebration, but only after exacting from Jacob his agreement to work another seven years for her (Genesis 29:28-30). Lifting the veil is part of the ancient Israelite-Jewish marriage ceremony and is symbolic of the groom taking possession of his bride as his lover or property.[16] In ancient Judaism, this part of the ceremony took place just before the consummation of the marriage as a symbol of becoming one in the marriage bed.[17] Ostensibly because of Laban's deceit, in Ashkenazi Jewish tradition the *badken* (cf. the Middle High German *bedecken* "to cover") ritual is observed, in which the groom places the veil over the face of the bride immediately before the ceremony.

The story of Queen Vashti in the Old Testament is sometimes interpreted to mean that she would not lift her veil, perhaps part of the "crown royal," for the princes and people to look upon her beauty at the king's court.[18] Her refusal to come at the king's command led to her replacement by Esther (Esther 1:11-19).

Relatively few allusions to veils in the Bible may actually refer to face veiling. Ruth held out her veil to receive six measures of barley from Boaz (Ruth 3:15), but it is not known if it was a face veil. When Isaiah speaks of the haughty daughters of Zion, he mentions veils in conjunction with "glasses [transparent garments],"[19] and the

---

shining, while a transparent veil surrounds her head in the form of a halo. Rachel . . . holds her left hand to her mouth as a sign of diffident reflection. For his part, Jacob is dressed as a shepherd and solemnly looks directly in front of himself. . . . Rachel's sister Leah gently urges her forward with a gesture of encouragement and lightly grasps her upper arm. For her part, Rachel, aware of the significance of the event, is looking toward her father, Laban." Stephen D. Ricks, *"Dexiosis* and *Dextrarum Iunctio*: The Sacred Handclasp in the Classical and Early Christian World," *FARMS Review* 18/1 (2006): 434, drawing on the astute description by Beat Brenk in *Die frühchristlichen Mosaiken in Santa Maria Maggiore zu Rom* (Wiesbaden: Steiner, 1975), 69.

16. However, Roland de Vaux, "Sur les voiles des femmes dans l'Orient Ancien," *Revue biblique* 44 (1935): 408, asserts that wedding ritual "requires the fiancée to remain covered until the newly wed are alone"; cf. van der Toorn, "Significance of the Veil," 331, 339.

17. "Veil," at en.wikipedia.org/wiki/Veil (accessed 29 December 2009).

18. Mohja Kahf, "From Her Royal Body the Robe Was Removed," in Heath, *The Veil*, 30-31.

19. Footnote in LDS Bible.

fine linen, and the hoods" (Isaiah 3:23). The veil referred to here may be a kind of cloak or wrapper. In the incident in which King Abimelech of Gerar desires Sarah and believes she is Abraham's sister, he speaks to Sarah of giving Abraham a thousand pieces of silver and of his being "to thee a covering of the eyes" (Genesis 20:16). One interpretation of this phrase is "implied advice to Sarah to conform to the custom of married women, and wear a complete veil, covering the eyes as well as the rest of the face,"[20] but "the phrase is generally taken to refer not to Sarah's eyes, but to the eyes of others, and to be merely a metaphorical expression concerning the vindication of Sarah."[21]

Other veils mentioned in the Bible include kinds of temple veils such as "the vail of the covering" for the ark of the testimony, a veil which was finely made of blue, purple, scarlet, and "fine twined linen of cunning work" (Exodus 40:21; 26:31; 36:35); the "vail before the mercy seat" (Leviticus 16:2), the "vail of the sanctuary (Leviticus 4:6), and the "vail of the testimony, in the tabernacle of the congregation" (Leviticus 24:3). Such veils were intended not so much to obscure as to shield the most sacred things from the eyes of sinful men, which purpose would also make sense in the veiling of women.

Face Veiling in the Hellenic World

Lloyd Llewellyn-Jones and Caroline Galt have both argued from plastic art representations and literary references that it was commonplace for women (at least those of higher status) in ancient Greece—following an ancient Near Eastern pattern—to cover their hair and face in public: "Greece is to be regarded as a Western branch of the old civilizations of Hatti, Mitanni, Babylon, Assyria, and the Levant, sharing in their cerebral processes and material

---

20. Matthew G. Easton, "Covering of the Eyes," in *The Illustrated Bible Dictionary*, rev. ed. (Grand Rapids, MI: Baker Book House, 1903), 172.

21. "Covering of the Eyes," at http://en.wikipedia.org/wiki/Covering_of_the_eyes (accessed 30 December 2009).

artefacts to such an extent that some modern hellenists are coming to regard Greece merely as a colony of the Near East."[22]

Face veiling in ancient Greece was not only a custom in the classic period,[23] but also in the Homeric age as well. The delectable English translation of Homer's *Odyssey* by T. E. Shaw (the pseudonym of T. E. Lawrence—the renowned "Lawrence of Arabia") gives several instances of face veiling: "As for her face she held up a fold of the soft wimple";[24] "she held the thin head-veil before her face";[25] "the queen stood with her gauzy veil before her face."[26] "Penelope," observes Lucinda Alwa, "whenever she appears before the abusive suitors, covers her face with her shining veils (*lipara kredemna*). . . . The *kredemnon*, as the veil of a married woman, obviously conveys the notion of chastity."[27] Odysseus, as an initiate, was saved from a storm at sea by binding his abdomen with a veil from the sea nymph Leukothea.[28]

Ovid's story of Pyramus and Thisbe in Book IV of his *Metamorphoses*, perhaps best known from the whimsical version of the tale found in Shakespeare's *Midsummer Night's Dream*, mentions a veil in the account of their star-crossed love. Thisbe's veil—dropped in haste at their appointed meeting place when she sees a lioness—is bloodied and shredded by the animal. Pyramus, upon finding

---

22. Lloyd Llewellyn-Jones, *Aphrodite's Tortoise: The Veiled Woman of Ancient Greece* (London: Classical Press of Wales, 2003), 7; cf. Caroline M. Galt, "Veiled Ladies," *American Journal of Archaeology* 35/4 (1931): 373-93. Classical, artistic depictions of veiling show "Greek women covering their heads, or much more rarely, their faces." Larissa Bonfante, review of *Aphrodite's Tortoise*, by Llewellyn-Jones, *International Journal of the Classical Tradition* 13/2 (2006): 285.

23. Llewellyn-Jones, *Aphrodite's Tortoise*, 61-66.

24. Homer, *Odyssey* 1.334.

25. Homer, *Odyssey* 16.416; 18.210.

26. Homer, *Odyssey* 21.65. These examples by Shaw (Lawrence) are cited in Hermann Haakh, "Der Schleier der Penelope," *Gymnasium* 66 (1959): 377.

27. Lucinda B. Alwa, "Veil and Citadel in Homer," *International Journal of the Humanities* 6/8 (2007): 135-44, at http://ho7.cgpublisher.com/proposals/740/index_html (accessed 29 December 2009); cf. Llewellyn-Jones, *Aphrodite's Tortoise*, 28-33.

28. Walter Burkert, "Concordia Discors: The Literary and the Archaeological Evidence on the Sanctuary of Samothrace," in *Greek Sanctuaries: New Approaches*, ed. Nanno Marinatos and Robin Hägg (London: Routledge, 1993), 187.

the mutilated veil, believes Thisbe is dead and kills himself. When Thisbe returns and finds Pyramus dead, she too kills herself with the same sword.

The Veiling of Women in Egyptian Mythology

It is significant that face veiling of women, not generally practiced in ancient Egypt, is mentioned by the Greek writer Plutarch (whose contemporary Hellenic society may not have engaged in veiling, but whose culture historically did) in his *Isis and Osiris*: "In Sais the image of Athena, which one also sees as Isis, contains the following inscription: 'I am the cosmos, the past, present, and future, no mortal has yet lifted my veil.'"[29] "Throughout the ancient world," observes Hugh Nibley, "the veil of the temple is the barrier between ourselves and both the hidden mysteries of the temple and the boundless expanses of cosmic space beyond. An example of the former is 'the veil of Isis,' which no man has lifted."[30]

Covering the Head in the Christian Tradition

Some head coverings mentioned in the Christian tradition may not necessarily refer to face veilings and may apply to both women and men. Edward Yarnold, in discussing Christian baptismal rites, states that "in some places a white linen cloth was . . . spread over the candidate's head."[31] Though not likely a strict face veiling, the covering was likely symbolic of the sacredness of the occasion. Theodore of Mopsuestia (ca. AD 350-428) believed that

---

29. Plutarch, *Isis and Osiris* 9. The following commentaries note that lifting the veil has sexual connotations: J. Gwyn Griffiths, *Plutarch's De Iside et Osiride* (Cambridge: University of Wales Press, 1970), 284; and Theodor Hopfner, *Plutarch über Isis und Osiris* (Prague: Orientalisches Institut, 1940-41), 84.

30. Hugh Nibley, "On the Sacred and the Symbolic," in *Eloquent Witness: Nibley on Himself, Others, and the Temple* (Salt Lake City: Deseret Book and FARMS, 2008), 376-77.

31. Edward Yarnold, *The Awe-Inspiring Rites of Initiation: The Origins of the RCIA* [Rite of Christian Initiation of Adults], 2nd ed. (Great Britain: Clark, 1994), 33, cited by Bryce Haymond, "Early Christian Face Veiling," www.templestudy.com/2008/07/22/early-christian-face-veiling (accessed 13 January 2010), who in turn seems to have been influenced by Matthew Brown, *The Gate of Heaven: Insights on the Doctrines and Symbols of the Temple* (American Fork, UT: Covenant Communications, 1999), 202 n. 90.

this covering was a sign of freedom in contrast to slaves—following an ancient Near Eastern pattern—who must have their heads uncovered.[32] According to an opposing view by St. Augustine, however, it was unveiling rather than veiling that symbolized freedom: "The veils are due to be removed from their head and this is a sign of freedom."[33] John the Deacon suggests that the veiling was symbolic of the priesthood since "priests of that time always wore on their heads a mystic veil."[34]

Baptismal candidates were veiled, "with their faces covered, in order that their mind might be more at liberty, and that the wandering of their eyes might not distract their soul."[35] After individuals have been exorcised in preparation for baptism, according to St. Cyril, the candidate will be breathed on and his face will be covered to secure for him peace of mind from the dangers of a roving eye. Veiling the face frees up the mind so the eyes or heart do not distract the ears from "receiving the means of salvation."[36] In 1 Corinthians 11, Paul discusses the covering of a woman's head (but not necessarily veiling) when she prays or prophesies, again perhaps in the context of avoiding distraction. A straightforward reading of Paul's text suggests that the veil (from the Latin *velare*, "to cover") helps define the relationship of God, man, and woman.[37] This practice has continued more in the sense of etiquette, courtesy, tradition, or elegance rather than for religious purposes. A Mennonite study of this passage by J. C. Wenger suggests that it could be that "Paul is here thinking of

---

32. Theodore, *Baptismal Homily* 2.19, in Yarnold, *Awe-Inspiring Rites of Initiation*, 179.

33. St. Augustine, *Sermon* 376.2, in *PL* 39:1669.

34. John the Deacon, *Epistula ad Senarium* 6, in *PL* 59:403.

35. Wolfred N. Cote, *The Archaeology of Baptism* (London: Yates and Alexander, 1876), 70.

36. Cyril of Jerusalem, *Procatechesis* 9, in *PG* 33:349.

37. Donald P. Goodman III, "Because of the Angels: A Study of the Veil in the Christian Tradition," at http://www.traditioninaction.org/religious/d006rpVeil_2_Goodman.htm (accessed 31 December 2009).

the veil as *a beautiful symbol of woman being the glory of the race, man's very queen.*"[38]

The liturgical feast of the Veil of Our Lady symbolized protection by the intercession of the Virgin Mary.[39] The assumption is that she must have worn a veil, pieces of which covered the original miraculous statue of Our Lady at Loretto and have since become relics.[40] In the Eastern Orthodox tradition of the tenth century, Mary interceded with her son for those who prayed to her for protection. After the prayer she spread her veil over the people as a protection.

In the Christian tradition the veil is worn during a "white" wedding. The veil represents the bride's purity and inner beauty, as well as her innate modesty. According to Alfred Jeremias, "The [Sumerian-Babylonian bridal veil] is indirect but certainly attested through mention of the night of a 'veiled bride.'"[41] The white diaphanous veils worn by traditional brides today may signify virginity (which earlier may have been represented by the bride's own long, flowing hair). Roman brides wore a brightly colored veil as a protection against evil spirits on their wedding day.[42]

Veiling in Early Islam

Clothing in early Islam likely emphasized modesty, as it did in Near Eastern Judaism and Christianity, and was not all that different from pre-Islamic Arabia.[43] The early Christian writer Tertullian, arguing on behalf of the veiling of virgins, observes that contemporary Arab women veiled themselves.[44] Once a year in

---

38. J. C. Wenger, *The Prayer Veil in Scripture and History: The New Testament Symbol of Woman as the Glory of the Race* (Scottsdale, PA: Herald, 1964), 10.

39. "Veil," at Wikipedia.

40. "Veil of Our Lady of Loretto," at http://www.ichrusa.com/saintsalive/veil.htm (accessed 19 January 2010).

41. Jeremias, *Der Schleier von Sumer bis heute*, 12.

42. "Veil," at Wikipedia.

43. Norman A. Stillman, "Clothing and Costume," in *Medieval Islamic Civilization: An Encyclopedia*, ed. Josef W. Meri (New York: Routledge, 2006), 1:159.

44. Tertullian, *De velandis virginibus* 17 (CSEL 76:102); cf. van der Toorn, "Significance of the Veil," 339. Note the full-body veils in Hugh Nibley, *The Ancient State: The Rulers and the Ruled* (Salt Lake City: Deseret Book and FARMS, 1991), 37, fig. 5A.

pre-Islamic Mecca, it was customary for young women to wear their fine clothes but to walk around unveiled to attract appropriate suitors. Once a husband was found, however, veiling was resumed. Veiling was typically practiced in urban areas but not among the Bedouin women in the desert.[45]

The Qur'an teaches modesty in dress for both men and women; modesty as such provides protection.[46] The idea of separation (ḥijāb) is also inherent in the Islamic texts cited for the precedence of veiling: "And say to the believing women that they cast down their looks and guard their private parts and do not display their ornaments except what appears thereof, and let them wear their head-coverings over their bosoms and not display their ornaments except to their husbands [and other men close to them]" (Qur'an 24:31). Another verse requests "your wives, your daughters, and the wives of true believers that they should cast their outer garments over their persons (when abroad). That is most convenient, that they may be distinguished and not be harassed" (Qur'an 33:59).

In the early Muslim community, strict veiling for women does not appear to have been the norm except for the wives of Muhammad, who had special status.[47] Apparently, it was only in the second Islamic century that veiling became common, where it was "first used among the powerful and rich as a status symbol." Rural and nomadic women typically did not veil and remained secluded in the home.[48] Veiling eventually became a customary practice of the Islamic community as a result of its presence in pre-Islamic Mecca.[49]

---

45. Riaz Hassan, *Faithlines: Muslim Conceptions of Islam and Society* (Karachi: Oxford University Press, 2002), 188.

46. Sherif A. Azim, "Part 15 - The Veil?" in *Women in Islam versus Women in the Judaeo-Christian Tradition: The Myth and the Reality*, at http://www.islamicity.com/mosque/w_islam/veil.htm (accessed 2 January 2010).

47. Stillman, "Clothing and Costume," 160.

48. "Historical Perspectives on Islamic Dress," in *Women in World History Curriculum* (1996-2009), at http://www.womeninworldhistory.com/essay-01.html (accessed 31 December 2009).

49. Hassan, *Faithlines*, 188.

Conclusion

While the veiling of women in the ancient world "was originally designed to mark a woman as the property of a man,"[50] veiling in the ancient Israelite and early Christian world was practiced to suggest purity, modesty, and holiness[51] as well as to reduce or eliminate the distraction of the hair or faces of women from others. As Nibley has astutely observed, the main purpose of the prayer circle, in which veiling is observed, is "the complete concentration and unity of the participants that requires the shutting out of the trivial and distractions of the external world."[52] The veiling of women had the function of emphasizing holiness and of eliminating distractions and maximizing focus on the religious task at hand. As a religious item, the veil in the Judeo-Christian tradition was intended to honor the woman and to emphasize her holiness, modesty, and purity. What is holiest among us—the most sacred precincts of the tabernacle or temple, and women—is protected with veils.

Stephen D. Ricks is professor of Hebrew and cognate learning at Brigham Young University.

Shirley S. Ricks is a senior editor at the Neal A. Maxwell Institute for Religious Scholarship at Brigham Young University.

---

50. Jastrow, "Veiling in Ancient Assyria," 215.
51. Cf. van der Toorn, "Significance of the Veil," 331, 338-39.
52. Hugh Nibley, "Early Christian Prayer Circle," in *Mormonism and Early Christianity* (Salt Lake City: Deseret Book and FARMS, 1987), 82.

CHAPTER 18

GOOD FRIDAY AND THE COPTS: GLIMPSES INTO THE DRAMA OF THIS HOLY DAY

Marian Robertson-Wilson

This tribute to my long-standing friend, S. Kent Brown, is written in commemoration of our first meeting, which took place in 1980 during an ARCE convention when we both participated in a special session devoted to Coptic studies. I wish you well, Kent and Gayle, my dear friends.

Introduction

Good Friday is known among the Copts either as Sublime Friday (yūm al-gumʿah al-ʿaẓīmah/يوم الجمعة العظيمة) or Friday of Sorrow (yūm al-gumʿah al-ḥazīnah/يوم الجمعة الحزينة), and for them it is the most solemn holy day of the year. Services are held from very early morning until after sundown and dramatically commemorate the events as they unfolded that fateful day. Sung almost in their entirety by the ranking officiant, his deacon, and the choir of deacons, these rituals present a vivid musical recollection of those extraordinary proceedings.[1] As Carolyn M. Ramzy has written, "No other

---

This article describes the services of the Coptic Orthodox Church of Egypt (al-kanīssah al-qibṭiyyah al-ʾurthūdhuksiyyah/الكنيسة القبطية الأرثوذكسية), which, according to legend, was established in Egypt ca. AD 48 by Mark the Evangelist, author of the Gospel of St. Mark. It is not to be confused with the Coptic Church of Ethiopia. For a succinct,

service compares to the melancholy of reliving Christ's death . . .
this pinnacle and most defining moment of Christianity."[2] It comes
as the culmination of Holy Week, or Holy *Paskha,* which begins on
Palm Sunday and continues throughout the week with special services every day. In fact, directly after the Palm Sunday liturgy, the
church is draped in black, the altar is closed, and there is no more
daily communion for the remainder of the week.[3]

Outline of the Good Friday Services

On Good Friday, with candles burning, wax and incense per-
fuming the air, the choir of deacons—now wearing sashes of dark
blue, purple, or black in lieu of their usual bright red,[4] and no longer
at their customary place in front of the iconostasis[5]—stand facing
each other on the north and south sides of the church (baḥrī/بحري
and qiblī/قبلي, respectively), where they may sing either together
or antiphonally (alternately back and forth) as the music demands.[6]

---

scholarly discussion of these two faiths, see Aziz S. Atiya, "Part I: Alexandrine Christianity: The Copts and Their Church," in *History of Eastern Christianity* (Notre Dame:
University of Notre Dame Press, 1968), 11-166. I would like to thank my good friends
and colleagues, Carolyn Magdy Ramzy and Nayra Atiya, themselves Copts, who graciously shared memories of their own Good Friday experiences, thereby bringing an
intimate, personal perspective to this account.

1. The officiant, ranked in order of ascending importance, could be the priest,
the bishop, the metropolitan (archbishop), or the Patriarch himself. See *The Rites of
Holy Paskha* (Coptic: (e)Pgōm (e)nte Pipaskha ethouab/ⲡϫⲱⲙ ⲛⲧⲉ ⲡⲓⲡⲁⲥⲭⲁ ⲉⲑⲟⲩⲁⲃ and
Arabic: ṭaqs ʾusbūʿ al-ālām/طقس أسبوع الآلم) (Cairo: The Coptic Church, 1981), 498; henceforth referred to as *Holy Paskha* (texts in Coptic and Arabic).

2. Carolyn Magdy Ramzy, letter to Marian Robertson-Wilson, Toronto, Canada, 22 September 2008, in possession of the author; henceforth referred to as "Letter No. 1."

3. Ramzy, "Letter No. 1," 1-2.

4. Ramzy, "Letter No. 1," 1.

5. The iconostasis is a partition, or screen, decorated with icons, which separates
the sanctuary—that particularly sacred area around the altar—from the rest of the
church.

6. *Holy Paskha,* passim; Ramzy, "Letter No. 1," 1-2; Nayra Atiya to Marian Robertson-Wilson, essay entitled "Good Friday or al-Gumʿa al-Hazeena" ("Hazeena" is an
alternate transliteration of the term "ḥazīnah"), Salt Lake City, 21 April 2009, in possession of the author; henceforth referred to as "Good Friday."

Set to special *Paskha* melodies, labeled "Hymns of Sorrow" (ʾalḥān al-ḥuzn/أَلْحَان الْحُزْن), some passages are rendered only in Coptic while others are sung first in Coptic, then Arabic.[7]

While the services are performed nonstop all day long, the Copts do adhere to the order of the regular canonical hours and celebrate the Good Friday events as follows:[8]

Morning Prayer (ṣalāt bākir/صلاة باكر), very early morning: recalling Christ in Gethsemane and his trial before Pilate.

Third Hour (al-sāʿah al-thalathah/الساعة الثالثة), ca. 9:00 a.m.: Christ derided, scourged, and nailed to the cross.

Sixth Hour (al-sāʿah al-sādissah/الساعة السادسّة), noon: The hour of crucifixion.

Ninth Hour (al-sāʿah al-tāsiʿah/الساعة التّاسعه), ca. 3:00 p.m.: Jesus's spirit delivered into the hands of his Father.

Eleventh Hour (al-sāʿah al-ḥādiyyah ʿashr/الساعة الحادية عشر), ca. 5:00 p.m.: A sword thrust into Christ's side; no bones broken. "For these things were done that the scripture should be fulfilled, A bone of him shall not be broken. . . . They shall look on him whom they pierced" (John 19:36–37).

Twelfth Hour (al-sāʿah al-thāniyyah ʿashr/الساعة الثانية عشر), ca. 6:00 p.m.: The burial—Joseph of Arimathea and Nicodemus retrieve

---

7. Coptic is the final stage of that ancient Egyptian tongue first written in hieroglyphics, subsequently transcribed with hieratic, then demotic characters, and lastly with letters of the Greek alphabet. After the Arabs invaded Egypt (AD 642), Arabic gradually replaced Coptic as the national language. Today very few Copts know Coptic—hence the need for some Arabic in their services. In fact, for Copts long since emigrated from their homeland to various countries about the world, other languages such as French and English are now heard in their services. For more details, see Carolyn M. Ramzy, letter to Marian Robertson-Wilson, Toronto, Canada, 3 May 2009, in possession of the author.

8. The canonical hours are special prayer services performed throughout the year by lay people in the city churches and by monks in the monasteries. For more details, see Ragheb Moftah et al., "Music, Coptic§The Canonical Hours," in *The Coptic Encyclopedia,* editor in chief Aziz S. Atiya (New York: Macmillan Publishing Company, 1991), 6:1724 (henceforth referred to as *CE*). For this outline of the Good Friday Hours and their topics, see *Holy Paskha,* 408.

Christ's body and wind it "in linen clothes with the spices, as the manner of the Jews is to bury" (John 19:40).

Each of these hours consists of scriptural readings, a commentary (ṭarḥ/ﻁﺮﺡ), and hymns that describe and illuminate the happenings of the hour at hand. They all follow the same general pattern, namely:

1. Lections from the Old Testament, primarily from the Pentateuch and the Prophets.
2. A lection from one of the Pauline epistles.
3. Lections from Psalms.
4. Lections from one of the four Gospels.
5. The ṭarḥ, which is an eloquent elaboration of the hour's events.

Appropriate hymns are interspersed into these lections that serve to intensify the emotion, and each hour then concludes with the prayer and benediction assigned thereto.

It is well beyond the scope of this article to cite all the texts—both spoken and sung—that are heard during this long day as well as describe the actions of the clergy, a sacred choreography. However, in hopes of giving the reader an idea of the spirit prevailing throughout, a few passages will be excerpted from some of these hours, beginning with the Sixth Hour, which, in elegizing the crucifixion itself, is in many ways the most vivid and heartrending.

Excerpts from the Sixth Hour

Old Testament lections:

> He was oppressed, and he was afflicted, yet he opened not his mouth: he is brought as a lamb to the slaughter. (Isaiah 53:7)

> Behold, God is my salvation; I will trust, and not be afraid: for the LORD JEHOVAH is my strength and my song; he also is become my salvation. (Isaiah 12:2)

And it shall come to pass in that day, saith the Lord God, that I will cause the sun to go down at noon, . . . I will send a famine in the land, not a famine of bread, nor a thirst for water, but of hearing the words of the Lord. (Amos 8:9, 11)

The choir of deacons then sings a series of five hymns that praise the Lord for condescending to sacrifice himself in order to redeem humankind.

Here is the text for the first of these hymns, "Thine is the power . . ." (Thōk te tigom/ ⲑⲱⲕ ⲧⲉ ϯϫⲟⲙ . . .):[9]

Thine is the power and the glory and the praise and dominion forever and ever. Amen.

Emmanuel, our God, our King: Thine is the power . . . , etc.

My Lord, Jesus Christ: Thine is the power . . . , etc.

My Lord, Jesus Christ, my good Savior:

My strength and my song is the Lord: He is become for me holy salvation.

Here is the last of these five hymns. Known as the *Trisagion* ("Thrice-Holy"), it was sung, according to legend, by Joseph of Arimathea and Nicodemus as they prepared and buried Christ's body after the crucifixion. The text is Greek, and it is also sung in the

---

9. The Coptic text reads as follows:

Thōk te tigom nem piōou nem pi(e)smou nem piamahi sha eneh, Amēn.

Emmanouēl pennouti penouro: Thōk te tigom . . . , etc.

Pachois Iēsous Pi(e) Christos: Thōk te tigom . . . , etc.

Pachois Iēsous Pi(e) Christos Pasōtēr (e)n agathos:

Tagom nem pa (e) smou pe (e)Pchois: afshōpi nēi eusōtēria efouab.

ⲑⲱⲕ ⲧⲉ ϯϫⲟⲙ ⲛⲉⲙ ⲡⲓⲱⲟⲩ ⲛⲉⲙ ⲡⲓⲥⲙⲟⲩ ⲛⲉⲙ ⲡⲓⲁⲙⲁϩⲓ ϣⲁ ⲉⲛⲉϩ ⲁⲙⲏⲛ

ⲉⲙⲁⲛⲟⲩⲏⲗ ⲡⲉⲛⲛⲟⲩϯ ⲡⲉⲛⲟⲩⲣⲟ: ⲑⲱⲕ ⲧⲉϯ ϫⲟⲙ . . .

ⲡⲁϭⲟⲓⲥ ⲓⲏⲥⲟⲩⲥ ⲡⲓⲭⲣⲓⲥⲧⲟⲥ: ⲑⲱⲕ ⲧⲉϯ ϫⲟⲙ . . .

ⲡⲁϭⲟⲓⲥ ⲓⲏⲥⲟⲩⲥ ⲡⲓⲭⲣⲓⲥⲧⲟⲥ ⲡⲁⲥⲱⲧⲏⲣ ⲛ̀ ⲁⲅⲁⲑⲟⲥ: ⲧⲁϫⲟⲙ ⲛⲉⲙ ⲡⲁⲥⲙⲟⲩ ⲡⲉ ⲛ̀ϭⲟⲓⲥ: ⲁϥϣⲱⲡⲓ ⲛⲏⲓ ⲉⲩⲥⲱⲧⲏⲣⲓⲁ́ ⲉϥⲟⲩⲁⲃ.

For this text, see *Holy Paskha*, 96–97.

Here are the incipits of the next three hymns:

This censer of gold (Taishourē (e)nnoub . . . /ⲧⲁⲓϣⲟⲩⲣⲏ ⲛ̀ⲛⲟⲩⲃ . . .)

Behold this man . . . (Phai etafenf e(e)pshōi/ⲫⲁⲓ ⲉⲧⲁϥⲉⲛϥ ⲉ̀ ⲛ̀ϣⲱⲓ . . .)

O, Thou Only-begotten . . . (O Monogenēs/ ⲟ̀ ⲙⲟⲛⲟⲅⲉⲛⲏⲥ . . .)

For the complete texts, see *Holy Paskha*, 447–53.

Greek Orthodox Church. However, the melodies for the Coptic and Greek versions are entirely different, the Coptic tune being the "Melody of the Cross" (laḥn al-ṣalbūt/الحن الصلبوت).[10] The text reads as follows:

> Holy God, who for us became a man, unchanging and remaining God.
> Holy and mighty, who in weakness obtained supreme power.
> Holy and immortal, who was crucified for us, who, by the cross, endured death in the flesh and passed judgment, and [who] in death conquered death, having become the immortal conqueror, having become the immortal conqueror.
> O Holy Trinity, have mercy on us.

The following phrases are then sung three times:

> Holy God; Holy and Mighty; Holy and Immortal,
> Thou [who wast] crucified for us, have mercy on us.

The hymn concludes with the Lesser Doxology:

> Glory to the Father and the Son, and the Holy Ghost, now and forever, and throughout all the eternities. Amen.[11]

---

10. See Marian Robertson, "The Good Friday *Trisagion* of the Coptic Church (A Musical Transcription and Analysis)," in *Miscellany in Honour of Acad. Ivan Dujčev* (Sofia, Bulgaria). While the editor has told me that this was published some time ago, not having seen a copy, I can give no further details about its appearance.

11. Here is the Greco-Coptic text:

Agios o Theos: o di ēmas an(e)thrōpos: gegonōs atreptōs ke minas theos.
Agios isshyros: o en asthenia to ypereshontēs isshyros epidixamenos.
Agios athanatos o (e)stavrōthis di ēmas o ton dia (e)stavrou thanaton ypominas sarki ke dixasōs ke en thanatō gegonōs yparshīs athanatos athanatos, gegonōs yparshīs athanatos.
Ē agia (e)trias eleēson ēmas.

ΑΓΙΟC Ò ΘΕΟC: Ò ΔΙ ЍΜΑC ΑΝѲΡѠΠΟC: ΓΕΓΟΝѠC ΑΤΡΕΠΤѠC ΚΕ ΜΙΝΑC ΘΕΟC.
ΑΓΙΟC ΙCΧΥΡΟC: Ò ЄΝ ΑCΘΕΝΙΑ ΤΟ ЎΠΕΡΕΧΟΝΤЋC ΙCΧΥΡΟC ЄΠΙΔΙΖΑΜΕΝΟC.
ΑΓΙΟC ΑѲΑΝΑΤΟC Ò ĊΤΑΥΡѠΘΙC ΔΙ ЍΜΑC Ó ΤΟΝ ΔΙΑ ĊΤΑΥΡΟΥ ΘΑΝΑΤΟΝ ЎΠΟΜΙΝΑC
CΑΡΚΙ ΚΕ ΔΙΖΑCѠC ΚΕ ЄΝ ΘΑΝΑΤѠ ΓΕΓΟΝѠC ЎΠΑΡΧΙC ΑѲΑΝΑΤΟC ΑѲΑΝΑΤΟC, ΓΕΓΟΝѠC
ЎΠΑΡΧΙC ΑѲΑΝΑΤΟC.
Ħ ΑΓΙΑ ΤΡΙΑC ЄΛΕЋCΟΝ ЍΜΑC.

Here is the Lesser Doxology:

As the chanting draws to an end, incense wafts through the air to accompany this lection from Psalms:

> Forsake me not, O Lord: O my God, be not far from me. Make haste to help me, O Lord my salvation. (Psalm 38:21-22)[12]

This lection is immediately followed by a reading from one of the Gospels, for example:

> And it was about the sixth hour, and there was a darkness over all the earth until the ninth hour. And the sun was darkened, and the veil of the temple was rent in the midst. (Luke 23:44-45)

At this moment the lights in the church are dimmed and the candles extinguished to symbolize the pervasive darkness.[13]

Near the end of the Sixth Hour the officiant chants an eloquent ṭarḥ proclaiming Christ's glory during the agony of his death. It begins:

> O ye inhabitants of Jerusalem, arise and comprehend this sight, for you hung Jesus, the Son of David, on a wooden cross and clothed him in a purple robe worthy of royalty and monarchs, and you placed a crown of thorns on his head, adorning the heavens with the beauty of the stars. The earth found in him the breath of life. . . . They carried his cross, following him like a king, victorious in war.

Doxa Patri ke Yiō ke Agiō (e)Pneumati: ke nyn ke aï ke is tous eōnas tōn eōnōn. Amēn. ⲆⲞⲜⲀ ⲠⲀⲦⲢⲒ ⲔⲈ ⲨⲒⲰ ⲔⲈ ⲀⲄⲒⲰ ⲠⲚⲈⲨⲘⲀⲦⲒ: ⲔⲈ ⲚⲨⲚ ⲔⲈ ⲀⲒ ⲔⲈ ⲒⲤ ⲦⲞⲨⲤ ⲈⲰⲚⲀⲤ ⲦⲰⲚ ⲈⲰⲚⲰⲚ. ⲀⲘⲎⲚ.

For these texts see *Holy Paskha*, 454; and *The Service of the Deacon* (khidmat al-shammās/خدمة الشمّاس) (Cairo: The Patriarchate, 1965), 315-16. [Texts in Coptic and Arabic]

12. Since the Copts use the Septuagint, their Psalm references differ from those in the King James translation, e.g., King James 38 = Septuagint 37. In every case, I cite the King James reference.

13. Other passages about the darkness can be found in Mark 15:33 and Matthew 27:45. Also see *Holy Paskha*, 454-61.

As the Sixth Hour ends, the lights of the church dimly come on, and the candles are relit as a sign that the darkness has lifted.[14]

Extracts from Subsequent Hours

As was mentioned, the Ninth Hour, ca. 3:00 p.m., recalls the moment of Christ's death. It begins with lections from the Old Testament, such as:

> Blow ye the trumpet in Zion, and sound an alarm in my holy mountain: let all the inhabitants of the land tremble: for the day of the Lord cometh, for it is nigh at hand; . . . And rend your heart, and not your garments, and turn unto the Lord your God: for he is gracious and merciful, slow to anger, and of great kindness, and repenteth him of the evil. (Joel 2:1, 13)

The hymns sung during the Sixth Hour are repeated, then the officiant chants from Psalms:

> Save me, O God; for the waters are come in unto my soul. . . . They gave me also gall for my meat; and in my thirst they gave me vinegar to drink. (Psalm 69:1, 21)

Lifting the censer, the officiant then chants passages from each of the four Gospels. Here are two extracts:

---

14. See *Holy Paskha*, 461, 467. Translated from the Arabic by Marian Robertson-Wilson.

These three hours of darkness during Christ's agony on the cross quite possibly correspond to the three hours of upheaval so vividly described in 3 Nephi 8:5–19 with that "great storm . . . and terrible tempest; and . . . terrible thunder, insomuch that it did shake the whole earth as if . . . to divide asunder. And . . . exceedingly sharp lightnings, such as never had been known in all the land" (vv. 5–7).

On a personal note about those three hours, my mother used to tell about the time when, on Good Friday, she went grocery shopping at midday in Burlingame, California (where we were then living), only to find all the stores closed and the streets empty. Upon inquiry, she learned from a passerby that on this holy day, from noon until 3:00 p.m., all businesses were shut down in memory of Christ's hours on the cross. With her Utah-Mormon background she was surprised and bemused at her innocent ignorance.

And at the ninth hour Jesus cried with a loud voice, saying, Eloi, Eloi, lama sabachthani? which is, being interpreted, My God, my God, why hast thou forsaken me? (Mark 15:34).

And when Jesus had cried with a loud voice, he said, Father, into thy hands I commend my spirit: and having said thus, he gave up the ghost. (Luke 23:46)

The Ninth Hour ends with the baḥrī side of the choir chanting, "Our Holy Messiah [Christ] came and suffered so as to save us by his suffering," and the qiblī responds, "And now we glorify him and exalt his name, for he showed us compassion, and sublime is his mercy."[15]

The Eleventh Hour, ca. 5:00 p.m., recalls how Joseph of Arimathea and Nicodemus retrieved Christ's body. The ṭarḥ begins:

O inhabitants of Israel, whose sins overwhelmed the air, behold the centurion, a foreigner, how he confesses the one crucified, and not only he, but those with him, they all cry out, "Verily this man is the Son of God." . . . And Israel did not understand that the Redeemer, Jesus Christ, through his suffering, sanctified the world forever.[16]

The Twelfth and final Hour, ca. 6:00 p.m., depicts the burial. The sanctuary is again opened and the altar now draped with a cloth suitable for the awaited vigil (see below). The church lights that had been dimmed are set to their brightest level, and the candles and censers are relit. The deacons have changed their sashes back from somber purple, blue, and black to their original bright red,[17] and the icon of the crucifixion is prepared while the officiant reads from Lamentations:

---

15. See *Holy Paskha*, 480. Text paraphrased from the Arabic by Robertson-Wilson.
16. See *Holy Paskha*, 487. Text paraphrased from the Arabic by Robertson-Wilson.
17. Ramzy, "Letter No. 1," 2-3.

I am the man that hath seen affliction by the rod of his wrath. . . . My strength and my hope is perished from the Lord: . . . [but] My soul hath them still in remembrance, and is humbled in me . . . therefore have I hope. It is of the Lord's mercies that we are not consumed, because his compassions fail not. (Lamentations 3:1, 18, 20-22)

The choir once again sings the hymn, "Thine is the power . . ." (see above), and then come lections from Psalms, which include these excerpts:

The Lord is my shepherd; I shall not want. . . . Yea, though I walk through the valley of the shadow of death, I will fear no evil: for thou art with me; thy rod and thy staff they comfort me. (Psalm 23:1, 4)

Thy throne, O God, is for ever and ever: the sceptre of thy kingdom is a right sceptre. (Psalm 45:6)

Passages chanted from all four Gospels recount how Joseph of Arimathea and Nicodemus wrapped Christ's body in clean linen, laid it in a new tomb and rolled a stone over the entrance while Mary Magdalene and other women watched from afar.[18]

At this point the congregants witness one of the most dramatic and memorable events of the entire day. As the officiant holds the cross aloft, he and the deacons gravely chant "Kyrie eleēson" ("Lord, have mercy") 412 times, turning first toward the east, then toward the west, then the north, and lastly toward the south, chanting 100 times at each turn. Finally, turning once again toward the east, they chant Kyrie eleēson twelve more times to the accompaniment of small brilliantly sounding hand cymbals (bil-nāqūs/بالناقوس).[19]

---

18. See *Holy Paskha*, 491-95. The New Testament passages can be found in Matthew 27:58-61; Mark 15:43-47; Luke 23:50-56; and John 19:38-42.

19. See *Holy Paskha*, 496; Ramzy, "Letter No. 1," 3. For more details about the small hand cymbals (al-nāqūs), see Marian Robertson-Wilson et al., "Music, Coptic§Musical Instruments," in *CE* 6:1738-39.

Immediately thereafter, as the choir sings the stately hymn "Golgotha," the officiant carries the icon of the crucifixion three times around the altar and three times around the church. As the procession returns to the sanctuary, the deacons circle the altar three more times; the officiant wraps the icon in a shroud of white linen, lays it on the altar, places a cross over it, and completely covers it (buries it as it were) under rose petals and spices—red roses signifying Christ's atoning blood—to re-create thereby a resting place befitting the highest, supreme sovereign of humankind.

The Twelfth Hour quickly ends with a final benediction: "Bless me unto repentance; forgive my sins; pray for me." The sanctuary door is closed once again, and this symbolic tomb is to be left undisturbed until the Easter service early Sunday morning.[20]

Meanwhile, as the people leave the chapel, the officiant and his deacons remain behind to keep vigil by chanting Psalms and other passages from the Old and New Testaments, each person taking a turn at reading a designated passage.[21]

To conclude this long holy day, the congregants break their daylong fast with a convivial meal, which may take place as a

---

20. See *Holy Paskha*, 496-99; Ramzy, "Letter No. 1," 1-3. Here is the Coptic text for the benediction:
(e)smou eroi: is timetanoia: Khō nēi evol gō (e)mpi(e)smou.
ⲥ̀ⲙⲟⲩ ⲉ̀ⲣⲟⲓ: ⲓⲥ ϯⲙⲉⲧⲁⲛⲟⲓⲁ: ⲭⲱ ⲛⲏⲓ ⲉ̀ⲃⲟⲗ ⲭⲱ ⲙ̀ⲡⲓⲥ̀ⲙⲟⲩ
A word about the hymn "Golgotha": One of the best known hymns in the entire Coptic repertoire, it describes the crucifixion of Christ at Golgotha between two thieves and recounts how Joseph of Arimathea and Nicodemus took Christ's body, prepared and placed it in a tomb, all while singing the *Trisagion* (see above). Consisting of some thirty-two verses, it is built on two musical themes. For a musical transcription of these themes, see Marian Robertson, "Music, Coptic§Description of the Corpus and Present Musical Practice," in *CE* 6:1723. For a transliteration and translation of the entire text, see Marian Robertson, "Revised Guide to the Ragheb Moftah Collection of Coptic Chant Recordings" (Salt Lake City: 2005), 2:121-24. Manuscript copies are housed in the Music Division at the Library of Congress; Rare Books and Special Collections Library at the American University in Cairo; Special Collections at the Harold B. Lee Library, Brigham Young University; and Special Collections at the Marriott Library, University of Utah, among other venues.

21. For more details about this vigil, see Ragheb Moftah and Martha Roy, "Music, Coptic§Canticles," in *CE* 6:1729.

communal gathering in the church basement or at home with beloved family members.[22]

Then, very early Sunday morning, the people return to celebrate
the long-awaited, highly anticipated Easter service, with its joyous
shout (first in Greek, then Coptic):[23]

> "Christ is risen, Truly he is risen."
> "Christos anestē, Alēthōs anestē."
> "Pi(e) Christos aftōnf, Ḥen oumethmēi aftōnf."

Conclusion

Although an article about the Coptic Good Friday services may
seem a bit esoteric and unusual for an LDS publication, the author
offers it as a way of broadening our understanding of another
venerable Christian tradition. We are all children of God, and the
more we may come to know about each other, the closer we may
draw to our Maker, ever constant, ever loving. It is in this spirit of
universal brotherhood that I have written.

Therefore, in fellowship, let us join the Coptic choruses
and sing together jubilant praises to Jesus Christ, our Lord and
Savior, who—by his suffering on the cross, his resurrection and
atonement—brought all humankind the greatest, most precious gift
of all, even life eternal.

*Marian Robertson-Wilson, a researcher in Coptic music, is a consultant to
the Music Division of the Library of Congress.*

---

22. This meal must still conform to the restrictions imposed by Lent, known by
the Copts as the "Great Fast" (al- ṣūm al-kabīr/الصوم الكبير), which will end only after the
Easter service early Sunday morning. Having begun some fifty-five days before Easter,
it is a period during which Copts are asked to abstain from all meat, fish, dairy, and
other animal products as well as alcohol. One typically Egyptian staple for this Good
Friday meal could be "Fūl Nābit" (فول نابت), a soup of skinned, sprouted fava (broad)
beans, boiled in a broth seasoned with salt and cumin. Ramzy, "Letter No. 1," 1, 3; N.
Atiya, "Good Friday," 2.

23. Here are the Greek and Coptic phrases:
ⲭ̅ⲣⲓⲥⲧⲟⲥ ⲁⲛⲉⲥⲧⲏ . . . ⲁⲗⲏⲑⲱⲥ ⲁⲛⲉⲥⲧⲏ.
ⲡⲓⲭ̅ⲣⲓⲥⲧⲟⲥ ⲁϥⲧⲱⲛϥ-ⲃⲉⲛ ⲟⲩⲙⲉⲑⲙⲏⲓ ⲁϥⲧⲱⲛϥ.
See *Holy Paskha*, 607.

яо

Two Crucified Men:
Insights into the Death of
Jesus of Nazareth

Andrew C. Skinner

O n a certain day about two thousand years ago, in a small and relatively obscure province of the Roman Empire, a man in the prime of his life took his last breath as he hung nailed to a cross outside a nearby city wall, suffering the final stages of punishment for some offense against the state. As a victim of crucifixion, the man experienced one of the most painful, terrifying, gruesome, and humiliating ways to die that has ever been conceived. The name of the province to which I refer was Judea. The name of the city was, of course, Jerusalem. And the name of the man was . . . Yehohanan ben Hagkol.

Perhaps some were expecting the name of the victim to have been Jesus of Nazareth. He is, without doubt, the most famous and important of all persons ever crucified, but Yehohanan ben Hagkol is important in his own right—even though he is not mentioned in any historical sources and we know almost nothing about his life. Yet, Yehohanan ben Hagkol's physical remains provide us with the *only known* archaeological evidence for the practice of crucifixion in the ancient Roman world, and therefore his circumstance tells us much about the physical aspects of the crucifixion of Jesus of Nazareth and the horrors he endured.

Yehohanan's physical remains were discovered accidentally in 1968 in the north Jerusalem suburb of Giv'at ha-Mivtar, some 15 km from the Old City of Jerusalem. Yehohanan was crucified sometime between AD 7 and 70—the period roughly contemporaneous with Jesus.[1] One study even opines that "Jehoḥanan was crucified closer to the time of Jesus' own crucifixion."[2] He was judged to have been between twenty-four and twenty-eight years of age at the time of crucifixion.

Historical sources inform us that thousands of people like Yehohanan ben Hagkol in Roman Palestine were put to death by crucifixion during the period between Herod the Great and the destruction of Jerusalem in AD 70. The historian Josephus reports that during a revolt that broke out in Jerusalem after the death of Herod in 4 BC, the Roman leader Quintilius Varus (46 BC-AD 9) crucified two thousand rebellious Jews.[3] There is documentary evidence that crucifixions continued through the years. As the threat of war between the Jewish nation and Rome loomed large in AD 66, Roman Procurator Gessius Florus ordered that Jewish troublemakers be "first scourged and then crucified."[4] Note here that scourging was used as punishment before administering crucifixion, just as reported in the Gospels (Matthew 27:26; Mark 15:15; John 19:1) and the Book of Mormon (Mosiah 3:9). Perhaps the capstone event in the history of crucifixion took place when Titus (AD 39-81) laid siege to Jerusalem, built an earthworks around it, captured those attempting to escape, and crucified them opposite the city walls. The daily tally of crucifixion victims was five hundred, sometimes

---

1. Rockefeller Museum flier, "The Crucified Man from Giv'at Ha-mivtar" (Jerusalem, 1990). Also, Rockefeller Museum exhibit placard, 1990.

2. Joe Zias and James H. Charlesworth, "Crucifixion: Archaeology, Jesus, and the Dead Sea Scrolls," in *Jesus and the Dead Sea Scrolls*, ed. James H. Charlesworth (New York: Doubleday, 1992), 284.

3. Josephus, *Jewish Antiquities* 17.295, trans. Ralph Marcus and Allen Wikgren, Loeb Classical Library (Cambridge: Harvard University Press, 1963), 8:509.

4. Josephus, *Jewish Wars* 2.306, trans. H. St. J. Thackeray, Loeb Classical Library (Cambridge: Harvard University Press, 1927), 2:443.

more! "The soldiers, out of rage and hatred, amused themselves by nailing their prisoners in different postures; and so great was their number, that space could not be found for the crosses."[5] The practice of crucifixion in the empire was finally abolished by Constantine in the fourth century.[6]

The ossuary (casket for bones) containing Yehohanan's physical remains was of the type used in the reburial process common in Roman Palestine. The ossuary had Yehohanan's name engraved on it, and its dramatic contents included a right heel bone, with a four-and-one-half-inch crucifixion spike still embedded in the bone. The spike was bent over at the pointed end, indicating perhaps that the spike had hit a knot while being driven into the wood on which Yehohanan was crucified. Other skeletal remains in the ossuary included the victim's shin bones, which initial examiners said had been broken on purpose, and a right forearm, which examiners thought showed evidence of a spike having been driven into the victim's wrist as part of the crucifixion process. Though other scholars have since reevaluated these initial claims regarding the shinbones and forearm and find the evidence inconclusive,[7] there is no question about ben Hagkol's crucifixion.

The grisly action necessary to have produced the physical evidence of Yehohanan's horrible death would have required each foot of the condemned man to be nailed laterally on opposite outside edges of an upright pole or stake, so that the victim's legs and feet straddled it. The cross to which Yehohanan was nailed was composed of two parts: an upright piece set in the ground, sometimes

---

5. Josephus, *Jewish Wars* 5.451, in Thackeray, *Jewish Wars*, 3:341. For the entire story, see Josephus, *Jewish Wars* 5.446-51.

6. Zias and Charlesworth, "Crucifixion: Archaeology, Jesus," 278.

7. Zias and Charlesworth, "Crucifixion: Archaeology, Jesus," 280. Joseph Zias and Eliezer Sekeles, "The Crucified Man from Givʿat ha-Mivtar—A Reappraisal," *Biblical Archaeologist* 48/3 (September 1985): 190. This earliest report of the reassessment is less tentative than latter ones—omitting any words like "inconclusive," or "in our estimation." Perhaps the perspective which time brings allowed scholars to be less strident and declarative.

referred to as a *stipes* (pole), and a detachable crossbar called a *patibulum*. The Gospel writers uniformly referred to Jesus's cross as simply a *stauros*, meaning "stake."

Scholars who worked on the sobering discovery of Yehohanan's remains tell us that written sources support the inferences deduced from Yehohanan's physical remains—"that the condemned [party] never carried the complete cross. . . . Instead only the crossbar was carried, to the place [where] the upright piece was set in the ground."[8]

Further forensic evidence from Yehohanan's physical remains tells us that when his feet were nailed to the upright portion of the cross, "an olive wood plaque was put between the head of each nail and the foot, probably to prevent the condemned [person's feet] from pulling free of the nail. Evidence for this consists of [olive] wood fragments found below the head of the nail [embedded in Yehohanan's heel]," as determined from careful examination by scholars from the Department of Botany at the Hebrew University in Jerusalem.[9]

The scholars and scientists who worked on ben Hagkol's remains have made two other comments worth noting. First, "It is important to remember that death by crucifixion was not caused by the traumatic injury of nailing; rather, hanging from the cross resulted in a painful process of asphyxiation, in which the two sets of muscles used for breathing—the intercostal muscles and the diaphragm—became progressively weakened. In time, the victim expired as a consequence of inability to continue breathing properly."[10] Quite literally, victims of crucifixion drowned in their own fluid that accumulated in the lungs. The implication here is clear: it would have been impossible to resuscitate a dead victim of crucifixion (as some anti-resurrection advocates have claimed about Jesus).

---

8. Zias and Eliezer, "Crucified Man," 190.
9. Zias and Eliezer, "Crucified Man," 190.
10. Zias and Eliezer, "Crucified Man," 190.

According to the second comment: "We do not know the crime for which [Yehohanan ben Hagkol] was sentenced to a death of agony on the cross. However, historical sources tell that the Romans adopted crucifixion for the execution of slaves, prisoners and rebels."[11]

Jesus of Nazareth

This brings us to the most famous case of crucifixion in all of history—Jesus of Nazareth. For, in truth, the understandings derived from the physical remains of Yehohanan ben Hagkol, and from the insights of scholars who investigated ben Hagkol's case, can be combined with historical and prophetic sources, including scripture, to provide us with a clearer picture of what likely happened to Jesus and thus increase our appreciation for him—which, in turn, may help to teach us profound lessons about committed discipleship in the face of significant suffering.[12]

The scriptural record indicates that Jesus's crucifixion was preceded by several exhaustive hours of teaching, redemptive suffering, and sheer endurance, first in the Upper Room where he performed the ordinances of the sacrament and the washing of the feet, then in Gethsemane where he bled from every pore as God the Father withdrew his life-sustaining Spirit, for the first time, during the last twenty-four hours of the Son's mortal life,[13] and finally during his arrest and abuse-filled arraignments before the Jewish high priest, the "council" or Sanhedrin, the Roman prefect, Pontius Pilate, and the tetrarch of Galilee, Herod Antipas.

Scholars writing about Yehohanan ben Hagkol's remains asserted that crucifixion was applied to slaves, prisoners, and rebels. That Jesus was treated as all of these—a slave, common criminal,

---

11. Rockefeller Museum flier, "The Crucified Man from Giv'at Ha-mivtar."

12. We know that the kingdom of the blessed will be made up of those "who had offered sacrifice in the similitude of the great sacrifice of the Son of God, and had suffered tribulation in their Redeemer's name" (D&C 138:13).

13. Brigham Young, in *Journal of Discourses*, 3:205-6. Also, see the discussion in Andrew C. Skinner, *Gethsemane* (Salt Lake City: Deseret Book, 2002), 100.

rebel, and political insurrectionist—from the moment of his arrest onward, and that his execution was thus a foregone conclusion, is seen in several individual actions taken against him.

Jesus's execution was an unalterable decision well before his arrest—a "done deal," so to speak. Two days before the Feast of Passover, and therefore at least forty-eight hours before his arrest, there were "assembled together the chief priests, and the scribes, and the elders of the people, unto the palace of the high priest, who was called Caiaphas, and consulted that they might take Jesus by subtilty, and kill him" (Matthew 26:3-4; see also Luke 22:1-4). As a result of this final conspiratorial conference, Jesus's fate was sealed.

The first of the individual actions against Jesus that show him being treated presumptively as a criminal came as he emerged from Gethsemane. He was, in the words of Elder Bruce R. McConkie, "led away with a rope around his neck, *as a common criminal*, to be judged by the arch-criminals who as Jews sat in Aaron's seat and who as Romans wielded Caesar's power."[14] With the rope around his neck, Jesus became, perhaps unintentionally, the symbolic reenactment and the foreseen fulfillment of the Yom Kippur scapegoat of Mosaic law that was led to the edge of the wilderness to perish on the Day of Atonement while bearing the sins of the covenant people. These sins had been transferred to the scapegoat through the laying on of hands by the high priest, as recorded in Leviticus 16:21-22:

> And Aaron shall lay both his hands upon the head of the live goat, and confess over him all the iniquities of the children of Israel, and all their transgressions in all their sins, putting them upon the head of the goat, and shall send him away by the hand of a fit man into the wilderness:
>
> And the goat shall bear upon him all their iniquities unto a land not inhabited: and he shall let go the goat in the wilderness.

---

14. Bruce R. McConkie, "The Purifying Power of Gethsemane," *Ensign*, May 1985, 9, emphasis added.

This, of course, is an apt metaphor for Jesus and his salvific mission, but it in no way absolves the conspiratorial leaders of the Jewish nation of their shameful deeds and unjust treatment of the Innocent One.

Second, the Gospels report in varying degrees of detail that as Jesus was arraigned before various Jewish tribunals he was subjected to the kind of verbal and physical abuse merited by slaves and criminals. Each of the Gospels has some kind of an account of the punishment and indignities endured by Jesus, first at the hands of the former high priest, Annas; then the current high priest, Caiaphas, and his servants; and then the council. The Greek text clarifies the exact nature of the abuse heaped on Jesus:

- Matthew 26:67 says: "they spat (*eneptusan*) into his face," "they struck (*ekolaphisan*) him," and "they slapped (*erapisan*) him." The meaning of *ekolaphisan* (from *kolaphizō*) is to strike or punch with a clenched fist; whereas *erapisan* means to strike with an open palm.[15] The difference is somewhat clouded in the King James Version. But it is an important distinction since slapping (with open palm) is merited by slaves—the lowest rung on the social ladder in the Mediterranean world.
- Mark 14:65 is the fullest account of the punishments delivered and says: "some began to spit (*emptuein*) on him," "to cover (*perikaluptein*) his face," "[to] strike (*kolaphizein*) him," "and the servants received him with slaps (*rapismasin*)." This is significant because here it is servants of the high priest who slap Jesus—indicating that he is regarded as lower than the servants themselves, the *hupēretai*, which is a Greek word meaning those who "do hard service,"[16] or those next to slaves in social order. Jesus is treated as being lower than a Jewish slave.

15. See the discussion in Adam Clarke, *The New Testament of Our Lord and Savior Jesus Christ . . . Marginal Readings and Parallel Texts: A Commentary and Critical Notes*, new ed. (Nashville: Abingdon, n.d.), 5:262.

16. H. G. Liddell and R. Scott, *A Lexicon: Abridged from Liddell and Scott's Greek-English Lexicon* (Oxford: University Press, 1976), 736.

- Luke 22:63–64 uses a different vocabulary in describing Jesus's abusive treatment: "the men, holding him in custody were ridiculing (*enepaizon*) him," "beating (*derontes*) him," and "blindfolded (*perikalupsantes*) him." Luke's use of the word *derontes*, from the root *dero*, implies a different kind of beating than slapping or cuffing with closed fist. In classical Greek it means "to skin, flay," also "to cudgel, thrash."[17] Significantly, this same root is used previously by Luke when reporting Jesus's own teachings about discipleship, which he himself set in the context of the master-slave relationship. The King James Version reads: "And that servant [here the Greek uses *doulos* or slave], which knew his lord's will, and prepared not himself, neither did according to his will, shall be beaten with many stripes" (Luke 12:47). One notes here that the kind of beating the slave receives in Jesus's hypothetical story is exactly the kind that Jesus received in actuality at his arraignment before the high priest and council, according to Luke, thus pointing again to Jesus's status as slave.

- John 18:22 is unique in that it reports that the first abusive treatment Jesus received came before he ever stood before Caiaphas or the Sanhedrin. According to John, Jesus was first taken to Annas, a former high priest in the days of Jesus's youth and father-in-law of Caiaphas. None of the other writers mention Annas, who seems to have been something of a behind-the-scenes power broker within the structure of Jewish leadership. The implication seems to be that if Annas found Jesus worthy of conviction, then Caiaphas would move ahead freely. Another indicator of Annas's preeminence, or influence at least, is seen in the fact that five of his sons went on to become high priests. Annas had been appointed high priest by the Roman legate Quirinius, at age 37. He ruled as high priest from AD 7 to 15, when he was deposed by Valerius Gratus. In Annas's

---

17. Liddell and Scott, *Lexicon*, 155.

presence Jesus was slapped (*rapisma*) by a servant (*hupēretōn*), who "struck Jesus with the palm of his hand."

The implication in John is clear: the treatment Jesus received was geared toward slaves who were guilty of misdeeds. In this context it seems significant to note that originally only slaves were crucified, though later, provincial freedmen were added to the list. Roman citizens were exempted under every circumstance.[18]

It must also be noted that though Jesus received all the physical and emotional indignities and vexations that the real archcriminals (to use Elder McConkie's words) could hurl at him, Jesus sought no revenge, though it was completely within his power to do so (Matthew 26:52-53). He bore all punishment with meekness—that sublime quality of exhibiting poise in the face of provocation—and thus surpassed even the meekness possessed by his great foreshadower-prophet, Moses (see Numbers 12:3 and Moses 1:6).

Third, the witnesses brought to bear against Jesus, as well as the charges leveled against him, clearly show that he was already regarded as a rebel worthy of death by crucifixion. According to Matthew and Mark, Jesus was charged with prophesying that he would personally destroy and rebuild the temple. "And there arose certain, and bare false witness against him, saying, We heard him say, I will destroy this temple that is made with hands, and within three days I will build another made without hands" (Mark 14:57-58). Jewish leaders were so intent on making sure Jesus was adjudged worthy of death on account of a capital offense that they "sought false witness against Jesus, to put him to death" (Matthew 26:59). The nature of the charges against Jesus are explained by Elder James E. Talmage: "The plan of the conspiring rulers appears to have been that of convicting Christ on a charge of sedition, making Him out to be a dangerous disturber of the nation's peace, an

---

18. See the discussion of Kaufmann Kohler and Emil G. Hirsch, "Crucifixion," in *Jewish Encyclopedia* at http://www.jewishencyclopedia.com/view_friendly.jsp?artid =905&letter=C (accessed 14 June 2011).

assailant of established institutions, and consequently an inciter of opposition against the vassal autonomy of the Jewish nation, and the supreme dominion of Rome."[19]

Jesus was also vulnerable to the charge of blasphemy because his supposed prophecy of the destruction and rebuilding of the temple amounted to a messianic claim, as seen in the high priest's inquiry as to whether or not Jesus really thought he was the Messiah. In fact, Caiaphas seems to have equated the title "Christ" (Messiah) with the title "Son of God," as noted by Matthew. "And the high priest answered and said unto him, I adjure thee by the living God, that thou tell us whether thou be the Christ, the Son of God" (Matthew 26:63). In this instance the Gospel of Mark uses "Son of the Blessed" (14:61) instead of the more assertive "Son of God," based perhaps on an original Aramaism, but meaning the same. John 1:49 further indicates that the Messiah was also assumed to be the King of Israel during Jesus's day. Nathanael affirms to Jesus, "Rabbi, thou art the Son of God; thou art the King of Israel." Thus, in first-century Judaism three titles went together; they were the equivalent of one another: Messiah (Christ), Son of God, and King of Israel. Jesus of Nazareth was correctly identified by all three epithets. In response to the high priest's direct question about his identity, Jesus left no room for doubt. As he did when he was first arrested in Gethsemane, Jesus identified himself by using the divine name "I am" (Mark 14:62)—the term by which Jehovah identified himself on Sinai (Exodus 3:14). This "was an unqualified avowal of divine parentage, and inherent Godship."[20] In this Jesus was guilty of nothing except telling the truth.

Caiaphas tore his clothes when he heard Jesus's answer—an ancient custom performed either to convey shock, outrage, or grief or to signify the death of a family or community member (Genesis 37:34; Numbers 14:6; 2 Samuel 1:11). Then Caiaphas immediately forestalled any verdict other than guilty: "He hath spoken

---

19. James E. Talmage, *Jesus the Christ* (Salt Lake City: Deseret Book, 1962), 624-25.
20. Talmage, *Jesus the Christ*, 626.

blasphemy; what further need have we of witnesses? . . . What think ye? (Matthew 26:65-66). To these carefully orchestrated manipulations, the entire council responded, "He is guilty of death" (Matthew 26:66). Jesus was now "had" on all counts. As had been determined before his Jewish trial ever began, Jesus would be crucified. He had been treated as a slave during the proceedings. After his Jewish arraignment he was a convicted criminal and rebel, found guilty of blasphemy and sedition.

When Jesus was delivered to Pontius Pilate, the Roman prefect or governor (Matthew 27:2), there occurred what amounted to a second trial. The charge against him at this juncture seems to have distilled around the specific claim that he was "king of the Jews," as reported in all four Gospels (Matthew 27:11; Mark 15:2; Luke 23:3; John 18:33). Some see in this charge "a secular equivalent of a messianic claim."[21] As Luke indicates, the Jewish leaders apparently wanted Pilate to believe that Jesus's intent was to rebel against Roman rule. "And they began to accuse him, saying, We found this fellow perverting [Greek, *diastrephonta* "misleading"] the nation, and forbidding to give tribute to Caesar, saying that he himself is Christ a King" (Luke 23:2). That this was the charge that ultimately made him worthy of death in Roman eyes is further supported by the content of the *titulus* or plaque placed on the top of his cross, "THIS IS THE KING OF THE JEWS" (Luke 23:38). At the heart of this claim to being king of the Jews was, again, sedition. The Jewish leaders wanted Rome to believe that Jesus had set himself up as ruler in juxtaposition to the sanctioned Jewish authorities. Therefore, Jesus was a rebel of the worst kind, religious and political.

The Cross

The modern commentators who have discussed the other crucified man of this essay, Yehohanan ben Hagkol, emphasize that

---

21. Dale Patrick, "Crimes and Punishment, Old Testament and New Testament," in *The New Interpreter's Dictionary of the Bible* (Nashville: Abingdon, 2006), 1:802.

the evidence indicates that the configuration of ben Hagkol's cross, as well as those of others, was in two parts, a detachable crossbar (which the condemned persons carried to the place of their executions) and an upright piece set in the ground to which the crossbar was attached.[22] Secular sources support this assessment. An important writer, Plautus, refers to a victim carrying a crossbar throughout the city and then being fastened on a cross.[23] Since no executions were allowed within Jerusalem's walls (Numbers 15:35; 1 Kings 21:13; Acts 7:58), processions led to the site or sites of crucifixion outside the city. In Jesus's case, the procession was led by a centurion and accompanied by at least a quaternion (four soldiers) to keep the procession moving (John 19:23). One of the soldiers carried the sign (*titulus*) on which the condemned man's name and crime were written and which was later fastened to the top of the cross (Matthew 27:37; Mark 15:26; Luke 23:38; John 19:19-22).

Biblical references indicate the possibility that the upright piece to which Jesus's crossbar was fastened was a tree whose branches had been trimmed off. The apostle Paul seems to refer to this in his discussion of Christ's many-faceted redemptive act: "Christ hath redeemed us from the curse of the law, being made a curse for us: for it is written, Cursed is every one that hangeth on a tree" (Galatians 3:13). Paul was quoting Deuteronomy 21:23, which may be viewed as a prophetic reference made by Moses to the future crucifixion of the Savior (the book of Deuteronomy consisting of Moses's final three sermons). This Deuteronomic passage was used by later Jews to emphasize the abhorrent nature of crucifixion as a way to die, that is, "*cursed* is every one that hangeth on a tree." Paul was saying that Jesus redeemed every one of us from the impossibility of being perfected through the Mosaic law by being crucified on a tree, even though it was an abhorrent and degrading form of death.

---

22. Zias and Sekeles, "Crucified Man," 190.
23. Plautus, *Carbonaria* 2.

The apostle Peter also refers to the tree as the method of Jesus's crucifixion. He speaks of our Savior as the one "who his own self bare our sins in his own body on the tree, that we, being dead to sins, should live unto righteousness: by whose stripes ye were healed" (1 Peter 2:24).

Crucifixion (Hebrew verb תלה) on "the tree" was also mentioned in the *Temple Scroll* as punishment for special offenses against the true community of Israel (Qumran covenanters):

> If a man slanders his people and delivers his people to a foreign nation and does evil to his people, you shall hang him on a tree and he shall die. On the testimony of two witnesses and on the testimony of three witnesses he shall be put to death and they shall hang him on the tree. If a man is guilty of a capital crime and flees (abroad) to the nations, and curses his people, the children of Israel, you shall hang him also on the tree, and he shall die. But his body shall not stay overnight on the tree. Indeed you shall bury him on the same day. For he who is hanged on the tree is accursed of God and men. You shall not pollute the ground which I give you to inherit.[24]

One important reason why condemned persons may have been crucified on well-rooted, trimmed trees may be connected to the reason why the condemned also carried only the crossbar (*patibulum*) and not the entire cross to their crucifixions. There was a shortage of wood. Josephus indicates that wood was so scarce in the Jerusalem area during the first century AD that the Romans had to travel ten miles outside the city to procure timber for their siege.[25]

---

24. 11Q Temple 64:6-13. See Geza Vermes, trans., "The Temple Scroll," in *The Complete Dead Sea Scrolls in English*, rev. ed. (London: Penguin Books, 2004), 218. See also Yigael Yadin, *The Temple Scroll: Text and Commentary* (Jerusalem: Keter, 1977), 2:288-91. The *Temple Scroll*, longest of all the Dead Sea Scrolls, is one of the most important, referred to by some scholars as the sixth book of the Torah.

25. Josephus, *Jewish Wars* 5.522-23.

The scarcity of wood thus affected the economics of crucifixion to the point that crossbars needed to be reused, and existing trees that could be repeatedly used facilitated the process.

Crucifixion may have originated in Persia long before the Romans adopted it, although one source puts its beginnings in Egypt.[26] Wherever it started, there is no doubt that it was one of the most horrific forms of execution ever invented by humankind. According to the Roman writer Cicero and the Jewish historian Josephus, crucifixion was the worst, most pitiable form of death![27] Cicero, arguably Rome's greatest statesman, detested crucifixion, calling it the "cruelest and most disgusting penalty," the "extreme and ultimate punishment for slaves."[28] (Again, we see the connection between Jesus's implied status as slave and the punishments he had to bear.) The Roman writers Juvenal, Suetonius, Horace, Pliny, and Seneca all have appalling things to say about crucifixion. In fact, the words *cross* and *crucify* actually derive from the Latin word for torture, *cruciare*. The nail found embedded in ben Hagkol's heel bone goes a long way toward substantiating historical assessments.

Crucifixion was state-sponsored torture, calculated to produce the greatest amount of suffering over the longest possible period before death. Being a public event or spectacle, Rome's aim in supporting crucifixion, more than individual punishment, was deterrence or prevention. "Whenever we crucify the condemned, the most crowded roads are chosen, where the most people can see and be moved by this terror. For penalties relate not so much to retribution as to their exemplary effect."[29] Crucifixion has also been called state-sponsored terrorism.[30]

---

26. Joseph W. Hewitt, "The Use of Nails in the Crucifixion," *Harvard Theological Review* 25/1 (1932): 40.

27. See Cicero, *Against Verres* 2.5.165; Josephus, *Jewish Wars* 7.203.

28. Cicero, *Against Verres* 2.5.165, 169.

29. Ps. Quintilian, *Declamations* 274; Ps. Manetho, *Apotelesmatica* 4.198–200; Aristophanes, *Thesmophoriazusae* 1029, quoted in Craig A. Evans, "Crucifixion," in *The New Interpreter's Dictionary of the Bible*, 1:807.

30. Richard Neitzel Holzapfel, *A Lively Hope: The Suffering, Death, Resurrection, and Exaltation of Jesus Christ* (Salt Lake City: Bookcraft, 1999), 64.

Frederick W. Farrar's summary of the effects of crucifixion is still one of the best and most succinct:

> A death by crucifixion seems to include all that pain and death can have of the horrible and ghastly—dizziness, cramp, thirst, starvation, sleeplessness, traumatic fever, tetanus, publicity of shame, long continuance of torment, horror of anticipation, mortification of untended wounds, all intensified just up to the point at which they can be endured at all, but all stopping just short of the point which would give to the sufferer the relief of unconsciousness. The unnatural position made every movement painful; the lacerated veins and crushed tendons throbbed with incessant anguish; the wounds, inflamed by exposure, gradually gangrened; the arteries, especially of the head and stomach, became swollen and oppressed with surcharged blood; and while each variety of misery went on gradually increasing, there was added to them the intolerable pang of a burning and raging thirst. . . . Such was the death to which Christ was doomed.[31]

Truly, Jesus of Nazareth came to earth and suffered the very worst that men ever inflicted.[32]

The use of nails was particularly grisly and effective in achieving desired aims. Ben Hagkol's remains substantiate the New Testament account of nails being used in Jesus's crucifixion. Many other literary sources confirm that nails were the usual way of crucifying individuals. Though the scriptures themselves do not describe the actual scene of Jesus being nailed to the cross, we know nails were used: "The other disciples therefore said unto [Thomas], We have seen the Lord. But he said unto them, Except I shall see in his hands

---

31. Frederick W. Farrar, *The Life of Christ* (New York: Dutton, 1884), 440, quoted in Bruce R. McConkie, *Doctrinal New Testament Commentary* (Salt Lake City: Bookcraft, 1976), 1:816.

32. See the excellent summary in Richard L. Anderson's, "The Ancient Practice of Crucifixion," *Ensign*, July 1975, 32-33.

the print of the nails, and put my finger into the print of the nails . . . I will not believe" (John 20:25).[33]

In addition to confirming the New Testament record, ben Hagkol's physical remains also provide a graphic visual reminder of the fulfillment of Isaiah's messianic prediction of Jesus's trauma some seven centuries before it actually occurred.

> And I will clothe him with thy robe, and strengthen him with thy girdle, and I will commit thy government into his hand: and he shall be a father to the inhabitants of Jerusalem, and to the house of Judah.
>
> And the key of the house of David will I lay upon his shoulder; so he shall open, and none shall shut; and he shall shut, and none shall open.
>
> And I will fasten him as a nail in a sure place; and he shall be for a glorious throne to his father's house.
>
> And they shall hang upon him all the glory of his father's house, the offspring and the issue, all vessels of small quantity, from the vessels of cups, even to all the vessels of flagons.
>
> In that day, saith the Lord of hosts, shall the nail that is fastened in the sure place be removed, and be cut down, and fall; and the burden that was upon it shall be cut off: for the Lord hath spoken it. (Isaiah 22:21-25)

In this passage, Isaiah, whose entire book constitutes a powerful witness of both the first and the second comings of the Messiah, describes the multifaceted role of a ruler and redeemer in the guise of a servant of God named Eliakim (a name that means "God shall cause to rise" and is itself messianic).

1. He would be given the government, or right to rule (v. 21).
2. He would be a father to the house of Judah (v. 21).
3. He would be given "the key of the house of David" (v. 22).

---

33. See also Jesus's own testimony as the risen Lord in 3 Nephi 11:14-15.

4. He would be fastened to something as "a nail in a sure place" (v. 23).

5. Upon him would be "hung," or placed, the glory of his father's house (v. 24).

6. He would be involved in the removing of the burden associated with "the nail that is fastened in the sure place" (v. 25).

Indeed, in one way or another this list describes the mission and ministry of Jesus of Nazareth, for by virtue of his mortal life and atoning sacrifice, he alone fits the characteristics enumerated by Isaiah:

1. He alone possesses the government—the power and authority to rule in heaven and on earth—and he will do so at his second coming (D&C 58:22).

2. He is the father, or king, of the Jews (as the title on his cross rightly declared; Matthew 27:37), and he alone is the spiritual father of Israel and of all who obey him (Mosiah 27:25). Indeed he may rightfully be called the Father through divine investiture of authority: "The Father has honored Christ by placing his name upon him, so that he can minister in and through that name as though he were the Father; and thus, so far as power and authority are concerned, his words and acts become and are those of the Father."[34]

3. He alone possesses the "key of the house of David," the symbol of absolute power and authority (both monarchial and priestly) invested in the true Messiah, who descends literally from Israel's greatest monarch, King David (Revelation 3:7).

4. He was in very deed fastened to the cross both *as* and *with* "a nail in a sure place" (Isaiah 22:23).

5. He had the glory of his Father's house placed upon him during the last week of his ministry when he referred to the Jerusalem temple not as "my Father's house" (which he had done at the

---

34. Joseph Fielding Smith, *Doctrines of Salvation* (Salt Lake City: Bookcraft, 1954–56), 1:29–30.

beginning of his ministry; John 2:16) but rather as "my house" (after his triumphal entry; Matthew 21:13).

6. Last, but not least, he alone is the one who took upon himself the great "burden" referred to by Isaiah, and who removed that burden from the world when "the nail that [was] fastened in the sure place [was] removed" (Isaiah 22:25). In other words, Jesus the Messiah removed from us the burden of physical and spiritual death when he completed the atonement (that is, after he was removed from the cross, buried, and resurrected).

Several sources, both LDS and non-LDS, assert that nails or spikes were driven through Jesus's wrists in addition to the palms of his hands for fear that the weight of his body would cause it to tear away from the cross. Medical authorities attest that it "has been shown that the ligaments and bones of the wrist can support the weight of a body hanging from them, but the palms [alone] cannot."[35] Thus, the nails driven into Jesus's wrists securely fastened him to the cross and fulfilled Isaiah's prophecy of the nail fastened in the sure place. There is hardly a more powerful image in scripture for Latter-day Saints than the one Isaiah uses of the nail in the sure place. It links the physical act of Jesus's crucifixion with the profoundest rituals and most sacred ordinances in Latter-day Saint theology and practice, such as the sacrament.

By expertly pounding nails through the wrists of a victim's outstretched arms and hands, without breaking bones or piercing major blood vessels, and yet crushing or severing important nerves, "excruciating bolts of fiery pain in both arms" were produced, as well as "paralysis of a portion of the hand." Additionally, "ischemic contractures and impalement of various ligaments by the iron spike

---

35. William D. Edwards, Wesley J. Gabel, and Floyd E. Hosmer, "On the Physical Death of Jesus Christ," *Journal of the American Medical Association* 255/11 (21 March 1986): 1460. Though criticized by some scholars for the historical portion of its discussion of crucifixion, as well as trying to "validate" Christianity, the medical information is most helpful.

might produce a clawlike grasp."[36] When the victim was nailed to the crossbar and lifted into place on the stake, or tree, the victim's arms would bear the full weight of his body. As the victim sagged and more weight was put on the wrists, excruciating pain would shoot along the fingers and up the arms. To relieve some of the pain in the hands, wrists, and arms, the victim would push down on his feet to raise himself up with the result that searing pain would shoot up the legs from the nail wounds in the feet. At some point, waves of cramps would sweep over the muscles of the legs and feet, causing throbbing pain as well as the inability to push upward and relieve the pain and pressure in the arms and wrists. Also, with the arms stretched out on the cross, breathing became increasingly difficult. Air could be drawn into the lungs but not exhaled, and asphyxiation eventually resulted.[37] When the legs of victims were broken, as reported in John 19:31-33, death resulted much more quickly because of the added shock to the body and the inability of the victim to raise up his body and stave off asphyxiation.

However, it is still fair to say that crucifixion was an agonizingly slow way to die. Under normal circumstances, a crucified body was left hanging on the cross to rot and be picked at by birds and insects. It is believed that this sometimes occurred while the victim was still alive, even if just barely. This, combined with the unnatural and contorted position of the body on the cross contributed to the victim's misery. Jesus's horrible circumstance was attested to by Israel's ancient psalmist: "I am poured out like water, and all my bones are out of joint: my heart is like wax; it is melted in the midst of my bowels" (Psalm 22:14). Yehohanan ben Hagkol's similar circumstance (contorted position) was alluded to by the

---

36. Edwards, Gabel, and Hosmer, "On the Physical Death of Jesus Christ," 1460.

37. See the summary in C. Truman Davis, "A Physician Testifies about Crucifixion," *Review of the News* (14 April 1976): 39.

obscure inscription on his ossuary, which indicates that he was posthumously nicknamed the "one hanged with knees apart."[38]

The Two Tombs

The location of ben Hagkol's ancient tomb in modern North Jerusalem is not an insignificant detail. It suggests some important considerations in determining both the place of Jesus's crucifixion as well as the location of his tomb, which was originally the property of Joseph of Arimathaea (Matthew 27:57-60). The latter was a respected member of the great Sanhedrin, who knew Jewish law and attendant issues regarding burials. As he would have been aware, a major issue to be considered regarding tomb placement in the Second Temple period of Jerusalem's history was ritual purity.

In first-century Palestine there existed a prohibition against placing burial sites to the west of Jerusalem for at least two important reasons. First, because prevailing winds in the Holy Land are from the west, if the dead were buried west of the city the odor of decomposing bodies could be carried through the city. It should be remembered that Jews did not embalm their dead prior to burial, but left corpses to decompose in the tomb before re-interring the remaining bones in an ossuary of the kind containing Yehohanan ben Hagkol's bones. Second, though the scent of decaying corpses was certainly unpleasant, far worse was the condition of ritual impurity those corpses conveyed. Jews believed that ritual uncleanness or impurity was a consequence of any and all contact with dead bodies, and this impurity was even conveyed secondarily, through contact with other persons who came in contact with the dead. Indeed, impurity could be carried over the city by the prevailing winds and thereby cause all living inhabitants of Jerusalem to become ritually impure or defiled.[39] Thus, Jerusalemites placed their tombs to the

---

38. Yigael Yadin, "Epigraphy and Crucifixion," *Israel Exploration Journal* 23 (1973): 22.

39. On this point, see the excellent discussion in Jeffrey R. Chadwick, "Revisiting Golgotha and the Garden Tomb," *Religious Educator* 4/1 (2003): 16.

north, east, or south of the Holy City to control at least one source of ritual defilement. Yehohanan ben Hagkol's tomb is dramatic witness to this policy.

The prohibition against tombs to the west of Jerusalem especially involved the temple. From about 20 BC onward, Herod the Great and his successors supervised the expansion of the temple and Temple Mount, making it the architectural jewel of the Mediterranean world. Modern scholars working in the Holy Land have shown that the beliefs and practices of the Pharisees were the basis for most Jewish practices, including those involving the temple, during the Herodian period. The Pharisees predominated in the Sanhedrin during this time. Pharisaic tradition "would not have permitted tomb construction anywhere directly west of the expanded Temple Mount because wind passing over western tombs would also have passed over the sacred temple enclosure, thus defiling it and anyone in it."[40]

It now becomes clear how the issue of ritual impurity impacted the location of the crucifixion and entombment of Jesus of Nazareth. Some well-known New Testament scholars have concluded that since "burial customs in the first half of the first century C.E. [AD] preclude burials and their attendant impurities west (windward) of the Temple, then the crucifixion and burial of Jesus could not have taken place at the site of the Church of the Holy Sepulchre, which is almost exactly due west of the Holy of Holies."[41] The Holy of Holies was the most sacred portion of the Jerusalem temple, the holiest spot on earth, and was to be guarded above all else. Thus the location of the crucifixion and entombment of Jesus was not near the Church of the Holy Sepulchre.

The linking of the locations of Jesus's crucifixion and burial follows from the Gospel narratives, especially John.

---

40. Chadwick, "Revisiting Golgotha and the Garden Tomb," 17.

41. John J. Rousseau and Rami Arav, *Jesus and His World* (Minneapolis: Fortress, 1995), 169.

> Now in the place where he was crucified there was a garden; and in the garden a new sepulchre, wherein was never man yet laid.
>
> There laid they Jesus therefore because of the Jews' preparation day; for the sepulchre was nigh at hand. (John 19:41–42)

That Jesus's tomb was located in a real garden and not some over-grown weed patch, as some have suggested, is confirmed by Mary Magdalene on the first Easter morning when she initially supposed she was talking to the "gardener" (John 20:15).

While we do not know if Yehohanan ben Hagkol was crucified near his burial site north of Jerusalem's Old City walls, we believe that Jesus's crucifixion and burial took place to the north of the city. While no crucifixions took place within Jerusalem's walls, Jesus's crucifixion was *near* the city (John 19:20). We know also that the crucifixion was within moderate calling distance of a nearby road. People passing by the site derided Jesus on the cross (Matthew 27:39; Mark 15:29), and bystanders heard him cry out, but misunderstood and thought he was calling to Elijah. What he actually said was, "Eli, Eli . . . My God, my God" (Matthew 27:46–47; Mark 15:34–35). This may indicate that there was just enough distance between the road and the cross to prevent some passersby from hearing clearly or picking up nuances of speech. In truth, this ultimate cry of pathos from the cross is fulfillment of the ancient psalmist's messianic prescience: "I will say unto God my rock, Why hast thou forgotten me?" (Psalm 42:9).[42] In Jesus's situation we see the psalm literally being acted out.

As Jesus hung on the cross, he endured great humiliation, per-haps even greater than was the common lot of all crucifixion vic-tims.[43] The synoptic Gospels report that passersby, as well as the

---

42. The Hebrew of Psalm 42:9 (42:10 in Hebrew) is slightly different from Mat-thew's (or Mark's) report of "Eli, Eli, lama sabachthani" (Matthew 27:46). The Hebrew reads, *"lamah shakachtani."*

43. All victims were crucified alongside the most crowded roads for maximum humiliation (see Quintilian, *Declamations* 274), but the Gospels seem to report an extra

members of the gathered crowd, mocked and ridiculed him. These included some of the same ones who had engineered the whole conspiracy (the chief priests, scribes, and elders). They not only railed at him and reviled him, wagging their heads as one might do to a fool who had been told better, but also twisted his own words to make those words appear to be the height of foolishness and arrogance. "Thou that destroyest the temple, and buildest it in three days, save thyself" (Matthew 27:40). "He trusted in God; let him deliver him now . . . for he said, I am the Son of God" (Matthew 27:43). "Save thyself, and come down from the cross" (Mark 15:30). "Let Christ the King of Israel descend now from the cross, that we may see and believe" (Mark 15:32). "He saved others; let him save himself, if he be Christ, the chosen of God" (Luke 23:35). One notes that the crowd also regarded as true the charges brought against Jesus by the false witnesses who appeared before the Sanhedrin—that of fomenting rebellion through destruction of the temple and rebuilding it according to his own scheme.

All of these statements, as well as the general scene at the cross that they depict, hark back to Psalm 22:7-8, a poetic messianic prophecy of incredible insight found in ancient Israel's hymnbook (the book of Psalms): "All they that see me laugh me to scorn: they shoot out the lip, they shake the head, saying, He trusted on the Lord that he would deliver him: let him deliver him, seeing he delighted in him."

There is another significant factor that bears on the location of the crucifixion of Jesus. From Mosaic times onward, Levitical requirements for animal sacrifices and offerings dictated that they be made "on the side of the altar northward before the Lord" (Leviticus 1:11). In other words, tabernacle and temple sacrifices of animals were to be slaughtered north of the great altar of burnt offering or brasen altar (Exodus 27:1-2; 39:39) during the days that the Tabernacle and First Temple (Solomon's) existed, and north of the great altar

measure of humiliation for Jesus.

of sacrifice, "in the area to the north of the Court of the Israelites,"[44] during the days of the Second Temple (Zerubbabel's and Herod's).

Since all animal sacrifices (burnt, peace, sin, etc.) symbolized the great and last sacrifice of the Son of God (Alma 34:13–14), down to exact details, it seems essential to look for the location of the crucifixion and entombment of Jesus north of the great altar of the Jerusalem temple, outside Jerusalem's city walls, near a thorough-fare, constructed in harmony with rules pertaining to ritual purity.

Calvary

The synoptic Gospels report that at the ninth hour, three o'clock in the afternoon, on a Friday (the eve of Passover), Jesus took his final breath (Matthew 27:46, 50; Luke 23:44–46). He endured the torture of the cross for six hours, having been nailed to it at the third hour or 9:00 a.m. (Mark 15:25). Unlike with Yehohanan ben Hagkol's circumstance, we are fortunate to have preserved for us the specific name of the place where Jesus was crucified—*Golgotha* (Aramaic) or *Calvary* (Latin), meaning "skull."

Perhaps the name denoted topographical features (tradition proposes the site to have been an old stone quarry), or maybe it was a symbolic name representing death much the same way the image of a skull and crossbones connotes death in modern times. It has even been suggested that Golgotha may have been so named because executed criminals were buried nearby, and the skulls or bones from interred bodies became exposed, on rare occasions, due to the ravages of animals or the elements. This seems problematic since leaving any portion of a corpse unburied was contrary to Jew-ish law and would have been rectified immediately.[45]

Beyond its specific association with the crucifixion and burial of Jesus, the term *Golgotha* is not attested in ancient sources. It could well have been a local term, contemporary with Jesus's time only.

---

44. Miriam Feinberg Vamosh, *Daily Life at the Time of Jesus* (Herzlia, Israel: Palphot, 2001), 23.

45. Talmage, *Jesus the Christ*, 667.

It seems significant that the Joseph Smith Translation of Matthew 27:35; Mark 15:25; and John 19:17 change the word *skull* to *burial*, that is "Golgotha . . . the place of a burial," indicating perhaps that the proper noun *Golgotha* was associated with the nearby entombment of crucifixion victims and not how it looked topographically. At any rate, the Joseph Smith Translation substantiates the view that the place of Jesus's crucifixion was very close to his burial.

Conclusion

Truly, the discovery of Yehohanan ben Hagkol's tomb and physical remains continues to impress and educate new generations of students of the Bible. It helps flesh out the picture of Jesus's crucifixion by suggesting intriguing parallels. However, there are also dissimilarities between Jesus's circumstances and those of Yehohanan ben Hagkol. One of the striking differences we see is that Yehohanan was buried with the remains of another adult as well as a male child who was three to four years old at the time of his death. This fits with the inscription on the ossuary in which the remains were found: "Yehohanan and Yehohanan ben [son of] Yehohanan." According to scholarly estimation, "There is now no doubt that the son was buried with the father, which was a common Jewish practice during the Second Temple period."[46] It is also possible that Yehohanan was buried in a family plot. This is very different from Jesus's interment. He was buried alone, in a borrowed tomb; "none were with [him]" (D&C 133:50).

Perhaps the most important difference between the tombs of Yehohanan ben Hagkol and Jesus of Nazareth again center on their contents, the very thing that made the 1968 discovery possible. Ben Hagkol's tomb was filled with bones; Jesus's tomb is empty. And that is the heart of the matter: Jesus of Nazareth was resurrected; he is a physical being who lives in the heavens; he lives to bless and nurture mortals on this earth; he lives to rule and reign as Lord, King, and God for eternity. Nothing can substantiate that fact—no

---

46. Zias and Charlesworth, "Crucifixion: Archaeology, Jesus," 280.

archaeological discovery, no artifact, no item of material culture—nothing except one thing: the witness of the Holy Spirit.

Andrew C. Skinner is the Richard L. Evans Professor of Religious Understanding and professor of ancient scripture and Near Eastern studies at Brigham Young University.

CHAPTER 20

ჯ❧

4Q521 AND WHAT IT MIGHT
MEAN FOR Q 3-7

Gaye Strathearn

I am personally grateful for S. Kent Brown. He was a committee member for my master's thesis, in which I examined 4Q521. Since that time he has been a wonderful colleague who has always encouraged me in my academic pursuits.

The relationship between the Dead Sea Scrolls and Christianity has fueled the imagination of both scholar and layperson since their discovery in 1947. Were the early Christians aware of the community at Qumran and their texts? Did these groups interact in any way? Was the Qumran community the source for nascent Christianity, as some popular and scholarly sources have intimated,[1] or was it simply a parallel community? One Qumran fragment that

---

1. For an example from the popular press, see Richard N. Ostling, "Is Jesus in the Dead Sea Scrolls?" *Time Magazine*, 21 September 1992, 56-57. See also the claim that the scrolls are "the earliest Christian records" in the popular novel by Dan Brown, *The Da Vinci Code* (New York: Doubleday, 2003), 245. For examples from the academic arena, see André Dupont-Sommer, *The Dead Sea Scrolls: A Preliminary Survey* (New York: Macmillan, 1952), 98-100; Robert Eisenman, *James the Just in the Habakkuk Pesher* (Leiden: Brill, 1986), 1-20; Barbara E. Thiering, *The Gospels and Qumran: A New Hypothesis* (Sydney: Theological Explorations, 1981), 3-11; Carsten P. Thiede, *The Dead Sea Scrolls and the Jewish Origins of Christianity* (New York: Palgrave, 2001), 152-81; José O'Callaghan, "Papiros neotestamentarios en la cueva 7 de Qumrān?," *Biblica* 53/1 (1972): 91-100. None of these arguments has been embraced by the majority of scholars.

may provide an important window into this discussion is 4Q521.[2] Although a fragmentary text, it clearly describes the eschatological expectation of activities that are remarkably close to activities found in a hypothetical document known as Q, which scholars have (re)created from the gospels of Matthew and Luke. It identifies Jesus as the Coming One (*ho erchomenos*), the figure anticipated by John the Baptist who would "baptize . . . in [holy] spirit and fire" (Q 3:16).[3] In addition, the Coming One gives sight to the blind, makes the lame to walk, cleanses the lepers, heals the deaf, raises the dead, and preaches to the poor (Q 7:22). In 4Q521 we read of eschatological events that will take place at the coming of the messiah: the release of captives, opening the eyes of the blind, straightening out the twisted, healing the badly wounded, raising the dead, and proclaiming good news to the poor (4Q521 2 II, 8 and 12). Both Q 7:22 and 4Q521 are based on a particular messianic interpretation of Isaiah 61—a healing and preaching messiah—that was not a common Jewish expectation in the first century AD.[4] Prior to the discovery and publication of 4Q521, however, this interpretation seemed to be peculiar to the Christian tradition. 4Q521 challenges that assumption.

The similarities between the two texts have divided scholars over the importance of 4Q521 for the study of early Christianity. Thomas Hieke notes that "the role of the messianic figure in 4Q521 is doubtful and the relationship of Qumran texts to Q completely unclear." For him, the value of 4Q521 is that it is "an important witness to the fact that certain texts and motifs from the Book of Isaiah are prolific and well-known in the discourse of Early Judaism."[5]

---

2. Émile Puech, *Qumrân grotte 4, XVIII: Textes Hébreux (4Q521-4Q528, 4Q576-4Q579)*, DJD XXV (Oxford: Clarendon, 1998), 1–38.

3. All quotations from Q are taken from James M. Robinson, Paul Hoffmann, and John S. Kloppenborg, eds., *The Critical Edition of Q* (Minneapolis: Fortress, 2000).

4. The Masoretic Text (MT) of Isaiah 61:1 does not include "giving sight to the blind," but the phrase is found in the Septuagint (LXX). In the MT "giving sight to the blind" is found in Isaiah 35:5 and Psalm 146:8.

5. Thomas Hieke, "Q 7,22—A Compendium of Isaian Eschatology," *Ephemerides Theologicae Lovanienses* 82/1 (2006): 179.

Frans Neirynck concludes that "it would be too rash a conclusion . . . to suggest that 'New Testament writers' may have known 4Q521."[6] In contrast, however, James M. Robinson has mused that "the list of healings from Isaiah may not be original to Q for it is remarkably similar to the Qumran fragment 4Q521."[7] John J. Collins has gone even further. He claims that the author of Q either knew of 4Q521 or "at the least . . . drew on a common tradition."[8] Thus George J. Brooke correctly summarizes, "Whether we conclude that Jesus must have known of this tradition directly from a Qumran source or that it was mediated to him some other how, the details of the similarities are too great to be brushed aside."[9]

In drawing these conclusions about 4Q521 and Q, however, none of these scholars seems to have appreciated the significance of the material in column III of 4Q521's second fragment where, as Émile Puech has noted, there is fragmentary evidence for an expectation of the coming of an eschatological Elijah.[10] Therefore, 4Q521 and Q 3-7 share not only the expectation of a healing and preaching messiah, but also an interpretation of Malachi 4:5-6 (Heb. 3:23-24) that an Elijah figure would be associated with the coming of this messiah. In this paper I will suggest that this additional factor strengthens Collins's conclusion that the author of Q either knew of 4Q521 or drew from common material. If it is the latter, however, we have no evidence for the common material. Therefore, I will argue that the Q community knew of 4Q521 and that therefore we

---

6. Frans Neirynck, "Q 6,20b-21; 7,22 and Isaiah 61," in *The Scriptures in the Gospels*, ed. Christopher M. Tuckett (Louvain: Leuven University Press, 1997), 58.

7. James M. Robinson, "The Matthean Trajectory from Q to Mark," in *Ancient and Modern Perspectives on the Bible and Culture: Essays in Honor of Hans Dieter Betz*, ed. Adela Yarbro Collins (Atlanta: Scholars Press, 1998), 131 n. 12.

8. John J. Collins, "The Works of the Messiah," *Dead Sea Discoveries* 1/1 (1994): 107.

9. George J. Brooke, *The Dead Sea Scrolls and the New Testament* (Minneapolis: Fortress, 2005), 262.

10. Émile Puech, "Some Remarks on 4Q246 and 4Q521 and Qumran Messianism," in *The Provo International Conference on the Dead Sea Scrolls: Technological Innovations, New Texts, and Reformulated Issues*, ed. Donald W. Parry and Eugene Ulrich (Leiden: Brill, 1999), 559-61.

are in a position to address the question of why John the Baptist plays such a prominent role in the first third of Q, a document primarily concerned with Jesus's sayings.

The Prophet and the Messiahs in Qumran and 4Q521

Florentino García Martínez writes, "the large number of [messianic] references inserted in every kind of literary context, including legal contexts, testifies to its importance for the Qumran community."[11] Although there is no monolithic messianic expectation, there was an expectation of more than one messianic figure. These figures are variously described performing both political and religious functions, liberating the community from the physical and spiritual oppression of its enemies, interpreting the law, acting as an eschatological judge, and providing an atonement.[12] In addition, one passage indicates that the community rules would be in force "until the coming of the prophet, and the Messiahs of Aaron and Israel" (1QS IX, 11: *'d bw' nby' wmshykhy 'hrwn wysr'l*).[13] Thus, in conjunction with the messianic figures, we note the expectation of a prophet. Lawrence H. Schiffman interprets this phrase to mean that the two messiahs will be "announced by an eschatological prophet."[14] This interpretation is in keeping with the position of *nby'*, which precedes the messianic construct in the sentence.[15]

---

11. Florentino García Martínez, "Messianic Hopes in the Qumran Writings," in *The People of the Dead Sea Scrolls*, ed. Florentino García Martínez and Julio Trebolle Barrera; trans. Wilfred G. E. Watson (Leiden: Brill, 1995), 189.

12. For a discussion, see García Martínez, "Messianic Hopes," 161–89.

13. The original scribe apparently misspelled the word for prophet as *ny'*. The ב has been added above the line of the text. See James H. Charlesworth et al., eds., *The Dead Sea Scrolls: Hebrew, Aramaic, and Greek Texts with English Translations* (Tübingen: Mohr, 1994), 1:40. The anticipation of the coming of a future prophet is also found in 1 Maccabees 4:46; 14:41.

14. Lawrence H. Schiffman, *Reclaiming the Dead Sea Scrolls: Their True Meaning for Judaism and Christianity* (New York: Doubleday, 1995), 324.

15. In this passage *mshykh* only has reference to Aaron and Israel and not to the prophet, although García Martínez believes that he was still a messianic figure ("Messianic Hopes," 186–88).

Unfortunately, the text does not delineate more fully for us the functions of this prophet. There are, however, references in other Qumran materials that enhance our understanding of this figure. 11Q13 seems to describe an eschatological prophet who is identified as "the messenger" who is "anointed of the spirit" (11Q13 II, 15-19).[16] Although the text at this point is fragmentary, it is clear that the prophet's role is to announce salvation, and the context implies that he will introduce the judicial action of the messianic figure, Melchizedek. Similarly, 4Q175 contains a pastiche of texts that the community interprets messianically, including Deuteronomy 18:18-19: "I would raise up for them a prophet from among their brothers, like you [i.e., Moses], and place my words in his mouth, and he would tell them all that I command them. And it will happen that the man who does not listen to my words, that the prophet will speak in my name, I shall require a reckoning from him" (4Q175 5-8).[17] Thus the prophet, who is associated in some way with Moses, acts as a mouthpiece for Yahweh on earth. In addition, this prophet in 4Q175 is specifically identified with a messianic figure who will destroy the enemies of the covenant people (4Q175 12-13, drawing on Numbers 24:17).

Although 4Q175 makes the association of the eschatological prophet with Moses, at least fragmentary evidence reveals that the Qumran community also looked for a prophetic Elijah figure. 4Q558 reads, "therefore I will send Elijah be[fore . . .],"[18] which phrase clearly presupposes Malachi 4:5 (Heb. 3:23). The Masoretic text of Malachi reads, "Behold I will send the prophet Elijah to you before

---

16. The word *prophet* is not used in the extant text, but it has generally been accepted that the messenger refers to a prophet. See Marius de Jonge and A. S. van der Woude, "11Q Melchizedek and the New Testament," *New Testament Studies* 12 (1966): 306-7; and García Martínez, "Messianic Hopes," 186.

17. Unless noted otherwise noted, I have taken all scrolls translations from Florentino García Martínez, *The Dead Sea Scrolls Translated: The Qumran Texts in English*, trans. Wilfred G. E. Watson, 2nd ed. (Leiden: Brill; 1996).

18. Collins, "Works of the Messiah," 106. See J. Starcky, "Les quatre étapes du messianisme à Qumran," *Revue biblique* 70 (1963): 498.

the great and terrible day of the Lord comes" (cf. Sirach 48:10). The context for this verse is established by Malachi 3:1, "Behold, I will send my messenger, and he shall prepare the way before me [i.e., Yahweh]." Beth Glazier-McDonald has convincingly argued that the messengers in Malachi 3:1 and Elijah in Malachi 4:5 (Heb. 3:23) "are one and the same."[19] She notes that Yahweh sent both individuals (*shlkh*), their arrival is near (*hnh*), and both of their missions are to prepare the people for the coming of Yahweh. We have already outlined the Qumran community's expectation of an eschatological prophet in association with the messianic age. The relationship, if any, between the "prophet like Moses" and Elijah in the minds of the Qumran community is impossible to establish given the fragmentary nature of texts from Qumran, but what is important here is that they did anticipate a prophetic figure and that Malachi's prophecy was known to them.[20] This concept from Qumran is important because Malachi's prophecy is not commonly found in Second Temple literature, although the messenger becomes important for the Q community (Q 7:27).

We place 4Q521 within this messianic spectrum. The editor of this text, Émile Puech, paleographically dates it to the first quarter of the first century BC, although he notes that our present text is probably a copy of an earlier document.[21] He argues that its author was an Essene. Not all scholars agree with the attribution of the text to the Essenes, but Puech notes some thematic and verbal parallels with other Qumran material.[22] He gives two main reasons why these connections are not more numerous: (1) the fragmentary

---

19. Beth Glazier-McDonald, *Malachi: The Divine Messenger* (Atlanta: Scholars Press, 1987), 263.

20. 4Q253a 1 I, 1–4 also includes a quotation from Malachi. Once again we are dealing with a fragment, but the quotation that precedes the promise of Elijah's return is from Malachi 3:16-18.

21. Puech, *Qumrân grotte 4*, 36.

22. For an example of a scholar who does not believe that 4Q521 was an Essene document, see Geza Vermes, *The Complete Dead Sea Scrolls in English* (New York: Penguin, 1997), 391.

nature of the text and (2) its origins within the first generation of the Qumran community before much of the characteristic theology had developed. Most important, for Puech, "the dual messianism attested in this scroll appears to recommend the allocation of the composition of this work to the Essene movement."[23] The purpose of the text seems to be to encourage the pious to persevere because the messianic era and time of judgment were imminent.[24]

The largest fragment (fragment 2) contains three columns. The text of column II reads as follows:

1 [for the heav]ens and the earth will obey his Messiah,[25]

2 [and all] that is in them will not turn away from the commandments of the holy ones.[26]

3 Be encouraged, you who are seeking the Lord in his service!

4 Will you not, perhaps, encounter the Lord in it, all those who hope in their heart?

5 For the Lord will observe the devout, and call the just by name,

6 and upon the poor he will place his spirit, and the faithful he will renew with his strength.

7 For he will honor the devout upon the throne of an eternal royalty,

8 freeing prisoners, giving sight to the blind, straightening out the twisted.

9 Ever shall I cling to those who hope. In his mercy he will jud[ge,]

23. Puech, *Qumrân grotte 4*, 38.

24. Puech, *Qumrân grotte 4*, 38.

25. Puech suggests that the *mshykhw* could be read as a defective form of the plural ("Some Remarks on 4Q246 and 4Q521," 554-55). I, however, have opted for the singular reading for two reasons: (1) because of the parallel with "his spirit" in line 6 and (2) because the standard plural form *mshykhyh* is found in one of the fragments, 4Q521 8 9. Florentino García Martínez, "Messianische Erwartungen in den Qumranschriften," *Jahrbuch für biblische Theologie* 8 (1993): 182-83.

26. Although García Martínez has translated *qdwshym* as "holy precepts," I have followed Puech in translating it as "holy ones" or saints (*Qumrân grotte 4*, 11).

10 and from no one shall the fruit [of] good [deeds] be delayed,

11 and the Lord will perform marvelous acts such as have not existed, just as he sa[id]

12 for he will heal the badly wounded and he will make the dead live, he will proclaim good news to the poor[27]

13 give lavishly [to the need]y, lead the exiled and enrich the hungry.

14 [. . .] and all [. . .] (4Q521 2 II, 1-14)

The text then breaks off. Column III of fragment 2 continues as follows:

1 and the law of your favor. And I will free them with [. . .][28]

2 . . .the fathers towards the sons [. . .]

3 who blesses the Lord in his approval [. . .]

4 May the earth rejoice in all the places [. . .]

5 for all Israel in the rejoicing of [. . .]

6 and his scepter. . .[. . .]

7 . . .[. . .]

Seven items should be noted with this text as we investigate its significance for Q. First, its messianic nature is established in the very first line of column II with the word *mshykhw*. My reading of the text is in contrast to that of Jean Durhaime, who believes that the first two lines represent the end of a passage on the messiah and the saints and thus infers that these lines are thematically distinct from what follows.[29] The paragraph break in the text may support

---

27. Although García Martínez has translated *ʿnwym* as "meek" I have translated it as "poor," which is the more common meaning.

28. Émile Puech originally restored the lacuna in context as follows: "And I will liberate them by [the word of your mouth (?) for] it is sure: 'The fathers are going/returning to the sons.'" "Une apocalypse messianique (4Q521)," *Revue de Qumran* 60/15 (1992): 495; see Puech, "Some Remarks on 4Q246 and 4Q521," 554. However, in his critical edition he leaves the lacuna blank but discusses the possibility of this restoration (*Qumrân grotte 4*, 19).

29. Jean Durhaime, "Le messie et les saints dans un fragment apocalyptique de Qumrân (4Q521 2)," in *Ce Dieu qui vient: Études sur l'Ancien et le Nouveau Testament*

this reading. However, there are more compelling reasons to see a coherency between the first two lines and the rest of the text. As Collins points out, any attempt to dissociate them "ignores the string of allusions to Psalm 146 in lines 1-9."[30] Additionally, the suffix in *mshykhw* serves to link the first line to those that follow. Although we are limited by not having the text that preceded line 1, there is good reason to understand the suffix in reference to the *adonai* of lines 3, 4, and 11. In every instance where *mshykhw* is attested in the Hebrew Bible, the suffix refers to Yahweh.[31] Likewise, the only other definite example of *mshykhw* in the nonbiblical Qumran texts, 4Q377 2 II, 5, refers to Moses as the anointed of the Lord God of Abraham. In 4Q521 the author seems to have made a conscious effort to use *adonai* instead of the tetragrammaton because his sources in Psalm 147 and Isaiah 61 use the latter.[32] Puech suggests that this shift may reflect the author's desire to avoid any misuse of the divine name.[33]

Second, the phrase *heaven and earth* in line 1 is probably a "figure of speech (merism) for the expression of 'totality,'" as we find in the Hebrew creation story.[34] Although Puech and García Martínez translate the construct *shmᶜ l* as "listen to," it can also mean "obey" (Genesis 3:17; Judges 2:20; Exodus 15:26) and, given the parallelism with line 2, that seems to make better sense here.[35] Thus line 1, in

---

offertes au Professeur Bernard Renaud, ed. Raymond Kuntzmann (Paris: Cerf, 1995), 267.

30. John J. Collins, "A Herald of Good Tidings: Isaiah 61:1-3 and Its Actualization in the Dead Sea Scrolls," in *The Quest for Context and Meaning: Studies in Biblical Intertextuality in Honor of James A. Sanders*, ed. Craig A. Evans and Shemaryahu Talmon (Leiden: Brill, 1997), 235 n. 38.

31. See 1 Samuel 2:10; 12:3, 5; 16:6; 2 Samuel 22:51; Psalms 2:2; 18:50 (Heb. 18:51); and 20:6 (Heb. 20:7); 28:8; and Isaiah 45:1.

32. This is not a surprising development since the Hebrew Bible often links the two titles (e.g., Genesis 15:2; Deuteronomy 3:24; 9:26; Joshua 7:7).

33. Puech, *Qumrân grotte 4*, 36.

34. John Sailhamer, "Genesis," in *The Expositor's Bible Commentary with the New International Version of the Holy Bible*, ed. F. E. Gaebelein, 12 vols. (London: Pickering and Inglis, 1979-92), 2:23. See Puech, "Some Remarks on 4Q246 and 4Q521," 555.

35. In French Puech uses *écouteront*, which can mean "listen to" or "hearken to" (*Qumrân grotte 4*, 11; "Une apocalypse messianique," 486). In his English publication he used the phrase *listen to* ("Some Remarks on 4Q246 and 4Q521," 553). See García Martínez, *Dead Sea Scrolls Translated*, 394. Others who translate it as "obey" are James D.

essence, means that all things in heaven and earth (cf. Deuteronomy 10:14) will obey God's messiah. While "all things" certainly includes the notion of all people, it may also have broader connotations. Joel 3:15-16 indicates that this totality of "the heavens and the earth" also includes creations such as the sun, moon, and stars. We certainly have examples where the elements obey human directives (see Joshua 10:12-13; 1 Kings 17).

The third point concerns the debate over who performs the eschatological deeds in lines 7-13. Grammatically the subject is clearly *adonai*.[36] The question may be asked *how* God will accomplish these acts. Would he use a human agent?[37] Clear instances in the Hebrew tradition show where God's agents assume responsibilities normally associated with God.[38] Although Psalm 146:5-8, one of the biblical texts that stands behind 4Q521, does not mention any human agent, in the Septuagint of Isaiah 61:1 God specifically anoints his agent to proclaim good news (*bśr*) to the poor, bind up the brokenhearted, proclaim liberty to the captives, open the prison to those who are captive, and open the eyes of the blind.[39] In fact, in none of the attested uses of the verb *bśr* in the Hebrew Bible is God the subject.[40] Likewise, while it is clear that the power

---

Tabor and Michael O. Wise, "4Q521 'On Resurrection' and the Synoptic Gospel Tradition: A Preliminary Study," *Journal for the Study of the Pseudepigrapha* 10 (1992): 151; and Collins, "Works of the Messiah," 99.

36. *Pace* Tabor and Wise, "4Q521 'On Resurrection,'" 149-55. For a critique of their reconstruction, see García Martínez, "Messianic Hopes," 170.

37. Hans Kvalbein, "The Wonders of the End-Time: Metaphoric Language in 4Q521 and the Interpretation of Matthew 11.5 par.," *Journal for the Study of the Pseudepigrapha* 18 (1998): 87-88; and Collins, "'Herald of Good Tidings,'" 234-35.

38. Cf. *Psalms of Solomon* 17:26; Isaiah 60. See also Edward P. Meadors, "The 'Messianic' Implications of the Q Material," *Journal of Biblical Literature* 118 (1994): 260.

39. Cf. also Isaiah 42:1-9, where God acts through an agent to give sight to the blind. Thus Hieke observes, "it is noteworthy that both Isaian texts [Isaiah 42:1-9 and 61:1] deal with an eschatological figure different from God who will bring the final redemption and salvation in the name of the Lord." Hieke, "Q 7,22," 180.

40. Tabor and Wise, "4Q521 'On Resurrection,'" 157-58. See also Collins's assessments: "It is surprising [in 4Q521] . . . to find God as the subject of preaching good news. This is the work of a herald or messenger" ("Works of the Messiah," 100), and "the suspicion arises that God is supposed to work through an agent here. Works

to heal the sick and raise the dead originates with God in Hebrew literature (cf. Psalm 103:2-3), he invariably uses a human agent to accomplish the task (see 1QapGen^ar XX, 22-29; 1 Kings 17:17-23; Sirach 48:5; 2 Kings 5:1-15).

We must seriously consider the implication of this fact for our understanding of 4Q521. If it is acknowledged that God is often, or even usually, represented as performing his mighty deeds through a human agent, who is there in 4Q521 who could be that agent? Although it is possible that it may be the holy ones (*qdwshym*) in line 2, as we have already noted, the suffix attached to *mshykh* in line 1 already ties the messiah to *adonai* in the lines that follow. Therefore, I would argue, although the ultimate source of these eschatological deeds is clearly God, it is well within the realm of Hebrew religious tradition to see him acting through an agent, and the only agent mentioned in this text that makes sense is the messiah. The totality of the "heaven and earth" that obey the messiah would then include not just humans but also other natural elements. In this context it would also refer to humans along with their burdens, diseases, and afflictions.

Fourth, God, through his messiah, is the giver of life in 4Q521: "he will make the dead to live" or, as Puech translates it, "he will raise the dead."[41] This attribution seems to be loosely based on Isaiah 26:19. Robert Eisenman translates the verb *khwh* as "resurrect."[42] It must be noted, however, that the Hebrew gives no indication of whether the messiah would revive the dead to a state of mortality or immortality,[43] although fragment 5 of 4Q521 may support his

---

performed through an agent would, of course, be nonetheless the works of God" ("Herald of Good Tidings," 234-35).

41. Puech, *Qumrân grotte 4*, 11.

42. Robert H. Eisenman, "A Messianic Vision," *Biblical Archaeology Review* 17/6 (1991): 65.

43. The verb has the sense of "live," "sustain life," to be "revived," or to "give life." Ludwig Koehler, Walter Baumgartner, and Johann J. Stamm, eds., *The Hebrew and Aramaic Lexicon of the Old Testament*, trans. M. E. J. Richardson et al., 5 vols. (Leiden: Brill, 1994-2000), s.v. חיה, 1:309-10.

translation. The text is fragmentary, but reads, "He [i.e., the Lord] shall open [graves] and he shall o[pen (?)] and [   ] and the Valley of Death in [   ] and the Bridge of the De[ep]" (5 II, 8-12).[44] It seems clear that the raising of the dead in this instance is associated with the judgment in Sheol and therefore with the resurrection.

That the messiah is associated with the resurrection is also not surprising. Other Hebrew texts, such as *2 Baruch* 30 and *4 Ezra* 7, indicate that the resurrection takes place during the time of the messiah, but in neither of these texts is there any indication that the messiah brings about the resurrection. In this aspect 4Q521 is unique. Some may argue that it is precisely this point that proves that 4Q521 describes the eschatological deeds of God rather than of the messiah. But the subject of healing the mortally wounded and causing the dead to live must be the same as the person who will bear good tidings to the poor, and these are the works of an agent. Also, as we noted above, God is never the subject of *bśr* in the Hebrew Bible. Therefore it is not only possible, but entirely likely that the immediate subject for the rest of the deeds in this line is also God's agent. Again, we must acknowledge that the best candidate for that agent in this fragment is the messiah mentioned in 4Q521 2 II, 1.

Fifth, what does it mean that the messiah will "proclaim good news to the poor"? A similar phrase is found in the Hodayoth (i.e., the Thanksgiving Scroll found among the Dead Sea Scrolls), "herald of your goodness, to proclaim to the poor the abundance of your mercies" (1QHᵃ XXIII, 14). But in 4Q521 the author is clearly indebted to Isaiah 61:1. Both the terms *proclaim good news* and *poor* are important for our investigation. *Bśr* means "to bring news."[45] With the exception of 1 Samuel 4:17, in the Hebrew Bible, it denotes

---

44. English translation from *The Dead Sea Scrolls Reader: Additional Genres and Unclassified Texts*, ed. Donald W. Parry and Emanuel Tov (Leiden: Brill, 2005), 160-61.

45. Koehler, Baumgartner, and Stamm, *The Hebrew and Aramaic Lexicon of the Old Testament*, s.v. בשר, 1:163-64.

good news.[46] In Isaiah 61 the good news is that Yahweh's anointed agent will "bind up the broken hearted, proclaim liberty to the captives and free those who are bound." In 4Q521 the good news is similar but is extended to include all the wonders that the Lord will perform through his messiah. Of course, the importance of Isaiah 61 to the messianic understanding at Qumran is not isolated to 4Q521.[47] We have already noted above the eschatological prophet mentioned in 11Q13. In this text, the prophet is described as a "messenger" (the nominalized form of *bśr*). His role, which is to "comfort the afflicted" and "watch over the afflicted ones of Zion," is substantively the same as the messianic activities described in 4Q521.[48]

Sixth, it is also significant that 4Q521, following Isaiah 61, designates the recipients of the message as *the poor*, a term that has already been used in 4Q521 2 II, 6 to describe the faithful.[49] In commenting on Isaiah 61:1, John L. McKenzie delineates the poor even further as "the devout core of the faithful."[50] Given the context of 4Q521, his description seems appropriate. The communal lifestyle of the Qumran community is well known, and the term *poor* seems to be a self-designation for the community (see 1QM XI, 7-9; XIV, 7-8; 1QH VI, 3).[51] Of course, the Qumran community was not the only group concerned with the poor. We have already noted that the poor are the recipients of the good tidings of Isaiah 61:1, but

46. For example, see Jeremiah 20:15, where it is used in parallel with *smkh* "to rejoice," and 2 Samuel 1:20, where it is used in parallel with both *smkh* and *ʿlz* "to exult."

47. Collins, "'Herald of Good Tidings,'" 225-40.

48. See also *Psalms of Solomon* 11:1, where the "good news" is that "God has been merciful to Israel in watching over them," in *The Old Testament Pseudepigrapha*, ed. James H. Charlesworth (Garden City: Doubleday, 1985), 2:661.

49. *ʿnwym* is in parallel with *ʾmwnym*. The scrolls use two words to designate the poor: *ʿnwym* and *ʾbywn*. E. Bammel argues that in the Qumran texts "there is no clear distinction between the terms." *Theological Dictionary of the New Testament*, ed. Gerhard Friedrich (Grand Rapids: Eerdmans, 1968), 6:896-98.

50. John L. McKenzie, *Second Isaiah* (Garden City: Doubleday, 1968), 181.

51. Poor is also frequently used in the Hodayoth to describe the righteous (1QH[a] VI, 3; IX, 36; X, 32, 34; XI, 25; XIII, 13, 16, 18, 22).

they are also important in numerous other passages.[52] These passages specifically deal with Yahweh's concern for the poor, but they do not, as we have noted with the scrolls, use the term as a divine self-designation. In this respect the Qumran community seems to have the earliest attested use of *poor* in this way.

The dominating picture portrayed in fragment 2 column II is that God, through his messiah, will not only vindicate the righteous (lines 5-6), but he will also heal those who would have otherwise been denied access to any office in the community because of their physical deformities (1Q28a II, 3-9).[53] The difficulty with this reading in 4Q521 is that it is perhaps the earliest document we have that associates teaching and healing with the messiah. This position is in stark contrast to the messianic activities of battle and judgment found in other sources such as the *War Scroll* (1QM), 11Q13, Psalms of Solomon 17, *1 Enoch* 37-71, *2 Baruch* 39-40, and *4 Ezra* 12-13. Yet it is precisely the combination of teaching and healing that give evidence in Q that Jesus was the Coming One (Q 7:22).

The final point of importance for our discussion moves away from the eschatological activities of God, through his messiah, in column II and focuses on the fragmentary text in column III. Here we have a clear reference to Malachi's prophecy that before the day of the Lord, Elijah will turn the hearts of the "fathers towards the sons [. . .]." While scholars generally recognize the importance of this line for understanding the messianic interpretation of the fragment, they disagree on the way that it should be interpreted. For example, Brooks argues that the anointed in column II "should be understood as *Elijah redivivus* and the text understood to be describing

---

52. For example, Psalms 40:17; 70:5; 86:1; 109:22; 112:9; Proverbs 13:7; 14:31; 17:5; 28:6; Isaiah 3:15; 14:32; 29:19; *Psalms of Solomon* 5:11; 15:1.

53. García Martínez, "Messianic Hopes," 169. Kvalbein has argued that the healings in line 8 were spiritual rather than physical ("The Wonders of the End-Time," 87-110). I agree, however, with Hieke's corrective: "It is doubtful whether the Isaian texts (as well as 4Q521) were always read only metaphorically: How is an eschatological renewal worthwhile, if there are still sick people, blind, deaf, lame? To read the eschatological promises 'only' as metaphors lets these powerful texts faint and sound rather cynical" ("Q 7:22," 178 n. 17).

how God will act through him, as he has done through Elijah in the past, including raising the dead."[54] Collins also argues that the two columns refer to a single individual, but he indicates that there is no distinction between the prophet and the royal messiah. He claims that 4Q521 describes a single prophetic messiah possessing the combined traits.[55] Puech, however, argues that it refers to two distinct people, a new Elijah who announces the royal messiah.[56] Two points seem to favor Puech's reading of two individuals. First, 1QS IX, 11 identifies a prophetic figure in distinction to other messianic figures. Second, 4Q521 8 9 contains a plural form of *mshykh* (*mshykhyh*) and would seem to indicate two different figures. If this interpretation is correct, then 4Q521 may be our earliest evidence for positing a relationship between the messenger/Elijah mentioned in Malachi and the coming of the messiah.

Editorial Activity in the Early Q Sections

We now turn to Q, which is a hypothetical document that scholars have (re)constructed. They have noted numerous verbal similarities between many of Jesus's sayings in the Gospels of Matthew and Luke and suggest that these similarities can be explained if both gospels used a source that concentrated on the sayings of Jesus. The discovery of the *Gospel of Thomas* in the Nag Hammadi Library, which contains 114 sayings of Jesus with only limited narrative context, proves that some early Christians did indeed collect Jesus's sayings.[57]

---

54. George J. Brooke, "Parabiblical Prophetic Narratives," in *The Dead Sea Scrolls after Fifty Years: A Comprehensive Assessment*, 2 vols., ed. Peter W. Flint and James C. VanderKam (Leiden: Brill, 1998-99), 1:277.

55. Collins, "Works of the Messiah," 103-6. John S. Kloppenborg Verbin follows Collins and assumes that the messiah in 4Q521 is an Elijah figure. *Excavating Q: The History and Setting of the Sayings Gospel* (Minneapolis: Fortress, 2000), 123.

56. Puech, "Some Remarks on 4Q246 and 4Q521," 559-60. See García Martínez, who argues that it refers to a royal or Davidic messiah ("Messianische Erwartungen," 182-85).

57. For a detailed discussion on Q, see John S. Kloppenborg, *The Formation of Q: Trajectories in Ancient Wisdom Collections* (Philadelphia: Fortress, 1987). While I have no problem accepting that a document such as Q existed and that it represents early

Even though Q consists primarily of a collection of sayings, numerous scholars have noted evidence of editorial activity.[58] Here we are interested specifically in the editorial activity evidenced in the reconstruction of the respective missions of John the Baptist and Jesus and their subsequent relationship to each other. In this editing we see the christianization of the title "the Coming One" in an effort to acknowledge the primacy of Jesus and thus attract John's followers into the Q community.[59] In doing so it appears that the editor has drawn upon traditions that were already developed to some extent in 4Q521.

Q opens, after a possible unrecoverable incipit, with John the Baptist crying repentance in the wilderness (Q 3:7-9). He preaches repentance and predicts destruction for those who fail to return to their covenantal obligations—in this case, the terms of God's covenant with Abraham. Receipt of the associated covenant blessings requires, for John, much more than familial bloodline. Rather it is one's actions that qualify a person for either the covenant

---

attempts of Christians to record Jesus's sayings, I do not accept many of the assumptions that scholars have developed from Q. For a perspective that cautions against some of these assumptions, particularly for a Latter-day Saint audience, see Thomas A. Wayment, "A Viewpoint on the Supposedly Lost Gospel Q," *Religious Educator: Perspectives on the Restored Gospel* 5/3 (2004): 105-15.

58. Dieter Zeller, "Redactional Processes and Changing Settings in the Q-Material," in *The Shape of Q: Signal Essays on the Sayings Gospel*, ed. John S. Kloppenborg (Minneapolis: Fortress, 1994), 116-30; Kloppenborg, *Formation of Q*; Migato Sato, "The Shape of the Q-Source," in *Shape of Q*, 156-79; Arland D. Jacobson, *The First Gospel: An Introduction to Q* (Sonoma: Polebridge, 1992); James M. Robinson, "The Sayings Gospel Q," in *The Four Gospels, Festschrift for Frans Neirynck*, ed. F. van Segbroeck et al. (Louvain: Leuven University Press, 1992), 361-88. Latter-day Saints recognize that the Book of Mormon was created through the editing process of both Mormon and Moroni. Mormon tells us on a number of occasions that "a hundredth part of the proceedings of this people . . . cannot be contained in this work" (Helaman 3:14; see Words of Mormon 1:5; 3 Nephi 5:8; 26:6; and Moroni in Ether 15:33). In other words, they had to choose what to include and what to exclude. In addition, their direct editorial voice is seen in the Words of Mormon and 3 Nephi 5:12-13, and indirectly through statements such as "and thus we see" (e.g., Alma 12:21-22; 24:19; 28:14; 30:60; Helaman 3:28; 6:34; Ether 14:25).

59. Robinson, "Matthean Trajectory," 149-54.

blessings or the corresponding curses for disobedience (Deuteronomy 27:14-28:6).

Yet it is clear in this Q pericope that John's mission does not include the carrying out of any punishments. Instead, the role of spiritual axeman belongs to another. Thus he declares: "I baptize you in water, but the Coming One (*ho erchomenos*) after me is more powerful than I, whose sandals I am not fit to take off. He will baptize you in [holy] spirit and fire. His pitch fork is in his hand, and he will clear his threshing floor and gather the wheat into the granary, but the chaff he will burn on a fire that can never be put out" (Q 3:16b-17). John's ministry is thus subordinated to that of the Coming One. The title is an interesting one because in the first century AD the Coming One was not normally a messianic title. Its only use in the Hebrew Bible is in Psalm 118:26a, where the immediate context shows that it refers to pilgrims to Jerusalem. However, Christians later reinterpreted Q in terms of an eschatological figure (Q 13:34-35), and Mark and John in terms of Jesus (Mark 11:9; John 12:13),[60] even though nothing in this Q text specifically identifies the Coming One with Jesus. David R. Catchpole argues that for the historical John the title referred to God who brings judgment upon the people,[61] but, as in 11Q13, in Q it may also have referred to the Son of Man, a supernatural agent of God's judgment.[62] In any case it is clear from this pericope that John's role is a subordinate

---

60. Robinson, "Sayings Gospel Q," 363.

61. David R. Catchpole, *The Quest for Q* (Edinburgh: Clark, 1993), 68, 239.

62. Catchpole, *Quest for Q*, 239. John's expectation of the Coming One as an agent of divine judgment may have been influenced by the Qumran community. See 4Q252 5 1-7, where the messiah is described as the messiah of righteousness and the expression that "[the thou]sands of Israel are 'the feet'" highlights the military context of the promised royalty (García Martínez, "Messianic Hopes," 162). See also 4Q161 3 18-22, where the "shoot of David . . . will rule over all the peoples and Magog [. . .] his sword will judge all the peoples." Perhaps the most compelling point from a conceptual, if not a linguistic, perspective is 1Q28b V, 20-29. In this text the "prince of the congregation" renews the covenant of the community (cf. John's role in Q 3:8) and strikes the people with the power of his mouth. "With your sceptre may you lay waste the earth. With the breath of your lips may you kill the wicked."

one, whether the Coming One referred specifically to God or to his agent. This passage, however, is the springboard for Q's later discussion on the significance of Jesus's ministry, which in Matthew is introduced by John's delegation asking Jesus, "Are you the Coming One (*ho erchomenos*)" mentioned in Q 3:16b, or should we look for another (Matthew 11:3)? Jesus's response recorded in Q not only defines his own mission, but also its relationship to John's.

First let us look at Q's description of Jesus's mission. "And in reply [i.e., Jesus] said to them: 'Go report to John what you hear and see: the blind regain their sight and the lame walk around, the skin-diseased are cleansed and the deaf hear, and the dead are raised and the poor are evangelized'" (Q 7:22). Rudolf Bultmann believed that this passage was "originally independent, and used by the community in the composition of an apophthegm."[63] But finding this passage in Q is somewhat surprising for a number of reasons. First, although not explicitly stated, our passage infers that Jesus is indeed the Coming One of Q 3, but not in the sense that John may have anticipated. Instead of an agent of judgment we find a miracle worker, and John S. Kloppenborg is correct to point out that "there is no indication that John expected a miracle-worker"[64]—hence Q 7:23, "And blessed is whoever is not offended by me." Second, related to the first, is the fact that we have listed here a number of miracles when Q is generally uninterested in miracles. This fact causes Robinson to muse that the passage "would have been more at home in the Σημεῖα [Semeia] Source used in the Gospel of John!"[65] Likewise Arland Jacobson frets over the fact that the "one type of miracle in Q linked to the manifestation of the kingdom is exorcism (Q 11:20)," and yet exorcism is not even mentioned in Q 7:22.[66] Third, this passage is a pastiche of Isaianic references associated with Isaiah's de-

---

63. Rudolf Bultmann, *The History of the Synoptic Tradition*, trans. John Marsh (New York: Harper & Row, 1963), 23.

64. Kloppenborg, *Formation of Q*, 107.

65. Robinson, "Sayings Gospel Q," 364.

66. Jacobson, *First Gospel*, 112.

scription of the coming time of peace (Isaiah 61:1-2 LXX; 29:18-19; 35:5; 42:6-7), but which have been edited "with Jesus' miracles in view."[67] Therefore one is left to ponder why, in a document with so little interest in miracles per se, 7:22 is the defining passage in Q of Jesus as the Coming One.

Points such as these have led scholars to question the assumption that Q 7:22 represents a dominical saying of Jesus while little unanimity yet exists regarding its editorial history. Kloppenborg, who believes that Q 7:22 is a post-Easter editorial composition,[68] represents one end of the continuum, while at the other end Catchpole believes that "everything in this tradition [i.e., the Jesus/John pericope] *apart from* the six-fold list in Q 7:22 is Q editorial."[69] However Catchpole's position is not as definite as one might think from reading this statement. In a footnote, he does allow for some editorial work in Q 7:22 by admitting that "we cannot rule out the further possibility, even probability, that some of the actions listed are additions to the original list." In particular, he identifies the phrases *lepers are cleansed* and *the dead are raised up.*[70] Jacobson agrees and argues that the raising of the dead "derives from the Jesus tradition rather than from Isa. 26:19."[71] Kloppenborg cites the phrase *lepers are cleansed* as the primary reason for his post-Easter dating.[72]

In drawing these conclusions, however, none of these authors seems to be aware of 4Q521 (although in a later monograph Kloppenborg does refer to it).[73] Yet this fragment from Qumran provides some important insights into the issue at hand. Healing of the lepers is not part of the wonders expected during the Jewish eschaton, nor is it mentioned in Isaiah 61; its absence in 4Q521 may strengthen

---

67. Kloppenborg, *Formation of Q*, 108; Robinson, "Sayings Gospel Q," 363-65.

68. Kloppenborg, *Formation of Q*, 107.

69. Catchpole, *Quest for Q*, 239, emphasis added.

70. Catchpole, *Quest for Q*, 239 n. 30.

71. Jacobson, *First Gospel*, 113.

72. Kloppenborg, *Formation of Q*, 108.

73. His discussion here, however, does not address the impact of 4Q521 for his assessment of Q 7:22 as a postresurrection saying (Kloppenborg Verbin, *Excavating Q*, 123).

both Cathchpole's and Kloppenborg's arguments that it represents an editorial element. On the other hand, 4Q521 forces us to reassess the editorial nature of raising the dead in this list of miracles.[74] I have argued here that 4Q521 had a tradition of a messiah raising the dead. The difference between Qumran and Q, however, is that while the Qumran community interpreted the phrase in terms of the eschatological resurrection, the Q and later Matthean communities interpreted it simply in terms of a revivification to mortality. This difference may indicate either of two positions: (1) the Q and Qumran communities were working from a common text that they interpreted independently, or (2) the Q community knew of 4Q521 and massaged it to fit their own circumstances since the resurrection does not appear to be theologically important for Q.

A case can be made for the latter of the two positions. In every other instance where Q quotes scripture it references a single passage.[75] In Q we find no other example of creating a scripture from a number of different passages,[76] a fact that makes Q 7:22 unique. Yet we find the creation of such a scriptural pastiche similar to that found in 4Q521. Given that the original of 4Q521 predates the first century BC, the direction of influence can only go one way. In addition, no other extant text that I am aware of combines the three characteristics of giving sight to the blind, raising the dead, and evangelizing the poor as a sign of the messianic kingdom. Giving sight to the blind and evangelizing the poor are based on either Isaiah 61:1 LXX or, possibly, a combination of Isaiah 61:1 and Psalm

---

74. So also Neirynck, "Q 6,20b-21; 7,22 and Isaiah 61," 59.

75. Hieke notes, "obviously the Q community is deeply rooted in the knowledge and appreciation of Jewish Scripture. This becomes clear in detail in the temptation narrative (Q 4), where Jesus only quotes core sentences of Scripture, especially from the most important texts of the Torah, and does not say a single word of his own. There seems to be a great interest in the community responsible for the Q text to relate Jesus closely to well known parts of Scripture" ("Q 7,22," 177).

76. Q 4:4 = Deuteronomy 8:3 LXX; Q 4:8 = Deuteronomy 6:13a; Deuteronomy 10:20a LXX; Q 4:10-11 = Psalm 91:11-12 LXX; Q 4:12 = Deuteronomy 6:16 LXX; Q 7:27 = Exodus 23:20a-b or Malachi 3:1a LXX; Q 13:35 = Psalm 117:26 LXX.

146:8; but raising the dead is loosely based on Isaiah 26:19. Again, no other Hebrew text creates this particular pastiche of Isaianic, plus or minus Psalmic, passages, with the exception of 4Q521. This point cannot be overemphasized. Moreover, it seems clear that the message of Q is that when John identified the Coming One in Q 3, he was referring to a known prophetic figure.[77] The problem, however, is that no single place in the Masoretic Text anticipates someone with all the qualifications listed in Q 7:22. Although Isaiah 61:1 LXX is an important pretext, the closest text is 4Q521.

A close parallel text, however, does not necessarily prove dependence.[78] After all, the list of end-time wonders is not identical in both texts. Kloppenborg Verbin notes that "most of the items listed in Q 7:22 (except deafness and leprosy) [occur] in 4Q521."[79] We have already noted above that the healing of the lepers is probably a later addition to Jesus's list; but what of the other differences? It is strange that Kloppenborg Verbin does not also include lameness in the items not mentioned in 4Q521, and he does not include any explanation. The question is whether we can also understand the additions of deafness (kōphos) and lameness in terms of Q editing. In addition to the combined acts of giving sight to the blind, raising the dead, and evangelizing the poor, 4Q521 also includes acts of liberating the prisoners and straightening out the twisted. The concept of liberating the prisoners in 4Q521 2 II, 8 (mtyr 'swrym) may come from Isaiah 61:1 (l'swrym pqḥ-qvḥ), but the Hebrew is the same as that in Psalm 146:7 (mtyr 'swrym), and raising up those who are bowed down clearly comes from Psalm 146:8. No immediate direct connection appears between these last two activities and the list in Q 7:22, but suggesting dependence requires an explanation of these apparent absences.

---

77. Robinson, "Matthean Trajectory," 131. 4Q521, however, may suggest that the prophecy was extracanonical.

78. Neirynck, "Q 6,20b-21; 7,22 and Isaiah 61," 58.

79. Kloppenborg Verbin, Excavating Q, 405 n. 72.

Let us examine the miracle of healing the *kōphos*. The Greek word *kōphos* can refer to someone who is deaf (Mark 7:37), mute (Matthew 15:31), or both.[80] In Q 7:22 the verb clearly indicates that the affliction is deafness rather than muteness. In addition, the stigma of being *kōphos* was sometimes associated with being possessed of a devil (Luke 11:14; Mark 9:25). This latter association is certainly how Matthew interpreted Q 7:22's phrase *the deaf hear*. In chapters 8 and 9 Matthew has brought together a number of miracles that serve as examples of each of the miraculous actions of the Coming One mentioned in Q 7:22. His example for "the deaf hear" is the miracle in Matthew 9:32-33. This interpretation does not work well in English, but in Greek both passages describe the man being *kōphos*. In this case the *kōphos* is specifically described as being "possessed of a devil" (*daimonizomenos*).[81] But how does this relate to 4Q521? 4Q521 does not have a corresponding passage about healing the deaf or casting out demons. Instead it has the phrase *liberate the prisoners*. Hieke speculates "whether Q might have contained such a sentence, since both, Matthew and Luke, had strong reasons to omit this aspect: According to both gospels, John the Baptist is imprisoned, and Jesus did not manage or even attempt to set him free."[82] If he is correct, then Q would have a very good reason to reinterpret this phrase in 4Q521. In addition, Edward P. Meadors has convincingly demonstrated that Q has reinterpreted liberating the prisoners as the casting out of devils. He points out a precedent for such an interpretation already in 11Q13 II, 1-13.[83] Is it just coincidence that Q is independently interpreting the liberating of captives as healing the *kōphoi*, or was the editor aware of 11Q13's interpretation and then applied the same interpretive framework to

80. Herodotus, *Histories* 1.34.

81. Here Matthew has incorporated healings from Mark's gospel to illustrate the healing capacities enumerated in Q 7:22. Linden E. Youngquist, "Matthew and Q" (PhD diss., Claremont Graduate University, 2003), 107-15.

82. Hieke, "Q 7,22," 181.

83. Meadors, "'Messianic' Implications," 262-63.

4Q521? It seems a logical step since in Q the casting out of devils is one of only two miracles mentioned (11:20). If so, then we can easily account for this discrepancy between 4Q521 and Q 7:22.

The phrase *straightening out the twisted* in 4Q521 is more problematic. Q may simply have taken the miracle of healing a lame man from Isaiah 35:6, but then we would again have to explain the pastiche approach to scripture that is otherwise not found in Q. If, on the other hand, Q 7:22 is dependent on 4Q521, then it must have reinterpreted the phrase about those who are twisted as the lame who are healed. I recognize that this interpretation is a tough sell linguistically because no specific connection exists between being lame (Heb. *pskh*, Gk. *chōlos*) and twisted (Heb. *kpp*). So why would Q reinterpret being twisted as being lame? Unfortunately, *kpp* does not have many attestations. In the Qumran texts, 4Q385 2 10 is the only other certain attestation where *kpwpym* (straightening out) and *zwqp* (raising up) are found together, although it has been reconstructed in 4Q501 1 4. The context in 4Q385 is the restoration of Israel through the covenant, using the physical symbols of sight, connecting of bones and sinews, and covering with skin as metaphors for Yahweh's bestowal of life. The author then asks, "when will these things happen?" Unfortunately the text containing Yahweh's reply is fragmentary. All we can read for certain is the phrase *a tree will bend over and straighten up* (*ykp 'ts wyzqp*). The lacuna makes it difficult to determine how the author understood this phrase in the context of what preceded it. Five attestations of *kpp* occur in the Hebrew Bible (Psalms 57:6 [Heb. Psalms 57:7]; 145:14; 146:8; Isaiah 58:5; Micah 6:6). Some of these texts describe a state of sacral humility (Isaiah 58:5; Micah 6:6; Psalm 57:6) or distress/humiliation (Psalms 145:14; 146:8), but none of these uses is particularly helpful for understanding how Q could have interpreted it as the healing of the lame. But the Akkadian cognate *kapāpu* and the use of *kpp* in the Talmud suggests a broader semantic range that includes a physical, and not just an emotional or spiritual, component.[84] Thus, although being used in a very figurative sense, Hebrews 12:12–13 associated the straightening of paralyzed knees (*paralelumena gonata anorthōsate*; the same Greek word used in Psalms 145:14; 146:8 LXX for *kpp*) with the healing of the lame. It is conceivable, therefore, that Q has reinterpreted the Hebrew *kpp* with the Greek *chōlos*.

But what would be Q's motivations for this interpretation? The simple answer is that it was not uncommon to combine the attributes of lameness (*chōlos*) with blindness (*tuphlos*).[85] If Q were to reinterpret any of the activities of 4Q521 as being lame, it would be "straightening out the twisted" (*zwqp kpwpym*) because it immediately follows "giving sight to the blind" (*pwqkh ʿwrym*) in line 8. The implication for my argument here is that the Q editor reinterpreted *kpp* as *chōlos* because he wanted to include Q's other miracle, the healing of the centurion's son, within the pastiche of Jesus's healing miracles. While not explicit in Q, this would assume that the Q editor understood the son's malady as associated with being *chōlos*. Matthew, "standing as he did in the Q heritage,"[86] seems to have shared this assumption in his editing of the Q miracle since his description of the son being a paralytic has a semantic range that includes being lame.[87]

In summary then, Q 7:22 is a pastiche of activities that the Q editor has used to interpret John's figure, the Coming One. Rather

---

84. *Kapāpu* can refer to a woman's bent nose; "*kapāpu*," in *Assyrian Dictionary of the Oriental Institute of the University of Chicago*, ed. A. Leo Oppenheim (Chicago: Oriental Institute, 1971), 8:175.

85. In LXX see Leviticus 21:18; Deuteronomy 15:21; 2 Samuel 5:6, 8; Job 29:15; Malachi 1:8. See also Matthew 15:30, 31; 21:14; Luke 14:13; 1QM VII, 4; 11Q19 LII, 10; Philo, *Questions and Answers on Genesis* 3:28.

86. Robinson, "Matthean Trajectory," 132.

87. Johannes P. Louw and Eugene A. Nida, eds., *Greek-English Lexicon of the New Testament Based on Semantic Domains*, 2 vols., 2nd ed. (New York: United Bible Societies, 1989), 1:273. Catchpole argues that "there is an underlying tradition historical relationship between the two stories [the healing of the Centurion's son in Matthew and the healing of the paralytic in Mark], even if not one of direct literary dependence." David R. Catchpole, "The Centurion's Faith and Its Function in Q," in *Four Gospels*, 520–21.

than being an agent of divine judgment, the Coming One is described in terms of his healing and preaching activities. As Kloppenborg notes, the title has clearly been infused "with specifically Christian content."[88] Yet the editor's reinterpretation of what it meant to be the Coming One is based primarily on an interpretation of Isaiah 61 that was unknown prior to the publication of 4Q521. In other words, our Q editor did not just fabricate the list in order to prove that Jesus was indeed the Coming One but seemed to be working from a tradition of messianic expectation that was already in place. The editor used that tradition, based on 4Q521's interpretation of Isaiah and Psalms, to describe Jesus's mission. We can understand both major Q editings of 4Q521, therefore, as a desire to incorporate both of the Q miracles within the pastiche of messianic activities that proved to the Baptist loyalists that Jesus was indeed the Coming One.

4Q521 and the Mission of John the Baptist in Q 3

But what of John's mission? We have already noted that his mission of repentance was distinct from the mission of the Coming One. Yet the Q editor is very careful not to discard either the prophet or his mission. Rather, his place in the Q community is central to the first third of the document. Not only is John a prophet, but he is "more than a prophet" (Q 7:26) and one of the children of Wisdom (Q 7:35); "among those born of women there is none greater" (with the exception of Jesus, Q 7:28). He is also specifically identified as the messenger referred to in Malachi 3:1 (Q 7:27). These points have led Christopher M. Tuckett to conclude, "Much of this material probably had a complex pre-history behind it before it ever reached Q."[89]

In recent years scholars have debated the Christian assertion here in Q and other synoptic passages that John the Baptist

---

88. Kloppenborg, *Formation of Q*, 107.

89. Christopher M. Tuckett, *Q and the History of Early Christianity: Studies on Q* (Edinburgh: Clark, 1996), 109.

is linked with Elijah. Morris M. Faierstein argued that there is no pre-Christian evidence that Elijah was considered to be a messianic forerunner. Rather, he notes, scholars relied upon later Rabbinic and Christian tradition and retrojected them into Second Temple Judaism.[90] Dale C. Allison, however, argues that Faierstein has gone too far. While the idea of Elijah as forerunner might not have been widespread, it was at least known in some quarters.[91] 4Q521 would seem to support Allison's position that, although not widespread, the idea was not original with the New Testament.

Why then was Q so interested in John as the Elijah forerunner? Kloppenborg and others have suggested that the editing of the first Q segment arose in an effort to "attract Baptist disciples into the Christian fold."[92] Rather than simply acknowledging John as the leader of his own religious group, Q 3-7 cleverly maintains his importance while at the same time subordinating him to Jesus; the Q community thereby allowed the Baptist disciples to join the Q community without losing face. In addition to this scenario, I would suggest that Q is also aware of a tradition from the Qumran community of a prophet associated with the messiah and used it to justify incorporating passages about John to fulfill that aspect of their messianic collage. The important parallels that we have noted between Qumran and Q suggest such a conclusion. If this is the case, then one further detail must also be explored. Qumran knew of more than one prophetic figure in association with the messiah. The more common is a "prophet like Moses" and then briefly a prophet in the mold of Elijah. If Q knew of the materials from the Dead Sea, then why did the editor prefer Elijah to Moses?

---

90. Morris M. Faierstein, "Why Do the Scribes Say That Elijah Must Come First?" *Journal of Biblical Literature* 100 (1981): 75-86.

91. Dale C. Allison, "Elijah Must Come First," *Journal of Biblical Literature* 103 (1984): 256-58.

92. Kloppenborg, *Formation of Q*, 107; Robinson, "Sayings Gospel Q," 361-62; and Catchpole, *Quest for Q*, 61-62.

The key seems to lie in Malachi's description of Elijah's role and the substance of John the Baptist's message of repentance. Some scholars have understood Malachi 4:5-6 (Heb. 3:23-24) to be a later addition to the text,[93] perhaps referring to a dissolution of family life during the Hellenistic period.[94] Even if this is the case, another level of interpretation other than reconciliation within the nuclear family is possible. The term *fathers* can also be interpreted in relation to the covenant.[95] Throughout the Hebrew Bible the plural term *fathers* usually refers to ancestors—and the quintessential positive ancestors are Abraham, Isaac, and Jacob, who represent the covenant.[96] A return to these fathers represents a return to covenantal status.

This understanding of Elijah in Malachi is particularly appropriate given Elijah's confrontation with the priests of Baal on Mt. Carmel. As Elijah confronted the priests he turned to the people and challenged them: "How long halt ye between two opinions? if the LORD be God, follow him: but if Baal, then follow him" (1 Kings 18:21). Elijah's subsequent dialogue with the Lord shows that he understood his actions with the priests to be a matter of covenantal fidelity (see 1 Kings 19:10, 14). What is interesting is Elijah's prayer after his miraculous quashing of the priests of Baal, "O Yahweh, God of Abraham, Isaac, and Israel, let it be known this day that you are God in Israel, and that I am your servant, and that I have done all these things at your word. Answer me, Yahweh, answer me, that this people may know that you, Yahweh, are God, and that you have *turned their hearts back*" (1 Kings 18:36-37, emphasis added). Although acknowledging Yahweh's power, Elijah's actions that day sought to return the people to the covenant and thus they "turned

---

93. C. C. Torrey, "The Prophecy of 'Malachi,'" *Journal of Biblical Literature* 17 (1898): 7.

94. Glazier-McDonald, *Malachi: The Divine Messenger*, 254.

95. Andrew E. Hill, *Malachi: A New Translation with Introduction and Commentary* (New York: Doubleday, 1998), 388.

96. See, for example, Genesis 48:15-16; Exodus 3:15-16; 4:5; Deuteronomy 1:8; 6:10; 9:5; 29:13; and 30:20.

their hearts back." Although the word *turned* (*hsbt*) is different from that of Malachi (*hshyb*), the substance of the message is the same. Elijah was therefore the perfect choice for Malachi's prophecy because he was already associated with the turning of hearts.

As we then move to consider why Q preferred the Elijah model over that of Moses, we are reminded of the substance of John the Baptist's imploring with the multitude that they "bear fruit worthy of repentance and do not presume to say to yourselves, 'We have as forefather Abraham!'" (Q 3:8). Jacobson argues that this passage is "probably a redactional addition, integrated into its context by picking up the theme of bearing fruit from Q 3:9."[97] If he is correct, then Q's editor is making a specific statement about John's audience—that they refuse the call to repentance by "invoking national privilege,"[98] as epitomized in their appeal to their father Abraham. John's original designation of his audience as a "generation of vipers" counteracts their claims to Abraham. They may well have been lineal descendants of Abraham, but spiritually they were not because their actions did not reflect such. John's cry for repentance could therefore be understood as a cry for a spiritual turning back to Abraham.[99]

One wonders whether the Israelites in 1 Kings 18 reacted similarly to Elijah's condemnation! The fact that Elijah specifically invoked "Yahweh, God of Abraham, Isaac, and all Israel" implies as much; otherwise the invocation would have been meaningless. Thus both Elijah's and John's audiences would have understood the importance of the figure of Abraham in their blood lineage, but neither group was acting as if the covenant of Abraham was the center of their lifestyle. Yahweh through Elijah turned the hearts of the Israelites back, and John the Baptist would do likewise through his

---

97. Jacobson, *First Gospel*, 82.

98. John S. Kloppenborg, "The Formation of Q and Antique Instruction Genres," in *Shape of Q*, 145.

99. The Hebrew behind the Greek *metanoia* is *shuv*, the same word used for "turning" in Malachi 4:6 (Heb. 3:24).

cry of repentance. The Q editor could therefore play on this scenario by portraying John as a prophet like Elijah.

Conclusion

It is not, I think, happenstance that in the editorial process the Q editor has incorporated themes that we have noted in relationship to Qumran and specifically 4Q521—that is, the portrayal of a healing and preaching messiah who is associated with a prophetic Elijah figure. Dieter Zeller reminds us that "no OT quotations refer to a wonder-working and preaching messiah," and yet we find here two communities drawing on such a tradition.[100] Similarly, Faierstein and Allison remind us that no widespread pre-Christian tradition associated Elijah with the messiah, and yet we here find these same two communities drawing on such a tradition.[101] Two possibilities for these occurrences avail themselves. Either both communities were dependent on an otherwise unknown common tradition, or the Q community knew of the Qumran tradition found in 4Q521. If the former, then it seems that these two communities preserve the only attestation to such a tradition. In this paper, I have argued for the latter. Thus Q 7:22 does not represent a direct interpretation of Isaiah, specifically Isaiah 61:1, but an editing of 4Q521's reinterpretation of Isaiah and Psalms.

Josephus informs us that the Essenes were not exclusive to Qumran but dwelled in every city.[102] Presumably that included Galilee, where it would have been possible for them to come into some kind of contact with the Q community.[103] Both the Essenes and the Q community had an understanding of a healing and preaching

---

100. Zeller, "Redactional Processes," 123 n. 32.

101. Faierstein, "Why Do the Scribes?" 75-86, and Allison, "Elijah Must Come First," 256-58.

102. Josephus, *War* 2.8.4.

103. It seems clear that other New Testament authors were familiar with teachings from the Qumran community. James H. Charlesworth, "The Dead Sea Scrolls and the Historical Jesus," in *Jesus and the Dead Sea Scrolls*, ed. James H. Charlesworth (New York: Doubleday, 1992), 1-74.

messiah. Although we have noted the similarities of healing the blind and especially raising the dead and evangelizing the poor, I have argued that we can understand some of the other differences as a Q editing of 4Q521. In addition to the parallels mentioned, the relationship of the form of Q 7:22 to the scrolls is also significant. The Q editor has clearly gathered together a collection of miracles and activities from a number of Isaianic passages and brought them together as a pesher to show their fulfillment in Jesus. This is an unusual editorial activity for Q but one that is common in the scrolls. Finally, we also see both texts associating an Elijah-type prophetic figure with the messiah—something that is difficult to support from other contemporary Jewish texts. 4Q521, therefore, should be viewed as another source on the trajectory from nascent Jewish messianism to the Christian development of Jesus as the Messiah.

Gaye Strathearn is associate professor of ancient scripture at Brigham Young University.

CHAPTER 21

❦

HOW RICH WAS PAUL?
...AND WHY IT MATTERS

John W. Welch

Working with Kent Brown on several New Testament projects has been an extraordinary honor and a joy in my life. Knowing especially of his spiritual and rigorous affinities to the gospel of Luke, and through Luke to Luke's likely traveling companion Paul, I offer the following musings about Paul's extraordinary backgrounds. Above all, Paul was a totally dedicated and consecrated disciple of Jesus Christ. Whatever time, talents, and resources he possessed—and it certainly appears that in all respects Paul was copiously endowed and equipped to carry out the extremely challenging calling that was given to him and to all the apostles of Jesus Christ—Paul placed them fully and gladly on the altar of spiritual sacrifice. These are virtues that Kent Brown has always deeply admired and, in so emulating these early Christian examples, has become both a wonderful follower and articulate leader, like Paul himself to all those around him.

Some Questions

Reading the writings of the apostle Paul is a daunting task, and the difficulties are only exacerbated because little is known about this extremely influential and complex man. He seems to come almost out of nowhere. Tarsus may have been as unknown to the Jewish Galileans as it is to modern readers: they knew the name of this city, to be sure, but possibly not much more. Throughout his life Paul proceeds to go just about everywhere. Nowhere was beyond his desired reach; Caesar's Rome was just a doorway that he hoped would help him achieve his goal of converting the entire known world to Jesus Christ. What kind of man was this *doulos,* this servant (or slave) of his spiritual Master? Had he himself grown up as the son of a common laborer? Or perhaps did he herald from the privileged aristocracy? And what difference might the answer make in how we read Paul today? Responses to these questions have gravitated in various directions.

In 1985, Jerome Murphy-O'Connor published in *Bible Review* a charming article on Paul's missionary travels, entitled "On the Road and on the Sea with St. Paul,"[1] concerned mainly with the means and manner by which Paul got around. Using detailed sources from the world of the New Testament, Murphy-O'Connor paints a vivid picture of the perils, hardships, and discomforts (including the bedbugs) that faced travelers in the eastern Mediterranean during the first century, and he creates a material context in which readers can begin to reconstruct various social, cultural, and economic aspects of Paul's travels.

Murphy-O'Connor's particular portrait of Paul, however, is largely based on the assumption that Paul was not a man of means. "Paul was not a rich man," we are flatly told:

> The impression he gives in his letters is that he had no significant personal financial resources. He seems to have had nothing beyond what he could earn and the sporadic gifts sent to him by various churches (2 Corinthians 11:8–9; Philippians 4:14). As an itinerant artisan, a tent-maker (Acts

---

1. Jerome Murphy-O'Connor, "On the Road and on the Sea with St. Paul," *Bible Review* 1/2 (1985): 38–47. This view was nuanced somewhat in 2004 by Murphy-O'Connor; see text accompanying notes 12–13 below.

18:3), he was far better off than an unskilled worker of the laboring class, but no artisan became rich. It would have been as much as Paul could do to earn his daily bread, even if he had enjoyed a stable situation with a regular clientele.[2]

The question of Paul's financial status, however, is critical not only to understanding his energetic ability to get around by land or by sea, but also to assessing the metaphors, ideologies, and paradigms within which this enigmatic man spoke, taught, and wrote. How should modern readers socially and economically situate Paul's comments about masters and slaves? Or about family relations and prevailing urban society? Or about making donations to Jerusalem or paying taxes to Rome? How do we position his stance toward the pervasive culture of honor and shame or the prevailing patron-client institution of his day? How do we understand his socially laden comments on being "no more strangers and foreigners" but becoming "fellowcitizens" (Ephesians 2:19) and inheriting even as sons? How do we see his personal standing in relation to the social values that he promotes, such as charity (1 Corinthians 13), obedience (Ephesians 6:5-9; 1 Timothy 6:1-2), unity (Ephesians 4:1-16), being rich in good works (Philippians 2:12-18; 1 Timothy 6:17-21), and avoiding hypocrisy (Romans 2:17-24)? Several theses—many of them more religiously or theologically important than the rather mundane conclusion that Paul traveled principally on foot precisely because he was poor—depend on assumptions about Paul's personal economic, social, and political status. Divergence among scholars on these views invites a renewed look at this interesting subject.

Previous Opinions

Murphy-O'Connor's view that Paul was a poor craftsman is reminiscent of the writings of the work of Gustav A. Deissmann on early Christian society. As Deissmann asserted, Paul was "a simple

---

2. Murphy-O'Connor, "On the Road and on the Sea with St. Paul," 39.

man," whose economic base was a relatively humble trade.[3] He oddly assigned Paul to the lower or middle class based on his literacy and language usage;[4] in reaching this conclusion he followed the arguments of early church fathers, such as John Chrysostom, who also saw Paul as a common man who had come from an undistinguished family.[5]

Deissmann's view, though perhaps widely shared among Bible readers, finds less support among scholars today, who typically hold the opposite view, although with considerable variations on this theme. Several hold that Paul was wealthy throughout his lifetime. For example, A. N. Wilson, the prolific biographer of such figures as Tolstoy, C. S. Lewis, Milton, and Jesus, sees Paul's trumpeted self-sufficiency and his successful trial at Jerusalem as proof that he was independently wealthy clear to the end of his life.[6] For other scholars, including the well-known Martin Hengel and Joseph Fitzmyer, Paul's Roman citizenship and his educational background necessarily presuppose significant monetary resources of his family.[7] Several other writers support the idea that Paul came from a family with wealth and high social standing, but they question his own status and means during the time of his apostolic ministry. F. J. Foakes-Jackson, for example, describes Paul's independent financial position as being attributable to the wealth of his family, who may well have held a good deal of social prestige and lived in "easy circumstances," but nevertheless he notes that Paul felt the pinch of poverty at times

---

3. Gustav A. Deissmann, *Paul: A Study in Social and Religious History*, trans. William E. Wilson (New York: Hodder and Stoughton, 1957), 48.

4. Deissmann, *Paul*, 51.

5. John Chrysostom, *Hom. de laud. S. Pauli* 3 (PG 50:491). In expressing this opinion, perhaps Chrysostom was projecting his own ascetic values back onto the apostle.

6. A. N. Wilson, *Paul: The Mind of the Apostle* (New York: Norton, 1997), 52.

7. Martin Hengel, *The Pre-Christian Paul* (Philadelphia: Trinity, 1991), 1-39; Joseph A. Fitzmyer, *The Acts of the Apostles* (New York: Doubleday, 1998), 144-45; see also Sherman E. Johnson, *Paul the Apostle and His Cities* (Wilmington, DE: Glazier, 1987), 31-33.

because of the sacrifices and inconveniences that clearly accompanied his ministry.[8] A century ago, W. M. Ramsay asserted that Paul, though formerly acquainted with wealth and status, was only the destitute nephew or relative of his rich extended family during his ministry.[9] More recently, N. A. Dahl has opined that Paul came from a family of wealth but "probably knew want more often than plenty" during his time as a preacher, surviving by the work of his own hands, possibly because he had been disinherited by his family for his conversion to Christianity.[10] Ronald Hock has even argued that Paul, who came "from a relatively high social class,"[11] willingly accepted a life of significant poverty, knowing that affluence would have eluded him as he plied "his trade in a social world that was highly hostile toward" his missionary work.[12] In 2004, Father Murphy-O'Connor argued once again in his very fine book, *Paul: His Story* (a much-expanded version of his 1985 article, introduced above), that Paul likely lived primarily off of almsgiving, although here Murphy-O'Connor allows that it was "not impossible that he was funded by his family," for his parents might have remained "prosperous into a ripe old age."[13] He dismisses the idea, however, that Paul earned money from his family's tentmaking trade because his "total dedication" to his religious endeavors would have left "little or no time to earn a living,"[14] and

---

8. F. J. Foakes-Jackson, *The Life of St. Paul: The Man and the Apostle* (New York: Boni & Liveright, 1926), 63–64.

9. William M. Ramsay, *St. Paul the Traveler and Roman Citizen* (New York: Putnam, 1904), 34–35.

10. N. A. Dahl, *Studies in Paul* (Minneapolis: Augsburg, 1977), 35–36.

11. Ronald F. Hock, "Paul's Tentmaking and the Problems of His Social Class," *Journal of Biblical Literature* 97 (1978): 564. For latest reflections, see Ronald F. Hock, "The Problem of Paul's Social Class: Further Reflections," in *Paul's World*, ed. Stanley E. Porter (Leiden: Brill, 2008), 7–18.

12. Ronald F. Hock, *The Social Context of Paul's Ministry: Tentmaking and Apostleship* (Philadelphia: Fortress, 1980), 35.

13. Jerome Murphy-O'Connor, *Paul: His Story* (Oxford: Oxford University Press, 2004), 14.

14. Murphy-O'Connor, *Paul: His Story*, 13.

thus, all the more, it would appear that his upbringing was highly privileged and his resources were ample.

This sample of opinions about Paul's wealth illustrates the breadth of possibilities that still remain to be explored. Effectual conclusions may always elude us, especially because the surviving evidence, coming almost exclusively from the New Testament, is not only scarce but also often inconsistent or inconclusive. At times, Paul seems to have the means and education of an upper-class Roman citizen; in other situations, he seems to be as destitute as an unrefined lowly laborer. Thus, the question of Paul's wealth must be approached, not as a single question, but rather as a series of inquiries regarding various aspects of Paul's life. Examined in this way, it seems that on every count Paul was quite rich throughout his life, and perhaps even very rich indeed.

Paul's Background, Education, and Acquired Legal Acumen

Despite the lack of information about Paul's background, most scholars accept the idea that his family was most likely one of considerable means and status. Paul was born during the Hellenistic diaspora into the home of a Pharisee who was also a Roman citizen. As a virtual citizen of three worlds, Paul acquired an education that was culturally rich, and his background was probably privileged and affluent.

Paul introduces himself in Jerusalem as both a Jew and a native of Tarsus in the province of Cilicia (Acts 21:39; 22:3). Tarsus was the capital of Cilicia, with a reputation among Greeks in the Hellenistic world as a center of Greek philosophical and literary education. One must assume that he studied to some extent in the local gymnasium or, if that would have been too Greek for a Pharisaic Jew, that he had tutors who taught him well. His Greek vocabulary is large and distinctive: by my computer count, 55 percent of the vocabulary words used in the Greek New Testament are used by him alone. Teachers of Greek, and apparently of Hebrew and Latin as well, would probably have been easily available in Tarsus, especially to a person of means.

As a sizeable trading city built upon the highway that connected the Syrian city of Antioch with the wealthy Roman province of Asia in eastern Turkey, Tarsus attracted many people of diverse origins, languages, and cultures, including a population of Hellenized Jews.[15] In this cosmopolitan setting, Paul probably witnessed early on the ways of the business world and became familiar with people from Greece, Asia, Galatia, Cyprus, Damascus, and beyond. Growing up in the provincial capital would also have exposed Paul to men of influence and power. Even as a boy, the son of a Roman citizen would have conversed occasionally with a wide spectrum of important officials in the marketplace, under the columned porches, and around the seats of government—places that he would frequent later in Philippi, Athens, Corinth, and Ephesus.

But more than that, Paul went on to receive his highest formal education in Jerusalem under the tutelage of Gamaliel, a scholar of Jewish law and a rabbi of great repute and influence among the Jewish people (Acts 5:34; 22:3). How would an ordinary Jewish boy from Tarsus ever manage to get admitted into the educational care of such an instructor? How would such a youth travel all the way to Jerusalem? Not by walking, one may assume. Since no scholarship funds gave equal opportunity to the poor or common folk in these days, one can only assume that Paul's family had significant financial resources to make this educational experience possible. Speaking of Paul's extraordinarily privileged educational background, "both religious and secular," Murphy-O'Connor concludes, "This was an expensive privilege, and was not available to the vast majority of Jews. Someone, presumably his parents, had to pay for it. . . . Paul clearly did not have to go to work either as a child or as a young man."[16]

---

15. Arthur Darby Nock, *St. Paul* (New York: Harper & Brothers, 1938), 22-23.
16. Murphy-O'Connor, *Paul: His Story*, 4.

And Paul's upper-class education paid off. His talents and training evidently brought him rapid success, bringing him respect and uncommon opportunities. As a young man he was already known and trusted by the Sanhedrin, whose leaders entrusted him with the official responsibility of arresting Christians in Damascus and returning them to Jerusalem to stand trial for blasphemy. This would have been an important commission. Perhaps this charge was entrusted to him precisely because he was the son of an influential father and, as a Roman citizen, could have commanded respect before Roman officials in the Roman province of Syria. Otherwise, this stewardship seems a bit out of the league of a young "college student," even assuming that he had received a high recommendation from his mentor, Gamaliel, or others. Moreover, on the road to Damascus, Paul was traveling with a group of men who appeared to be his subordinates. Even as a relatively young man he seemed to be fully in charge of them, and they seemed obligated, either as underlings or servants, to take care of him after he was temporarily blinded.

In addition, Paul's writings reflect the deep influence of both the Greek and Jewish cultures on his education. Paul's letters are illustrative of a man who enjoyed an education similar to that of other wealthy, upper-class men of his day. Many of the metaphors that he so richly employs throughout his letters are drawn from the domains of law, business, politics, and leisure,[17] and they would have been naturally on the lips of men of means. He seems conversant with several philosophies of his day.[18] His writings reflect the Greek oratory tradition as well as "Hellenistic anthropology, [and] Stoic methods of argumentation."[19] He uses Greek philosophical

---

17. David J. Williams, *Paul's Metaphors: Their Context and Character* (Peabody, MA: Hendrickson, 1999), esp. chaps. 6–12.

18. See, for example, Troels Engberg-Pedersen, *Paul and the Stoics* (Edinburgh: Clark, 2000); Bruce W. Winter, *Philo and Paul among the Sophists* (Cambridge: Cambridge University Press, 1997).

19. Calvin J. Roetzel, *Paul: The Man and the Myth* (Columbia: University of South Carolina Press, 1998), 22–23.

terminology in his letters to Corinth and Colossae. Indeed, the Hellenistic elements of Paul's education make it difficult for Peter and the other apostles to understand him at times (2 Peter 3:16). The structure of his letters imitates the refined models of the ancient rhetoricians, such as Quintilian, although the ethical content is Jewish in nature.[20] With great skill, Paul utilizes Greek rhetorical forms and philosophical ideas to further his own arguments, as has been especially observed in regard to his defense in the letter to the Galatians or before the Areopagus in Athens.[21] At the same time, he readily quotes and expounds on the meanings of scripture in both the Hebrew and Greek versions and modes of interpretation. He knows the Greek Septuagint translation of the Jewish scriptures intimately and quotes from it profusely.

His phenomenal ease and success within Jewish, Greek, and Roman courts of law particularly suggest that his training in the law was superb as well. Virtually everywhere Paul went, he wound up in court, and he loved being thrown into those legal briar patches. Every time, he wiggled out of the problem or won outright, sometimes winning big, either by serving the Sanhedrin; impressing the Roman proconsul Sergius Paulus on Cyprus; escaping from Jewish prosecutors in Antioch, Iconium, and Lystra; asserting his rights in Philippi; settling a case in Thessalonica; obtaining a stay of action from the high court of Athens; winning a major victory over Sosthenes before Gallio, the proconsul in Corinth; exposing illegal magicians in Ephesus; or defending himself upon arrest, initially before the temple guards in Jerusalem and subsequently before Roman governors in Caesarea. In each case he acquitted himself masterfully.

It is difficult to imagine that Paul's multifaceted, religious, literary, and philosophical education could have been open to anyone

---

20. Johnson, *Paul the Apostle and His Cities*, 33.

21. See, for example, Hans Dieter Betz, "Galatians," in *Anchor Bible Dictionary*, ed. David Noel Freedman (New York: Doubleday, 1992), 2:873.

but the most privileged and prosperous members of society. Most likely, the exceptional wealth and status of Paul's family made this all possible. His extensive knowledge, huge vocabulary, and impressive command of literary techniques are attributes possessed by members of the upper class, those with enough money to buy instruction and with the leisure time (*scholia*, from which the English word *school* derives) in which to study.

The Business of Tentmaking

Luke records that Paul stayed and worked with Aquila and Priscilla in Corinth because they, like he, were tentmakers (*skēnopoioi*) by trade (Acts 18:3). Deissmann, considering this reference to Paul's trade, concludes that Paul, as a tentmaker, could not possibly be conceived of as a well-educated and literate person, but at best a simple laborer of the lower classes who wrote clumsily with "a workman's hand deformed by toil."[22] However, this view is now rejected.[23]

Deissmann's main error lay in his failure to consider the craft within the context of Paul's world. Tentmaking was no small-scale profession in ancient times. Because inns were filthy or nonexistent, tents were luxury items for wealthy travelers and, more importantly, they were standard equipment for Roman legions, especially during the winter. Tents were large and expensive, measuring ten Roman square feet inside and housing eight men.[24] In addition to tents, a tentmaker would likely have been responsible for the manufacture of other military gear and clothing, leather products, and perhaps also *cilcium,* a thick material made from goat hair, for which Tarsus was famous.[25]

Moreover, tentmakers probably worked in leathers, canvas, and heavy fabrics for many commercial applications. In addition to making tents, members of Paul's business community would have

---

22. Deissmann, *Paul*, 48–49.
23. Hock, "Paul's Tentmaking," 556–57.
24. Wilson, *Paul*, 29.
25. Hengel, *Pre-Christian Paul*, 17.

made sacks for grain, awnings for shops, sails for ships, and very large coverings for public spaces. Tentmaking was an important business in the world of the New Testament.

We do not know the profession of Paul's father or how Paul became involved in this trade. Hock believes that Paul learned tentmaking from his father, and indeed Pharisees had a duty to teach their sons a skill: "Eduard Meyer even assumed that 'his father had a factory in which tents were made.'"[26] Be that as it may, if Paul's family was wealthy and had been involved with any large degree of volume production of tents or other products, slaves must have been part of the family work force. No business of any significance could be conducted in Paul's day without the labor of people who were indentured to the master or in servitude of one kind or another. In that case, Paul probably grew up with domestic servants (slaves) in the home.

In Corinth or elsewhere, items produced by tentmakers were in high demand, and the tools of this trade were readily portable. Therefore, Paul's business probably suited his itinerant lifestyle and was potentially quite lucrative. He lived and worked in "downtown" Corinth with Aquila and then moved in with Justus, whose house was right next door to the Jewish synagogue (Acts 18:7), probably in a good location close to the agora and civic center of this capital city of the Roman province of Achaia.

Paul's Roman Citizenship

The greatest potential evidence for the wealth and status of Paul and his family, however, is the Roman citizenship that Paul claimed to have held from birth (Acts 22:25-28). His family's economic standing was probably consistent with the rare procurement and maintenance of Roman citizenship, and that privilege probably translated into further economic advantages, especially for the pre-Christian Paul.

---

26. Hengel, *Pre-Christian Paul*, 15.

Roman citizenship was undoubtedly the most highly coveted symbol of wealth and status in the Roman world at this time; especially in the eastern Mediterranean where one can estimate that only 1 percent of males were citizens. It is unknown how Paul's father became a Roman citizen, but Paul claims that he acquired his citizenship by birth. It would seem more plausible that Paul's father or grandfather was given citizenship as an honor bestowed in recognition of some extraordinary act of service—perhaps in supplying a Roman general with tents or sails—than that the family's citizenship had been obtained by purchase. Indeed, Paul's Latin name Paulus may be a family name of the Roman patron through whom his citizenship derived. In any event, very few Jews in the first half of the first century held Roman citizenship. This was an extraordinary and powerful social privilege. Obtaining such status either came at great cost or was due to high-profile connections. It could be bestowed as a reward for a large-scale act of civil service or through the intercession of a wealthy and influential patron. Only a family of great importance in a prominent eastern city would have had means and influence enough to gain such a distinction.

But can we be sure that Paul truly was a Roman citizen? Although scholars such as Ramsay, Hengel, and A. N. Sherwin-White have accepted Paul's allegation at face value, the matter of his citizenship has recently been the subject of much skepticism and is worth addressing.

One of the most recent of these skeptical studies appeared in 1998. In *Paul: The Man and the Myth,* Calvin J. Roetzel summarizes the four main arguments that have been advanced against Paul's Roman citizenship by such distinguished scholars as W. W. Tarn, E. R. Goodenough, and Victor Tcherikover. First, it was rare for Jews to be granted citizenship in the East, and even then it was reserved for wealthy, influential people who were "profoundly attracted to Hellenistic and Roman culture." This would not seem to describe a Pharisee such as Paul's father. Second, since citizens were required to participate in the civic cult and to offer sacrifices to the state gods, the deep religious commitment of Paul's family would have conflicted with the obligations associated with citizenship. Third, it is puzzling why Paul did not save himself from imprisonment and arrest by asserting his citizenship earlier in Philippi and Jerusalem (one must assume that for some strange reason Paul was not wearing the toga on these occasions, which he would have been entitled to wear, but only as a Roman citizen). Finally, one may be suspicious of Paul's claim of citizenship because it serves Luke's theological interests in legitimizing the Christian movement. Based upon these four objections, Roetzel concludes that the evidence weighs against the historicity of Paul's citizenship.[27]

This conclusion, however, seems a bit hasty. Just because citizenship was rare among Jews in the East does not disprove the legitimacy of Paul's claim. One percent of the general population in the eastern Mediterranean would have held Roman citizenship at this time. Acts correctly presents Paul's citizenship as an unusual and unexpected status for a person in Paul's world. Moreover, Roetzel bases his assertion on the assumption that Paul's family could not possibly have been among the wealthy and influential members of society, but that only begs the crucial question.

The conditions of Roman citizenship to which Roetzel refers do not actually conflict with Paul's strict piety. Participation in the civic cult, the making of offerings to local gods, and participation in religious festivals were not obligatory for all Roman citizens in Paul's time. During this period Philo of Alexandria, whose family was extremely wealthy, remained avidly Jewish while participating actively in the social and political world of Roman Egypt and attending banquets, theater, and sporting events.[28] If a person stayed out of court where oaths and sacrifices were required of litigants and witnesses (as Paul advises in 1 Corinthians 6) and stayed

---

27. Roetzel, *Paul*, 20-21.
28. Peder Borgen, "Philo of Alexandria," in *Anchor Bible Dictionary*, 5:334.

out of major trouble with the public law demanding oaths of loyalty to the emperor (as occurred in the case of the Sicarii at Masada and in Egypt), people could simply avoid the need to participate in Roman religious cultic activities. There was no punishment for remaining uninvolved.

Paul's silence about his citizenship prior to his arrest on the Temple Mount in Acts 21 does raise a very interesting question. Likewise, one may well wonder why he did not use his citizenship preemptively on other occasions to avoid treatment terrible enough that he feared he might not escape it alive (2 Corinthians 1:8). Why does he not mention his personal status in his epistles as a metaphor or in contrast to his citizenship in God's kingdom? Perhaps the mind of Paul in these instances can be understood by exploring possible reasons for such silence. Might it have been more expedient for Paul *not* to declare his citizenship too saliently? Since Roman citizenship was so rare, a diplomatic Paul may have been reluctant to boast of his elite status for fear of alienating himself from the general population to which he was preaching. Furthermore, it seems that Paul thought of himself more as a citizen of Tarsus than of Rome, and as Sherwin-White explains, Paul viewed his Roman citizenship as "a personal privilege to be invoked if and when necessary."[29] Perhaps he did not try to save himself too quickly by invoking his personal privileges as a Roman citizen, knowing that his companions would then be left without a similar defense. Roman citizenship in the East was not a way of life but more of an honorary title. Hellenistic Romans considered citizenships similar to honorary titles and often collected them as such.[30] Eastern citizens could not vote without traveling to Rome and very rarely made use of this status to enter the Roman army or provincial politics.[31] Perhaps Paul did not dwell on his citizenship in his writings because

29. A. N. Sherwin-White, *Roman Society and Roman Law in the New Testament* (Oxford: Oxford University Press, 1963), 180.

30. Sherwin-White, *Roman Society and Roman Law*, 178.

31. Sherwin-White, *Roman Society and Roman Law*, 176–77.

its privileges seemed so distant from and irrelevant to the normal life of himself or those around him. Then again, perhaps he does actually say more than that about citizenship when he promises his converts that they are now no longer foreigners and aliens but full citizens in the kingdom of God (Ephesians 2:19).

Finally, should one doubt the reality of Paul's citizenship because it appears to serve Luke's theological agenda? If one gives any credence whatever to the main events reported in the last part of the book of Acts, there can be little doubt about the authenticity of Luke's claim. After Paul's arrest in Jerusalem, he was given legal protections that would have been extended only to a Roman citizen. He was sent from Jerusalem under guard to the Roman governor Felix at Caesarea. When Felix learned that Paul was from the Roman province of Cilicia, he agreed to hear him (Acts 23:35). After remaining at Caesarea in Felix's custody for two years, Paul rebutted the right of the Jews to try him and invoked his right as a Roman citizen to have his case tried before Caesar (Acts 25:10–11). He then traveled under light Roman guard to Rome, where he remained for two years (Acts 28:30). None of this high-level privileged treatment would have been possible without the diplomatic passport of Roman citizenship.

Under Roman law, the penalty for laying false claim to Roman citizenship was death, at least potentially. As such, one would think that the crime of forging Roman citizenship was rarely committed and then only quite foolishly. It is not unlikely that Paul would have been required to prove his claim of citizenship at several points, either by producing documents in his possession or by obtaining an examination of records in Rome. Paul's actions do not portray any lack of confidence that such a perjurer might feel as he waited two years in Caesarea for the transfer of his trial to Rome. Too many of Luke's own readers in Ephesus, Corinth, or Rome would have personally known Paul and his status for Luke to have risked fabricating a blatant hoax of Roman citizenship.

The arguments against the veracity of Paul's statement being questionable, there seems to be little reason to reject his claim that he was a citizen by birth and as such was fully entitled to the legal rights of a Roman citizen. This rare honor would have been available to his family only at great cost and would have conferred extraordinary privileges; thus Paul's Roman citizenship supports the assertion that his family was one of very significant means and status.

Paul's Financial Resources during the Time of His Ministry

Even if Paul came from a privileged family in Tarsus, his economic condition during the time of his ministry raises yet another question. Could he have started out rich but then become poor?

Much evidence in the New Testament suggests that Paul possessed significant personal means throughout his ministry. Above all, he could afford to travel extensively with companions throughout his life. Travel in Paul's world was not cheap. Travelers typically traveled in a company, taking with them food, clothing, and supplies, as well as feed for their livestock. Wagons were costly, at least those that would not break down.[32] Paul surely walked on many journeys, as he did from Troas to Assos in Acts 20:13-14; but on that occasion he could have stayed with his companions who preferred to go by sea. Perhaps Paul wanted to visit friends or preach in a few public places along the way.

All through his ministry, Paul was apparently able to afford parchment and ink. Paul had access to books and written materials and had the means to hire a scribe by which he wrote lengthy letters. His habitual writing is characteristic of a man of means.

Paul went straight to the capital cities of the provinces of Asia, Macedonia, and Achaia. He was not intimidated in these circumstances. He maintained himself in the impressive urban center of Corinth for a year and a half, and in the metropolis of Ephesus for a

---

32. Murphy-O'Connor, "On the Road and on the Sea with St. Paul," 39.

significant period of time (Acts 18:11; 19:10). He knew how to handle and transmit international transfers of money, and he was able to organize and direct several branches of the church. Paul even converted wealthy people such as Erastus, a major benefactor of public works in Corinth (Romans 16:23), and he "had wealthy and powerful friends at Ephesus."[33] Paul seemed fully at ease in such upper-class roles and environments.

He boldly returned to Jerusalem and, with one of his gentile converts, entered the temple filled with Pharisees. He knew what he was getting into and acted with confidence, returning to the domain of his former coreligionists, who were in control of the all-important and extremely wealthy temple complex in Jerusalem.

Paul was held in special custody by Felix and Festus in Caesarea for a lengthy period of time (Acts 24:27). It seems unlikely that these governors would have accommodated Paul as a "house-guest" for such a long time, even if under house arrest, if he had not been a man of great influence and social stature. Under Roman law, according to Justinian, the proconsul determined "whether someone is to be lodged in prison, handed over to the military, entrusted to sureties, or even on his own recognizances. . . . He normally does this by reference to the nature of the charge brought, the honorable status, or the great wealth, or the harmlessness, or the rank of the accused."[34] In asserting his rights as a Roman citizen to have his case heard by the Emperor himself, Paul no doubt hoped that his legal success in Rome would be even more stunning than it had been before the Proconsul Gallio in Corinth, for an empire-wide verdict in his favor would set a favorable precedent protecting Christians throughout the empire from Jewish arrest and prosecution. Thus, Paul wanted to stay "in chains," or in custody; his status as a famous defendant in fact opened to him doors of publicity in high forums before King Agrippa and presumably also in Rome. Felix and Festus

---

33. Sherwin-White, *Roman Society and Roman Law*, 90.
34. Justinian, *Digest* 48.3.1.

no doubt would have preferred to dispose of this case more quickly; but more than that, they would not want to offend their superiors in Rome by mishandling the case of an influential Roman citizen from a neighboring province.

Acts also says that Felix "had hopes of a bribe from Paul; and for this reason sent for him often and talked with him" (Acts 24:26 NEB). Obviously, Felix must have believed that Paul had the financial means to afford such a payment or this strategy would have made no sense.

In Rome, Paul was able to rent a large house, an insula (Acts 28:30), where he lived for two years and received "all that came in to him," evidently a fair number of people. How did he afford this property if he did not have considerable wealth at his disposal? Nor could Paul have assured Philemon that he would pay any debts incurred by the slave Onesimus if Paul were without resources (Philemon 1:18).

Nevertheless, along with these evidences of Paul's wealth, his letters also contain indications that he labored strenuously during the course of his ministry. Paul speaks of "labour and travail," "labouring night and day" (1 Thessalonians 2:9), and "working with our own hands" (1 Corinthians 4:12). Hock cites these references, along with two others (1 Corinthians 9:19; 2 Corinthians 11:7), as evidence for Paul's manual laboring at a trade during his missionary journeys. Paul, he argues, practiced his demeaning trade in order to avoid being an economic burden on his fledgling churches, jeopardizing their survival and risking a reduction in the number of converts. Hock ultimately argues, however, that Paul's language about "labor" testifies to his upper-class origins, not to his impoverishment, for Paul speaks as one who is demeaned by the manual labor he must perform.[35]

---

35. Hock, "Paul's Tentmaking," 558–60.

Paul's lack of funds on these occasions may, of course, have been a temporary problem caused by being on the road for such a long period of time. A. N. Wilson supports this view:

> In the 50s he writes as if he is a man who was once much richer than he now is, indeed, as a man who has become enslaved, and humiliated by the need to undertake manual work. . . . We can assume that, having been as it were the director of the family tentmaking business, he was thrown back on the necessity to work as an actual tentmaker in other people's business enterprises.[36]

On similar grounds, others have thought that Paul may have been disinherited by his family when he converted to Christianity; or he may have voluntarily foregone his personal wealth, sold all that he had, and devoted himself entirely to the cause of spreading the gospel.[37]

Today scholars still struggle to reconcile the inconsistencies between the evident wealth and status of Paul's family with the picture of the apostle later laboring at a trade to support himself. But the arguments of those who question the wealth of Paul on the basis of his rhetoric concerning labor must consider several further points.

First, one cannot safely assume that Paul's words to the Corinthians and Thessalonians referred to laboring at tentmaking rather than to religious or charitable labors. The physical hardships of proselytizing were numerous; the rigors of land and sea travel alone were draining enough to sap or claim lives. Combined with long hours of walking, healing, preaching, and conversing in the scorching summer sun, these journeys alone certainly could have caused Paul to remind his converts of his stressful and burdensome work. Because Paul was in Thessalonica only a few days, it seems unlikely

---

36. Wilson, *Paul*, 80.
37. Johnson, *Paul the Apostle*, 31, and Dahl, *Studies in Paul*, 36.

that he set up shop and began plying much of a trade there. His work was more religious than economic.

Second, what was the nature of the work that Paul was forced to do? As previously discussed, tentmaking could easily have been a large-scale business demanding a variety of economic and business skills. Whether Paul actually worked with his hands under Aquila and Priscilla or instead served as an overseer, administrator, financial advisor, materials purchaser, or investor in their enterprise is left unsaid. The author of Acts only records that Paul remained with them and worked, but it is unclear in what capacity. Obviously, he could have been useful to them as an able administrator or in many ways other than as a menial handworker.

Finally, in considering the possibility that Paul was disinherited by his family over religious differences, one must remember that in Paul's time no sharp distinction existed between Christianity and other sects of Judaism. "Paul was simply a Jew who had an ecstatic experience; he was not a Jew becoming a Christian. The very word did not exist when he had the experience," Wilson reminds us.[38] Furthermore, good evidence shows that Jews often moved from one sect to another without being disinherited. Josephus himself is an example. It would, therefore, be unlikely that Paul was disinherited by his family for his religious beliefs or practices.

Reading Paul in This Light

So what difference might this view of Paul and his wealthy situation make in understanding Paul, his personality, biases, teachings, and actions? In terms of understanding Paul's personality, it is important to recognize that all people in the ancient Mediterranean did not necessarily think alike on issues such as family values, kinship, marriage, dress, appearance, honor, and shame. One's economic station in life would tend to make a major difference from one person to the next. Bruce Malina and Jerome Neyrey have led

---

38. Wilson, *Paul*, 80.

the way,[39] and Ben Witherington has followed suit,[40] in trying to reconstruct the "archaeology of ancient personality" in general and to apply Malina and Neyrey's social scientific conclusions to the case of the apostle Paul in particular. Their conclusions can be augmented by an appreciation of Paul's associations with wealth.

Malina and Neyrey identify a number of elements that comprise an ancient person's self-concept and personality. In terms of "pedigree," Paul emphasizes his "honorable origins," as an "honorable and full member of an ancient, honorable ethnic group, as well as a person rooted in noble poleis."[41] Such a boastful self-presentation bespeaks one who is of high social and economic status. From what he says about his education, accomplishments, deeds of the soul, and deeds of fortune, Malina and Neyrey conclude that Paul "presents himself as utterly dependent on group expectations and the controlling hand of forces greater than he: ancestors, groups, God. He was a typically group-oriented person."[42] While one may readily agree with this conclusion, it may now be asked how Paul's wealthy background and condition would have affected his posture within the groups that comprised his circles of association. In the ancient world, for example, "although elites knew they had little if any control over their fortune, they were deemed responsible for how they dealt with events that cropped up in life."[43] In this light one can see how Paul, in honorable elite fashion, responded admirably and indelibly to the callings, fortunes, and responsibilities that unexpectedly interrupted his trip to Damascus and beyond. Paul repeatedly speaks of "his afflictions at the hands of others and his shameful physical treatment,"[44] perhaps doing this especially because such hunger, homelessness, persecution, beatings, death

39. Bruce J. Malina and Jerome H. Neyrey, *Portraits of Paul: An Archaeology of Ancient Personality* (Louisville: Westminster John Knox, 1996).
40. Ben Witherington III, *The Paul Quest* (Downers Grove, IL: InterVarsity, 1998), 39.
41. Malina and Neyrey, *Portraits of Paul*, 204.
42. Malina and Neyrey, *Portraits of Paul*, 217.
43. Malina and Neyrey, *Portraits of Paul*, 31.
44. Malina and Neyrey, *Portraits of Paul*, 210, 220-24.

threats, and inclement misfortunes would have been seen by himself as well as in Mediterranean societies generally as being unbecoming of a man of substantial means and good fortune.

Witherington focuses on elements of personality such as family relations, perceptions of one's body, and the dyad of honor and shame. He ignores the factor of poverty or wealth in his analysis, yet one would think that material status would have a significant impact on one's personality and self-perception. For example, the rich would not think the same as the poor on matters such as family and marriage. The poor would be lucky to marry with any dowry or financial means at all, and they would have a difficult time imagining themselves in a condition of physical and social well-being, let alone survival, without the daily support of a spouse to sustain the household, of working children to keep the farm or craft running, and of the older generation to provide the places of residence and land to cultivate from the traditional holdings of the family. Could a poor man, in such a world, glibly say to all single men and widowed women that it is good for them to remain single? (1 Corinthians 7:8). I think not. At least a poor person would have a hard time assuming that his audience would see this as an ideal state; but an aristocratic person might easily assume that a life of unconnected, unencumbered freedom was exactly the way to live, and indeed many wealthy Roman men at this time were avoiding marriage and the duties of being a husband and father, much to the chagrin of Roman imperial leaders. But the point is that such a lifestyle was the luxury of the few, never the attitudes or practices of the plebs.

Regarding bodily appearance, only the rich could fuss much about their appearance; and indeed, for Roman aristocrats, exotic cosmetics and expensive clothing were all the rage in the first century. In this world, in which "it was possible to tell what sort of person someone was by close analysis of their appearance and body characteristics,"[45] one can readily understand why Paul might have been so self-conscious and apologetic about his looks (Galatians 4:13-15). The tone of Paul's comment here is revealing, for a poor man would not have been expected to look anything but poor and infirm, with unimpressive flesh or eyes. But a man of high station in society would have some explaining to do if his appearance were not up to the normally expected standards.

Likewise, in a world in which "every social interaction that took place outside one's family or circle of friends was perceived as a honor challenge,"[46] matters of honor and shame were extremely important. Yet, here again, honor meant something different to people who enjoyed a superior social and economic position. Giving and accepting gifts, for example, was a matter of the honor-and-shame culture, for gift-giving was "seen as an honor challenge," and accepting brought a loss of honor, unless one could respond with a reciprocal gift of comparable or higher value.[47] On the one hand Paul avoided the duties of accepting gifts from anyone so that he could remain a servant to all (1 Corinthians 9:19). But on the other hand, this was something that only a socially superior person could well afford to do: "For a social superior to [refuse gifts or favors] was more common than the other way around."[48] Now however one reads Paul in these contexts, it seems inescapable that wealth and political and social status have an immense bearing on how such cultural traits manifested themselves among the people of the Roman Empire during Paul's lifetime. While one can learn much from Witherington's very insightful attempt to reconstruct Paul's personality based on social scientific evidence about the social norms and character profiles that mainly comprised elements regarding family values, body language, and the *agonistic* world of honor and shame, it would be helpful to distinguish between how

---

45. Witherington, *Paul Quest*, 39.
46. Witherington, *Paul Quest*, 47.
47. Witherington, *Paul Quest*, 47.
48. Witherington, *Paul Quest*, 49.

these elements manifested themselves among the rich and the poor in general, let alone in Paul's life and personality in particular.

In terms of his social frame of reference, Paul's extensive use of metaphors has been wonderfully detailed by David J. Williams,[49] and in his writings one can find another way in which Paul's wealthy background and persistent worldview aid our understanding of him and his delivery. Williams classifies into a dozen categories Paul's rich and memorable linguistic and rhetorical uses of socially situated metaphors such as armor, foundations, squalor, mirrors, reaping, olive cultivation, pedagogy, adoption, inheritance, slavery, citizenship, guarantees, travel, and sporting competitions.[50] Interestingly, most of these metaphors belong decidedly to the world of the well-traveled, widely experienced, upper-class overseer of major social and economic affairs, such as urban life, the legal arena, the business worlds of marketing and banking, travel by land and by sea, military tactics and administration, and public celebrations and major civic events. Thus, Paul refers to the generosity of God as "riches" (*ploutos*, Romans 2:4), to salvation in terms of "reward" (*misthos*, Romans 4:4), and to eternal life in terms of inheritance (*klēronomos*, Romans 4:13–14). My point is not that a poor person could not use such words, but to a wage earner wages were a good thing, unbefitting the wages of sin; to a wealthy person, however, being reduced to the plight of a day laborer, who had to live from hand to mouth, was exquisitely unappealing, although I agree with Todd Sill that this does not necessarily mean that Paul loathed manual labor.[51] When Paul then refers to himself as a "servant" or slave (*doulos*, Romans 1:1) of Jesus Christ, this image—coming from the lips of one who grew up with a silver spoon in his mouth—is a stunningly arresting

---

49. Williams, *Paul's Metaphors*.

50. These metaphors are summarized conveniently in John F. Hall and John W. Welch, *Charting the New Testament* (Provo, UT: FARMS, 2002), chart 15-12.

51. Todd D. Still, "Did Paul Loathe Manual Labor? Revisiting the Work of Ronald F. Hock on the Apostle's Tentmaking and Social Class," *Journal of Biblical Literature* 125/4 (2006): 781–95.

and emphatically self-effacing personal introduction. When he casts himself as an ambassador of the Lord (2 Corinthians 5:20; Ephesians 6:20), he uses a powerful term that was the proper word "in the Greek East for the emperor's legate."[52]

In this regard, Philo presents an interesting comparison to Paul. Philo came from a phenomenally wealthy family and had several affinities toward Stoicism, embracing, for example, "the classic Stoic paradox that only the wise man is 'rich.'"[53] Paul similarly warned that the riches of the world were less than the fulfillment of God's purposes (Romans 11:12-13) and that God's wisdom is clearly greater than the wisdom and wealth of the world (1 Corinthians 1:20), for those who do good works are the ones who are truly rich (1 Timothy 6:18). Such attitudes, on the parts of Paul and Philo alike, reflect "the studied indifference of Stoicism, and also with the settled social and economic position many Stoics had."[54] Indeed, even more, "a survey of Near Eastern ethical tradition reveals this as a familiar situation: almost every source that exhibits a degree of hostility to wealth, from ancient Babylonian works to contemporary Jewish pseudepigraphical literature, shows evidence of aristocratic production."[55] In an odd way, those who have had wealth are most likely to be dismissive of it. "Indifference to wealth comes most naturally to those who have inherited it, as Plato acutely observed (Rep. 1.330)," and certainly Philo and Paul apparently both reflect this phenomenon.[56]

Speaking so comfortably, knowledgeably, and intimately on such a wide range of activities bespeaks a person who belongs to a highly sophisticated segment of that society. While some metaphors used by Paul speak of ordinary parts of family and country life, even in these categories Paul takes a rather highbrow

---

52. Williams, *Paul's Metaphors*, 151.

53. David Mealand, "Philo of Alexandria's Attitude to Riches," *Zeitschrift der neutestamentliche Wissenschaft* 69 (1978): 259.

54. Mealand, "Philo," 260.

55. T. Ewald Schmidt, "Hostility to Wealth in Philo of Alexandria," *Journal for the Study of the New Testament* 19 (1983): 85.

56. Mealand, "Philo," 260.

posture, for raising olives (used elaborately in Romans 11) was not the task of unlanded peasants, and understanding the rules of such family-law matters as adoption and inheritance, as Paul's meta- phors presuppose,[57] was not the domain of lowly folk. I suppose that one might argue that Paul learned all these things while in his wealthy childhood and continued to use them as lively metaphors throughout his ministry, but I think not. Paul's ongoing use of all these metaphors signals to readers that he was comfortably conver- sant throughout his life with the social circles that produced these upper-crust metaphors. Indeed, if he had not been, why would he have continued to use such metaphors when writing to his newest converts, many of whom must have come from the lower rungs on the social ladder?

In terms of thinking about Paul's main teachings, a perspective of wealth may well help to accentuate and inform our understand- ing of his key points of emphasis. For example, he portrays God as a powerful soldier with a two-edged sword (Hebrews 4:12), as the preeminent judge of the world (Romans 3:6), as having "riches both of . . . wisdom and knowledge" (Romans 11:33), and as the ultimate conqueror over all powers and principalities (Romans 8:31, 37-38). He speaks often of the "grace" of God, which can be understood as seeing God as the supreme patron in a typical beneficium-officium relationship between a patron and client that was so fundamental to social and political networkings in the Roman world. He describes the atonement of Jesus Christ in terms of being "reconciled" (Romans 5:10), which draws on language from the making of peace treaties between two previously warring parties.

Paul has much to say about the law in various contexts (for example, Romans 3:27-31; 7:1-13; 1 Timothy 1:8-11; Galatians 3:10- 22), as one would expect from a man who was thoroughly trained in the Jewish law and familiar with Roman law. Paul knows the law,

---

57. See for example F. Lyall, *Slaves, Citizens, Sons: Legal Metaphors in the Epistles* (Grand Rapids, MI: Zondervan, 1984).

as only the elite part of society would have known. Under Roman law, "things had to be done in precisely the right way. Scrupulous attention was paid to form: the correct formulae had to be used, and the proper days had to be observed in bringing matters before the courts."[58] As Paul speaks of mankind's need for an "advocate," because people do not know what to say in petitioning God (Romans 8:26-34), or of "justification," meaning legal exoneration (Romans 4:25; 5:18), or of being "called" or "summoned," Paul shows inside familiarity with the workings of the Roman legal system. Paul also knows well the public laws of citizenship, as well as the private laws concerning adoption and the differences between adopted sons and natural sons in the laws of intestate succession regarding essential real property, as David Williams shows.

In 1 Thessalonians 2:14-16, Paul not only uses the marketplace imagery of weighing on the scales, but he does so from the vantage point of the merchant or lender, not the ordinary consumer. "Paul speaks of 'treasuring up' [thēsaurizeis] in Rom 2:5, in the [technical] negative sense of adding entry to entry on the debit side of the ledger," and in Philippians 4:17 he hopes "that the Philippians' gift to him would be credited to their account in God's ledger with interest accruing."[59] In Colossians 2:13-15, he uses the financial terms for the making and the cancellation of debts that assume conversance with the world of financiers, and the conversion of a loan into a gift through forgiveness of personal indebtedness.[60] Second Corinthians opens with an impressive "cluster of metaphors from the business world," such as the word bebaiōn, which is used in the Greek papyri for a legal guarantee that certain commitments will be carried out, which altogether reflects a comfortable familiarity with the high business world of guaranteeing property ownership and handling the amortization of payments against an obligation.[61]

---

58. Williams, *Paul's Metaphors*, 141.
59. Williams, *Paul's Metaphors*, 185.
60. Williams, *Paul's Metaphors*, 182-83.
61. Williams, *Paul's Metaphors*, 179-80.

Paul knows, apparently from close encounters, the social ills of the wicked upper class of society around him (2 Timothy 3:1-9; Philippians 3:1-3; Titus 1:10-16). He looks forward to the second coming of Christ as the arrival of a major visiting dignitary being received by the rulers of the city going out to meet him (1 Thessalonians 4:17).[62] Paul's letters are laden with instructions about leadership, with firm words of correction, and with administrative directives about church policies and practices, including worship, meetings, the sacrament, making donations, purchasing meat in the marketplace, and avoiding any contact with pagan idolatry. When one hears Paul speaking of marriage, husbands, wives, incest, fornication, widows, children, slaves and masters, and many other topics, it is easier to appreciate his practical wisdom and perspectives, realizing that he speaks with the voice of managerial experience and administrative acumen that most often accompanies a life of high-level involvement in business relations and social organizations.

Conclusion

The wealth and status of the apostle Paul are widely debated topics. A preponderance of evidence, however, supports the idea that Paul came from a family of significant means. His education and background, his profession, and his status as a Roman citizen all indicate that Paul was accustomed to prosperity and unfamiliar with destitution and subsistence living, despite the long-held beliefs of some to the contrary. If this is so, I draw one overarching conclusion: Paul made enormous social and financial sacrifices in becoming a Christian. His own declaration, "I have suffered the loss of all things" (Philippians 3:8), implies that he started out with much to lose. He probably consecrated a vast amount of money to enable him to travel and correspond extensively, and he certainly exhausted his very significant social capital to win audiences among important people of wealth and status. But more than that,

---

62. Williams, *Paul's Metaphors*, 193 n. 2.

when we read Paul's advice on numerous topics, ranging from slavery, civil disobedience, ideal virtues, and charity to wealth itself, modern readers will want to remember where Paul was coming from—and above all understand that he had put his money where his mouth was. Since "it is easier for a camel to go through the eye of a needle, than for a rich man to enter into the kingdom of God" (Mark 10:25), Paul's personal sacrifices and absolute devotion become all the more impressive.

John W. Welch is Robert K. Thomas Professor of Law and editor in chief of BYU Studies *at Brigham Young University.*

Works of S. Kent Brown

Books and Articles

1970

"A Guide to Literature on Religion" (brochure). Providence, RI: Brown University Press, 1970. 10 pages.

1973

"James the Just and the Question of Peter's Leadership in the Light of New Sources." In *Sidney B. Sperry Symposium Papers*, 10-16. Provo, UT: BYU Press, 1973.

1974

With C. Wilfred Griggs. "The Messiah and the Manuscripts." *Ensign*, September 1974, 68-73.

"Jesus and the Gospels in Recent Literature: A Brief Sketch." *Dialogue: A Journal of Mormon Thought* 9/3 (1974): 71-73.

With C. Wilfred Griggs and Thomas W. Mackay. "Footnotes to the Gospels." *Ensign*, October 1974, 52-54.

1975

With C. Wilfred Griggs and Thomas W. Mackay. "Footnotes to the Gospels: The Sermon on the Mount." *Ensign*, January 1975, 30-31.

With C. Wilfred Griggs and Thomas W. Mackay. "Footnotes to the Gospels." *Ensign*, February 1975, 50-51.

With C. Wilfred Griggs and Thomas W. Mackay. "Footnotes to the Gospels." *Ensign*, March 1975, 34-35.

With C. Wilfred Griggs. "The 40-Day Ministry." *Ensign*, August 1975, 6-11.

With C. Wilfred Griggs. "The Apocalypse of Peter: Introduction and Translation." *BYU Studies* 15/1 (1975): 131-45.

"Jewish and Gnostic Elements in the Second Apocalypse of James." *Novum Testamentum* 17 (1975): 225-37.

1980

"The Ostraca of the Coptic Museum: A Preliminary Report," *Newsletter of the American Research Center in Egypt*, no. 111 (Spring 1980): 38-42.

"Biblical Egypt: Land of Refuge, Land of Bondage." *Ensign*, September 1980, 44-50.

"Extracanonical Literature: The Dead Sea Scrolls and the New Testament." In *A Symposium on the New Testament*, 45-49. Salt Lake City: Church Educational System, 1980.

1981

"Microfilming Coptic Records in Egypt: Report of a Research Development Trip." *Newsletter of the American Research Center in Egypt*, no. 114 (Spring 1981): 11-17.

"Microfilming." *Bulletin d'Arabe chrétien* 5/1-3 (1981): 79-86.

1982

"Autocephalos." In *Dictionary of the Middle Ages*, 13 vols., edited by Joseph R. Strayer, 2:9-10. New York: Scribner's, 1982.

1983

"The Dead Sea Scrolls: A Mormon Perspective." *BYU Studies* 23/1 (1983): 49-66.

"The Four Gospels as Testimonies." In *The Eleventh Annual Sidney B. Sperry Symposium Papers*, 43-56. Provo, UT: BYU Press, 1983.

"The Seventy in Scripture." In *A Symposium on the Old Testament*, 27-32. Salt Lake City: Church Educational System, 1983.

1984

"Jesus among the Nephites: When Did It Happen?" In *A Symposium on the New Testament*, 74-77. Salt Lake City: Church Educational System, 1984. Revision reprinted by FARMS (Provo, Utah), 1989.

"Lehi's Personal Record: Quest for a Missing Source." *BYU Studies* 24/1 (1984): 19-42.

"History and Jeremiah's Crisis of Faith." In *Isaiah and the Prophets*, edited by Monte S. Nyman, 103-18. Provo, UT: BYU Religious Studies Center, 1984.

"Microfilming Coptic and Arabic Manuscripts in Egypt." *Coptologia* 5 (1984): 63-67.

With Robert J. Matthews and Victor L. Ludlow. "The Joseph Smith Translation of the Bible: A Panel." In *Scriptures for the Modern World*, edited by Paul R. Cheesman and C. Wilfred Griggs, 75-99, especially 80-88, 92-94. Provo, UT: BYU Religious Studies Center, 1984.

1985

"Approaches to the Pentateuch." In *Studies in Scripture, Volume Three: The Old Testament*, edited by Kent P. Jackson and Robert L. Millet, 13-23. Salt Lake City: Randall Book, 1985.

"Microfilming Coptic Records in Egypt: Report of a Research Development Trip." In *Acts of the Second International Congress of Coptic Studies, Roma, 22-26 September 1980*, edited by Tito Orlandi and Frederik Wisse, 27-29. Rome: CIM, 1985.

1986

"Trust in the Lord: Exodus and Faith." In *The Old Testament and the Latter-day Saints: Sperry Symposium 1986*, 85-94. Salt Lake City: Randall Book, 1986.

"The Testimony of Mark." In *Studies in Scripture, Volume Five: The Gospels*, edited by Kent P. Jackson and Robert L. Millet, 61-87. Salt Lake City: Deseret Book, 1986.

"The Nag Hammadi Library: A Mormon Perspective." In *Apocryphal Writings and the Latter-day Saints*, edited by C. Wilfred Griggs, 255-83. Provo, UT: BYU Religious Studies Center, 1986.

"Coptic and Greek Inscriptions from Christian Egypt: A Brief Review." In *The Roots of Egyptian Christianity*, edited by Birger A. Pearson and James E. Goehring, 26-41. Philadelphia: Fortress, 1986.

1987

"Whither the Early Church?" in *Studies in Scripture, Volume Six: Acts to Revelation*, edited by Robert L. Millet, 276-84. Salt Lake City: Deseret Book, 1987.

With C. Wilfred Griggs. "The Postresurrection Ministry." In *Studies in Scripture, Volume Six: Acts to Revelation*, edited by Robert L. Millet, 12-23. Salt Lake City: Deseret Book, 1987.

1988

"Whither the Early Church?" *Ensign*, October 1988, 6-10.

1989

"Man and Son of Man: Issues of Theology and Christology." In *The Pearl of Great Price: Revelations from God*, edited by H. Donl Peterson, 57-72. Provo, UT: BYU Religious Studies Center, 1989.

1990

"The Seventy in Scripture." In *By Study and also by Faith: Essays in Honor of Hugh W. Nibley on the Occasion of his Eightieth Birthday (March 27, 1990)*, 2 vols., edited by John M. Lundquist and Stephen D. Ricks, 1:25-45. Salt Lake City: Deseret Book, 1990.

"The Exodus." *Ensign*, February 1990, 54-57.

"The Exodus Pattern in the Book of Mormon." *BYU Studies* 30/3 (1990): 111-42.

"A Communiqué: Microfilming the Manuscripts of the Coptic Orthodox Church in Egypt." In *Coptic Studies: Acts of the Third International Congress of Coptic Studies (Warsaw, 20-25 August, 1984)*, edited by Włodzimierz Godlewski, 71-73. Warsaw: Państwowe Wydawnictwo Naukowe, 1990.

1991

"Nephi's Use of Lehi's Record." In *Rediscovering the Book of Mormon*, edited by John L. Sorenson and Melvin J. Thorne, 3-14. Salt Lake City: Deseret Book and FARMS, 1991.

"Act of Peter," "Apocalypse of Peter," "Butler, Alfred Joshua," "Discourse on the Eighth and Ninth," "Evetts, Basil T.A.," "Gospel of the Egyptians," "Gospel of the Truth," "Keimer, Ludwig," "Ladeuze, Paulin," "Ostracon," "Plato's Republic," "Prayer of Thanksgiving," "Thunder, Perfect Mind." In *The Coptic Encyclopedia*, edited by Aziz S. Atiya. New York: Macmillan, 1991.

"The Preservation on Microfilm of Coptic and Arabic Manuscripts for Posterity—A Serious Challenge." *Newsletter of the American Research Center in Egypt*, no. 153 (1991): 7-11.

"Apostle," "Gethsemane," "Israel: Overview," "Lehi." In *The Encyclopedia of Mormonism*, edited by Daniel H. Ludlow. New York: Macmillan, 1991.

1992

"Alma's Conversion: Reminiscences in His Sermons." In *The Book of Mormon: Alma, The Testimony of the Word*, edited by Monte S. Nyman and Charles D. Tate Jr., 141-56. Provo, UT: BYU Religious Studies Center, 1992.

"Egypt, History of (Greco-Roman)," "Egyptian, The," "Sayings of Jesus, Oxyrhynchus," "Souls, Preexistence of," "Truth, Gospel of." In *The Anchor Bible Dictionary*, 6 vols., edited by David Noel Freedman. New York: Doubleday, 1992.

"The Prophetic Laments of Samuel the Lamanite." *Journal of Book of Mormon Studies* 1/1 (1992): 163-80.

1993

"The Book of Hosea." In *Studies in Scripture: 1 Kings to Malachi*, edited by Kent P. Jackson, 4:61-67. Salt Lake City: Deseret Book, 1993.

"An Easter Calendar on Limestone." In *Acts of the Fifth International Congress of Coptic Studies*, 2 vols., edited by David W. Johnson, 2:79-90. Rome: CIM, 1993.

"Moses and Jesus: The Old Adorns the New." In *The Book of Mormon: 3 Nephi 9-30, This Is My Gospel*, edited by Monte S. Nyman and Charles D. Tate Jr., 89-100. Provo, UT: BYU Religious Studies Center, 1993.

1994

"The Exodus: Seeing It as a Test, a Testimony, and a Type." *Tambuli*, March 1994, 34-43; this article was published in the *International Magazines* in twenty-three other languages as well, e.g., "Der Exodus: Prüfung, Zeugnis und Beispiel." *Der Stern*, March 1994, 34-43.

Edited with Donald Q. Cannon and Richard H. Jackson. *Historical Atlas of Mormonism*. New York: Simon and Schuster, 1994.

1997

"Oxyrhynchus." In *The Oxford Encyclopedia of Archaeology in the Near East,* edited by Eric M. Meyers, 4:194-95. New York: Oxford University Press, 1997.

Edited and introduced: Yigael Yadin, "Masada: Herod's Fortress and the Zealot's Last Stand." In *Masada and the World of the New Testament,* edited by John F. Hall and John W. Welch, 15-32. Provo, UT: BYU Studies, 1997.

"A Case for Lehi's Bondage in Arabia." *Journal of Book of Mormon Studies* 6/2 (1997): 205-17.

1998

Edited and introduced: Jacques Tagher, *Christians in Muslim Egypt: An Historical Study of the Relations between Copts and Muslims from 640 to 1922,* translated from Arabic by Ragai Makar. Altenberge, Germany: Oros Verlag, 1998. xx + 294 pages.

Edited: "Planning Research on Oman." *Journal of Book of Mormon Studies* 7/1 (1998): 12-21.

A study guide for the movie "The Prince of Egypt" (DreamWorks). 25 pages.

From Jerusalem to Zarahemla: Literary and Historical Studies of the Book of Mormon. Provo, UT: BYU Religious Studies Center, 1998. xi + 169 pages.

1999

"'The Place That Was Called Nahom': New Light from Ancient Yemen." *Journal of Book of Mormon Studies* 8/1 (1999): 66-68.

2000

"Jesus' Sermon on the Last Days: Matthew 24." In *Brigham Young University 1999-2000 Speeches,* 69-77. Provo, UT: Brigham Young University, 2000.

Edited with Daniel H. Ludlow and John W. Welch. *A Light to All the World: The Book of Mormon Articles from the Encyclopedia of Mormonism.* Provo, UT: FARMS, 2000. xvii + 323 pp., with index of scriptural passages.

"Marriage and Treaty in the Book of Mormon: The Case of the Abducted Lamanite Daughters." In *The Disciple as Scholar: Essays on Scripture and the Ancient World in Honor of Richard Lloyd Anderson*, edited by Stephen D. Ricks, Donald W. Parry, and Andrew H. Hedges, 1-18. Provo, UT: FARMS, 2000.

"Seventy." In *Encyclopedia of Latter-day Saint History*, edited by Arnold K. Garr, Donald Q. Cannon, and Richard O. Cowan, 1091-93. Salt Lake City: Deseret Book, 2000.

2001

With David R. Seely. "Jeremiah's Imprisonment and the Date of Lehi's Departure." *Religious Educator* 2/1 (2001): 15-32.

Edited with Kaye T. Hanson and James R. Kearl. *Finding God at BYU.* Provo, UT: BYU Religious Studies Center, 2001.

2002

"The Temple in Luke-Acts." In *Revelation, Reason, and Faith: Essays in Honor of Truman G. Madsen*, edited by Donald W. Parry, Daniel C. Peterson, and Stephen D. Ricks, 615-33. Provo, UT: FARMS, 2002.

"New Light from Arabia on Lehi's Trail." In *Echoes and Evidences of the Book of Mormon*, edited by Donald W. Parry, Daniel C. Peterson, and John W. Welch, 55-125. Provo, UT: FARMS, 2002.

With Richard Neitzel Holzapfel. *Between the Testaments: From Malachi to Matthew.* Salt Lake City: Deseret Book, 2002. xx + 268 pages, 10 maps and chronological chart.

Mary and Elisabeth: Noble Daughters of God. American Fork, UT: Covenant Communications, 2002. 122 pages, one map.

2003

"The Arrest." In *From the Last Supper through the Resurrection: The Savior's Final Hours,* edited by Richard Neitzel Holzapfel and Thomas A. Wayment, 165-209. Salt Lake City: Deseret Book, 2003.

"Abraham," "Alma²," "Anoint," "Brazen Serpent," "Covenant People of the Lord," "Curse, Cursing(s)," "Exodus, the," "Fiery Flying Serpents," "Goodly Parents," "Hiss and a Byword," "Isles of the Sea," "Israel, House of," "Jacob¹," "Lamanites, Twenty-four Daughters of," "Lehi, Book of," "Lehi, Journey of, to the Promised Land," "Man, Creation of," "Moses," "Mosiah, Book of," "Nephi, First Book of," "Nephi's Psalm," "Rend, Rent." In *Book of Mormon Reference Companion,* edited by Dennis L. Largey et al. Salt Lake City: Deseret Book, 2003.

2004

"Jerusalem Connections to Arabia in 600 B.C." In *Glimpses of Lehi's Jerusalem,* edited by John W. Welch, David R. Seely, and Jo Ann H. Seely, 625-46. Provo, UT: FARMS, 2004.

Voices from the Dust: Book of Mormon Insights. American Fork, UT: Covenant Communications, 2004. xvi + 216 pages, 2 maps, 1 chart.

2005

"Zacharias and Elisabeth, Joseph and Mary." In *The Life and Teachings of Jesus Christ: From Bethlehem through the Sermon on the Mount,* edited by Richard Neitzel Holzapfel and Thomas A. Wayment, 91-120. Salt Lake City: Deseret Book, 2005.

With Richard D. Draper and Michael D. Rhodes. *The Pearl of Great Price: A Verse-by-Verse Commentary.* Salt Lake City: Deseret Book, 2005. xi + 447 pages.

2006

"The Twelve." In *The Life and Teachings of Jesus Christ: From the Transfiguration through the Triumphal Entry,* edited by Richard Neitzel Holzapfel and Thomas A. Wayment, 98-124. Salt Lake City: Deseret Book, 2006.

With Richard Neitzel Holzapfel. *The Lost 500 Years: What Happened between the Old and New Testaments,* a special illustrated edition. Salt Lake City: Deseret Book, 2006. xx + 179 pages, 10 maps, 6 charts.

Edited with Peter N. Johnson. *Journey of Faith: From Jerusalem to the Promised Land.* Provo, UT: The Neal A. Maxwell Institute for Religious Scholarship, 2006. ix + 172 pages, fully illustrated.

"The Manuscripts of the Gospel of Judas." *BYU Studies* 45/2 (2006): 15-20.

With Richard Neitzel Holzapfel and Dawn C. Pheysey. *Beholding Salvation: The Life of Christ in Word and Image.* Salt Lake City: Deseret Book and BYU Museum of Art, 2006. xi + 116 pages, fully illustrated.

"Refining the Spotlight on Lehi and Sariah." *Journal of Book of Mormon Studies* 15/2 (2006): 44-57.

2007

"Ammonihah: Measuring Mormon's Purposes." In *A Witness for the Restoration: Essays in Honor of Robert J. Matthews,* edited by Kent P. Jackson and Andrew C. Skinner, 165-75. Provo, UT: BYU Religious Studies Center, 2007.

"The Hunt for the Valley of Lemuel." *Journal of Book of Mormon Studies* 16/1 (2007): 64-73.

2009

With assistance from Aida el-Sayed. *The Ostraca of the Coptic Museum in Old Cairo, Egypt.* Piscataway, NJ: Gorgias, 2009. xiii + 377 pages.

2011

"The Savior's Compassion." *Ensign*, March 2011, 51-53.

Book Reviews

Review of *Nag Hammadi Codices III, 2 and IV, 2: The Gospel of the Egyptians*, by Alexander Böhlig and Frederick Wisse with Pahor Labib. *Bulletin of the American Schools of Oriental Research*, no. 228 (December 1977): 78-79.

With C. Wilfred Griggs and H. Kimball Hansen. Review of *April Sixth*, by John C. Lefgren. *BYU Studies* 22/3 (1982): 375-83.

With C. Wilfred Griggs and H. Kimball Hansen. "Afterwords" (on *April Sixth* by J. Lefgren). *BYU Studies* 23/2 (1983): 252-55, especially p. 255.

Review of *Der Herrenbruder Jakobus und die Jakobustradition*, by Wilhelm Pratscher. *Journal of Biblical Literature* 109 (Spring 1990): 162-64.

Review of *LDS Perspectives on the Dead Sea Scrolls*, edited by Donald W. Parry and Dana M. Pike. *FARMS Review of Books* 10/2 (1998): 141-46.

Films

Golden Road, executive producer for a 60-minute documentary on the fabled incense trail that ran from southern Arabia into the Mediterranean region. 2005.

Journey of Faith, executive producer for a 90-minute documentary on the journey of Lehi and Sariah from Jerusalem to the New World. 2005.

Journey of Faith: The New World, executive producer for a 90-minute documentary on the Book of Mormon in the New World. 2007.

Messiah: Behold the Lamb of God, executive producer for a seven-part documentary on Jesus Christ. 2010.

CITATION INDEX

Subject Index